Thabo Mbeki
and the
Battle for the Soul
of the ANC

# Thabo Mbeki
# and the
# Battle for the Soul
# of the ANC

WILLIAM MERVIN GUMEDE

ZEBRA

Published by Zebra Press
an imprint of Struik Publishers
(a division of New Holland Publishing (South Africa) (Pty) Ltd)
PO Box 1144, Cape Town, 8000
New Holland Publishing is a member of Johnnic Communications Ltd

**www.zebrapress.co.za**

First published 2005

3 5 7 9 10 8 6 4

PUBLISHING MANAGER: Marlene Fryer
MANAGING EDITOR: Robert Plummer
EDITOR: Marléne Burger
PROOFREADER: Ronel Richter-Herbert
COVER AND TEXT DESIGNER: Natascha Adendorff
TYPESETTER: Monique van den Berg
INDEXER: Robert Plummer
PRODUCTION MANAGER: Valerie Kömmer

Set in 10 pt on 13.65 pt Minion

Reproduction by Hirt & Carter (Cape) (Pty) Ltd
Printed and bound by Paarl Print, Oosterland Street, Paarl, South Africa

ISBN 1 77007 092 3

www.imagesofafrica.co.za

IMAGES OF AFRICA
PHOTO LIBRARY

To my mother Sophia,
and my wife Ylva

# Contents

# Preface

THIS IS NOT AN OFFICIAL BIOGRAPHY OF THABO MBEKI OR OF THE African National Congress. It is instead a political biography of Mbeki and the ANC in power. Indeed, the book critically evaluates the ANC's difficult transition from liberation movement to governing party and its attempts to modernise the ANC by transforming it into a heavily centrist party, while still retaining its mass support base.

Simultaneously, the ANC has tried to modernise apartheid South Africa's isolated economy, while making a brave attempt to kick-start the political, social and economic renewal of the African continent. Both processes have been heavily contested within the ANC alliance in what insiders call 'the battle for the ANC's soul'.

The book uses Mbeki's leadership and presidency of the ANC and the country as an entry point to these dramatic events, and endeavours to explain how his twin pursuit of economic and political reform has been based on tight control of the ANC by centralising decisions, making sure that sympathetic leaders are elected and policing public critics of the movement.

The idea for this book was conceived in late 2000, following several years of observing and reporting on South Africa's tumultuous transition from apartheid to democracy. I was motivated at least in part by my deep frustration over the inadequacies of some of the earlier works I had read on this vital period in the country's development, and also by a compelling ambition to add some diversity to existing accounts of the ANC in government.

Many of my sources agreed to be interviewed on condition of total anonymity, while others were willing to talk provided that I did not attribute certain comments to them. I have honoured their wishes, because the information and insights they provided was invaluable, and would otherwise not have seen the light of day.

Some sections of the book are based on my own political and economic reports while working as a journalist for the *Sunday Independent* and *Financial Mail*, and research papers that have formed part of my academic studies.

I could not have produced this book without the generous support of my family, friends, colleagues and ANC activists. Many thanks to the publishers, Zebra Press, for their enthusiasm and, more importantly, their boundless patience. Special thanks to Georgina Hatch, who was involved at an early stage, Marlene Fryer, who took over with the same enthusiasm, Robert Plummer, Ronel Richter-Herbert and Monique van den Berg. I would also like to thank Marléne Burger, for her considerate editing of the book.

I am also grateful to my former colleagues at the *Financial Mail*, especially my editor there, Peter Bruce, who persuaded me to make the presidency my 'beat'. Former colleague and friend Ferial Haffajee has been a valuable sounding board and resource, while the habitually sceptical Aminarth Singh helped panel-beat rough early ideas.

My former editor at the *Sowetan*, John Dludlu, was a treasured mental sparring partner, while Amrit Manga, Duma Gqubule and Farouk Chothia gave generously of their time and opinions.

Much appreciation to my erstwhile co-workers at the *Sunday Independent*: Newton Kanhema, Brendan Seery, Lloyd Coutts, Peta Krost, Benita van Eyssen, Christina Stucky, Blackman Ngoro, TJ Lemon, Maureen Isaacson and John Battersby. Chris van Gass at *Business Day* was a pillar of support, and my colleagues at the Media Institute of Southern Africa, who had to soldier on with little contribution from me during the last three months of the writing process, deserve a special accolade.

My thanks also to Patrick Bond, Suren Pillay, Febe Potgieter, Chris Matlhako, Anna Weekes, Karima Effendi, Veerle Dieltiens, Kenneth Creamer, Julian Jacobs, Mike Makhura, Melissa Levin, Badian Maasdorp, Rhoda Kadalie, Iraj Abedian, Peter Vale and Asghar Adelzadeh for being critical sounding boards. My old friend Leslie Dikeni could always be relied on to point out the counter-arguments, and I am deeply indebted to the late Sipho Maseko, professor of politics at the University of the Western Cape, whose tragic passing robbed South Africa of a great intellectual at a time when the country most needs critical and engaging intellects.

Many thanks to the Press Fellowship Programme at Wolfson College, Cambridge University, and the Sir Halley Stewart Trust for their financial support. The generosity of John Naughton, Bill Kirkman and Hilary Pennington made my time at Cambridge a cherished and enriching experience, while Richard Synge, who diligently read through the early tentative drafts, was liberal in his encouragement.

I am also indebted to William Beinart at St Antony's College, Oxford University, who gave me the opportunity to present seminars on the politics of modern South Africa at which I tested out of some of the ideas now included in this book. The African Studies Centre at Leeds University and the London School of Economics offered similar opportunities.

Hugh Lewin and the Institute for the Advancement of Journalism in Johannesburg have been immensely helpful over the years, not least in helping me to secure funding. Here, at last, is the result! The staff at Johnnic Publishing library in Johannesburg were always helpful and professional.

Many thanks to Ellen Mickiewicz and Laurie Bley at the DeWitt Wallace Center for Communications and Journalism, and the Terry Sanford Institute for Public Policy at Duke University, North Carolina, where I did valuable early thinking and writing. Ariel Dorfman at Duke provided immensely fresh and inspiring pep talks about the lessons of Chile and Latin America. Deep appreciation to the University of the Witwatersrand politics department, especially Tom Lodge, Sheila Meintjies and Stephen Louw.

I derived great benefit from the lively conversations with Jacques Monash in Amsterdam on the modernisation of centre left parties, and his insights into the Dutch Labour Party were most useful. Phil Noble's ideas on modern political party campaigns were invaluable, and I owe special thanks to Esther Palsgraaf and everyone else at the Amsterdam Maastricht Summer University.

Marianne Peters, who managed against all odds to help me obtain funding to study at Utrecht University, deserves her very own bouquet of gratitude.

Technically, the first ideas for this book germinated as I listened to the passionate lectures of the late Geoff Mungham, my former dissertation supervisor, and Kevin Williams, on the changes in the UK's New Labour Party. Hans Henrik Holm at Aarhus, Denmark, taught me valuable lessons on Scandinavian social democracy, and my 1999 Euro MA class deserves three hurrahs for being such good company and early guinea pigs.

Tebogo Seokolo offered many a meal, inspiration and intense debate on the latest political developments at home while I was in Amsterdam, as did Nadira Omarzjee, Crystal Orderson and that dear friend of South Africa, Jasteena Dhillon, now based in Afghanistan. Leonard Martin, formerly from the politics department at Aarhus University, spent long hours talking to me about South African politics, and the late Uncle Vernie February at Leiden University was of tremendous help. I am saddened that he won't be able to read the final product.

Karen Munkholm of the Danish Social Democrats in Copenhagen, now mediating in Sri Lanka, provided both hospitality and much early encouragement.

Many thanks to those who willingly agreed to read parts of the manuscript: Helga Jansen, Donna Andrews, Judith February, Saleega Zardad, Adiel Kamedien, Cecyl Esau and Terry Bell in Cape Town; Ebrahim Fakir in Johannesburg; Kerry

Cullinan in Durban; Hein Marais in Geneva; Phumzile Ludidi in Cambridge; Sean Jacobs in New York; Victor Chimbwamba and Laurie Nathan in London; Martha Lucia Moreno in Bogotá.

My appreciation to Kerstin Rodny and Michael Rosen in Halmstad, Sweden, who listened with so much interest and patience, and, most of all, my love and thanks to my family, my wife Ylva, and sons Lars Andile and Emil Alexander, who not only accepted so graciously the amount of time spent on this project, but who lent me their ears when I laboriously read through the chapters at the oddest hours imaginable. Ylva provided valuable comments, Lars Andile tried his best and Emil Alexander must have wondered why there was so much fuss about a 'bloody book'. And the late Anthony Sampson, who had been such a valuable source of support and inspiration in the writing of this book, and with many other projects I've been involved with in the past few years.

Finally, the opinions expressed in this volume are entirely my own, and I take full and final responsibility for the contents.

WILLIAM M GUMEDE
JOHANNESBURG, SEPTEMBER 2004

# Abbreviations

| | |
|---|---|
| **ANC:** | African National Congress |
| **ANCYL:** | African National Congress Youth League |
| **ANCWL:** | African National Congress Women's League |
| **AU:** | African Union (successor to the Organisation of African Unity) |
| **AZAPO:** | Azanian People's Organisation |
| **BC:** | Black Consciousness |
| **BCM:** | Black Consciousness Movement |
| **BEE:** | Black Economic Empowerment |
| **BEECom:** | Black Economic Empowerment Commission |
| **CODESA:** | Convention for a Democratic South Africa |
| **COSATU:** | Congress of South African Trade Unions |
| **CPSA:** | Communist Party of South Africa (later renamed South African Communist Party) |
| **DA:** | Democratic Alliance |
| **DTI:** | Department of Trade and Industry |
| **EU:** | European Union |
| **FDI:** | Foreign Direct Investment |
| **FOSATU:** | Federation of South African Trade Unions |
| **GATT:** | General Agreement on Tariffs and Trade |
| **GCIS:** | Government Communications and Information System |
| **GDP:** | Gross Domestic Product |
| **GEAR:** | Growth, Employment and Redistribution |
| **GNU:** | Government of National Unity |
| **ICT:** | Information and Communications Technology |
| **ICU:** | Industrial and Commercial Workers' Union |
| **ID:** | Independent Democrats |
| **IDC:** | Industrial Development Corporation |
| **IFP:** | Inkatha Freedom Party |

| | |
|---|---|
| ILO: | International Labour Organisation |
| IMF: | International Monetary Fund |
| ISP: | Industrial Strategy Project |
| JSE: | Johannesburg Stock Exchange, now known as the JSE Securities Exchange SA |
| LDC: | Least developed country |
| LPM: | Landless People's Movement |
| MDC: | Movement for Democratic Change |
| MDM: | Mass Democratic Movement |
| MERG: | Macroeconomic Research Group |
| MK: | Umkhonto we Sizwe (armed wing of the ANC) |
| NAFCOC: | National African Federated Chambers of Commerce |
| NAIL: | New Africa Investments Limited |
| NALEDI: | National Labour and Economic Development Institute |
| NAM: | Non-Aligned Movement |
| NCOP: | National Council of Provinces |
| NEC: | National Executive Committee (of ANC) |
| NEDLAC: | National Economic Development and Labour Council |
| NEF: | National Economic Forum |
| NEPAD: | New Partnership for Africa's Development |
| NGO: | Non-governmental organisation |
| NLC: | National Land Committee |
| NP: | National Party (later renamed New National Party, NNP) |
| NUM: | National Union of Mineworkers |
| NUMSA: | National Union of Metalworkers of South Africa |
| OAU: | Organisation of African Unity |
| PAC: | Pan Africanist Congress |
| PCAS: | Policy Coordination and Advisory Service |
| RDP: | Reconstruction and Development Programme |
| SABC: | South African Broadcasting Corporation |
| SACOB: | South African Chamber of Business |
| SACP: | South African Communist Party |
| SACTU: | South African Congress of Trade Unions |
| SADC: | Southern African Development Community |
| SADF: | South African Defence Force (later South African National Defence Force, SANDF) |
| SANCO: | South African National Civic Organisation |
| SANGOCO: | South African National Non-governmental Coalition |
| SANNC: | South African Native National Congress (later the African National Congress) |
| SAP: | South African Police (South African Police Services (SAPS) after 1994) |
| SASM: | South African Students' Movement |
| SMME: | Small, medium and macro enterprise |
| SECC: | Soweto Electricity Crisis Committee |

| | |
|---|---|
| **TAC:** | Treatment Action Campaign |
| **TGWU:** | Transport and General Workers Union |
| **TRC:** | Truth and Reconciliation Commission |
| **TUCSA:** | Trade Union Council of South Africa |
| **UDF:** | United Democratic Front |
| **WTO:** | World Trade Organisation |
| **ZANU-PF:** | Zimbabwean African National Union Patriotic Front |
| **ZCTU:** | Zimbabwe Congress of Trade Unions |

# — I —

# Freedom's
# Long Walk

Chiefs of royal blood and gentlemen of our race ... We have discovered that in the land of their birth, Africans are treated as hewers of wood and drawers of water. The white people of this country have formed what is known as the Union of South Africa – a union in which we have no voice in the making of the laws and no part in their administration. We have called you, therefore, to this conference, so that we can together devise ways and means of forming our national union for the purpose of creating national unity and defending our rights and privileges.

– Pixley ka Isaka Seme, 1912[1]

For it is not true that the work of man is finished
That man has nothing more to do in the world
But be a parasite in the world
That all we now need is to keep in step with the world.
But the work of man is only just beginning
And it remains to man to conquer all the violence embedded
   in the recesses of his passion
And no race possesses the monopoly of beauty, of intelligence, of freedom
There is a place for all at the rendezvous of victory.

– Aime Cesaire, 'Return to my Native Land'[2]

Yesterday is a foreign country; tomorrow belongs to us.     – Thabo Mbeki[3]

S LEEPY BLOEMFONTEIN WOKE TO AN UNFAMILIAR BUZZ. FROM THE FARTHEST corners of South Africa they came, by train, on foot and horseback, to this windswept city in the middle of the veld, deep in the rugged interior. For one day, the natives were *baas* in this consummate Afrikaner capital of an erstwhile Boer republic, the Orange Free State. It was 8 January 1912, a date that would be etched in the memory of all South Africa as the founding day of the African National Congress, known at the time as the South African Native National Congress.

The historic conference opened with a moving prayer, a call to the Almighty to bring sanity to a land where one's skin colour at birth determined where you would go to school (if at all), how much education you could get, whom you could sleep with, where you worked (if it all), how high you could rise in society, how much you would be paid, where you would live, whether or not you could be treated for illness, and where you would be buried.

That morning, with tears in their eyes and in full voice, they sang that stirring hymn, 'Lizalise Dinga Dingalako Tixo We Nyaniso'[4] (Fulfil Thy Promise, God of Truth) by the seminal African composer, Tiyo Soga. The melody drifted out of the sandstone hall, past startled white passers-by, across the rolling prairie stretching towards the deep-blue African skies, before disappearing over the nearby flat-topped *koppies*. Another, more popular hymn, Enoch Sontonga's 'Nkosi Sikelel'iAfrika' (God Bless Africa), would also be rendered during the conference, with equal gusto and deep emotion. In due course, the ANC would adopt this as its official anthem, and more than half a century later, many newly free African countries would proclaim 'Nkosi Sikelel'iAfrika' the national song of their fledgling nations.

But it would be almost eight decades before the same hymn became the national anthem of a free, democratic, non-racial South Africa, and on that January morning, such a prospect lay deeply buried beneath an uncertain future.

It was a young African lawyer, Pixley ka Isaka Seme, who would bravely point expectation towards that future. The year before, at a special meeting of the South African Native Convention's executive committee, Seme had issued a clarion call for all the diverse opposition groups in South Africa to unite under a single banner in order to more effectively fight the growing disenfranchisement of blacks.

Formal black political organisations included the Natal Indian Congress (formed by Mohandas Gandhi in 1894) and the African Political Organisation, set up in 1902. In former colonies that had become provinces there were the Natal Native Congress, organised in 1900 by Josiah T Gumede, Martin Luthuli and Saul Msane, among others; and the Orange River Colony Native Congress and the South African Native Congress in the Western Cape.[5]

In 1910, Boer and Briton had buried the hatchet after the bitter Anglo-Boer War of 1899–1902 to form the Union of South Africa, in which blacks were regarded as second-class citizens. The cruel Natives Land Act of 1913 would reduce the entire black population to squatters, forcefully wresting control of the land on which they had homes, earned a living and hoped to be buried.

The groundwork for the historic launch of the ANC had been laid a number of years before, but assumed a new dimension when Seme, recently returned from studying at Columbia University and Jesus College, Oxford, joined forces with three more young black lawyers, Alfred Mangena, George D Montsioa and RW Msimang, and called for a conference to 'unite all the various African tribes in South Arica'.[6]

Seme was a political novice, equipped with the training and prestige of an attorney, and a strong sense of mission to bring about political unity among the African people. Seme, journalist Sol T Plaatje and others involved in the tricky negotiations in the second half of 1911 had in mind a movement that would not only unite politically active Africans and their separate organisations in different parts of the country, but also achieve a social unity of the chiefs, as representatives of traditional forms of authority and influence; of the new generations of mission-educated Africans who were now ready to assume the leadership in political affairs of their people; and the masses who needed to be led.

Only with such an organisation could Africans overcome the political disabilities confirmed by the 1910 Act of Union, and would they be able to make 'their grievances known and considered' by both 'the government and the people of South Africa at large'.[7]

Late that Monday afternoon, when Seme's motion proposing the establishment of the Congress was passed unanimously, few were in doubt that they had taken a vital step in the history of their people. Many saw the formation of the Congress as equal in significance to the achievement of the whites-only Act of Union, which brought the former Boer republics and British colonies together under a single flag.

The Reverend John Dube, an educationist and editor of *Ilanga lase Natal*, was elected president general. Seme became treasurer, and Plaatje, a self-educated newspaper editor and novelist, became secretary general. Thomas Mapikela, president of the Free State Native Congress, would act as speaker, and George Montsioa would be the recording secretary. The Reverend EJ Mqoboli of the Wesleyan Church filled the post of chaplain-in-chief, and the vice-presidents were Walter Rubusana, of the Cape Native Congress, Meshach Pelem, of the Bantu Union in the Eastern Cape, Sefako Makgatho, president of the Transvaal Native Congress, and Alfred Mangena, South Africa's first African barrister. Eight chiefs were elected honorary presidents.

Dube, to his own surprise, was elected *in absentia* – he had injured himself in a bad fall from a horse and was represented by his brother, Charles. Ahead of the conference it was widely expected that the Reverend Walter Rubusana from East London, translator of the Bible and the first and only African candidate elected to the Cape Provincial Council, would be the founding president.[8]

John Dube was an impressive figure. He was seen as the right man to achieve the vital tribal unity the Congress hoped to achieve. He was also considered to be above the fray of the competing Cape and Transvaal political axes, which traditionally dominated both black and white politics in South Africa. Ordained as a clergyman by American missionaries in Natal, he had travelled to the US as a young man to further his education. Seeing the parallels between black South Africans and their American counterparts, he was strongly influenced by the black educator Booker T Washington.

Indeed, in accepting the presidency of the Congress, he proclaimed Washington his 'patron saint' and 'guiding star'. However, another influential black American scholar, WEB DuBois, who urged political organisations to capture their rights, also left his mark on the early debates. American thinking was prevalent among the new leaders, many of them having studied in the US before furthering their education in Britain. At the turn of the century, as many as 400 blacks from South Africa were studying abroad.

Plaatje[9] was the ideal choice as secretary general. He was instrumental in persuading the leaders of the two main African political organisations in the Transvaal, namely the Native Congress and the Native Political Organisation, to bury their differences and cooperate in setting up a single, national political body. In addition to many years of experience as a newspaper editor, Plaatje was a familiar political spokesman, had clerical experience in the Cape public service, had a well-known Protestant capacity for hard work – essential in building up any new movement – and could speak all South Africa's major indigenous languages.

The executive was representative of the new African elite, striving for national advancement despite the economic colour bar and restricted educational opportunities for blacks that blocked their advancement. The founding leaders came from the more moderate and conservative stream. Industrial action was not contemplated as a means of obtaining redress for the growing number of grievances among black people. For most of its history, the ANC's leadership would shift between moderate and conservative on the right, and radical on the left.

The organisation was modelled on the American congress, and contained elements of British parliamentary structure and procedure, such as a speaker and an upper house of chiefs. The founders deliberately ensured that the offices of president, secretary general and treasurer created three separate power blocs within the organisation. The constitution referred to the ANC as a 'Pan African Association'.[10] The founding fathers planted the roots of organisational culture in espousal of internal democracy, the right to dissent, a highly consultative style of leadership, adherence to rules and norms set out in the constitution, and regular elections.

The ANC's mission was to achieve African unity and serve as a pressure group in defence of African rights. It sought the removal of racial discrimination to open the way for African participation in the economy and gradual inclusion in the country's political institutions. The nationalism[11] that the ANC advocated was that of a multinational state with the different population groups participating in a gradually widening parliamentary democracy.

Like the whites – Afrikaners and English-speakers – blacks, encompassing Africans, Coloureds and Indians, would contribute to the rich and evolving patterns of South African society. The ANC's ideology was that of an 'outward-looking' nationalism, respectful of past traditions, yet based on the universal principles of equality, liberty and justice. The new society was to be a legal structure based on a non-racial ethic that would ensure justice, peace and good government. These would remain the fundamental political tenets until the 1940s, when the role of the African majority in the liberation struggle was redefined within the non-racial ethic.

The founders hoped that by bringing their complaints to the attention of the authorities through the moderate means of explanation, petition and deputation, they would be given a fair hearing, and that action would be taken on their grievances. Successive white governments would not only prove hard of hearing, but the early moral persuasion and moderate agitation would be answered with the iron fist: brutal state violence and even more repression by the white minority government. Over the ensuing decades, thus, the ANC's methods of protest would change from consultation with the authorities to non-collaboration, followed by passive resistance and eventually armed struggle.

The Congress's baptism of fire came with the introduction of the notorious Natives Land Act of 1913 – one of the pillars of the legalised disenfranchisement of blacks – and the outbreak of the First World War in 1914. The war placed the ANC in a bind. South Africa had rallied to Britain's side and sent troops to the European theatre to fight Germany. The irony was that the war was fought both for and with the help of the colonies.[12] Many of the overseas territories were given the impression that they would be freed after the war. Thousands of blacks answered the call to arms, and many died on foreign soil. The ANC initially softened its criticism of the government so as not to endanger the war effort.

In 1915, South Africa defeated the German forces in neighbouring South West Africa, which would later become Namibia, and took control of the country. The ANC protested against the incorporation of the territory as a fifth province of South Africa, and the status of South West Africa would remain a burning issue until Namibia attained independence in 1989. The ANC was angered and indignant over the fact that even in war, General Jan Christiaan Smuts, then minister of defence, tried to prevent blacks from fighting against whites in South West Africa, despite the fact that hundreds of them were fighting and dying in Europe.[13]

The 1913 Land Act was one of the most important pieces of legislation in South Africa's history. Under the terms of the legislation, only 7.3 per cent of the total land surface in the country was set aside for African occupation. Black people were unceremoniously evicted from land that was not in the arid and hostile areas reserved for their use by the government, and forced to seek work on the mines and white farms. In his book *Native Life in South Africa*, Plaatje movingly described the awful consequences for the Kgobadi family, which were mirrored in hundreds of communities:

> Mrs Kgobadi carried a sick baby when the eviction took place, and she had to transfer her darling from the cottage to the jolting ox-wagon in which they left the farm. Two days out the little one began to sink as a result of privation and exposure to the road, and the night before we met them its little soul was released from its earthly bonds. The death of the child added a fresh perplexity to the stricken parents. They had no right or title to the farm through which they trekked: they must keep to the public roads – the only places in the country open to the outcasts if they are possessed of a travelling permit. The deceased child had to be buried, but where, when and how?[14]

The anguish caused by the Land Act was captured in a heart-rending song by RT Caluza, 'Sikalel' Iswe La Kiti'[15] ('We Cry for Our Country'), which gave voice to the anxiety and frustration of thousands.

Many blacks settled in cities such as Johannesburg, but most became migrant workers, travelling to the mines to work and returning home to the rural areas once a year with part of their wages. Unlike many of the other issues that concerned the Congress, such as rail travel or employment by the government, the Land Act threatened the very livelihood of all Africans, and provided an opportunity to mobilise the movement in a way no other issue could.

The question of how the Congress should respond to the land issue would still be vexing the ANC when it came to power in South Africa more than eight decades later. At the time, however, moderate leaders argued against suggestions by their more radical colleagues in support of militant action, such as strikes and protests. The moderate group argued that the Congress should achieve its aims through persuasion, for example by appealing to Britain, the colonial power, and they won the day. But when the Congress sent a delegation to Britain in 1914 to protest the Land Act, appeals for equality were met with hostility by the British government.

Before the delegation's departure, Dube controversially expressed a willingness to compromise on the land issue, saying he did not object in principle to separation of the races 'as far as it can be fairly and practically carried out'.[16] His statement followed a government offer to increase the land 'allocated' to blacks, but maintain segregation, with blacks having local self-government in the form of 'native councils'. Although Dube later rescinded his apparent support for segregation, his view, shared by conservative elements in the Congress, had sown discord. Seme, in particular, was outraged, and Dube's handling of the land issue would see him resign as president under pressure at the 1917 national conference.

In 1913, black women burst onto the political scene in a campaign against the pass laws in the ultra-conservative Orange Free State. Until the 1930s, the pass laws, used to control the black population's movements, were confined to men, since so few women lived in urban areas. The Orange Free State was the exception, and on 6 June, a large crowd of women marched to the mayor's office to present a petition against the pass laws. They were all arrested, and simmering opposition turned into open defiance.

The incident marked the start of a widespread passive resistance campaign, pioneered by South African Indian Congress leader Mohandas Gandhi. Resistance flagged during the Second World War, but the Free State provincial authorities were eventually forced to amend the pass laws, and the campaign led to the formation of the Bantu Women's League (BWL), led by Charlotte Maxeke, a graduate of Columbia University in the USA, under the aegis of the ANC. However, it would not be until 1943 that women were accorded full membership and voting rights. At the same time, the BWL was replaced by the ANC Women's League.[17]

The rise of communism in Europe did not leave South Africa untouched. The Internationalist Socialist League was formed in 1915 after a group, unhappy with South Africa's participation in the First World War, broke away from the ruling white Labour Party. The success of the 1917 Bolshevik Revolution in Russia captured the imagination of South African radicals, and in 1921 the International Socialist League would combine with other socialist organisations to form the Communist Party of South Africa. Founded largely by white immigrants – trade unionists from Britain and left-leaning émigrés from Eastern Europe – the party would emit a passionate call to socialism, but retain a slavish obedience to the new Soviet Union.

Amid post-revolutionary fervour, the Industrial Workers' Union (ICU) – the first mass-based black trade union movement – was founded in 1919. Led by Clements Kadalie, the embryonic trade union toiled for improved working conditions and higher wages, and became the most active and popular organisation in rural and urban areas. One of its earliest actions was a daring strike by dockworkers in 1919.

Meanwhile, the ANC was entering a dip. It still clung to the idea of using petitions, and within months of the end of the First World War, sent a delegation to Britain to seek recognition for the rights of Africans in the Union of South Africa. Sol Plaatje, Selope Thema, Josiah Gumede and LT Mvabaza[18] handed over a memorandum to the British government in London, demanding a revision of the Act of Union so as to remove the colour bar in the economy and political institutions of South Africa. The request was ignored yet again, and this was the ANC's last serious attempt at securing direct British intervention in South Africa.

At war's end, expectations were high that political emancipation and social and economic justice for Africans might be near. ANC members felt that the war effort had proved African loyalty, and that this should merit civil rights and liberty. At the ANC's 1919 conference, the new president, Sefako Makgatho, revealed that Richard Winfrey, secretary for agriculture in British prime minister Lloyd George's cabinet, had written to Plaatje in 1917 that 'at the close of the War we shall do all in our power to help you regain that justice and freedom to which as loyal British subjects your people are justly entitled'.[19]

Nothing came of this promise, and as the first decade of the twentieth century drew to a close, there was widespread anger among blacks over the pernicious effects of the Land Act. Suffering from an acute shortage of land in the rural areas, yet thwarted by official discrimination from pursuing their economic fortunes in the cities, African urbanisation was increasing. A series of droughts increased both the flow of migrant labourers and food prices.

Afrikaners were also leaving the *platteland*, resulting in amplification of the poor-white problem, which in turn led to mounting white insistence on an industrial colour bar to ensure preferential employment. Several well-known Africans were ousted from the few jobs in the public service that blacks were allowed to hold in order to make room for whites. The post-war recession also led to increased black taxation and lower spending on African schools, just as the demand for education was growing.

The movement of Africans was restricted by the forced use of passes, and the pass laws were not only a source of annoyance, but also prevented Africans from changing jobs or embarking on industrial action, thus ensuring that their labour was available only on the mines or the farms. 'Petty' racism, for example on trains and in post offices, created in blacks a deep sense of humiliation and heightened the sense of injustice. A number of incidents of whites shooting blacks saw the perpetrators appearing before outrageously biased juries and being given lenient sentences or acquittals, thus intensifying African resentment and anger. With no representation or access to the government, the situation for Africans was bleak.

Not surprisingly, black anger began to spill into the streets in the form of strikes and demonstrations. The ANC called for a 'free, compulsory and public system of native education',[20] and in 1919 the Transvaal organisation led a campaign against the pass laws. The government responded with terrible violence, and the Congress recoiled, moving back to protest by petition and using the limited government channels at their disposal.

Significantly, having failed to capitalise on the widespread black anger in order to build a mass base or a powerful national organisation, the ANC was soon eclipsed by new and more radical organisations, many with socialist and communist roots, which had begun recruiting black workers.

In the biggest action of its kind up to that point, 42 000 African mineworkers embarked on a militant strike in 1920 to protest their inhumane working conditions. The ripple effect spread to the black higher-education sector, where protests broke out. Although the ANC supported the strike and related industrial action, its generally cautious strategy caused its profile to sag.

In the 1920s, the government introduced a colour bar to stop blacks from holding semi-skilled jobs in some industries. The ICU won some spectacular victories through militant action before it collapsed towards the end of the decade, but the ANC leadership continued to support non-violent protest – meetings with the authorities, deputations and petitions – to which the only response was more and even harsher violence and oppression on the government's part. Naively, Congress leaders continued to propagate a strategy of moral assertion and focus on the limited equality of opportunity for blacks. Failure by the ICU and the ANC to cooperate on a mass scale prevented the organisational forces of black resistance being turned into a powerful political machine.

In 1922, the all-white Communist Party had marched under the shameful banner 'Workers of the World, Unite and Fight for a White South Africa',[21] but not long afterwards a drive to recruit blacks made it the first non-racial political organisation in South Africa, and the first generation of radical African communists, men like Albert Nzula, Johannes Nkosi, Moses Kotane, Edwin Mofutsanyana and JB Marks, soon emerged from within its ranks.

Blacks were increasingly attracted to the non-racist party, and, in accordance with instructions from Moscow that blacks should be at the core of attempts to create a socialist society in South Africa, recruitment among blacks was stepped up. The combined efforts of the ICU and the Communist Party created the first left-wing organisation open to Africans.

In 1925, the ANC adopted its tri-coloured flag: black for the people, green for the land and gold for the resources. By the mid-1920s, more radical leaders, inspired by the Soviet Union and led by Josiah T Gumede, tried to shake up the ANC by infusing it with heightened radicalism, and attempted to reposition the organisation firmly to the left.

Gumede attended the inaugural congress of the League Against Imperialism in Brussels in February 1927 on behalf of the ANC. James La Guma represented the Communist Party, and D Colraine went on behalf of the Trade Union Council (TUC). Communists, socialists and anti-colonial freedom fighters from all over the world attended the congress, including India's Jawaharlal Nehru.

Afterwards, Gumede and La Guma visited Germany, where they addressed large crowds in Berlin under the auspices of the German Communist Party. Following one speaking engagement, Gumede attended a political meeting in Berlin with some of the delegates who had been in Brussels. Otto Schnudel, a delegate from

Switzerland, said of Gumede: 'I was present at that meeting ... Josiah Tshangana Gumede and I were standing side by side. He towered over most of those present with his tall, powerful figure.'[22]

Most of the whites he had met until then had treated Gumede with contempt, but in Berlin, for the first time, he stood as an equal among people of all races, colours and beliefs, united in brotherhood with the purpose of putting an end to the contemptible system of colonialism. Gumede was so overwhelmed by this experience that his eyes filled with tears. 'I am so happy!' he stammered. Then he drew himself up and added: 'I am going to fight.'[23]

From Berlin, Gumede proceeded to the Soviet Union to attend the commemoration of the October Revolution in Moscow. His visit left a lasting impression on him, and on returning to South Africa, Gumede called for a united front of communists and non-communists, and for the ANC to take a much more militant stance in the struggle for liberation. At the organisation's national conference in 1927, militants, led by Gumede, joined battle with conservatives for the 'soul' of the ANC. The leftists were frustrated with the ANC's cautious approach under the leadership of Zaccheus R Mahabane, who had succeeded Sefako Makgatho as president in 1924. Mahabane, a Methodist clergyman and at heart a moderate, had headed the Congress during its eclipse by the ICU.

The radicals won the day, and Gumede was elected president general. Fellow communist Eddie J Khaile, the ICU's financial secretary and one of the first Africans elected to the Communist Party's central committee, became secretary general. The ANC was now firmly under control of the left.

Gumede, a founder member and one of those who framed the ANC's constitution in 1919, had become a radical after the disillusionment of having the Congress's demands rejected by England and Versailles in the same year. During the war he had edited *Ilanga lase Natal*, the weekly publication founded by Dube, and was deeply involved in the groundbreaking African mining strike in 1920.

However, conservatives soon balked at the more militant and egalitarian approach espoused by Gumede. One chief complained: 'The Tsar [of Russia] was a great man in his country, of royal blood like us chiefs and where is he now? If the ANC continues to fraternise with them [the communists] we chiefs cannot belong to it.'[24] The chiefs and the conservatives formed an alliance to replace the leftist leadership, and at the ANC's national conference in 1930, Gumede was voted out of office, placing control once again in the hands of the moderates.

The old guard rallied around Pixley ka Isaka Seme, who captured the presidency by 39 votes to 14. Gumede remained president of the League of African Rights, presiding over an executive that comprised both communists and non-communists.

The Communist Party was also plunged into crisis, with anyone deviating from the Moscow line being purged, in keeping with Stalin's exorcism of dissenters in the Soviet Union. Founder members WH Andrews and SP Bunting were the first to be expelled, and even Kotane was ousted, though he was later reinstated. Writing under the pseudonym of A Lerumo,[25] Michael Harmel observed in *Fifty Fighting Years*, his history of the Communist Party of South Africa:

> A harshly intolerant, ultra-left period ensued in the leadership ... A purge of 'right-wing opportunists' extended to the summary expulsion of WH Andrews and a number of other members who were trade union officials, as well as SP Bunting. The proceedings were arbitrary in the extreme. The members concerned were not faced with the charges or given a chance to reply ... There was no possibility of any appeal.[26]

As the Communist Party's slide continued, Seme extended an olive branch to chiefs in the ANC. He focused his presidency on African economic empowerment and self-help in a forerunner to post-1994 black economic empowerment, aimed at building a black business class. Seme moved to establish a national fund for business ventures that would allow Africans to 'regulate their own standard of living' and 'supply the needs of their own people'.[27] They would produce their own cotton, leather, wool and timber for the manufacture of their own clothes, boots, bags, blankets and furniture. Seme's close ally, DDT Jabavu, lamented: 'Seek first the kingdom of money and the ownership of the soil and many other things will be added unto you.'[28] Another ally, George Champion, said that without a 'black capitalist class' there could be 'no hope of liberation'.

However, Seme's 'autocratic' leadership soon began to antagonise even his close allies, and differences between the left and the right led to a split in 1930 and formation of the short-lived Independent ANC. The ensuing decade would see the ANC decline into nothing more than a 'talkshop', as one critic put it. Plaatje described 1931 as a 'barren' year, while Selope Thema, another veteran, observed that there had 'never been such inactivity and apathy since the organisation's launch in 1912'.

At the 1933 Bloemfontein conference, Mahabane and senior stalwarts challenged Seme, accusing him of packing the hall with his supporters and weeding out dissenters before votes were taken. Mahabane left the conference in disgust, while Thomas Mapikela declared the gathering unconstitutional before vacating the speaker's chair. Seme's proposal for organisational reform, which included giving the president the power to appoint his own 'cabinet' or National Working Committee, caused intense bitterness and was rejected by grassroots supporters in 1936.[29]

May 1933 saw the introduction of a coalition government formed by the National and South African Parties, led by General JBM Hertzog as prime minister and Jan Smuts as his deputy. In December 1934 the two parties merged to form the United South African National Party. The government was confronted with the devastation of the Great Depression, which had hit South Africa hard when speculation over whether or not the country would follow Britain and move away from the gold standard precipitated a flight of capital.

Many whites now joined the long-suffering blacks in ever-longer unemployment and poverty queues as the Depression swept rural Afrikaners off the farms and into the cities. In the urban environment, they faced direct competition with black workers, who were also streaming in from the reserves, mostly arid and non-arable rural areas designated by the authorities. The government's response was to implement a programme of state-led job creation for whites and unleash harsh restrictions on black rights.

In May 1935 the Representation of Natives Bill and the Native Trust and Land Bill were tabled in parliament. Known as the Hertzog Bills,[30] the first curtailed the Cape African franchise and called for the creation of a Native Representative Council with advisory status on so-called 'native' issues, while the second consolidated the restriction of African landholding rights to the reserves designated by the 1913 Land Act.

Under Seme's conservative leadership, the ANC had become virtually defunct. The ICU was on a downward spiral to oblivion, despite pockets of support in Natal. The Communist Party was paralysed in an orgy of purges. Political activists tried to find avenues in new organisations such as the All-African Convention, the National Liberation League and the Non-European United Front.

The stirrings of another world war had the same galvanising effect on blacks as the outbreak of hostilities in 1914. The Italian invasion of Ethiopia in 1937 sent political fever soaring among blacks, who generally identified with the victims of Mussolini's aggression and were hoping that the fascists would 'bite the African dust'.[31] Huge 'Hands Off Ethiopia'[32] demonstrations were organised in the main cities, and furious debate was elicited by the question: Should blacks go to war for a white South Africa or not?

With the rise in prominence of new black communists as war loomed, the Communist Party were given a new lease on life and began riding a wave of popularity. It organised night schools and ran welfare projects, but its uncritical support of Moscow and Russian leader Joseph Stalin forced it to make several dramatic ideological somersaults. In accordance with the Soviet–Nazi pact, it agitated fiercely against a war, only to turn 360 degrees two years later when the Germans invaded Russia. It was all very confusing. Prime Minister Jan Smuts pushed South Africa into joining the war on the side of the Allies, and once again many blacks enlisted voluntarily.

But not even war was a bulwark against discrimination. Black South Africans were banned from carrying arms, and when black stretcher bearers were buried in a mass grave along with whites after intense fighting at Sidi Rezegh in Egypt, South African Army Headquarters ordered that their remains be dug up and placed in separate graves for whites and blacks.[33]

Mahabane turned the new grassroots political fervour to his advantage, mobilising support against Seme's lethargic leadership at the 1937 conference by arguing that fresh blood was needed to steer the ANC. Seme was voted out by angry delegates demanding change and replaced by Mahabane, whose star appeared to be rising once again. The Reverend James Calata, a capable organiser, was elected secretary general.

Calata, an Anglican clergyman from Cradock in the Eastern Cape and one of the early radical clerics in the mould of liberation theologians, is widely credited with doggedly reviving the organisation. He set off in 1936 on a tour of dormant ANC branches, and it took him until 1939 to visit local organisations in all four provinces.[34]

Others who breathed new life into the ANC during this period were Selope Thema, CS Ramohanoe (later president of the Transvaal Congress), and the talented young communists JB Marks, Moses Kotane and Edwin Mofutsanyana. Govan Mbeki, Gert Sibanda, ZK Matthews and AB Xuma, who returned to South Africa in 1939 after qualifying as a medical specialist abroad, also emerged as potential leaders. Calata, an organisational genius, persuaded Xuma to stand for the ANC's presidency in 1940, when he defeated the incumbent Mahabane by 21 votes to 20.

Xuma's election set the seal on the ANC's revival, while Matthews, a lecturer in social anthropology and native law and administration at Fort Hare, who had already made a name for himself in education circles abroad, added new intellectual vigour to the national executive.

The 1940 conference marked an important ideological turning point for the ANC, which resolved to formulate a comprehensive race relations policy for a 'Christian Democracy'.[35] The objective would be to progressively abandon racial discrimination and pursue the logic of equal opportunity to the ultimate – African dominance in the political and economic life of South Africa. The conference also resolved to build a mass membership so as to show that it 'fully represents the voice of the African people'.[36]

Xuma vigorously adopted the non-racist theme, and although not new, it brought a sense of purpose to the centre. At the same time, he pushed for representation of Africans at all levels of representative government and for reversal of the ownership restrictions imposed by the Land Act. The removal of all statutory restrictions against Africans[37] was high on his list.

The Second World War heralded the revival of black politics in South Africa, which was bolstered by dramatic economic changes. War production gave rise to immense industrial expansion, based on foreign investment and dependent on cheap black labour. Wages for black workers were far below the subsistence level, and African trade unions were becoming more and more militant.

In 1942, Smuts, by now prime minister, introduced War Measure 145,[38] which outlawed all strikes, to counter a rash of industrial action by Africans. But illegal protests continued, with residents of Alexandra, north of Johannesburg, for example, organising a bus boycott against increased fares, which they were too poor to pay. In the bitter cold of the highveld winter, thousands of people walked the ten miles to and from work rather than pay the higher fares, and after nine days, the bus company capitulated.

When fares were increased again a year later, the boycott was renewed. This time, the buses stood idle for seven weeks until the operators backed down.

The Second World War against Nazism and fascism gave new impetus to the concepts of freedom and self-determination, especially for people living in and struggling for the independence of colonial Africa and Asia. Under Xuma's presidency, the ANC introduced structural changes and laid the basis for a mass political movement. In 1943, it committed itself to a policy of universal adult suffrage and set up the Women's League, with Xuma's wife, Madie Hall Xuma, as president. An African American from Georgia, she was a social worker with a master's degree from Columbia University who greatly influenced the ANC's links with the American civil rights movement.[39]

In December 1943, the ANC adopted a new comprehensive policy statement, called 'Africans Claims', drafted under the leadership of Xuma by a committee including Matthews, Kotane, Marks and Mofutsanyana. The policy pegged the demand for African rights in South Africa to the Atlantic Charter, the declaration of intent issued by Winston Churchill and Franklin D Roosevelt in August 1941. The Atlantic Charter supported the right of all peoples to self-determination and set in motion the end of the colonial era after the Second World War.

The African Claims called for all forms of racial domination everywhere to be eradicated, and demanded self-government for colonial nations. They also demanded the abolition of the pass laws and the industrial colour bar, as well as the introduction of free, compulsory education and full citizenship rights, including the vote. The liberation of South Africa was viewed as part of the broader anti-imperial struggle by the colonies, but when Xuma sent a copy of the African Claims to Smuts with a request for a meeting, he angrily dismissed the document as 'propagandist',[40] and refused to meet with Xuma.

All these events and influences, and government's failure to fulfil promises of reforms, incited a mood of defiance in a new generation of activists, including Nelson Mandela, who wanted an even more radical ANC. JB Marks, Moses Kotane,

Edwin Mofutsanyana and Dan Tloome were also among the new crop of African communists.

Also in 1943, AP Mda, a teacher who went on to become a lawyer, Nelson Mandela, Walter Sisulu, Oliver Tambo, Robert Resha, William Nkomo, Jordan Ngubane and others formed a Youth League. They hoped that it would 'galvanise'[41] the ANC, which they saw as the 'symbol and embodiment of the Africans' will to present a united front against all forms of repression', but which had been 'organisationally weak', regarding itself as 'a body of gentlemen with clean hands' and failing to give a positive lead.

Although Xuma had ushered in a new era for the ANC, the young radicals wanted him to go further still. When first approached by Walter Sisulu, Nelson Mandela, Oliver Tambo and Anton Lembede, the son of farmworkers so poor that they wore clothing made from sacks, Xuma was reluctant to support formation of a Youth League, but although he treated the young radicals with reserve, he was essentially on good terms with them.

Initially, the league was manifestly anti-communist and objected to the united front of Africans, Coloureds, Indians and whites espoused by the mother body, on the grounds that other groups were 'hijacking' the African struggle. In April 1944, Lembede was elected the ANC Youth League's president, and Tambo its secretary. Mandela, who was involved in the final drafting of a basic policy document drawn up by Mda, said they felt the ANC leadership had paid no attention to the question of organising a mass movement. Through the Youth League, the young activists aimed to stimulate the ANC's development into a powerful liberation movement with African nationalism as its creed.

Their goal was 'true democracy', and to achieve it the league would struggle for the removal of discriminatory laws and the full citizenship that would give Africans direct representation in parliament. Land would be divided among farmers and peasants of all population groups in proportion to their numbers. Trade unions would have full recognition, there would be free compulsory education for children, supplemented by mass adult education, and African culture would assimilate the best elements of European and other cultures.

By this time, Xuma had formed a united front with the leaders of the Communist Party of South Africa and the South African Indian Congress, founded by Mohandas Gandhi in 1894, to oppose the pass laws. The campaign was precipitated by the government's rejection of parliamentary moves to repeal the pass laws and orders for the mass arrest of pass offenders. The agreement between AB Xuma, Yusuf Dadoo and GM Naicker, that the ANC and SAIC would work together for full franchise rights, was called the Doctors' Pact, because all three were medical doctors.

Mandela, Mda, Lembede, Sisulu and Tambo, whom Bram Fischer called the Young Turks, were still determined that the ANC should go it alone. They felt that cooperation with Indians and communists was undermining the ANC's own struggle, and tried to force African communists to resign from the Communist Party if they wanted to remain in the ANC. However, a motion to this effect made by the group at a national ANC conference was defeated. Among the most respected ANC activists at the time were the communists JB Marks, Moses Kotane and Gaur Radebe, Mandela's mentor.

Strikes by mineworkers were turning points in South Africa's liberation struggle more than once, and the 1946 action, the largest in African political history, was no different. According to unofficial estimates, 100 000 miners downed tools under the banner of the African Mineworkers' Union.

The plight of the country's 308 000 black miners, the most vital component of the national economy, was dire and exploitation was rife. Mostly migrant workers, they were paid a pittance. Their families in the Transkei and Ciskei lived in abject poverty, suffering greatly from malnutrition and disease. Many workers died or were injured daily in mining accidents, or succumbed to serious work-related illnesses. There was no sick leave, annual leave or payment for overtime.

The strike leaders, Kotane and Radebe, had long warned the Chamber of Mines about growing dissatisfaction among black mineworkers over their miserable conditions. The strike, which saw police armed with rifles, bayonets and batons violently driving the men back to work, was a call for a minimum wage in accordance with 'the New World's principles for an approved standard of living subscribed to by our government at the UNO (United Nations Organisation)'.[42]

Smuts, the leader of the mainly English-speaking governing United Party and a much revered statesman in the West, had been at the United Nations a year earlier and had helped draft the Preamble to the UN Charter, which affirmed 'faith in fundamental human rights, in the dignity of the human person, in the equal rights of men and women'.[43] Xuma, who was lobbying the UN, ironically remarked in reference to the prime minister's involvement: 'When we ask for bread, we get lead.'

The miners' strike was broken within a week, defeated not only by the government's endorsement of police brutality, but also by the complicity of the employers represented by the Chamber of Mines. Police reinforcements were deployed at every mine, and the chamber implemented a policy of housing workers in tribal-based compounds. At least nine miners were killed and 1 248 injured by police action.

Not until the 1980s would black unionism on the mines become a major political force in the form of the National Union of Mineworkers (NUM), built by leaders such as Cyril Ramaphosa into South Africa's biggest, richest and most powerful trade union.

The brutal repression of the 1946 strike reinforced the belief of the Young

Turks, like Mandela, that the time had come for action, and that the ANC's cautious approach needed to change. In 1947, Lembede died after a long illness, and Mda was elected president of the Youth League, with Tambo as vice-president and Mandela as secretary.

Lembede's death was an incalculable loss for the Young Turks, but his ideas would both inspire and divide his colleagues for years to come. The league had cobbled together a programme of action, and was ready to confront Xuma with their dissatisfaction over the direction of the ANC and his cautious leadership.

The great wave of decolonisation in Africa began with Ghana in 1956, but, as early as 1947, the granting of independence to India ignited a new fervour within liberation movements in South Africa. While acknowledging that Xuma had built a large membership base for the ANC, as shown by the organisation's bank balance of £3 000, a princely sum at the time, the Young Turks stepped up their campaign for a more aggressive approach. Mandela, who had a high personal regard for Xuma, concurred with the criticism of his leadership.

Shortly before the ANC's annual conference, Tambo, Sisulu, Mda and Mandela were delegated by the Young Turks to convey their feelings to Xuma. It was a difficult meeting, which took place at Xuma's home in Sophiatown. Xuma was determined to keep the ANC on its chosen course, while the young radicals were convinced that the time had come for action and change. The lesson of the mine strike had confirmed their belief that without the workers – the masses – there could be no effective political advance.

They suggested a programme of action similar to Gandhi's non-violent protests in India, and Sisulu impressed on Xuma that the ANC leaders had to be willing to violate the law and, if necessary, go to jail for their beliefs.

The meeting continued late into the night, and ended with Xuma angrily dismissing the Young Turks as arrogant after they issued an ultimatum: they would not support his re-election as president general unless he accepted their programme of action.

By the time Xuma showed them the door, public transport had stopped running for the night and the Young Turks faced a long walk home on streets that had no lights. Tambo mumbled that Xuma could at least have offered them a lift, but fortunately the ever-resourceful Sisulu knew a family nearby, who agreed they could sleep on the floor overnight.

The Young Turks began looking for someone with the same stature as Xuma who would be willing to accept their programme of action and stand against the incumbent leader in the forthcoming election. They approached ZK Matthews, but he considered them naive and immature and turned them down. At the last minute they found James Moroka, a medical doctor like Xuma and a respected activist, though not even an ANC member at the time. He endorsed their programme of action but, to their dismay, persisted in referring to the ANC as the African National Council.

Apartheid was legalised in 1948, when the National Party came to power with a small majority and immediately began codifying white domination and segregation. The Population Registration Act classified each individual by race, causing immense personal suffering, while the Group Areas Act divided races and tribes in urban and rural areas. The government forcefully removed all 'non-Europeans' living in areas henceforth designated 'white'.

Africans were to be called Bantu and were to be retribalised in terms of the Bantu Authorities Act. A huge sense of alarm and trepidation arose among blacks, who demanded some form of determined action against the expected unleashing of brutal Afrikaner nationalism. The Youth League's programme of action fell on eager ears at the ANC's 1949 conference, with the organisation's left wing finding common cause in the call for radical action, despite the Youth League's fierce opposition to communists in the ANC.

The conference became a battleground, with the conservatives ranged against the alliance between the Young Turks and the newly confident left. The conservatives voted for Xuma and the continuation of the ANC's cautious approach. The younger supporters cast their ballots for Moroka and radical change, and won the day.

Sisulu scraped through to be elected secretary general by a single vote. Mandela was among the new members of the National Executive Committee (NEC), which included moderates, communists and other Youth League representatives, all sworn to vigorous execution of the programme of action, which had been enthusiastically adopted by the conference.

Sisulu's appointment was especially significant. For the first time the ANC would have a full-time secretary who would be paid a salary and occupy an office in downtown Johannesburg.

The programme of action called for national freedom and self-determination,[44] and rejected apartheid and white leadership motivated by the idea of domination. Arguing that new weapons had to be employed in the struggle, it called for the ANC to organise a national strike in protest against the government's reactionary policies. For the first time the ANC endorsed majority rule, and Mandela observed that whereas the leadership had previously acted 'in the apparent hope that by pleading their cause they would persuade the authorities to change their hearts and extend to them all the rights they were demanding', pressure would now be used 'to compel the authorities to grant their demands'.[45]

The Suppression of Communism Act, passed in 1950,[46] had a far-reaching political impact, directed as it was against a much broader target than the estimated 2 000 communists in South Africa at the time, and declaring the Communist Party illegal. During the 1940s, communists had been elected as

Native Representatives to parliament, and as members of the Johannesburg and Cape Town city councils. But, as Senator Joe McCarthy cast his anti-communist net across America, South Africa's minister of justice, CR Swart, announced that he had investigated the growth of communism in Africa in company with Sir Percy Sillitoe, head of Britain's Secret Service.

The new legislation had a uniquely South African flavour. Communism included any doctrine that aimed at 'bringing about any political, industrial, social or economic change within the Union by the promotion of disturbance or disorder, by unlawful acts or omissions or by the threat of such acts or omissions'. The minister of justice was given the power to 'name' any person considered to be a communist and to ban such people from membership of certain organisations. The penalty for furthering the aims of a banned organisation was up to ten years in prison.

Ironically, the law brought the Communist Party closer to the ANC, especially the Young Turks, including Mandela. Sisulu was the first to argue that the clampdown on the communists, was a threat to all opposition groups. Mandela, though moving towards pragmatism, was still opposed to collaborating with the communists, and, when the party's Johannesburg branch joined forces with the Transvaal ANC and Transvaal Indian Congress to propose a May Day strike in protest against the suppression, many of the Young Turks were suspicious.

Mandela and a group of Youth League members would violently disrupt several Communist Party meetings held in preparation of the May Day protest. At a meeting in the Johannesburg suburb of Newclare, Mandela and other league members dragged Indian Congress leader Yusuf Cachalia off the platform. Mandela also disrupted a meeting at which the African communist, JB Marks, was making a speech about how white supremacy could be overthrown.

But mere months later, Mandela warned in the *African Lodestar* journal that the Suppression of Communism Act was not aimed so much at the Communist Party as at the ANC. From then on, Mandela would support joint action, even though this was contrary to the majority NEC view. The only exception was in June 1951, when he argued at an NEC meeting that Africans should go it alone, without whites, Indians or the communists. Moses Kotane, the general secretary of the Communist Party, did a great deal to convince the Young Turks, including Mandela, to change their stance.

Walter Sisulu was the first to come round. At a 'Vote For All' campaign initiated by the Communist Party and the Indian Congress, he was persuaded by Ismail Meer, Maulvi Cachalia and JN Singh to mobilise black and white against racial discrimination. Mandela and Tambo were so annoyed by Sisulu's conversion that they refused to take the train back to Orlando with him, and did not speak to him for some time afterwards. Both would later become converts themselves, however.

At the ANC's national conference in 1952, Chief Albert Luthuli was elected president, and a decision was taken to embark on a massive countrywide campaign of defiance against apartheid laws.

Luthuli was a devout Christian of unquestionable integrity. He defied a 1952 government ultimatum to withdraw from liberation politics or face being deposed as a chief, and, as a committed non-racist, led the ANC to work closely with other races and communists. His leadership also helped nudge the Young Turks into embracing a much broader non-racist approach.

The Defiance Campaign was launched on 26 June 1952, with Mandela as 'volunteer in chief'.[47] The civil disobedience that lay at the core of the protest action gained massive support for the ANC, especially among the youth. The South African Congress of Trade Unions (SACTU) was formed in March 1953 as the first non-racial trade union, representing eight African and three Coloured unions, as well as white laundry workers. SACTU became a member of the Congress Alliance, and its successor, the Congress of South African Trade Unions (COSATU) would later form a tripartite alliance with the ANC and the Communist Party.

In 1954 the ANC launched a campaign against the introduction of inferior Bantu Education, deliberately crafted by the government to ensure that Africans remained forever hewers of wood and drawers of water. Parents and teachers alike boycotted schools offering Bantu Education.

Introducing the law that governed this second-rate system of education, then minister of native affairs HF Verwoerd stated: 'The Native must not be subject to a school system that draws him from his own community and misleads him by showing him the green pastures of European society in which he is not allowed to graze.'[48] The National Party considered adequate education for black children a three-hour daily session consisting of religious studies, gardening and rudimentary maintenance, learnt by carrying out odd jobs on the school premises.

Early in 1955, ZK Matthews, recently returned after a year at the Union Theological Seminary in New York, proposed at the Cape ANC's annual conference that a Congress of the People should be convened. 'I wonder,' he asked, 'whether the time has not come for the ANC to consider the question of convening a national convention representing all the people of this country, irrespective of race or colour, to draw up a Freedom Charter for the democratic South Africa of the future?'[49]

The ANC called for 50 000 volunteers to collect freedom demands, and on 26 June 1955 some 3 000 delegates, representing the ANC, SAIC, SACTU, the Communist Party, the Coloured People's Organisation and the Congress of Democrats, gathered in the veld at Kliptown, south of Johannesburg, to adopt the historic Freedom Charter.

The charter called for equal rights for all national groups, and demanded the nationalisation of mines, banks and monopoly industry, but this was not interpreted by the ANC as a call to socialism.

The staging of the non-racial Congress of the People outraged the ANC's Africanists. Most of the Young Turks, including Mandela, Sisulu and Tambo, had committed themselves to a broad, multiracial nationalism in alliance with the communists, but the Africanists opposed the Freedom Charter, which held that land belonged to everyone, and called for more militant action, as well as an end to cooperation with the communists and other races.

In September 1955, the government announced that black women were to be issued with passes restricting their movements. On October 27, the Federation of South African Women, formed a year earlier, staged a groundbreaking march on the Union Buildings in Pretoria, armed with 100 000 anti-pass petitions. The success of the anti-pass campaigns that followed highlighted the important and enduring role of women like Lilian Ngoyi, Ray Alexander, Frances Baard, Fatima Meer, Helen Joseph, Hilda Watts, Ida Mtwana, Josie Palmer, Bettie du Toit and many others in the quest for freedom.

Meanwhile, the turn to non-racialism in the ANC caused dissent within the movement. There were two streams of African nationalism within the ANC. One centred on Marcus Garvey's slogan 'Africa for the Africans', and called on whites to quit the continent or be driven into the sea. The other, supported by the Young Turks, was more moderate. The Youth League stated on its founding:

> We take account of the concrete situation in South Africa, and realise that the different racial groups have come to stay. But we insist that a condition for interracial peace and progress is the abandonment of white domination, and such a change in the basic structure of South African society that those relations which breed exploitation and human misery will disappear. Therefore our goal is the winning of national freedom for the African people and the inauguration of a people's free society where racial oppression and persecution will be outlawed.[50]

The Africanists launched a battle to reclaim the soul of the ANC from the 'leftist multiracial leadership'. Their strongest support was in Soweto, where the fiery Potlako Kitchener Leballo issued a journal, *The Africanist*, from his house, regularly denouncing the ANC's leadership. The Africanists, including some of Mandela's old comrades in the Youth League, attacked the leadership for moving closer to whites and communists, and at a special conference of the Transvaal ANC in February 1958 in Orlando, the Africanists made their move.

Leballo led the charge against a provincial leadership weakened by the fact that senior members such as Mandela and Sisulu were prohibited from attendance by the government. The meeting broke up in chaos, and the ANC's national executive had to use emergency powers to take over the Transvaal branch.

In April 1958 the Africanists opposed the national leadership's bid to organise a stayaway in protest against the whites-only general election by instructing people to go to work. Duma Nokwe, the ANC's assistant secretary general, called the failed stayaway 'bitterly disappointing [and] humiliating'. The national leadership was outraged by the open defiance of the Africanists and expelled Leballo at a secret meeting, but the most serious confrontation came at a crisis conference of the Transvaal ANC in November.

Luthuli opened the gathering with a warning that 'narrow African nationalism' would not be effective as a response to the government's Afrikaner nationalism. When a heated dispute arose over delegations and voting credentials, Tambo, secretary general of the ANC, tried to make peace between the Africanists and the leadership, but failed. In the eyes of the Africanists, Tambo, Mandela and Sisulu were the enemies. The issue remained unresolved, and the Africanists walked out of the conference. They later sent a letter to the NEC saying they had broken away to become custodians of the ANC policy as it was formulated in 1912.

Five months later, the Africanists launched the Pan Africanist Congress of Azania (PAC). At a conference in Orlando on 6 April, the public holiday marking the arrival of the first white settlers at the southern tip of Africa under Jan van Riebeeck of the Dutch East India Company in 1652, Robert Sobukwe – a formidable intellect, erstwhile secretary general of the ANC Youth League and a lecturer in languages at Wits University – was elected the PAC's first president.

In February 1960, Britain's prime minister, Harold MacMillan, warned stony-faced white members of South Africa's parliament that the wind of change was sweeping across colonial Africa.[51] Soon afterwards, forced by the launch of the PAC to adopt a more militant stance, the ANC embarked on a series of protests against the pass laws, with 31 March set as the date for the national launch.

But on 18 March, the PAC announced that it would stage a protest against the pass laws three days hence, thus pre-empting the ANC campaign by ten days. On 21 March, PAC leaders surrendered themselves to the police for refusing to carry passes, and in the township of Sharpeville, south of Johannesburg, a crowd of about 10 000 surrounded the police station. The police opened fire and shot dead sixty-nine people, including women and children, many in the back. The massacre was reported around the world and had far-reaching repercussions for the South African liberation movement.

Oliver Tambo, vice-president of the ANC, was instructed to leave the country and set up a mission abroad in order to canvass international support against the apartheid regime. The NEC had decided in June 1959 already that, in the event of a crisis, Tambo should go into exile. On 8 April the government, with the support of the opposition United Party, passed the Unlawful Organisations Bill, which declared both the ANC and the PAC illegal organisations. They would remain so for the next three decades, with the ANC and Communist Party alliance growing even stronger by virtue of being forced to operate underground.

On 16 December 1961, with Mandela as commander in chief, the ANC formed Umkhonto we Sizwe (the Spear of the Nation, or MK), the secret armed wing of the organisation. Initially involved only in organised acts of sabotage against government installations, MK would, in time, move to full-scale guerrilla warfare, but when it was launched it was such a radical departure from the ANC's stated policies that its existence was kept secret from even the president, Albert Luthuli, lest he veto the idea.

From 1962 onwards, liberation movements across southern Africa took up arms. In Angola, Portuguese forces faced both the FNLA and the MPLA. SWAPO's offensive in Namibia was followed by Frelimo in Mozambique and ZAPU and ZANU in Rhodesia. By 1967, a guerrilla front stretched across southern Africa from the Indian Ocean to the Atlantic. In the words of Martin Legassick, 'The unholy alliance of Smith (Rhodesia), Vorster (South Africa) and Salazar (Portugal) … has been forced to draw its battle lines roughly along the Zambezi: the whole of southern Africa has now become a single theatre of struggle.'[52]

When Luthuli learnt of MK's formation, he demanded explanations from those involved, and the ANC sent two senior leaders to his home at Groutville in Natal. After listening to Moses Kotane, Luthuli, who still had misgivings about the unilateral decision to embark on sabotage, accepted responsibility for MK as the ANC leader. As he told Kotane: 'When my son decides to sleep with a girl, he does not ask for my permission, but just does it. It is only afterwards, when the girl is pregnant and the parents make a case, that he brings his troubles home.'[53]

Mandela said of MK: 'At the beginning of June 1961, after long and anxious assessment of the South African situation, I and some colleagues came to the conclusion that as violence in the country was inevitable, it would be wrong and unrealistic for African leaders to continue preaching peace and non-violence at a time when the government met our demands with force.' He slipped out of the country in January 1962 to undergo military training and to garner support for the ANC from newly independent African countries. Soon after his return, he was arrested in Natal on 5 August.

On 11 July, the security police had raided Liliesleaf farm in Rivonia, north of Johannesburg, where MK's high command was holed up. Nelson Mandela, Govan Mbeki, Walter Sisulu, Denis Goldberg, Ahmed Kathrada, Raymond Mhlaba, Andrew Mlangeni and Elias Motsoaledi were convicted of treason on 12 June 1964 and sentenced to life imprisonment.

They were sent to the high-security prison on windswept Robben Island near Cape Town, and the government systematically set about arresting and banning all known anti-apartheid activists. Some, like Joe Slovo, joined Tambo in exile or left the country to undergo military training. It would take a few years before the ANC recovered from the shock of having its leadership echelon destroyed, and on 25 April 1969 the organisation met at Morogoro, in Tanzania, to take stock and reorganise.

The conference adopted the influential strategy and tactics document that endorsed an all-out struggle against the apartheid government on both a political and military level, and called for the establishment of underground structures inside South Africa, as well as an international campaign for support and assistance. It was at Morogoro that membership of the ANC was officially opened to all races and that Tambo was elected president.

In exile, the ANC looked to its communist allies for both guidance and material support, allowing the Communist Party to achieve a position of influence that it would hold until 1990, when the liberation movements were unbanned.

Inevitably, questions arose about where the power lay within the ANC. The long tradition of collective leadership, in which the president presided with the consent of the NEC, became subtly eroded into a system resembling the classic Leninist technique of democratic centralism: the governing body made decisions that every other organ or individual had to accept without dissent.

Amid complaints that the ANC's collective leadership had fallen prey to the SACP's caucus tactics, Alfred Nzo was appointed in June 1971 to investigate allegations of undemocratic decision-making. He concluded that many NEC members were merely informed of decisions that had been taken and were often unclear about who the decision-makers were.

Just as the early Africanists had begun to resent the domination of the communists, the ANC in exile found itself facing serious tensions between the communists and the nationalists. The issue came to the fore with the death in 1973 of Robert Resha, a harsh critic of the Communist Party's perceived domination of the ANC.

At Resha's memorial service in London, Ambrose Makiwane lambasted the 'small clique' of communists who had taken over the ANC and, afterwards, a group of eight nationalists, including Makiwane and his cousin Tennyson, attacked Tambo's leadership. Tambo tried to keep the Gang of Eight, as they became known, within the ANC fold, but in September 1975 the NEC voted to expel them.

The rebels formed their own organisation, the African Nationalist Congress, and asserted that Mandela was their leader. Mandela responded by sending a clear message from his prison cell that he continued to regard Tambo as his leader, and in due course most of the rebels returned to the ANC. Tennyson Makiwane joined the Transkei government of Kaiser Matanzima, however, and was killed in July 1980 by an assassin.

Tambo's leadership was under constant attack, and his response was to emphasise the need for unity above all else. However, the scrupulous care he took never to take a decision that would anger any single faction evoked criticism from the militants that he was weak and indecisive, while the Africanists saw his consensus style as proof that he was under the spell of the communists.

The MK leadership also came under attack. Young militants despaired of the approach adopted by Joe Modise and Andrew Masondo, and levelled accusations at the ANC leadership in general, and MK in particular, that a culture of internal democracy was non-existent, consultation was rare and dissent was not tolerated. As early as 1968 a group of MK defectors sought asylum in Kenya, alleging that there was widespread dissatisfaction in the camps in Tanzania.

They accused their commanders of extravagant living and favouritism, and claimed that the first guerrilla operation in Rhodesia was effectively a suicide mission designed to eliminate dissenters.[54] Two MK combatants who took part in the mid-1967 Wankie Campaign with guerrillas from ZAPU claimed their criticism of the operation had led to their imprisonment in an ANC camp in Tanzania.

Meanwhile, a bitter dispute that raged for several years and led to Mandela and Govan Mbeki not speaking to one another for a considerable time, arose among the prisoners on Robben Island over the question of internal democracy within the ANC.

In 1969, one of the five ANC units on the island proposed a discussion on institutions that formed part of the government's separate development policy, such as Bantu homelands and the Indian Council. Discord developed between factions led on the one hand by Mandela, backed by Sisulu, and by the left, which included Govan Mbeki and Raymond Mhlaba, on the other.

Together with MD Naidoo, they were all members of the High Organ, the ANC's leadership body on Robben Island, from 1965 to 1972, when it was decided that leaders would be elected on a rotational basis. Mbeki feared that Mandela wanted to abandon the ANC's decision to boycott apartheid institutions. 'Mandela and Mbeki represented polar opposites in attitudes and opinions,' according to a memorandum smuggled out of Robben Island and sent to Tambo.

Allegations also abounded that Mandela was about to unilaterally abandon the armed struggle. His status as the most senior leader on the island was placed in question, and after several failed attempts to resolve the dispute, the five-member High Organ had a 'long, frank' meeting with the four people involved before reaffirming Mandela's leadership of the movement on Robben Island.

Following the banning of the ANC and its move into exile, resistance inside South Africa became largely dormant. However, grassroots activism slowly revived in the 1970s on the back of resurgent trade unionism. The government had applied brutal methods to crush the burgeoning black trade union movement, making strikes and trade unions illegal and either banning or jailing trade unionists for long periods. In 1968, however, a labour dispute propelled 2 000 dockworkers in Durban to go on strike,[55] which triggered a new phase of rebellion that would lead to the effective collapse of apartheid in 1990.

At the end of 1971, 20 000 Namibian contract workers brought the mining industry to a standstill and disrupted the communication and transport industries until the South African army was called in to quell the strike. In October 1972, dockers in Durban and Cape Town again embarked on industrial action. Though fifteen workers were sacked, this strike was seen as a major victory that underscored the nascent power of black labour, as, for the first time, employers met workers' demands and granted a pay rise.

In 1975, the Portuguese colonies of Angola and Mozambique threw off the yoke of colonial rule, and, in June 1976, black grievances against Bantu Education in South Africa finally exploded. Tens of thousands of high school pupils took to the streets of Soweto to protest against the compulsory use of Afrikaans in schools, sparking an uprising in townships throughout the country that claimed more than 1 000 lives and ignited fury among the masses.

Many young activists were influenced by the concept of Black Consciousness, as expounded by the likes of Steve Biko and influenced by the writings of Amilcar Cabral and Frantz Fanon.

Interpretations of Fanon's call for a positive racial identity to overcome the psychological damage of discrimination were central to Black Consciousness, while Cabral's argument that racism and colonialism were interlinked was also espoused. One of the earliest symbolic moves towards a positive group identity based on race was the rejection, in 1970, of the negative label 'non-white' in favour of 'black'.

A number of the leaders of the 1976 uprising fled the country and joined the ANC in exile, while hundreds of radical young cadres joined MK. Among those who would later be deployed in leadership positions were Mosiuoa Lekota, Popo Molefe and Murphy Morobe.

Those who were imprisoned on Robben Island challenged the accepted truths of the elder statesmen such as Mandela, Sisulu, Kathrada and Mbeki, while the new generation of radical black religious leaders included the Reverend Frank Chikane, Archbishop Desmond Tutu and the Reverend Allan Boesak, all heavily influenced by religious leaders in the American civil rights movement and exponents of liberation theology, which was especially popular in Latin America.

According to Mongane Wally Serote, the new grassroots activists 'gave the ANC oxygen and new life, which the movement desperately needed'. The students and trade unionists brought with them a particular leadership style that emphasised internal democracy, freedom of expression, the right to dissent, consultation, regular elections and active opposition to a leadership cult.

Marxist Harry Gwala's detention in 1977 sparked a huge debate on Robben Island about the direction the ANC was taking. After serving an earlier sentence for political activities, he had joined a network that was secretly recruiting MK fighters and organising strikes, but he was caught in 1975 and sentenced to life imprisonment. Gwala endeared himself to the ANC youth, especially the 1976 activists who had been sent to Robben Island, and his presence gave rise to vigorous debate between the Marxists and the African nationalists, as Mandela's group was called. Gwala was determined to achieve a genuine workers' democracy in post-apartheid South Africa, and his arrival on the island strengthened the hand of older leftist radicals like Mbeki.

Gwala was housed in Section E among the young militants, dubbed the 'klipgooiers' (stone-throwers), and, almost immediately, this became a hotbed of Marxism, with both Gwala and Mbeki running political education classes for the inmates. Gwala believed that the ANC would seize power as the result of a decisive military victory, while Mandela, Sisulu and Kathrada saw the armed struggle as a means to force the apartheid government to the negotiating table. The Mandela axis saw the ANC as an independent organisation that welcomed members of all political hue, while Gwala and Mbeki considered the Communist Party the dominant force.

Mandela and his group believed that the Freedom Charter intended to establish a bourgeois democracy, which could be the prelude to a socialist state, but that in the interim the ANC should fight on the broadest front possible against racism, rather than against capitalism. Mbeki and Gwala believed that the Freedom Charter represented the workers and the oppressed, who were destined to destroy the capitalist class. The leaders in Mandela's section set out their views in a document codenamed Inq-M. Inq was the abbreviation of inqindi, meaning fist, as embodied by the Congress movement, while M stood for Marxism.

Asked to compile a summary of the arguments, Ahmed Kathrada tried to ameliorate revolutionary expectations by pointing out that South Africa was not ready to become a workers' state. South Africa's struggle was different from that in the East bloc, he noted, and the congresses had never said they stood for the dictatorship of the proletariat. Despite the fierce polemics, there was open debate and great tolerance for different viewpoints in the Robben Island 'university', and ultimately all the separate factions accepted the document.

The 1976 uprising caused the apartheid government to change its strategy and introduce limited reforms aimed at winning the support of some sections of the black community and placating the outside world. Washington still saw South Africa as an important ally and bulwark against communism.

Puppet local authorities were introduced in African townships, and Coloureds and Indians were granted representation in a tricameral parliament. None of these institutions had any real power and consisted of members selected by the apartheid regime for their pliability. Simultaneously, the government stepped up repression and the use of force, launching a dirty tricks campaign and officially sanctioning death squads, which killed hundreds of activists and caused countless others to disappear without trace.

Apartheid securocrats, heavily influenced by the writings of French general Andre Beaufre, devised a total strategy to combat what the regime believed was a Moscow-inspired total onslaught against white South Africa. Prime Minister PW Botha fully supported the military, political, psychological and diplomatic counter-offensive.

The introduction of black local authorities gave rise to the formation of civic groups opposed to the apartheid structures, and in many cases civic organisations developed from parent–student committees that had been formed to support education struggles. The South African Student Movement (SASM) was among the first organisations for black high school students, and played an important role in the 1976 uprising. In 1983, student rebels joined forces with the trade union movement and the churches to form the United Democratic Front (UDF), which played a decisive role in rejuvenating internal resistance and raised the consciousness of the ANC inside South Africa anew.

At the launch of the UDF in Cape Town, Boesak told an ecstatic crowd:

> We have arrived at a historic moment. We have brought together under the aegis of the UDF the broadest and most significant coalition of groups and organisations struggling against apartheid, racism and injustice since the early 1950s. We have been able to create a unity among freedom-loving people this country has not seen for many years. Indeed, I believe we are standing at the birth of what could become the greatest and most significant people's movement in more than a quarter of a century.

The government was soon on the defensive as a popular revolt swelled in African townships, swept through schools and drew in the emerging independent trade union movement. Neither increased oppression nor piecemeal reform would end resistance or crush the UDF.

Paying tribute to the important role in the transformation of South African politics played by the UDF from its launch on 20 August 1983 until it was disbanded on its eighth anniversary in 1991, Walter Sisulu said: 'The formation of the UDF decisively turned the tide against the advances made by the National Party regime.'[56]

As the UDF's star rose internally, the influence and effectiveness of the anti-apartheid movement abroad was growing rapidly. Extending to the media, churches, political parties, trade unions, even the Trotskyite left, it proved even more effective than the solidarity movements during the Spanish Civil War. But, as resistance mounted, the apartheid regime became increasingly brutal and vicious.

In 1985 the government declared a draconian state of emergency, detaining, torturing and killing thousands of opponents. Successive states of emergency until February 1990 would see the detention of 300 000 people, the banning of the UDF and its affiliates, and restrictions on all political activity by COSATU. The new-found resistance shook the apartheid regime to its very foundations and saw it enlisting allies, such as vigilante groups and warlords from the Natal-based Inkatha Freedom Party.

The South African Defence Force led raids into neighbouring countries to destroy ANC bases as part of a general strategy to destabilise governments that offered the organisation safe haven or logistical support. The government, in turn, poured massive support into rebel armies, such as those of Renamo in Mozambique and UNITA in Angola.

As international condemnation of the apartheid government's brutality escalated, the National Party was forced to recognise that the political crisis in South Africa could no more be resolved by an iron-fisted military response than by unilateral and cosmetic political reform and deals with discredited black leaders. The government was forced to accept that it would have to negotiate with the ANC, and this was largely due to the sustained pressure exerted by the combination of determined agitation by the UDF-led internal opposition and the international solidarity.

The organisation's leaders always saw themselves as subordinate to the ANC in exile. As Murphy Morobe put it, the UDF 'managed to get people to stand up and fight for their rights without any fear and to actually challenge authority'.[57]

The formation of the Congress of South African Trade Unions in 1984 was another watershed moment in forcing the apartheid regime to enter negotiations, as cracks began to appear in the alliance between business and the government over the economic cost of maintaining apartheid. International sanctions, coupled with the price of keeping apartheid's war machine functional, sent the national economy into a tailspin in 1984. International banks suspended long-term loans, and by the middle of 1985 South Africa had a foreign debt burden of $22 billion, of which more than half was due for payment in six months or less. On 27 August, finance minister Barend du Plessis admitted that South Africa could not meet its commitments and announced a freeze on repayments.

Economic leaders began to call for talks between the government and credible black leaders, and by 1988 Pretoria had agreed to participate in a UN-supervised handover of power in neighbouring South West Africa in return for the withdrawal of Cuban surrogate forces from Angola, signalling an end to two decades of South African security force involvement in soon-to-be-independent Namibia. Black South Africans rejoiced. They could sense that freedom was near.

Within the National Party, Botha's intractable leadership gave way, after a brief but bloody internal battle, to the more conciliatory policies of FW de Klerk. One of his first moves was to sound out major allies, Britain's Margaret Thatcher and Germany's Helmut Kohl, on reform. 'They assured me that I could expect strong support for a reasonable reform initiative,'[58] he reflected many years later. De Klerk also met with Joachim Chissano of Mozambique and Kenneth Kaunda of Zambia, who told him firmly that he could not swim against the tide of history.

In February 1990, De Klerk unbanned the ANC, SACP and all other liberation movements, reasoning that if the National Party government made the first move, the ANC alliance would be placed on the defensive. Without Soviet backing, the Nats argued, it would be impossible for the ANC to maintain an armed struggle, and the South African economy had become so widely devolved that a black government would have little room to manoeuvre if a radical overhaul of existing institutions was proposed.[59]

Fatally, the government believed its own propaganda, namely that the ANC alliance was a house divided, encompassing so many different political cultures that it would be incapable of functioning in a legal environment. Moreover, the Nats believed they would be able to build a strong enough alliance with the support of loyal Bantustan leaders and the Inkatha Freedom Party's Mangosuthu Buthelezi to create a coalition that might even win a democratic election or at least provide a powerful veto bloc.

After its surprise unbanning, the ANC expectantly moved its considerable head office from throbbing Lusaka to an uncertain Johannesburg, and began the arduous task of re-establishing itself inside the country.

The biggest battle for the soul of the ANC would be waged as it prepared to enter into negotiations with the apartheid government and embarked on the difficult transformation from a 'broad church' revolutionary liberation movement, consisting of several different strands, to a political party equipped to govern. Its biggest challenge would be to craft a new nation from the ruins of 300 bloody years of apartheid and colonialism, while at the same time overcoming the hangover of crippling poverty, unemployment, and inequality between predominantly rich whites and poor blacks.

# — 2 —

# Mbeki's
# Path to Power[1]

There is a heavy responsibility for a leader elected unopposed. He may use that powerful position to settle scores with his detractors, to marginalise ... to get rid of them and surround themselves with yes-men and women. His first duty is to allay the concerns of his colleagues to enable them to discuss freely without fear within internal structures.

    – **Nelson Mandela in his last speech as ANC president, December 1997**

I could not compromise my integrity crafting lies. I did not possess the passion for illusion, the love of guile, the worship of obfuscation and the desecration of the word that makes speechwriters.

    – **Seitlhamo (Thabo) Motsapi, poet, 29 April 2002, on quitting as speechwriter for the Thabo Mbeki presidency after just two months**

THABO MBEKI'S SPECTACULAR CLIMB TO THE TOP OF THE POLITICAL TOTEM pole, and hanging in there, was a combination of birth, luck, intelligence and ruthlessness. By contrast with many other liberation movements in Africa and the developing world, the ANC is in the enviably unique position of having leadership skill and talent in abundance. One could easily imagine any one of five other candidates comfortably sitting in the president's chair.

The assassination by white right-wingers in 1993 of the popular SACP general secretary Chris Hani – a fierce rival since they were youths – opened the door for Mbeki to capture the presidency. Before his untimely death, Hani had all the ANC big hitters punting for him. He was the protégé of legendary SACP chairman Joe Slovo, and internal kingmakers such as Winnie Madikizela-Mandela had urged him on to the presidency at the height of her charm and influence. The powerful security network built up by the ANC in exile was at his disposal, he was revered by the radical youth and he was gifted with a natural charm, charisma and intelligence.

The SACP had invested much in Hani's future. He rose swiftly through the ranks and was groomed for decades to be ready when the time came.

But when Hani died, the party's left-wing mantle fell on Cyril Ramaphosa, the charismatic former trade union leader and tough-as-nails constitutional negotiator turned businessman.

Ramaphosa could count on the UDF 'inziles' who had been absorbed into the ANC, and he also had the support of the trade union movement. He was the former general secretary of the National Union of Mineworkers (NUM), COSATU's largest affiliate. The mineworkers' unions had a glorious tradition of radicalism and for close to a century produced some of South Africa's most enigmatic African leaders, such as JB Marks and Moses Kotane.

However, in a series of rapid and ruthless political manoeuvres behind the scenes, grabbing his opportunities and with a massive boost from the powerful exile faction, Mbeki crushed Ramaphosa's spirited challenge and became president of the ANC in 1997, and thus also Mandela's heir apparent.

The exiles were sure that Mbeki, not only one of them but also one of Oliver Tambo's protégés, would protect their interests. To the powerful exile and ANC security nexus, Ramaphosa was an unknown factor, a danger, someone who might give the upper hand to the internal wing, with its different culture and tradition.

For Ramaphosa, the battle was already lost at the ANC's December 1994 conference. Even Mandela's partisan support counted for nothing. How was the decision made? Just as Jawaharlal Nehru had been singled out for leadership when the Congress Party of India took power after independence in 1947, Mbeki was anointed by the ANC's elders. Yet, ten years earlier, some had even seen Max, son of former ANC secretary general Walter Sisulu and a scion of the party's other influential dynasty, as a contender.

But by 1990, with Tambo at death's door and Mandela chosen to succeed him, it was a foregone conclusion within the tripartite alliance that either Hani or Mbeki would be the next leader. The only question was whose supporters could propel their man to the top job.

When Hani was assassinated, many of the exiles who would have voted for him switched their support to Mbeki. Tambo had made his preference clear to party elders such as Mandela, Sisulu and the rest of the ANC leadership, but Mandela nonetheless consulted with two other senior African liberation leaders, Kenneth Kaunda and Julius Nyerere.

Both endorsed Tambo's choice, but when Ramaphosa faltered, two ANC heavyweights with serious ambitions emerged to challenge Mbeki's ascent. Former Gauteng premier Tokyo Sexwale, widely recognised as South Africa's first television politician, and former ANC legal head Mathews Phosa, who was also the former provincial leader in Mpumalanga, entered the leadership race late and were swept aside with relative ease. In the process of elbowing out Ramaphosa, Mbeki had amassed sizeable and influential backing.

Heavily bruised politically, Ramaphosa, Sexwale and Phosa all quit active politics and went into business, though they remained members of the National Executive Committee. As behoves a loyal member of the ANC, all three have insisted ever since that they harbour no further presidential ambitions. ANC tradition dictates that no one ever openly declares a hankering for higher office, which is seen as contrary to the spirit of the party's culture. Indeed, one's chances of being elected to higher office are more likely to be boosted by feigned humility, declaring an aversion to the fruits of advancement and insisting that one is unequivocally prepared to serve in the lowliest capacity, if this is where deployment by the movement leads.

Who is Thabo Mbeki? No typical revolutionary, that much is obvious. Not for him the military fatigues so beloved of Hani, for example. Mbeki dresses distinctively, favouring houndstooth sports jackets or Cuban shirts. His pipe and favourite Bay Rum tobacco are never far from hand, projecting an image of sophistication and contemplation – the English intellectual. In some circles, his designer suits have earned him the name of a 'Gucci revolutionary'.

He has deliberately cultivated a look that exudes charm and projects an image of being reasonable, composed and shrewd. He was enthralled by Shakespeare while at Sussex University in the roaring sixties and never misses an opportunity to quote the great wordsmith. When Mandela celebrated his eightieth birthday, Mbeki borrowed from *King Lear* to describe how the iconic leader planned a rural retirement 'to tell old tales, and laugh, At gilded butterflies, and hear poor rogues talk of court news'.[2]

As the ANC's main public spokesman and later head of the movement's international affairs department, it was vital that Mbeki should rebut the caricature of the ANC cadre as a hothead wielding an AK47, the archetypal 'red under the bed' that the apartheid government loved to portray. Mbeki is suave and revels in the gentlemanly exchanges of diplomacy, but the soft exterior masks a deceptively tough negotiator. Afrikaner 'scouts' who made secret contact with the ANC during the 1980s were usually taken aback by the frontman's seeming moderation.

In exile, Mbeki was Tambo's right-hand man. In turn, the highly respected Tambo, who held together the different components of the ANC during the tough exile years, was Mbeki's mentor, guide and protector. Tambo himself had a great ability to put a human and friendly face on the ANC, and Mbeki learnt this art at the feet of the master. His diplomacy, style and ability to win over enemies are all traits that Mbeki acquired by osmosis during many years of accompanying

Tambo. He also learnt to mimic Tambo's speaking style, the way he played with his hands, the way he paused between sentences.

Under Tambo's protection, Mbeki was untouchable, even when he regularly outraged powerful sections of the ANC by making policy statements without consulting the movement's rank and file. Anyone with lesser protection would have been disciplined, demoted and pushed into the political wilderness. Despite being a senior official, Pallo Jordan was interned during the 1980s for wondering aloud about the rough tactics employed by personnel in the ANC's prison camps.

What makes Mbeki's conquest of Africa's most powerful liberation movement so spectacular is that, notwithstanding his international connections, he lacked a strong popular base both within the organisation and South Africa when the ANC was unbanned in 1990. Although internal support would be crucial in any bid for leadership, he was seldom seen at branch meetings, declined many party speaking engagements, kept a low media profile and made no effort to canvass popular appeal amid the sprawling communities of South Africa's homeless and landless, where both Hani and Winnie Madikizela-Mandela were familiar figures.

Mbeki was acutely aware that his talents, style and approach could be best put to use in meetings with barons of industry, international businessmen, foreign statesmen, leaders of the prickly right-wing opposition – both white and black – and sounding them out.

In the immediate aftermath of the ANC's unbanning, Mbeki was seen as soft and too distant from the masses. His meetings with local and international businessmen and diplomats in smoke-filled rooms and posh hotels were viewed with suspicion by the ANC's militant youth, student and civic affiliates, and by radicals in both townships and trade unions. The perception was that he was likely to make too many compromises, and the masses found it easier to relate to romantic revolutionary heroes such as Hani, Madikizela-Mandela, Slovo and the irrepressible Mac Maharaj.

An intellectual at heart, Mbeki was never an inspiring public speaker. His preferred theatre of operation was behind the scenes. In private, he was the master diplomat, silky, smooth and amiable. He was fascinated by the political chessboard, and saw his rise to the top as part of an absorbing chess game, with himself as the pivotal piece.

What counted in Mbeki's favour was his political pedigree. His father, Govan, was an influential African Marxist, a Robben Islander and a founding member of MK. Mbeki senior shared a pedestal with Mandela and Sisulu. 'I was born into the struggle,' Thabo would often quip, and he has undoubtedly immersed himself, body and soul, in the ANC. The movement is his family.

During the 1950s, his father had built the ANC's branch in the industrial city of Port Elizabeth into the best organised in the country, and, as a teacher, had developed a great love for English literature, which would rub off on his son.

Thabo was born in Idutywa, a village in rural Transkei, on 18 June 1942, one of Govan and Epainette Mbeki's four children. His mother still runs the cooperative store that she and Govan, two young but educated communists, started in 1940 on the red-blanketed slope that houses the village. Thabo was never close to his father, and political obligations prevented them from spending long periods together. Govan's people were Mfengu, or Fingoes, early converts to Christianity, well educated and affluent. White traders called them 'the Jews of Kaffirland', and they produced many of the region's elite – teachers, preachers, shopkeepers and public servants.

Epainette's family, the Moeranes, are from the equally elite Bafokeng clan and of similar background. Her father owned a successful dairy farm, and wheat and sorghum fields, and sent all seven of his children for tertiary education, an extraordinary feat for a black family in those days.

When the ANC launched its Defiance Campaign against the pass laws in 1952, Thabo, aged ten, and a cousin offered to be volunteers in Queenstown, a hub of radical activism in the Eastern Cape. The boys were told their time would come, and three years later, when his father became Cape leader of the ANC, Thabo was enrolled at school in the Port Elizabeth township of New Brighton.

Throughout his teens, Thabo was involved in black student politics, even dabbling in the Non-European Unity Movement, forerunner of the Trotskyite New Unity Movement in the Cape. He joined the African Students' Organisation (ASO), and in 1959 was expelled from Lovedale College at Alice in his matric year for organising a boycott.

Even Thabo was surprised that his interrupted schooling evoked no recriminations. 'My father never said anything about this [expulsion]. I raised the matter with my mother: Why doesn't this fellow say anything about this?' Mbeki asked his mother. 'Why don't you write to him,' his mother said.[3] Following his expulsion, Mbeki moved to Johannesburg, the political epicentre of the country, where he was taken under the tutelage of ANC grandees Walter Sisulu and Duma Nokwe.

At the age of sixteen, Thabo had a son of his own. This would be his only child, and he was only two years old when Thabo left the Transkei. In 1981, according to the young man's mother Olive Mpahlwa, Monwabisi Kwanda set off to find and join his father in exile. He disappeared without a trace, and though Mbeki has never spoken publicly about the youngster's life or presumed death, he did try, unsuccessfully, to find out what had happened to him.

Mbeki's younger brother Jama also disappeared, in Lesotho in 1983. Family members suspect that apartheid death squads had a hand in the fate of both men, but no one came forward to claim responsibility at the Truth and Reconciliation Commission.

Thabo completed his schooling through correspondence in 1961, and enrolled as an external student for a degree in economics with the University of London. He had been elected national secretary of the ASO, and his involvement in organising protests against Bantu Education drew the attention of the security police and caused him to be detained for six weeks.

In 1962, Thabo slipped out of the country to which he would not return for twenty-eight years, travelling through Botswana to Rhodesia, where he was arrested and held in a Bulawayo prison for several weeks. The white Rhodesian authorities intended to deport him back to South Africa and the waiting security police, but British Labour member of parliament Barbara Castle intervened after being lobbied by the ANC, and Mbeki was granted asylum in Tanzania by President Julius Nyerere.

From there, Thabo made his way to England, and obtained a master's degree in economics from the University of Sussex, a hotbed of student radicalism. It was the time of anti–Vietnam War protests, miniskirts, student uprisings, existentialism and the 'New Left'. His peers read the Manchester *Guardian* and wore denim jeans. Mbeki, the only black student in his year, favoured tweed cloth caps and a pipe – the 'Tory look'. His politics were orthodox left, but his professors imprinted on him an indelible suspicion of Soviet-style central planning.

Capetonian Kenny Parker, a former National Union of Students leader who was at Sussex at the same time as Mbeki, recalls: 'He was very conscious that he was representing South Africa … don't let the side down in public, as if to say, look how good we are; look how civilised we are. How can people like us be discriminated against back home?'[4]

His closest friends in exile were the Pahad brothers, Essop and Aziz, with whom he formed life-long bonds. He threw himself into the ANC's youth politics, and in 1964 organised a march protesting the proposed passing of the death sentence on his father, Mandela and the other treason trialists in South Africa. Many of his university friends remember him as having a calm and gentle nature, but being hard to pin down. One friend, Veronica Linklater, now a peeress in Britain's House of Lords, explains: 'He must have had to be very chameleon-like, really, straddling different worlds the way he did. One got the sense he kept his worlds in different compartments, and that they never really met.'[5]

He attracted the attentions of several Englishwomen and led an active social life, but avoided serious relationships. Many years later, when he was deputy president of South Africa and journalists bewailed the fact that he was an enigmatic character, he would respond: 'That's what women at Sussex told me.'[6]

After university, he went to work in the ANC's London office, imbibing his politics from the grand old men of the movement, Tambo and Yusuf Dadoo. According to Anthony Sampson, he was 'a charming and amusing companion, drinking and talking into the night with friends from very different fields: one became a leading art critic, another a liberal democrat baroness'.[7] Senior ANC officials warned him that he could endanger his leadership chances if he married outside the movement, and in due course the ANC arranged for him to wed Zanele Dlamini,[8] whose sister Edith became the wife of an English aristocrat, Wilfred Grenville-Grey.

After undergoing military training in the Soviet Union – a mandatory requirement for those cherry-picked as future ANC and SACP leaders – Mbeki was ready to commence his political apprenticeship. He started out as the understudy for ANC secretary general Duma Nokwe in the 1960s, then worked for Tambo until he returned from exile, and finally served as Mandela's aide from 1990. He joined the ANC head office in Lusaka to hone his skills under Tambo, and many watched his dizzy ascent with suspicion amid whispers of favouritism.

At a relatively young age, he was elevated to assistant secretary of the influential Revolutionary Council, which was responsible for plotting the overthrow of the apartheid government. Already at the heart of power within the ANC, Mbeki's next task was to learn the art of African diplomacy.

Any future ANC or black South African leader had to be familiar with the politics of the continent. A stint as the ANC representative in Swaziland was followed by a prime posting to Nigeria, black Africa's most powerful nation at the time and one with which the ANC envisaged working closely once it came to power.

In 1975, Mbeki was elevated to the National Executive Committee, but it was his appointment as political secretary in Tambo's office that opened the door to his future. Deftly turning the job into far more than a bureaucratic necessity, Mbeki was effectively in charge of the day-to-day functioning of the most powerful ANC office in exile.

His ability to turn small opportunities into major advantanges would stand Mbeki in good stead throughout his political career. As Tambo's gatekeeper and repository of the ANC's secrets, he cannily crafted his position into that of advisor and manager to such an extent that some privately expressed concern that he saw himself as the deputy president.

Other posts followed: director of information, secretary for presidential affairs, member of the elite political and military council.

Mbeki became the ultimate insider. Tambo shared his vast network of contacts and experience with the rising young star, confided in him and took him to meetings with international diplomats, politicians and statesmen.

By the late 1970s, Mbeki, influenced by Tambo's pragmatism, underwent an important Damascene change in his political thinking. It was not an overnight change, but one he came to gradually. Tambo, a deep Christian democrat, had slowly over the years started to embrace social democracy as practiced in the Scandinavian countries. He became a great friend of the Swedish Social Democratic Party leader Olof Palme. Palme, West Germany's Willy Brandt and Switzerland's Bruno Kreisky were trying to reinvent social democracy as a humane middle way between crass American capitalism and crushing Soviet-style communism; their mission appealed to Tambo, and, later, to his protégé Mbeki.

Moreover, by the late 1980s there was a widespread feeling among ANC cadres that the armed struggle was not going anywhere. Morale was low. A new strategy was needed to lift spirits.

Around the same time, Mbeki began privately telling close friends that he believed the ANC alliance with the Communist Party would have to be broken at some point, especially if the ANC gained power in a post-apartheid South Africa. In Mbeki's scenario, the ANC would govern as a centre-left party, keeping some remnants of trade union and SACP support, while the bulk of the alliance would form a left-wing workers' party. To many, the idea was premature at best, tantamount to heresy at worst. Militants in MK and the SACP were especially outraged, since many were already watching with alarm the growing influence of Mbeki the centrist on Tambo and the ANC leadership in Lusaka.

It didn't help that in 1978, Mbeki collaborated with American television network CBS on a documentary about the ANC called *The Struggle for South Africa*. His participation offered viewers an intimate and unprecedented glimpse of the habitually secretive organisation, evoking criticism from ANC and SACP militants that Mbeki's candour had revealed sensitive issues to the apartheid regime, thus endangering the lives of activists and soldiers.

In the early 1980s, Tambo appointed Mbeki to coordinate the ANC's diplomatic campaigns and spearhead the organisation's controversial new strategy to involve more white South Africans in anti-apartheid activities. Just as Mbeki had come to believe a few years earlier, the ANC now concluded that in order to bring down the apartheid regime it had to prise away some of the National Party's supporters, infiltrate the state and chip away at its foundations. Mbeki would also act as the link with anti-apartheid fronts in Western countries.

On 13 September 1985, when protests by black students and community groups under the umbrella of the United Democratic Front were at their fiercest, Mbeki held a clandestine meeting with leading South African businessmen at Mfuwe, a short distance from then President Kenneth Kaunda's game lodge in Zambia's Luangwa Valley. With the help of a good supply of Scotch, Mbeki charmed the nervous businessmen. 'The ANC supremo has a remarkable ability to instil confidence, even in the most fraught circumstances,' said Hugh Murray, a member of the delegation.[9]

There was great suspicion in the ANC, especially among the militants, about the motives of the business leaders, but Mbeki was instrumental in persuading Tambo to meet with them. Tambo, in turn, convinced some of the biggest sceptics, such as Hani and Maharaj, 'that we needed to talk to people whom we considered our enemies or adversaries'.

Mbeki believes that if he had failed to persuade Tambo, 'the [political] advances [negotiations for a democratic South Africa] we have seen would have been considerably delayed'.[10]

Despite his inherently centrist political instincts, Mbeki served on the SACP's central committee for a considerable time in exile. It was fashionable to be a member of 'the party' during the 1970s and 1980s – it afforded one 'intellectual clout' and proved one's 'radicalness'. But Mbeki came to imbibe Tambo's social democratic leaning and set his personal political compass by Harold Wilson's wing of the British Labour Party, which he greatly admired.[11]

Ever the strategist, Mbeki resigned from the SACP's central committee with the collapse of the Soviet Union in the late 1980s, and, after the ANC was unbanned, allowed his membership of the party to lapse. He was never a great fan of Soviet socialism or its Eastern European equivalent. He saw the bankruptcy of the regimes, and he cringed. After the comforts of London, African socialism held no appeal for Mbeki.

He toyed, for a while, with the Africanists, but found them intellectually weak and too immersed in the ethnic blame game. The cosmopolitan Mbeki was as far removed from narrow ethnic politics as anyone could possibly be, but this would not stop him from using the Africanists when he launched his bid to capture the presidency.

Mbeki's resignation from the SACP's central committee came at a time when a group of disgruntled Africanists[12] were complaining that the party's leadership was loaded with white and Indian communists. When he quit, it was seen as a move designed to embarrass the SACP leadership and ally himself with the sentiments of the Africanists. Some SACP leaders, including Slovo, never forgave Mbeki for resigning, and would vehemently oppose Mbeki's candidacy for crucial leadership positions in the early 1990s.

Mbeki's independent streak also raised the ire of the ANC's militant wing in 1988 when he stated publicly that the organisation would be prepared to drop its 'counterproductive' stance that there could be no normal sport in an abnormal society. The hardcore militants saw his attitude as premature, while the UDF was deeply irked by his pronouncement on a key feature of their efforts to breach the racial lines that divided organised sport in South Africa. Even ANC spokespersons in London and Lusaka were alarmed and strongly denied that Mbeki was expounding official policy.

At the same time that Mbeki was rocketing through the ANC's political ranks, the organisation's other wunderkind, Chris Hani, was making a name for himself as an MK commander. Among the young cadres in townships across South Africa and the ANC training camps further to the north, he gained the status of a struggle hero, the dashing soldier who is the stuff of legends.

Interestingly, when Tambo first cast around for an aide de camp, Hani was the man he chose. But Hani saw himself more in the mould of Che Guevara than a bureaucrat, and politely declined. For all the nurturing and grooming he would get from Tambo, Mbeki was thus only chosen for the plum position by default.

Just as the ANC moderates prepared Mbeki for a future leadership role, the SACP helped craft Hani into a left-wing, socialist alternative. The two men kept a mutually suspicious distance from one another, and at one point Hani, clearly with Mbeki in mind and backed by the SACP, fuelled the rivalry by blasting the 'armchair revolutionaries' at ANC headquarters.

When he returned from exile in 1990, Mbeki's reputation as the ANC's foremost diplomat and spokesman was well established. Businessmen, foreign envoys and the apartheid government saw him as someone they could talk to, unlike Ramaphosa, the firebrand trade unionist, or Hani, the guerrilla leader.

But within the organisation, not a single song – the liberation movement's ultimate tribute and measure of popular appeal – was dedicated to Mbeki.

The ANC that emerged from almost three decades underground consisted of four distinct strands with entirely different political cultures. The exiles, many of them urbane intellectuals like Mbeki, had attained political maturity in the capitals of the world, operating in utmost secrecy and under high standards of discipline to reduce the constant danger of infiltration by apartheid spies. By necessity, decisions were frequently taken by a few key leaders and conveyed on a strict need-to-know basis. Crucially, the exiles controlled the ANC's financial, intelligence and military networks, and any future leader would need their support.

The elders included Mandela, Sisulu, Mbeki's father and others who had served long terms of imprisonment on Robben Island. They had developed a highly consensual political style that canvassed the broadest possible opinion, no matter how long this took, before any decisions were made.

The internal wing, or 'inziles', had been represented by the UDF since 1983, and encompassed trade unions, church and civic groups, women's, student and parent organisations. Their style was one of grassroots consultation, mandate by the masses and robust political debate.

The fourth group consisted of the soldiers of Umkhonto we Sizwe, the ANC's armed wing. Operating from camps in countries such as Angola, Tanzania and Zambia, they had adapted their political style to the harsh conditions of bush warfare, with the command structure functioning as a tight and disciplined military unit. Their support lay firmly with the exiles.

The ANC's two major affiliates were COSATU and the SACP, and anyone with pretensions of leading the broad church of the most powerful anti-apartheid bloc would have to amass the support of all these factions.

When the ANC set about regrouping after it was unbanned, one of the first priorities was selecting a successor for a frail and sickly Tambo. Newly released after twenty-seven years in prison and seen as the consummate struggle icon, Nelson Mandela was the obvious choice, but who would be his understudy?

The person who captured this powerful position would be a heartbeat away from the ANC's top post, next in line to lead not only the organisation but also the country.

After consulting his closest advisors, Mbeki – head of international affairs at the time – made an early move for the deputy presidency at the ANC's national conference in Durban in July 1991. Hani's stunned supporters quickly recovered, and he entered the race at the last minute.

The looming battle between the two long-standing rivals threatened to split the ANC at one of the most critical junctures in its history. The elders, appalled at the prospect of division on the eve of tough negotiations with the apartheid government, proposed a compromise that saw both candidates withdraw in favour of the ageing Walter Sisulu.

As it happened, Hani was elected to the NEC by a landslide, while Mbeki polled the most votes for the National Working Committee, thus underlining his support among the ANC's leaders.

The conference was a watershed for Mbeki, offering rank-and-file members their first opportunity to get his measure. However, it also gave Hani's supporters a chance to portray Mbeki as a man whose appeal was rooted among whites and the business world.

Tambo, with Mbeki's vocal backing, chose the conference as the first public platform for a proposal that the ANC should support the lifting of sanctions against the South African government. Several diplomats, especially from the US, Britain and Germany, had been lobbying both Tambo and Mbeki for a signal to Western powers that it was time to reward FW de Klerk for initiating political change.

Tambo argued that the ANC needed to be seen as taking the lead rather than risk being caught off guard and categorised as hard line by foreign governments that were in any event ready to lift sanctions.

The proposal was rejected out of hand, but Mbeki's fear of the ANC being seen as 'hard line' by the West would crop up frequently in the future.

His detractors scored another victory by marshalling support from the left wing and the internal group to have Ramaphosa elected secretary general of the ANC. Mbeki was bitter, but after the election he invited Ramaphosa for a drink and lulled his rival into complacency by offering his full cooperation. 'Chief, consider us resources in your job,' was Mbeki's opening gambit in a plan to lure Ramaphosa into his camp.

Ramaphosa's outward charm masks a ruthless political instinct. Shrewd and hard-working, he commands enormous respect both within and outside the ANC. His skills honed by years of tough and often acrimonious bargaining on behalf of the powerful National Union of Mineworkers, he is a seasoned political infighter and few opponents would survive close political combat with him. Mbeki is the exception.

The differences between Ramaphosa and Mbeki were never ideological, since there is no great distance in thinking between the two. Ramaphosa was no less moderate than Mbeki, but he had the knack of maintaining the image of a radical trade unionist, and was popular with the ANC's rank and file.

Nor was there anything to choose between the abilities of the two men. Both had established solid reputations for their skills and talents, and both had allowed their SACP membership to lapse, though it was Mbeki who outraged the party leadership by not attending the SACP's 1991 national conference in Soweto.

Ramaphosa's supporters won a considerable victory and struck their biggest blow against Mbeki at the start of formal negotiations for a democratic South Africa. As the person who had spearheaded secret talks with the apartheid regime as far back as the late 1970s, Mbeki naturally expected to lead the ANC team at the talks table.

However, militants, including Slovo and Maharaj, lobbied successfully for Ramaphosa to head up the team on the basis of his vast experience as the NUM's chief negotiator, and because, as an inzile, he was intimately acquainted with the government's weak points. Ramaphosa was known as a tough bargainer well schooled in the art of brinkmanship, and Mbeki's preferred style of consensus politics would be no match for the hard men of apartheid. In any event, his camp argued, as the ANC's secretary general, it was fitting that Ramaphosa should lead the team.

For Mbeki, the decision was intensely painful, and one he would never forget. His frustration at having to take a back seat to Ramaphosa at the negotiating table would surface periodically, especially when talks became deadlocked.

It was part of the wily Ramaphosa's strategy to deliberately steer matters to breaking point at crucial moments. In a series of calculated risks, he reasoned that each time the talks resumed, the government would be willing to make additional concessions, just to keep the process alive.

Mbeki vigorously objected to this strategy, fearing the consequences of an irretrievable breakdown in negotiations, and made it plain that he wanted the talks to continue at all costs.

As the negotiations unfolded, Mbeki focused his attention and energy on wooing reluctant political groups to the table. The spectre of a right-wing coup or violent insurrection loomed large, and he worked tirelessly to bring the noisy white and black right-wing groups to the negotiating table.

The greatest danger lay in a right-wing alliance, but even on its own, the intractable and belligerent Inkatha Freedom Party could potentially scupper the delicate negotiations. Ironically, Mbeki had been involved in discussions between Tambo and Chief Mangosuthu Buthelezi in the 1970s that led to formation of the IFP as an ANC ally against the apartheid regime.

Since then, however, the IFP had switched allegiance, espousing free market policies that endeared it to Britain's Tory prime minister, Margaret Thatcher, German chancellor Helmut Kohl and American president Ronald Reagan.

Amid threats that KwaZulu-Natal would secede, thus plunging South Africa into the abyss of a Balkan-like collapse, Mbeki launched a series of meetings with representatives of the white right. A breakthrough came one night while former SADF chief Constand Viljoen and others were meeting at Mbeki's home to thrash out a solution to the right-wing demand of self-determination for the Afrikaner.

The key was Mbeki's knack for juggling with words until everyone was happy and felt that their specific concerns had been addressed. Having impressed on his guests that the Freedom Charter contained a clause stating that all national groups should enjoy equal rights, he delivered the coup de grâce.

'For national groups, read ethnic groups,' he said, shifting his steady gaze to each right-wing leader in turn.

The reference to ethnicity played straight into the sentiments of the assorted group and laid the foundation for the moderates, at least, to seek solutions through the ballot box. Clause 235 of the interim constitution recognised the right of national groups to self-determination.

Aided by Jacob Zuma, Mbeki played an equally important role in persuading the IFP to abandon its fighting talk at the eleventh hour in favour of participating in the first democratic elections.

Mbeki's approach to the IFP differed dramatically from that of Ramaphosa. The official ANC line was to make no concessions to the black right, and Ramaphosa publicly stated: 'We will crush Buthelezi and the IFP.'

Buthelezi was not only a man with an enormous ego, but also one who detested Ramaphosa for the disdain and disrespect with which he customarily treated the Zulu leader. At one point, an enraged Buthelezi lashed out at Ramaphosa with an injunction that as someone of royal blood, he would not allow himself to be treated in such humiliating manner by 'a commoner'.

From the beginning of 1994, Mbeki met with Buthelezi several times, making promises that went well beyond the ANC's position but were, in some instances, endorsed by Mandela. The strategy irked Ramaphosa and other ANC negotiators, but it did pay dividends.

Ironically, having invested heavily in delivering the IFP to the ballot box, Mbeki was denied the accolades. The ANC's left wing managed to engineer a situation that required Mandela to send Mbeki abroad at the crucial moment, thus allowing Slovo and Ramaphosa to tie up the loose ends with Buthelezi. Ramaphosa took the public credit for the deal, and Mbeki had yet another score to settle.

Ramaphosa's stature had been growing since 1993, when he helped Slovo negotiate the sunset clause that laid the foundations for power-sharing in a post-apartheid government. Following Hani's assassination in April 1993, the succession race had been narrowed to only two contenders: Mbeki and Ramaphosa.

Since the July 1991 conference, Mbeki had systematically been courting influential leaders and factions within the ANC alliance. At the same time, he began recasting his image to that of custodian in the formulation of ANC strategy.

Behind the scenes, Mbeki was playing a shrewd political game. Not having a mass power base of his own, he ran up credit with those who did – credit he would be able to call in when it came to election of the ANC leadership.

Anticipating his rivals' moves, planning a few steps ahead, building up formidable defences and setting his pieces for an all-out attack: this was Mbeki's game plan. The traits that make Mbeki such a formidable political player are his skill at choosing allies, granting favours to be called in at an opportune moment, and playing the endgame in the corridors of power or the telephone booth.

He is also adept at playing the Africanist card when it suits him – seldom in public, but he has the knack of knowing when and with whom to use it. In addition, Mbeki entered the succession contest wearing the tie of the ANC exiles' old boys' network and bearing the endorsement of the party elders.

Topping his agenda were meetings with the influential maverick Peter Mokaba, leader of the militant ANC Youth League, Winnie Madikizela-Mandela and Bantu Holomisa, the former Transkei homeland leader who commanded considerable support in the populous Eastern Cape and among the youth.

In due course, Mbeki would also assiduously court Mbhazima (Sam) Shilowa, general secretary of COSATU, to gain support for his centrepiece economic strategy, the market-friendly Growth, Employment and Redistribution (GEAR) strategy. The economic austerity programme was adopted in 1996 to stimulate market confidence, replacing the more expansionary Reconstruction and Development Programme (RDP), which was the ANC's 1994 election platform.

Mbeki would also charm former SACP general secretary Charles Nqakula, to blunt SACP resistance to GEAR, and leaders of the South African National Civic Organisation (SANCO), particularly the president, Mlungisi Hlongwane, to support the ANC's economic programme despite widespread protest organised by SANCO against the privatisation of local services, as envisaged by GEAR.

In spinning his web around the most radical elements of the ANC alliance, Mbeki's strategy was to listen attentively but promise nothing, yet somehow create the perception of a promise.

Madikizela-Mandela's support stretched across the key constituencies of SANCO, MK, the Women's League and ANCYL. In June 1993, she was elected chairperson of SANCO's arguably most powerful region, Southern Transvaal. Six months later, she defeated Albertina Sisulu to become president of the ANC Women's League.

Madikizela-Mandela was just beginning her political rehabilitation. Mbeki had told her he thought her ostracisation was unfair and promised to help her restore her reputation.

She hated Ramaphosa, firmly believing that he and former UDF leader Murphy Morobe were leading a cabal bent on hounding her out of the ANC. They had harshly criticised Madikizela-Mandela during the late 1980s over her own conduct and that of her supporters, amid allegations that they were conducting a reign of terror in Soweto.

Madikizela-Mandela was also convinced that Ramaphosa wanted Nelson Mandela reduced to a figurehead and planned to oust him as president of the ANC.

Mokaba had his own axe to grind with Ramaphosa. In June 1993, the young hothead was severely upbraided and publicly humiliated by Ramaphosa for chanting 'Kill the Boer, Kill the Farmer!' at a rally, despite the fact that the ANC had banned the slogan.

At a private meeting, Mbeki told Mokaba he considered Ramaphosa's chastisement harsh. At the very next meeting of the ANC Youth League, Mokaba engineered an endorsement of Mbeki as the organisation's next deputy president and Mandela's heir apparent.

He also formally requested the NEC to place Mbeki's candidacy on the agenda for its next meeting. Since Tambo's death in April 1993, the post of national chairman had remained vacant. Mandela was seventy-five and Sisulu eighty-one, and Mokaba argued that the time had come to inject younger blood into the ANC leadership.

In the run-up to the NEC meeting, Mokaba frequently expressed public support for Mbeki, describing him as 'most intelligent' and of the same calibre as Tambo, Mandela and Sisulu. As far as the Youth League was concerned, Mbeki was not only the right man for the job, but should be elected almost immediately rather than waiting for the next national conference.

Mokaba made it clear that Ramaphosa should remain secretary general, catching his supporters off guard and sparking a flurry of talks with the ANC's fourteen regional leaders in an attempt to block the ANCYL call.

Ramaphosa tried especially hard to get the powerful Pretoria–Witwatersrand–Vereeniging region to veto the proposal, and his supporters lambasted Mokaba for placing a 'private' ANC matter in the public domain, but to no avail. The sharpest criticism came from Tokyo Sexwale, another pretender to the ANC throne, who accused Mokaba of engaging in 'pendulum politics'.

But the die was cast, and Mbeki's final ascent to power had begun.

Ahead of the NEC meeting from 27 to 29 August, an internal assessment of the ANC was circulated to leaders. The report blamed Ramaphosa, as secretary general, for slipshod administration and lack of coordination between the regions and head office. He was accused of paying insufficient attention to regional reports, lacking control over the hiring and firing of personnel, and being 'inaccessible' to the regions.

According to the report, 'The briefing of regional secretary generals has stopped. National Executive Committee visits to the regions are more theoretical than practical and National Working Committee reports to the NEC inconsistent and unclear. There is a lack of financial planning and management, there is not enough accountability of staff at headquarters and a lack of discipline among the NEC and staff.'

The Ramaphosa camp saw this as a thinly veiled attempt to tie him to a desk at headquarters. If bureaucratic obligations forced Ramaphosa to quit as the ANC's chief negotiator, Mbeki would be the automatic replacement.

Ideally, Ramaphosa's supporters wanted to prevent the Mokaba proposal from even being discussed at the NEC meeting, but some of the elders were concerned that a bruising contest lay ahead. On the eve of the meeting, Sisulu suggested that as a compromise, academic Kader Asmal should be appointed ANC chairman.

Mandela agreed. Not only would this stave off a decision about the deputy presidency, but also dispel perceptions that a Xhosa cabal dominated the ANC leadership.

Realising that they had been trumped, Mbeki's supporters abandoned their bid for his election to the number two spot. Mokaba opposed the plan to appoint Asmal, demanding that the chairmanship be put to the vote, convinced that Mbeki would be voted in as chairman.

Despite opposition from Mandela and Sisulu to Mbeki's nomination for the post, he won a clear majority and immediately began transforming the hitherto largely ceremonial position into a formidable power base from which he would launch his bid for the ANC presidency.

In the second half of 1993, Mbeki further alienated the left wing by suggesting privately that at some point the ANC would dissolve the tripartite alliance with COSATU and the SACP, and go it alone. 'What will happen is that as you get a normal society ... then the ANC as a broad movement will begin to identify itself in terms of different schools of thought. Out of the same ANC you would get a social democratic party ... and so on,' he predicted.

Following its massive victory in South Africa's first democratic elections in April 1994, it was time for the ANC to govern. Mandela favoured Ramaphosa as his deputy, but in keeping with his consensus style, consulted with senior alliance leaders before making a final decision.

Sisulu, ANC treasurer Thomas Nkobi and Jacob Zuma, assistant secretary general at the time, insisted that the post should go to Mbeki. COSATU general secretary Sam Shilowa and John Gomomo, the president, Charles Nqakula, general secretary of the SACP, and SANCO leaders supported their recommendation.

Mandela had developed great respect for Ramaphosa's negotiating skills and strongly favoured a non-Xhosa as his deputy, and made it clear during consultations that his reluctance to appoint Mbeki had nothing to do with his competence. But he was anxious not to repeat the pattern of other African liberation movements dominated by a single ethnic group, and went so far as to appoint a commission chaired by Sisulu to look at how the NEC could best be restructured to represent a cross-section of South Africa's population.

What became known as the Mandela Initiative would have required a departure from the ANC's established nomination procedures, and it was rejected at the 1994 national conference in Bloemfontein. Mandela was severely criticised by some NEC members, with one charging that he was conducting himself like an 'old-style communist'.

As Mandela vacillated over the choice of a deputy, support for Mbeki mounted. Dullah Omar, Peter Mokaba and Winnie Madikizela-Mandela all threw their weight behind him. In desperation, Mandela asked Ramaphosa and Mbeki to decide which of them would stand down.

Neither was prepared to do so. According to Mbeki, at a civil if not cordial meeting 'I discussed with Cyril the need to act in a way that did not result in conflict and tensions within the movement, and that it was wrong to act in a manner that would feed the notion of competition [between us].'

In desperation, Mandela considered bypassing the ANC candidates and appointing opposition leaders De Klerk and Buthelezi as his deputies, but his co-leaders were adamant that at least one of the posts should go to an ANC member.

Slovo, Maharaj and Mohammed Valli Moosa added their voices to the growing choir of support for Ramaphosa, with Slovo actively arguing against Mbeki, but in the end Mandela deferred to the Sisulu group and offered Mbeki the job. As consolation, Ramaphosa was invited to accept the plum cabinet post as foreign minister, but he declined.

One door to the presidency remained open for Ramaphosa. If he could poll enough votes for the deputy presidency of the ANC at the national conference in December, he would be well placed to challenge Mbeki for the number one spot at the decisive 1997 national conference.

Mandela alone among the ANC's senior leadership backed Ramaphosa's bid. At a heated meeting sought by Mbeki, he demanded Mandela's total commitment to his candidacy, accusing the president of causing division within the organisation by continuing to support Ramaphosa on ethnic grounds.

Mandela backed down, and in October Ramaphosa told his closest advisors he was ready to throw in the towel and accept that he had lost the succession battle to Mbeki. On the first day of the December conference, Mbeki was elected unopposed as deputy president of the ANC. Ramaphosa would remain secretary general.

Votes for Mbeki's key allies – Holomisa, Mokaba and Madikizela-Mandela – were among the five highest polled at the conference.

Realising that the ANC was in danger of losing Ramaphosa's skills, Mandela, Sisulu and Asmal turned their attention to a way of accommodating him in the future running of the country. At the NEC's meeting in September 1995, they tabled a proposal for a government structure that included both a president and a prime minister.

The premier (Ramaphosa) would appoint a cabinet in consultation with the president (Mbeki), who would have the power to veto suggestions. The two executives would be expected to develop and implement government policy by consensus.

On paper, the proposal was tailor-made to exploit the considerable combined talents of Mbeki and Ramaphosa. Mbeki had a reputation as a brilliant diplomat, but his performance in the day-to-day running of the government was not highly regarded. Ramaphosa, on the other hand, had proved himself a brilliant organiser, both with NUM and during the difficult constitutional talks.

But the NEC, led by Mbeki's supporters, rejected the proposal, hostile to any dilution of presidential powers for their candidate of choice. They warned that the proposed structure could create competing centres of power and executive paralysis over cabinet appointments and policy-making.

The alternative, endorsed by the NEC, provided for a president and a deputy, both elected by the National Assembly. The president would not be a member of parliament, and, in addition to being the majority party leader in parliament, the deputy would 'perform such duties and functions as the president assigns him or her'.

A disappointed Ramaphosa had privately told friends after the December 1994 conference that he planned to quit active politics when his term as chairman of the Constitutional Assembly expired in 1996, and he did. Mandela pleaded with him to stay in government, but Ramaphosa was adamant that he preferred to leave. All that remained was for Mandela to promise he would secure a good position for Ramaphosa with mining giant Anglo American.

In the end, the man whose star had shone as brightly as most in the galaxy of future ANC leaders made one cardinal mistake. He was one of the few members of the tripartite alliance who dared to publicly spar with Madikizela-Mandela and Mokaba, both of whom commanded huge grassroots support, and who had aligned themselves with Mbeki.

The way was clear for Mbeki to claim the presidency, uncontested, at the ANC's 1997 national conference. He and his strategists chose former intelligence operative and KwaZulu-Natal MEC Jacob Zuma as his deputy. Not only was Zuma a trusted Mbeki ally, but, as far as anyone knew, he harboured no ambitions to become president. Mbeki did not want a deputy who might challenge him midway through his term, and with a benign Zuma at his side, he would be able to focus on transforming the ANC from its socialist orientation to a modern political party with centrist market-based policies. The ANC envisaged by Mbeki and his strategists would be shaped along social democratic lines, not unlike Britain's New Labour Party, the German Social Democratic Party and the Swedish Social Democratic Party.

In order to implement his programme of change, Mbeki would need close allies in the highest echelon of the ANC. But, as the crucial national conference neared, challengers for the position of deputy president began to emerge.

Tokyo Sexwale, an unorthodox politician who even had his own radio talk show for a spell, was the first to threaten what had been regarded as a done deal.

As premier of Gauteng, South Africa's wealthiest province, which includes both the economic hub of Johannesburg and the administrative capital of Pretoria, Sexwale had wide appeal among both black and white. He lacked Mbeki's political experience, but a deputy presidency would be the ideal platform from which to flex his muscle within the ANC.

However, rumours that he was a drug dealer prevented Sexwale's campaign from ever getting out of first gear. Devastated by the accusations, he quit politics for business, becoming one of South Africa's wealthiest former activists within a few short years.

His supporters muttered darkly that the damaging gossip had been deliberately planted from within the Mbeki camp, but nothing could be proved. Notably, rumours of impropriety, carefully timed to discredit political rivals, would become a familiar tactic of ANC leadership struggles, with fingers regularly pointing towards the growing band of Mbeki-ites. By the time accusations had been investigated and found baseless, the alleged offender would long since have been effectively neutralised as a political contender.

Popular Mpumalanga premier and budding Afrikaans poet Mathews Phosa was Zuma's next challenger. His nomination by the Youth League and the ANC's Mpumalanga branch raised the ire of the ANC leadership to the extent that Mbeki dispatched a delegation to persuade Phosa's supporters to rethink their position.

They refused to budge. 'Not even someone from the national or provincial structures can tell us to withdraw this candidacy,' said Jackson Mthembu, a member of the provincial legislature. When Mandela appealed to Phosa to decline the nomination in favour of consolidating support for Zuma, lest Madikizela-Mandela make herself available for election, Phosa remained non-committal, pointing out that it was up to the ANC's Mpumalanga branch to make a decision.

No one, thus, was more surprised than Phosa himself to learn while on a trip to France that he had withdrawn from the race. To his consternation, Mandela had made the announcement, but an even greater shock lay in store.

Phosa arrived home to rumours that he had been a spy for the apartheid regime and was deeply involved in corruption in Mpumalanga. Yet another unwanted bid for the deputy presidency had been successfully thwarted, but one more hurdle remained.

It was the Women's League on Zuma's home turf of KwaZulu-Natal that put forward Winnie Madikizela-Mandela's name for the ANC's second highest post. The leadership sent several emissaries, who urged her to step back for the sake of party unity, but the formidable 'Mother of the Nation' sent them all packing.

Every cog in the powerful party machine was engaged to knock Madikizela-Mandela out of the running. Safety and security minister Steve Tshwete used an interview with the daily, the *Star*, to accuse her of lacking discipline and bringing the ANC into disrepute. Under relentless pressure from the party leaders, Mavivi Myakayaka-Manzini, a close confidante of Mbeki and a member of the national executive of the Women's League, overruled the KwaZulu-Natal branch and announced that Madikizela-Mandela's nomination had been withdrawn.

At an ANCWL meeting in Johannesburg, Madikizela-Mandela threatened to resign if the campaign of vilification against her did not stop. Then she wrote a letter to the ANC's National Working Committee, accusing her former husband, Thabo Mbeki, Steve Tshwete, Cheryl Carolus and Ronnie Mamoepa of orchestrating efforts to malign her.

She used the media to accuse the ANC leaders of being arrogant and abandoning the impoverished masses who had voted the party into power, and lost no opportunity to capitalise on the government's lack of delivery.

It was one of the most intense public displays of the seething power struggle in the ANC, culminating in senior party leaders testifying against Madikizela-Mandela at hearings of the Truth and Reconciliation Commission.

And there was a back-up plan. The rules of nomination for office were changed, so that candidates for the five top positions had to secure 30 per cent of the votes from the floor, instead of the customary 10 per cent, before a nomination became valid. Both the ANCWL and the ANCYL were also stripped of their right to independently nominate candidates.

Against this background, the ANC met in December 1997 in Mafikeng. The two burning questions were whether or not Madikizela-Mandela would toe the party line and whether the leadership would approve GEAR.

On election day, a massive cheer went up when Madikizela-Mandela entered the hall, but only 127 of the 3 046 delegates raised their hands in support of her nomination as deputy president.

She asked for an adjournment in order to consult with her advisors, but Mbeki, who was chairing the session, ruled that it was an inopportune time for a break. Left with no alternative, Madikizela-Mandela conceded defeat, but her parting shot spoke volumes.

'Comrade Thabo,' she said, 'I think I understand what is happening here. To those comrades who nominated me, I apologise for having to decline.'[13] Mbeki was smiling.

Though both 'the chief', as he is known to the inner circle, and Zuma were elected unopposed, Mbeki did not have it all his own way. The party left wing secured the position of secretary general for NUM's Kgalema Motlanthe, with Thenjiwe Mtintso as his deputy.

Mbeki also failed to have Tshwete installed as party chairman in the face of a challenge from Mosiuoa Lekota, backed by a loose alliance of left-wingers and inziles.

The chairmanship battle turned bitter, inflicting new scars and opening old wounds. From the outset, it was clear that the Eastern Cape and KwaZulu-Natal would decide the result. Tshwete had cut his political teeth in the Eastern Cape and was confident that he could deliver the regional vote. Mbeki loyalist Dumisani Makhaye swung into action to bag the support of KwaZulu-Natal, a far harder nut to crack, despite being Zuma's traditional support base.

Lekota had an intimate knowledge of the political configuration in KwaZulu-Natal, having operated from there in the late 1980s and early 1990s, before becoming premier of the Free State. Lekota had tackled corruption and infighting among the ANC's provincial leadership head-on, only to be ignominiously replaced, mid-term, by SABC chairperson Ivy Matsepe-Casaburri.

Mbeki used Tshwete as the hatchet man, but the decision to redeploy Lekota as chairman of the National Council of Provinces would backfire on them. If anything, his grassroots support had surged after what was seen as unfair treatment by the party leadership, and despite all the firepower unleashed by the Mbeki camp in support of Tshwete, Lekota was elected party chairman on a wave of jubilation. He was carried shoulder high around the hall in a victory lap, and his supporters toyi-toyied late into the night as they savoured his victory. 'A good man has won deservedly,' was how one delegate from the Eastern Cape summed it up.

It still remained for Mbeki to secure majority support in the NEC, and he had laid the ground for this shortly before the conference opened.

A group of 'concerned' leftists, mostly from the SACP and COSATU, had drawn up a list of alternative candidates who they believed would act as a bulwark against the hegemony of the moderate Mbeki-ites. Just days before the start of the conference, Mbeki got wind of the plan and demanded that SACP general secretary Charles Nqakula identify those involved in the 'plot'.

Under enormous pressure from Mbeki, Nqakula and his deputy, Jeremy Cronin, censured the group leaders and instructed them to stop lobbying for left-wing domination of the NEC, or face disciplinary hearings and possible expulsion.

The last-ditch attempt by the ANC's militant wing to regain influence in the post-apartheid organisation was duly extinguished, and this was, in fact, the last real organised threat against Mbeki from the left.

Five years later, Mbeki would consolidate his support base within the ANC still further, and ensure that residual elements to the left were more marginalised than ever. But by then, his remodelling of both the ANC and the South African economy would be well advanced.

# — 3 —

# Escaping
# Mandela's Shadow

Upon this a question arises: whether it be better to be loved than feared or feared than loved? It may be answered that one should wish to be both, but, because it is difficult to unite them in one person, it is much safer to be feared than loved, when of the two, either must be dispensed with.

– Machiavelli, *The Prince*[1]

IT WAS SAID TONGUE IN CHEEK, BUT THERE WAS AN UNDERLYING AND SERIOUS reality when Thabo Mbeki told outgoing ANC president Nelson Mandela: 'I will never, ever be seen dead in your shoes, because you always wear ugly shoes!'[2]

From the moment he delivered his maiden address as the new head of the ANC at the party's December 1997 conference in steamy Mafikeng, Mbeki was determined to create his own image. Both internationally and at home, the need to separate himself from his larger-than-life predecessor became one of the driving forces of Mbeki's reign.

At times, the inevitable comparison with Mandela exasperated him and drove the sensitive Mbeki to despair. Once, he burst out: 'Yes, indeed. Mandela has much larger feet. I guess I could go back 27 years, and try going to jail, and then come out and wear funny shirts.'[3] Mbeki's closest friend and ally, Essop Pahad, doesn't care for the media's treatment of his boss either. 'Why do you people always have to compare Thabo with Madiba? Look, this is not fair,' he complains.[4]

To some extent, Mbeki became the victim of the ANC's own success. While Mandela was in prison, the organisation meticulously and successfully cultivated his image as a liberation icon. His successor was always going to be measured against the standard of a demi-god – an impossible challenge for even the most accomplished contender. The reality is that Mandela made many mistakes during his tenure, and those closest to him knew that he was often impetuous, stubborn and quick-tempered. But the myth remained intact. Just as millions of Indians sanctified Mohandas Gandhi when he retreated from politics, Mandela has been all but beatified.

The relationship between Mandela and Mbeki was every bit as complex as one might expect of two people drawn together by history but frequently at odds with one another. Mandela admits to having drawn inspiration from Gandhi, and perhaps the relationship between the Mahatma and India's first post-independence prime minister Jawaharlal Nehru[5] is the closest parallel in recent history to the Mandela–Mbeki relationship. Gandhi pushed Nehru to the pinnacle of the Indian Congress Party, and Mandela's blessing – albeit reluctant – carried Mbeki to the top in the ANC, despite opposition from formidable rivals such as Cyril Ramaphosa, Mathews Phosa and Tokyo Sexwale. Gandhi had personally favoured one of his most trusted lieutenants, Vallabhbhai Patel, but nevertheless backed Nehru, because logic dictated that he alone at the time had the vision, brains and courage to govern India.

In a letter explaining his decision to Patel, Gandhi wrote: 'A great organisation cannot be governed by affections, but by cold reason. I plump for Pandit Jawaharlal [Nehru] as ... the best person to represent the nation and guide ... in the right channels the different forces that are at work in the country.'[6]

Similarly, Mandela met with a disappointed Ramaphosa at his home and told him that he had endorsed Mbeki's election because this was what the organisation wanted, though his heart had been set on Ramaphosa.

Mbeki's political future was inextricably bound to Mandela, just as Nehru's had been to Gandhi, but Madiba's occasional admonishments drove him to distraction, starting with the first piece of unsolicited advice Mandela offered at the Mafikeng conference in 1997 where Mbeki was elected.

'The leader must keep the forces together, but you can't do that unless you allow dissent,' Mandela warned his putative successor. 'People should be able to criticise the leader without fear or favour. Only in that case are you likely to keep your colleagues together.'

It was vintage Mandela. He knew that people both in the ANC and outside were worried about Mbeki's intolerance and vindictiveness against those who differed from him. He was also aware that few ANC leaders would be bold enough to confront Mbeki on these issues, so he took it upon himself to do so.

It's not that Mbeki is not a democrat at heart, but rather that he appears to be politically schizophrenic. Where the ANC is concerned, he demands centralised control and an absence of dissent, with recalcitrant critics being ruthlessly marginalised. In his role as a regional conflict mediator, however, he is the most congenial of hosts, accommodating the views of everyone involved in a relaxed ambience and eventually arriving at an acceptable compromise decision.

This is the style of his mentor, Oliver Tambo, and of a traditional African chief presiding over a community council or kgotla.

At the apex of his power, Nehru wrote popular perceptions of himself in his diary: 'Vast popularity, a strong will directed to a well-defined purpose, energy, pride, organisational capacity, ability, hardness and, with all his love of the crowd, an intolerance of others and a certain contempt for the weak and the inefficient. His flashes of temper are well known and even when they are controlled, the curling of the lips betrays him. His over-mastering desire to get things done, to sweep away what he dislikes and build anew, will hardly brook for long the slow processes of democracy.'[7]

Gandhi once chided Nehru for appearing to believe at times that he alone had the power to turn back the tides of poverty and human misery. 'We have made you King Canute so that you may do it better than others,' Gandhi said ironically.[8]

After leaving office, and fully aware of Mbeki's insecurities, Mandela went out of his way not to undermine his successor. He tried scrupulously not to govern from the political graveyard, publicly backed Mbeki at every turn and defended him at crucial moments when Mbeki appeared to be faltering.

Throughout 2001, a year perceived by Mbeki's closest allies as his *annus horribilis*, he could count on Mandela's support when he was besieged by internal party wrangles; when the ANC's left wing brazenly flexed its muscle; when confidence in his presidency was shattered by his unorthodox views on the growing crisis in neighbouring Zimbabwe; amid his strange revelations of a plot by ANC grandees to replace him. But Mbeki's intransigence on the AIDS pandemic eventually drove Mandela to throw protocol out the window and angrily remonstrate with his successor.

In fact, away from public scrutiny, Mandela would often pick up the telephone to Mbeki and roast him over a policy issue he was unhappy with. Mbeki would refuse to take the calls or meet with Mandela, instructing aides to say he was 'busy'.

Jakes Gerwel, who was as close to Mandela as anyone, commented: 'I can't imagine that the two men would ever be shoulder slapping buddies who would daily spend time together in the same pub.'[9]

The way Mbeki tells it, Mandela would sometimes call and say: 'This is what I think, what is your view?' Or Mandela might say: 'I saw the statement that you made and I'm not quite happy with it.' Alternately, Mbeki might say: 'I don't think this is a correct position to take.'[10]

Throughout the world, Mandela has become the grand symbol of South Africa's transition from the brutality of apartheid to a liberal, non-racial democracy. His ability to forgive those responsible for his almost three decades of incarceration was the perfect foil to the naysayers who predicted that the conflict and divisions in South Africa ran too deep for peace and reconciliation ever to become reality.

Mandela's most valuable contribution to the fledgling democracy was to cobble together a broad-based consent for the new order. His purpose was to 'carve out a new breathing space where pulses could settle, enmities subside and affinities become recast'.[11] Throughout the transition, his leadership served both to maintain the poor black majority's trust and loyalty towards the ANC, and to alleviate the fears of the predominantly white middle class, pampered and pandered to during white rule, and frightened of black majority rule.[12]

Like Mbeki, Mandela is extremely conscious of his place in history. He wants to be remembered as the extraordinary man who emerged from twenty-seven years in prison without rancour, to lead a divided South Africa into the future. During an address at the University of Potchefstroom in February 1996, he said: 'I will pass through this world but once, and I do not want to divert my attention from my task – which is to unite the nation.'[13] Even more revealing was his next sentence: 'I am writing my own testament because I am nearing my end. I want to be able to sleep till eternity with a broad smile on my face knowing that the youth, opinion-makers and everybody is stretching across the divide, trying to unite the nation.'[14] Gandhi, too, dreamt of uniting India's diverse groups.

Mandela's broad societal authority was akin to that of a benign patriarch, guided by the principles of inclusivity. Indeed, his leadership stemmed largely from his moral authority. For Mandela, as for Gandhi, the moral integrity of a leader is crucial.

By contrast, Mbeki is generally considered a visionary, 'can-do' politician. One South African journalist described him as the 'kick-arse' president.[15] According to the erudite analyst Hein Marais, Mandela's key accomplishment was to 'rearrange' the political stage and nudge the players into getting used to the new configuration. If that is true, then Mbeki's role is that of director.

Where the Mandela era was about reconciliation, compromise and new symbols of unity, the Mbeki period is far more about hands-on governance and management, fine-tuning new institutions, and establishing and entrenching new power blocs and political relations.[16] Mbeki has often told close associates that Mandela could have done more for black advancement had he not prized reconciliation above all else. While Mbeki must still tread the same fragile path between black hope and white fear, his main focus has been on transformation of the economy. He would like to be remembered as the person who brought economic, political and social benefits and equality to black South Africans and who led a change in the economic, political and social fortunes of the African continent.

Mandela often upbraided white South Africans, but his rebukes were softened with broad smiles and warm hugs. Mbeki is diligent about reassuring whites that they have a home on South African soil, but makes it clear that this means they also have obligations. He will not accept white complacency or the hackneyed argument that whites have already done enough. Having allowed Anglo American and other major South African corporations to move their share listings to the foreign financial capitals of the world, Mbeki expects them to return the favour.

Projecting a good image has been a recurring theme in Mbeki's life. While a pupil at Lovedale College, the Eton of black education for Mbeki's generation, in the Eastern Cape, even though he was one of the main instigators of a school strike, he made sure that he was viewed as a diligent student. He was nevertheless expelled and made his way to Johannesburg, where he came under the political tutelage of ANC legends Walter Sisulu and Duma Nokwe.

Mbeki's introduction to the world of non-racial politics included house parties in the plush northern suburbs, late-night drinking sessions, jazz clubs and endless youthful discourses about revolution. It was during this period that he befriended Essop Pahad and first engaged the flamboyant Ronnie Kasrils in debate.

Recruited to the SACP in 1962, he spent long hours under tutelage discussing Marxism with Bram Fischer and Michael Harmel, Joe Slovo and Yusuf Dadoo. When he went into exile, he studied economics on his father's instruction and remained an active communist.

But by the mid-1970s, Mbeki had fallen out bitterly with Slovo, was at logger-heads with Chris Hani and would soon cut all ties with the SACP. Ironically, Slovo had initially taken to Mbeki and was a mentor to him. But in 1979 they clashed bitterly over the drafting of the ANC's *Green Book*, a cornerstone policy blueprint, cobbled together mostly by Slovo and the ANC's left. It proposed that the ANC change strategy and become a Marxist–Leninist liberation movement in the mould of Mozambique's Frelimo and Angola's MPLA. Both these liberation movements were at the time scoring spectacular successes, while the ANC struggled. Even Tambo, not a Marxist by any stretch of the imagination, accepted the proposal in an attempt to breathe new life into the ANC's campaign.

However, Mbeki objected strenuously, arguing that the SACP, and not the ANC, was a socialist party. He enlisted the support of the powerful veteran black communist, then SACP general secretary Moses Mabhida, who backed Mbeki. Tambo demurred. Slovo was furious, and he was one of the prime movers to sack Mbeki from the party's politburo in the early 1980s, ostensibly for non-attendance of meetings. Partly, the SACP objected to Mbeki's new strategy of talking to whites linked to the apartheid establishment.

The difference in Mandela's and Mbeki's leadership styles has as much to do with their individual personalities and a generation gap as their specific experiences of the ANC. For almost thirty years, Mbeki knew the ANC as an exile movement in which, largely for security reasons, decisions were taken by the top coterie of leaders, and lower-level members were simply expected to accept and obey. Consequently, he learnt to regard relationships in terms of power and ascendancy, seeing even his own career as an ongoing game of chess in which the objective is to checkmate all opponents.

Mandela spent most of his twenty-seven years of imprisonment on Robben Island, where consultation and cooperation were the lifeblood of the political culture. Moreover, from the 1940s to the early 1960s, when Mandela cut his political teeth, the spirit of democracy was paramount within the ANC. Political prisoners took their cue from that tradition and developed a complex but effective network of negotiation, discussion and decision-making that recognised the equity of all and reflected a strong aversion to any one person having overriding authority. Great democratic leaders are visionaries. They have an instinct for their nation's future, a course to steer, a port to seek. Through their capacity for persuasion, they win the consent of their people and call forth democracy's inner resources. Jeremy Cronin, one of South Africa's major left-wing theoreticians, sums up the contrast between Mandela and Mbeki as follows: 'Mandela leads by example. Mbeki leads by seeking to articulate a vision.'[17]

Mbeki is the quintessential behind-the-scenes man, preferring to lead from behind rather than in a visible, bold, populist way. Critics often use his rather secretive style to support their assessment of him as a conniving, ruthless politician, but he often acts as a prophet in the wilderness. At the height of the struggle he engaged in such taboos as talking to white South African businessmen to lure them towards negotiation and compromise. He called on the ANC to formally end the armed struggle without securing any guarantees in return from FW de Klerk's government, even though the majority view inside the organisation was that this was not only premature, but tantamount to capitulation.

Mbeki is a formal man, who dresses for a political rally as he would for a corporate board meeting. His smiles are perfunctory, and he seldom laughs out loud spontaneously. Though his elegant suits and cosmopolitan air charm outsiders, he cuts an awkward figure in the rough and tumble of the townships. When the rest of the ANC dances and sings at rallies, he is far happier surveying the activity from his chair. He prizes competence far more highly than charisma, he is intensely reclusive, and he rarely offers a glimpse into his private life. Even his father was sometimes irritated by Mbeki's rather excessive woodiness and formality.

Mandela is tall, he laughs easily (in speeches he often endearingly pokes fun at himself), he wears distinctive loose shirts, even on formal occasions, and he has opened many aspects of his life, including his messy divorce from Winnie, to public scrutiny. He has a genius for the simple gesture that speaks to the soul,[18] and endeared himself to white sports fans by wearing South African rugby captain François Pienaar's No. 6 jersey during the 1995 Rugby World Cup. The following year, it was the national cricket team that he charmed with an unscheduled 'good luck' telephone call.

Such gestures are alien to Mbeki, who lacks the common touch that comes so naturally to Mandela. During the 2004 election campaign, voters were genuinely astonished to find him on the stump, campaigning door to door in some of the poorest townships and informal settlements, kissing babies and hugging pensioners. It was a masterstroke by his professional image consultants, but once the votes were in, he retreated into his customary shell once more. Nevertheless, it was during that campaign that Mbeki finally stepped out from under the giant shadow cast by Mandela and came of age as a leader in his own right.

Unfortunately, under Mbeki, the stiff, aloof intellectual, the ANC government has come across as uncaring and distant. Mandela's popularity had much to do with expressions of empathy with society's most needy and deeds that seemingly manifested the ANC promise of building a caring community. Though Mbeki's aim is to improve the lot of the poor, visible compassion is not his strong suit.

His bald statement, that he knew no one who had AIDS at a time when millions were known to be infected, is a case in point. It hasn't helped that some of his closest allies, like finance minister Trevor Manuel, have dismissed calls for additional aid to the poor as fostering a culture of dependency.

For all his outward poise, Mbeki is shy. He is also a workaholic. No matter how punishing his week, he still finds time to churn out a 2 500-word *Letter from the President* that is posted on the ANC's website. In fact, Mbeki may be the only head of state who compiles a weekly 'blog'.

When Mandela once suggested privately that Mbeki should take a holiday, he declined, dismissing concerns that he had too much on his plate with 'I don't know how much is too much, but there are so many things that need to be done.'[19]

At times of great pressure, his mentor, Tambo, a devout Christian, would seek out a church or a quiet corner in which to pray. Mandela often sneaked off to the countryside to be alone or relax with a grandchild on his knee. Under strict instructions from his medical team to de-stress, Mbeki has become a keen amateur photographer and may occasionally be found on the golf course. But his favourite hobby is surfing the Internet.

His management style is hands-on, down to the smallest detail, and even as head of state, he insists on writing his own speeches. According to Frank Chikane, this involves a process that goes more or less as follows:

> All manner of information is assembled on the assumption that Mbeki will want to incorporate it. Responsible departments are asked for drafts. If he is travelling, transcontinental telephone calls and faxes may be required to gather quotes and anecdotes he has remembered reading and has asked

for. In the end, his entire staff collapses in bed, exhausted. At that point, Mbeki goes to work at his computer, surfing the Internet for information and putting his thoughts on paper. At five or six in the morning, he heads for the shower, ready to speak at nine or ten. Very little, if anything, of what others have prepared has survived. It can be a very frustrating process.[20]

While Mandela was the consummate delegator, Mbeki finds it almost impossible to leave important tasks to others. Herein lies the problem – it is impossible for the president to deal with minute policy tasks personally. Not surprisingly, when this happens, it often leads to policy blunders. When he became president, the novelty of South Africa having a black leader had worn off, and every government programme or instance of non-delivery was open to criticism. Having fought for the throne, Mbeki had to build an administration whose performance would prove that his ascendancy was warranted.

Making deals is what Mbeki does best. His readiness to resort to expediency carries the danger of being seen as somewhat underhand at times, but opportunistic deal-brokering may be exactly what South Africa needed to consolidate the infant democracy.

His position was not unlike that of former Brazilian president Fernando Henrique Cardoso,[21] who also started out as a left-wing intellectual, but once in power, moved firmly to the right, while still using the slogans of the left to defend his conservative policies. Cardoso[22] applied a strategy of co-opting powerful figures behind his economic reforms and aggressively marginalising his opponents, both in government ranks and outside.

Despite the opposition of the trade unionists, communists and most of the ANC's once powerful left, Mbeki introduced the conservative economic policy, GEAR, in 1996. His success in getting the ANC to adopt the policy was due partly to his grasp of the economic detail and partly to his skill at building an alliance between what appear, to the outsider, to be opposing groups.

In a crisis, Mbeki inevitably relies on his considerable diplomacy. When Mandela came into direct confrontation with his critics in the cabinet, such as his former wife Winnie, Pallo Jordan and Bantu Holomisa, Mbeki's approach was carefully calculated with an eye to the future.

Mbeki's choice of advisors and frontmen and women often baffles. His detractors complain that his inner circle is like a royal court, with his advisors telling him only what they know he wants to hear. There is strong evidence to suggest that he rewards loyalty far more readily than competence.

His advisors serve as the presidential gatekeepers, shutting out the critical voices. Men who control the president's schedule, such as Essop Pahad, have the power to block access to Mbeki, and even senior ANC leaders have problems getting an appointment.

During his first term in office, Mbeki was constantly looking over his shoulder, imagining opponents breathing down his neck. His road to the top was paved with bruised egos and shattered careers, but never was his paranoia more apparent than when he announced that his former rivals – Ramaphosa, Sexwale and Phosa – were conspiring to oust him in 2001.

Mbeki dislikes the media and rarely speaks to journalists. He has an excellent media team, headed by the urbane Bheki Khumalo, but direct access to the president, even if only in the form of regular media conferences, would do much to dispel his image as a secretive, unapproachable elitist. Surprisingly, he used the media to great effect in exile, but as president he has become increasingly suspicious of their motives, and his antipathy is shared by Pahad and Mojanku Gumbi, Mbeki's legal advisor.

His infrequent appearances at parliament and treatment of the opposition with what borders on contempt do not endear him to his critics. Pahad argues that, as president, Mbeki is not an MP, and that Jacob Zuma, as deputy president, is in charge of government business in the House. Mandela, on the other hand, seized every opportunity to put his views across in parliament, and, like India's Nehru,[23] made a concerted effort to inculcate respect for both the institution and the official opposition.

Mbeki has a frosty relationship with opposition party leaders. Mandela created a special forum where they could discuss policy differences with him or voice their concerns. Consequently, opposition leaders were less inclined to aggressively attack him, as they do Mbeki on his rare parliamentary appearances.

Mbeki obtains acceptance of his policies from within the tripartite alliance by means of what sociologist Sakhela Buhlungu calls 'Mbeki logic', as opposed to 'Madiba magic'. Whereas Mandela sought to 'win the voluntary cooperation' of all interest groups, Mbeki 'demands cooperation'.[24]

The hallmark of Mbeki's style is to stack up as much support as possible, and to isolate or marginalise those who stubbornly refuse to toe the line. His backers are expected to maintain their position in perpetuity, posing no future challenge to the leader. He is particularly hard on the ANC's left, which has the potential to derail his reforms and become a real alternative to the ANC in the long term, unlike any of the current ineffective opposition parties.

Mbeki's standard response has been to offer the harshest critics of his policies in the trade union movement sinecure government posts. If, like COSATU general secretary Zwelinzima Vavi and its president Willie Madisha, they don't take the bait, they are publicly ridiculed and shut out by the president and his allies.

The union leaders have been branded as newcomers to the struggle who understand neither the history nor tradition of the liberation movement and have been cast outside the struggle mythology.

When the RDP was scrapped in favour of GEAR, Mandela justified the shift in the ANC's economic policy as an essential compromise to ensure stability and secure the support of groups that had the potential to destabilise the country. Mbeki argued that the ANC had to adopt GEAR in order to modernise the economy and deal with the awful realities of a world in which the state could ensure development only if it entered into a joint enterprise with the private sector. Privately, he suggested that the markets still doubted that the ANC was really committed to economic prudence.

Mbeki has an unfortunate knack of assembling unlikely constituencies to back his programmes, then dropping them when they have outlived their usefulness. He knew he would need Madikizela-Mandela's support to become president, and pleaded with Madiba to give her another chance. Jordan, a fellow intellectual, was a potential rival, however, so he happily encouraged Mandela to fire him. Even though Holomisa had supported Mbeki's climb up the political ladder, he too presented a possible future rival, and Mbeki thus had no qualms about dumping him as well.

Vindictiveness comes easy to Mbeki, and often instils both fear and anger in those who experience it at first hand. Madikizela-Mandela and Holomisa were among the victims of his wrath. He used both of them to mobilise grassroots support for his bid to become president, and quickly discarded them once his objectives had been reached. Madikizela-Mandela became deeply embittered when Mbeki dumped her. It was she, after all, who had warned him that Mandela and others favoured Ramaphosa as the heir apparent.

Nor would she forget the public humiliation of being pushed away, so forcefully that she lost her hat, when she leaned down at a public rally on 16 June 2001 to kiss him hello. Madikizela-Mandela tacked a photograph of the altercation to her office wall, almost like a trophy. She also liked to display newspaper cartoons depicting Mbeki's failings and follies, especially those by the brilliant political cartoonist Jonathan Shapiro, or Zapiro as he is better known.

Mandela went to great lengths to facilitate a smooth transition for Mbeki. By the end of 1995, the ANC's deputy president was wholly in charge of the day-to-day running of the government and the cabinet, leaving Mandela to focus on what he saw as his primary task, namely nation-building and reconciliation. On a visit to London in 1997, Mandela explicitly stated: 'The ruler of South Africa, the *de facto* ruler, is Thabo Mbeki. I am shifting everything to him.'[25]

Long before his inauguration as president in 1999, Mbeki began expanding his office, rapidly increasing the size of his staff and bringing all his long-time allies into his 'kitchen cabinet.' His first major appointment was that of Essop Pahad, his close friend since they were students together in Sussex and a political street fighter of note. With Pahad as his parliamentary counsellor, Mbeki established a direct link with the legislature, parliament's important committees and the ANC caucus. Moss Ngoasheng and Vusi Mavimbela were appointed as his economics and political advisors respectively, and former UDF leader Frank Chikane became director-general in Mbeki's office.

A number of institutions were brought under Mbeki's control, most importantly the Government Communications and Information Service (GCIS), headed by his protégé, Joel Netshitenzhe. In June 1997, Mbeki established an important new unit in his office, the Coordination and Implementation Unit (CIU), which later evolved into the Policy Coordination and Advisory Service (PCAS). The PCAS is not accountable to any legislative body. When it was set up, no formal announcement was made and its functions were shrouded in mystery.

Mbeki's non-transparent way of operating irritated many, and some cabinet ministers warned that his office was becoming an economic 'super-ministry'. In 1996, he had put together a secretive twenty-four-member think tank called the Consultative Council to give him political advice. The council had no constitutional or administrative status and met monthly at Mbeki's Pretoria home.

Pahad was the convener, and members included a raft of people from both the government and external agencies: Shilowa, who was still general secretary of COSATU; SACP general secretary Charles Nqakula; Pahad's brother Aziz, another long-standing Mbeki friend; safety and security minister Sydney Mufamadi; defence minister Joe Modise; Durban-based human rights lawyer Linda Zama; Development Bank of Southern Africa chairman Wiseman Nkuhlu; and National Olympic Council of South Africa president Sam Ramsamy.

Not even the ANC knew the details of what the council discussed, or why, but Mbeki's ever-expanding 'empire' began to concern observers, including Mandela.

One morning, Mandela called his deputy to raise the issue with him. After being told several times by aides that Mbeki was 'busy', Mandela walked to his nearby residence in the government enclave of Bryntirion and demanded to see Mbeki, who was taking a shower.

It was after this that Mandela began to have doubts about Mbeki's suitability as his successor. The NEC was stunned when Mandela informed them at a meeting on 10 November 1996 that he had not yet chosen a successor, and that no one should assume it would be Mbeki.

'There has been a perception that I have already chosen my successor,' he said. 'There is talk that Comrade Mbeki is the heir apparent, but all this is not true. I have not chosen anyone to take over. The whole matter is in the hands of the congress.'[26]

Coming on the eve of a European tour that Mbeki would use to introduce himself to the leaders of ten nations, Mandela's warning was a bombshell.

'It's a misconception that I have already chosen a successor,' Mandela continued.

'What I have said is that we have a number of competent, gifted and experienced leaders. Any one of them could qualify. But if the leadership [of the ANC] elects Mbeki, I would support that, because he is competent and deserves that position.'[27]

Mbeki's arbitrary nature was never better illustrated than by his handling of the Truth and Reconciliation Commission's final report in 1998. On learning that the TRC, under Archbishop Desmond Tutu, had condemned the torture and execution of dissidents in ANC camps in Angola, Mbeki denounced the five-volume report without reading it.

'They are wrong,' he said. 'Wrong and misguided.'[28]

When the TRC refused to excise references to human rights violations in the camps, Mbeki went to court to prevent publication of the report. The Cape High Court turned down his application.

Mandela, by contrast, welcomed the report. 'I have no hesitation in accepting the report of the TRC, with all its imperfections,' he said. He made a point of publicly thanking Tutu for his work, and, in the face of Mbeki's attitude, several NEC members also contacted Tutu and some of the commissioners to express their gratitude and acceptance of the commission's findings.

Mbeki can be both impetuous and indecisive. According to Mandela, 'He would not confront problems in a direct manner as I have done. He is too diplomatic for that. He is sometimes criticised by our own people, who say he is indecisive when faced with a situation that requires firmness. But the man is an asset, not only to the ANC, but to the country as a whole.'[29]

Mbeki subscribes to the 'Third Way' of running a country, espoused by Britain's Tony Blair, Germany's Gerhard Schroeder and Sweden's Göran Persson – less government, market-related delivery, greater distance from unions and close proximity to business.

Essentially, Mbeki sees himself as the chief executive of SA Inc., and runs the government as if it were a major corporation, with the cabinet and the ANC's National Executive Committee as affiliates.

Whereas Mandela was 'more like a ceremonial head of state, more like a constitutional monarch, submitting himself with a strong sense of duty to the disciplines of party democracy through the Cabinet or ANC NEC',[30] Mbeki has consolidated power in the presidency, which is bigger, more powerful and has a far larger budget than under Mandela.

Mbeki is not one for the big hall meeting. He excels at formulating policy in small, bilateral groups, and resolves conflict by talking to the parties concerned individually and securing separate agreements. Official policy is increasingly the product of bilateral meetings.[31]

The dilemma facing governments that embark on reform is that broad consultation with diverse political forces may lead to inertia, while reforms imposed from above may be impossible to implement in the face of political resistance and economic incredulity. Mbeki appears to have embarked on a style described as 'mandatism' by Polish political economist Adam Przeworski.[32]

It is based on former British prime minister Margaret Thatcher's attitude: she told the people what she would do if elected, they voted for her, and she thus had a mandate to do what she had said she would; voters would have the chance to decide whether this, indeed, was what they wanted when they next went to the polls.

This means that from one election campaign to the next, the governing party requires no consultation with opposing political forces either in parliament or in any other sector in order to formulate and implement stated policies.

Mbeki's government and party reforms have tended to be initiated from above, as with GEAR. Thus they are launched by surprise, independently of public opinion and without the participation of organised political forces.

This technocratic style of policy-making sees governments demoralise their own supporters rather than compromise their programmes through public consultation. In the end, the electorate learns that it can vote, but not choose; legislatures feel they have no role in policy-making, and civil society perceives that its voice counts for nothing. The inherent danger of Mbeki's presidential style is that it tends to undermine representative institutions.[33] Consultation and negotiation are vital tools for the channelling of political conflict. If decisions are made elsewhere, representative institutions wilt. Conversely, involving people in the process of change and making them partners in the benefits and obligations of the state not only liberates popular energy, but also promotes popular support, which had been Gandhi's central teaching. Nehru only realised the value of democracy from below late in life, when his powers had already waned. Herein lies the lesson for Mbeki.

# — 4 —

# Was the ANC
# Trumped on
# the Economy?

The economists, by dint of their refusal to see that economic choices are practicable only if the political and social compromises that they imply are acceptable, are encouraging a utopian economism. — Samir Amin, 1993[1]

Reconciliation means that those who have been on the underside of history must see that there is a qualitative difference between repression and freedom. And for them, freedom translates into having a supply of clean water; having electricity on tap; being able to live in a decent home, and have a good job; to have accessible healthcare. I mean, what's the point of having made this transition if the quality of life of these people is not enhanced and improved? If not, the vote is useless! — Desmond Tutu, 1999[2]

WITH HINDSIGHT, IT IS CLEAR THAT THE NATIONAL PARTY WAS MASTERFULLY trounced by the ANC in the political poker game around the negotiating table in the early 1990s. However, many of those involved have since readily acknowledged that the ANC was outfoxed when it came to the economy.

When apartheid ended, South Africa needed to attain three goals simultaneously: constitutional democracy, industrial modernisation, and economic and social reform. But the ANC had no plan for the practical implementation of anything except donning the mantle of power after centuries of colonialism and oppression. There was a strangely naive expectation that the abolition of apartheid in itself would put an end to black economic deprivation. Saki Macozoma, former ANC MP and now a successful businessman, says the ANC calculated that 'the economic question would be dealt with once the democratic government was in place'.[3]

The single pillar on which the ANC's economic policy rested, even after its Harare conference in April 1990 that set out its basic economic views, was nationalisation. In his first public address after being released from prison, Nelson

Mandela chilled white hearts with his affirmation that 'nationalisation of the mines, banks, and monopoly industry is the policy of the ANC, and a change or modification of our views in this regard is inconceivable'.[4]

The Johannesburg Stock Exchange[5] tumbled immediately, but for almost a year afterwards Mandela religiously punted the same line as the only way to eradicate the economic inequalities of apartheid.

After all, he would remind his audiences, the National Party had nationalised key industries such as transport and heavy engineering in order to empower the Afrikaner, so why should blacks not take the same route?

The majority of NEC and ANC members shared this view, with the most militant factions going so far as to equate capitalism with apartheid. Yet, by the time Mandela was sworn in as South Africa's first black president in May 1994, the ANC had undergone a dramatic shift towards economic conservatism. Thabo Mbeki's talented minerals and energy affairs minister, Phumzile Mlambo-Ngcuka, says the change did not come overnight.[6]

The business community had realised as far back as 1985 that unless it eschewed apartheid, capitalism would be the victim. Those foolish enough to still insist that they would not talk to 'terrorists' were persuaded quickly enough after South Africa's humiliating debt repayment default that the ANC had to be included in their future, or there would be no future, in economic terms.

Since the 1960s, ANC president Oliver Tambo had lobbied Western governments, which were lukewarm, the Soviet Union and its allies, the developing world and Asian governments for support, with mixed results. From the early 1980s, with Mbeki in tow, Tambo embarked on a series of meetings with large corporations, especially those with South African links, in search of support for economic sanctions against the apartheid regime. Some companies, such as Citibank and General Motors, initiated talks with Tambo on the subject.

The Lancaster House Agreement, which had ushered in the independence of Zimbabwe in 1980,[7] was a seminal moment for the ANC. Zimbabwe's ill-prepared liberation movements were pressured by African leaders such as Zambia's Kenneth Kaunda and Tanzania's Julius Nyerere into making a hastily conceived deal with renegade white Rhodesian prime minister, Ian Smith. Tambo and other leaders realised that unless the ANC seized the initiative, the movement could face a similar fate.

Far better, he frequently suggested to Mbeki, to persuade the white South African establishment, including the business community, that the ANC was not the monster it had been painted by the National Party government. It would be tricky, as many militants were vehemently opposed to any form of negotiation with the enemy, so Tambo entrusted the task to his right-hand man, Mbeki.

Meanwile, certain white establishment groups within the country realised that a peaceful resolution to South Africa's problems must include the ANC. 'Verligtes' such as FW de Klerk's brother, Willem de Klerk, senior figures in Afrikaans churches, members of the academia, some business leaders and members of the opposition realised that an attempt had to be made to seek out the ANC.

In 1986, Mbeki drafted a proposal that the ANC should open talks, in the utmost secrecy, with business people, homeland leaders and Afrikaner dissidents in order to increase pressure on the apartheid government from within.[8] Such heresy fuelled speculation among activists that Mbeki was an enemy agent,[9] but he maintained his position that in order for the ANC to win over sceptical whites and influential Western governments, it needed to show a moderate face, especially on the economy.

Tambo endorsed the proposal unconditionally, and a flurry of meetings between the ANC and white establishment representatives took place in Britain and Zambia. Mbeki's eloquent and reasonable arguments reassured anxious Afrikaners, other white South Africans and Western liberals alike, but the ANC's left, particularly the SACP, was incensed, and Mbeki came into direct conflict with both Joe Slovo and Chris Hani.

Many years later, it would emerge that from his prison cell, Mandela was also trying to engage National Party strongmen in dialogue, even as the ANC's radical internal wing and MK were gearing up for a final armed push against the apartheid security forces to usher in the long-awaited revolution.

After the fall of the Berlin Wall and the collapse of the Soviet Union, Tambo advised Mbeki that a moderate approach, especially on the economy, would help turn the tide of events in the ANC's favour. In September 1989, Tambo suffered a stroke, leaving the movement rudderless. Mbeki assumed many of his duties, including overseeing the drafting of the Harare Declaration, the ANC's seminal policy statement after the organisation was unbanned in February 1990.

The left wanted the declaration to send a clear signal of revolutionary commitment that would resonate with the militant faction, but Mbeki and a slew of senior leaders felt the time had come to allay the fears of foreign governments, business and white South Africans who might otherwise be drawn to the right wing. However, the document made it clear that apartheid had created a legacy of such terrible proportions that extensive state intervention would be a prerequisite for reconstruction.[10]

Following Mandela's release from prison, the spectre of nationalisation dominated all dialogue. When he told leading businessmen at a lunch organised by veteran opposition politician Helen Suzman that only nationalisation could redress the inequalities created by apartheid, the All-Gold Index plunged by 5 per cent. Mandela had asked Suzman to introduce him to local captains of industry, and many of those who attended the luncheon later formed the nucleus of Mandela's economic advisory group during constitutional negotiations.

By the end of the ANC's first year as a legal organisation, nationalisation had become such an albatross that Mbeki, senior ANC strategists and the Brenthurst Group, as the business group became known, suggested Mandela should refrain from further public reference to the concept.

He listened, and, addressing business leaders in Pittsburgh, Pennsylvania, sought to reassure potential investors that an ANC government could be trusted. He said: 'The private sector must and will play the central and decisive role in the struggle to achieve many of the [transformation] objectives ... let me assure you that the ANC is not an enemy of private enterprise ... we are aware that the investor will not invest unless the security of that investment is assured. The rates of economic growth we seek cannot be achieved without important inflows of foreign capital. We are determined to create the necessary climate that the foreign investor will find attractive.'[11]

At the World Economic Forum in Davos, Switzerland, in February 1992, three left-wing delegates persuaded Mandela that the ANC would be wise to ditch nationalisation as the basis of its economic policy.

Wined and dined by the world's top bankers and industrialists, he initially persisted in his argument that the ANC intended doing nothing that countries such as Britain, Germany and Japan had not already done by relying on state-owned industry to rebuild their economies in the aftermath of global conflict. The Dutch minister of industry was sympathetic, but brutally frank. 'That was what we understood then,' she pointed out. 'But the economies of the world are interdependent. The process of globalisation is taking root. No economy can develop separately from the economies of other countries.'[12]

Like Britain's Tony Blair, Mandela's grasp of economics was somewhat rudimentary. He came from a generation of African nationalists who used the rather vague Freedom Charter, which calls for public ownership, as their economic touchstone. However, what finally convinced Mandela were the experiences of two avowed socialist states, China and Vietnam, whose leaders told him that the collapse of the Soviet Union had led them to embrace private enterprise.

Not surprisingly, ANC leaders expected post-apartheid South Africa to benefit from something akin to the Marshall Plan, the US-led initiative to rebuild Germany after the Second World War. ANC thinking was based on the fact that many Western countries and corporations were complicit in extending apartheid's lifespan through direct or indirect economic support for the hated regime. Such notions were soon quashed, however, when Western governments made it plain that the best the ANC might expect was a deluge of foreign investment if South Africa applied orthodox, market-friendly economic policies.

So when Mandela boldly proposed in late 1992 that the ANC should abandon nationalisation, the rest of the leadership emphatically rejected the idea. Trade union leader Alec Erwin – then still firmly on the left – stated angrily that COSATU objected to privatisation as an alternative to nationalisation. Mandela was accused of betraying the Freedom Charter, and the ANC economic conference vehemently rejected his proposal.

A youthful Tito Mboweni, who chaired the heated session, accepted a proposal from the floor that the issue be referred to a discussion group, which later presented a compromise proposal calling for public sector economic involvement to be expanded or reduced on a case-by-case basis. It was left to the drafting committee to finesse the concept into the ANC's *Ready to Govern* policy document, and Mandela and Mbeki made sure that the committee was packed with centrists.

A year later, Mandela and Mbeki would succeed in having nationalisation expunged from all ANC policy documents.

Going into negotiations with the South African government, the ANC was politically adept. Both the international network it had built to put pressure on apartheid's custodians and the guerrilla campaign waged against its security forces were successfully employed in support of the organisation's historical mission, namely full political rights for blacks.

Strategically, however, the ANC was guilty of a grievous omission, since it had never done its homework on the internal dynamics of South Africa's relatively developed industrial economy. Studies had been confined to the economies of Vietnam, Cuba, Mozambique, Angola and Zimbabwe – all foreign to the character of South Africa's existing model.

The position was exacerbated by the fact that throughout the 1980s the ANC had devoted its resources to building a military capability, even though from the middle of the decade the struggle arena extended to the workplace, mines, civic bodies, schools, universities, churches and the retail sector in the form of consumer boycotts.

The United Democratic Front had successfully mobilised opposition to bread-and-butter issues, ranging from township service charges to education, while the trade unions became a well-oiled mechanism for negotiating labour reforms with both industry and the government. When the UDF was absorbed into the movement and COSATU also deferred to the ANC, valuable potential economic negotiating skills were lost. Most of the former high-profile internal activists were in awe of the returned exiles, who were regarded as struggle heroes.

'As a liberation movement,' SACP deputy general secretary Jeremy Cronin has conceded, 'we were not well positioned, intellectually, theoretically in terms of policy formation, in terms of socio-economic transformation. It was understandable. We had been very focused on the political tasks, democratisation, mobilisation, fighting a guerrilla struggle.'[13]

Exactly how delinquent the ANC was can be seen from the fact that, after almost eighty years as a liberation movement, the organisation first formed a dedicated department of economic policy in 1990, with Trevor Manuel as the head. Consequently, the ANC entered the multiparty negotiations at a severe disadvantage against the ruling National Party's massive economic capacity, which included both the business community and all the state's resources.

In addition, with its own members at loggerheads over economic policy, the ANC was vulnerable to relentless pressure from local and international business, the media, and multilateral organisations such as the World Bank and International Monetary Fund (IMF).

Local business groups churned out sophisticated and slickly packaged ready-made economic scenarios and lined up selected foreign economists to give orthodox opinions, which would then be widely quoted. Adherents of redistribution were portrayed as the 'loony left', while praise was lavished on the centrists.

It was an onslaught for which the ANC was wholly unprepared. Key economic leaders were regularly ferried to the head offices of international organisations such as the World Bank and IMF, and during 1992 and 1993 several ANC staffers, some of whom had no economic qualifications at all, took part in abbreviated executive training programmes at foreign business schools, investment banks, economic policy think tanks and the World Bank, where they were 'fed a steady diet of neo-liberal ideas'.[14] It was a dizzying experience. Never before had a government-in-waiting been so seduced by the international community. Both the World Bank and the IMF sought to influence the ANC's economic policy, frequently warning against pursuing 'unorthodox' policies. Senior executives such as Stanley Fischer, then vice-president of development economics at the World Bank, regularly met with ANC heavyweights to counsel caution. Both the World Bank and the IMF went so far as to employ ANC centrists in their local offices.

South African business leaders joined the stampede to woo Mandela and other ANC leaders. Anglo American's Harry Oppenheimer was eager to entertain Mandela at his private estate, Brenthurst, while Anglovaal's Clive Menell hosted Mandela's first Christmas as a free man at his mansion, Glendirk, tucked away at the foot of Cape Town's Table Mountain.

While separated from his wife, Winnie, Mandela's home for several months was the palatial Johannesburg estate of self-made insurance tycoon Douw Steyn. Mandela's autobiography was launched from the home of the Auto & General founder.

The younger Mandela daughter, Zinzi, had a honeymoon partly financed by resort and casino king Sol Kerzner, and Mandela spent Christmas 1993 in the Bahamas as the guest of Heinz and Independent Newspapers chairman Sir Anthony O'Reilly.

Mbeki's father, Govan, was appalled at the influence of the Brenthurst Group on both his son and Mandela, while Harry Gwala, the ANC's influential leader in KwaZulu-Natal, denounced the 'capitalist influence' on ANC economic policy. Walter Sisulu privately cautioned Mandela about the growing perception that the ANC's economic policy had been hijacked by big business.

But Mandela and Mbeki were desperate to dispel predictions that a black government in South Africa would go the same way as those in countries north of the Limpopo River. Mbeki, in particular, would have no truck with anything that could be vaguely construed as Eastern European socialism or its African equivalent. He would later admit that Zimbabwe and Tanzania served as valuable lessons on the pitfalls of state-led spending sprees. Both Mandela and Mbeki were convinced that for a black government to gain respect in the West, it needed to follow economic and social policies modelled on those of Britain, Germany and the United States. Mbeki and others of his generation had seen African and Eastern European socialism in action, and wanted nothing to do with it.

Mbeki toiled ceaselessly to prevent any group from steering the ANC towards a socialist nirvana, but he knew that the only sure way to prevent this was by wresting control of the alliance's economic machinery from the SACP and COSATU. It was no accident that Trevor Manuel was the first head of the ANC's department of economic policy.

Along with Cheryl Carolus and Dullah Omar, Manuel had been one of the UDF centrists, and had propelled himself to the top of the organisation in the Western Cape by elbowing out the charismatic torchbearer of the left, Johnny Issel. With Mbeki's backing, Manuel marshalled enough support to prevent the SACP's man, Sisulu's son Max, from heading up the economic structure.

The department's first policy statement was cautious:

> The engine of the economy of a developing, non-racial and non-sexist country should be the growing satisfaction of the basic needs of the impoverished and deprived majority of our people. We thus call for a programme of growth through redistribution which acts as a spur and in which the fruits of growth are redistributed to satisfy basic needs.[15]

But by April 1992, Manuel made it clear that 'nationalisation will only be used as a last resort'.[16]

COSATU leaders, concerned since the late 1980s that the ANC seemed to have no clear and ready economic policy strategy, had launched research and a series of workshops, publishing the results as *Our Political Economy: Understanding the Problems*.[17] The main elements of the suggested growth path rested on massive investment in training and development; comprehensive extension of basic services and infrastructure; adding value to raw materials; large-scale redirection of investment into productive capacity, technological innovation and research; reorientation of the manufacturing sector to produce affordable commodities for the mass market; rural development and land reform.

Out of this came the COSATU blueprint for growth through redistribution, which was adopted at the trade union federation's economic policy conference in March 1992. Alec Erwin, the former militant general secretary of the Federation of South African Trade Unions (FOSATU), was the patron of COSATU's academic economists, and until shortly before taking his seat in the cabinet, would fiercely insist that growth could be achieved only through redistribution. One of Mbeki's finest internal coups would be to lure Erwin into his economic camp, thus pulling the plug on COSATU's dominance of the tripartite alliance's economic thought.

Sympathetic local and international economists, who were becoming increasingly worried about the perceived paucity of the ANC's policy proposals, set up the Macroeconomic Research Group (MERG) in 1992 under the leadership of Vella Pillay. A former advisor to the Bank of China, he was widely expected to be the ANC's first Reserve Bank governor.

MERG's first report reiterated the concept of growth through redistribution, but the ANC leadership had already shifted firmly to the centre, and Mandela and Mbeki, who feared it could be construed in business circles as socialist, did not welcome the proposal. It was time to sideline both Pillay and MERG.

Foreign diplomats began showing unusual interest in MERG's activities, with both the British and US ambassadors dropping in unannounced at Pillay's office to inquire about the progress of policy formulation. Walter Sisulu had warned Pillay at a private meeting early in 1993 that new pressure was being brought to bear on the ANC over its economic policy, but Pillay ignored the danger signals and would later admit he had been politically naive.[18]

Manuel and Mboweni were among the ANC leaders sponsored by the World Bank and IMF for training in orthodox international economics,[19] and Mbeki would have little trouble persuading them to abandon growth through redistribution.

In November 1993, Mandela withdrew an earlier offer to write the foreword for MERG's document, *Make Democracy Work*, lest he be seen as endorsing the Pillay group's proposals. In terms of the MERG blueprint, state investment in social and physical infrastructure – housing, education, health, electrification and road development – would account for more than 50 per cent of growth in the first phase of ANC governance. The state would apply a strategic mix of incentives and regulations to improve industrial performance and exercise more control over the Reserve Bank.

South Africa's white business community went on the attack. Economist Terence Moll labelled the plan 'macroeconomic populism' and 'a dangerous fantasy'.

Counter-proposals from the private sector included the Mont Fleur scenarios, Nedcor and Old Mutual's *Prospects for a Successful Transition*, and insurance conglomerate Sanlam's *Platform for Investment.*

Unlike the political aspects of the constitutional negotiations led by Cyril Ramaphosa, the economic talks took place behind closed doors, allowing the centrists free rein on compromises. When confronted by NEC members asking for report-backs, Mbeki downplayed the discussions as 'technical' and merely 'administrative'.

COSATU leaders were growing increasingly anxious over the free hand given to Mbeki and his economic negotiating team, and general secretary Jay Naidoo warned Mbeki that the trade unions would not be dictated to by anyone, including the ANC. He also reaffirmed that as far as economic policy went, the intention was

> of necessity, to influence and lobby all the political organisations we can. The most important is the ANC. So we make no bones that we wish to influence the ANC – and in return, they seek to influence us. What we are doing is raising the issue of the orientation of ordinary people, of workers. We want to promote the economic debate, not stifle it. We are not prepared as trade unionists to go the same way as those under Kaunda and Mugabe. We want our key rights in legislation. We are not interested in blind faith.[20]

Anger at the ANC economic negotiators spilt over at COSATU's July 1991 conference, where members slammed what they saw as attempts by Mbeki and his centrist ANC allies to take control of the trade union movement or 'subvert it from within'.[21]

Naidoo recalled: 'The issue of economic negotiations was of central concern to COSATU. Because the ANC is a political organisation, its focus has been primarily on political issues. We were not trying to usurp the ANC's position. COSATU has always been a political player and intends remaining a political player, even if we have an ANC government in power.'[22]

The situation became so serious that COSATU considered sending its own team of negotiators into the arena. Indeed, in November 1991, COSATU demanded that FW de Klerk set up a 'macroeconomic negotiating forum' to negotiate separately for a new economic dispensation. The leadership at COSATU's conference in December 1991 decided to continue being represented at the talks by the ANC. If COSATU took a seat at the table, the leadership argued, a raft of other interest groups could be prompted to do the same, making the process even more cumbersome than it already was.[23] Though some trade unionists, especially those in the National Union of Metalworkers of South Africa, demanded that COSATU negotiate as an independent force, the leadership position carried the day.

In September 1993, COSATU convened a special national congress to debate the adoption of a reconstruction and development programme, which would be presented to the ANC. The intention was that COSATU would persuade the ANC to adopt the programme as its election platform, and in this they would succeed. Although the final RDP document adopted by the ANC was revised many times in an attempt to make it more acceptable to the business community, it retained the core elements of the COSATU proposals, famously promising 'a better life for all' in the form of a million houses over a five-year period, basic services such as electricity and water, and free education for the previously disadvantaged.

Prior to 1994, the majority of tripartite alliance members believed that an ANC government's economic policy would be based on those of the Soviet Union, Eastern Europe or Cuba. However, when constitutional negotiations got under way in South Africa, several governments that had evolved from former liberation movements in the developing world were in deep economic crisis.

The Social Democratic Party in Sweden, the Labour Party in the Netherlands, the Pan Hellenic Socialist Party in Greece and the socialists under François Mitterand in France were not faring well either, and the ANC could not adopt any of the established European socialist models with confidence.

According to former communist and ANC negotiator Mac Maharaj, 'there were no examples to learn from or use as a guide'.[24] He said, 'We could not go it alone. Countries that did, such as Sweden, had the space to do so with the Cold War still raging and the world being bipolar. The ANC came to power at the end of the Cold War in a unipolar world. We had no room to manoeuvre.'[25]

Maharaj pointed out that African states which had chosen to deviate from established economic models, such as Tanzania under Julius Nyerere and Egypt under Gamal Abdel-Nasser, continued to suffer from underdevelopment.

With Francis Fukuyama's 'end of history' thesis ringing in their heads, the ANC had no appetite for risk. Jeremy Cronin explained:

> The triumph of neo-liberalism was at its zenith in the early 1990s. So for a combination of reasons, including the sheer power, the ideological and hegemonic power of the neo-liberal model and the weakness of the left, which may have been with us through the twentieth century, but had become apparent in the 1990s, whether from panic or deep concern, laden with the responsibilities of governing, they were persuaded of certain aspects, not necessarily the whole package. The core aspects of the neo-liberal paradigm became very influential in government circles and in leading parts of the ANC.[26]

Meanwhile the ANC, influenced by Mbeki, appointed Stan Greenberg, former advisor to the US Democratic Party, as its policy advisor. His success in skilfully turning the Democratic Party into a party of fiscal discipline had impressed Mbeki and many of his centrist allies. Greenberg was instrumental in pushing the ANC to adopt policies that appealed to a broader audience.

Among the costliest agreements reached at the Convention for a Democratic South Africa (CODESA) was the honouring of contracts for public servants. The sunset clause that protected apartheid-era government employees from wholesale retrenchment was designed to prevent disgruntled state employees from destabilising the transition from apartheid to democracy, but its cost would be exorbitant. One of the most far-reaching compromises agreed to by the ANC guaranteed the full benefits of all public servants who left voluntarily, imposing a huge financial burden on the incoming government of national unity (GNU).

Slovo argued that it would probably take years for the ANC to assume control of the levers of government, and that meanwhile the existing public service was needed to keep the massive state machine running. In the same spirit, the ANC agreed to a continuation of established economic policies by the GNU, and Mandela's first cabinet would include National Party veterans in the key economic portfolios of finance and mineral and energy affairs. Chris Stals would remain governor of the Reserve Bank, which would maintain its independence and boost confidence in the financial markets.

The Reserve Bank is directly responsible for monetary and interest rate policy, which impacts on fiscal and industrial policies as well as the state of the economy. 'South African Reserve Bank independence meant that democratic parliamentary control over these critical areas of economic policy has been removed altogether or at least potentially undermined.'[27]

Strenuous attempts by the World Bank and the IMF to influence the new democracy's policies finally bore fruit in November 1993, when ANC negotiators signed an $850-million IMF Compensatory and Contingency Financing Facility. Mbeki was a member of the working group on transitional government arrangements,[28] and the loan was intended to support South Africa's balance of payments following the decline in agricultural exports and the increase in imports caused by a prolonged drought. As a condition of the loan, the IMF required an undertaking by a 'legitimate' body that the economy would be responsibly managed and that South Africa would sign the General Agreement on Tariffs and Trade (GATT), thus locking the ANC into prudent economic policies.

The secret letter of intent that accompanied the loan pointed out the dangers of increases in real wages in the private and public sector, stressed the importance of controlling inflation, promised monetary targeting, and trade and industrial liberalisation, and argued in favour of the virtues of market forces over regulatory interventions.

Similarly, the ANC's land reform policies were based on the World Bank's

1993 willing-buyer, willing-seller principle, protection of private property and market-related compensation for expropriations. The intention was to ensure stability in the rural areas, maintain the existing white commercial farmers and extend black commercial farming. Scant attention was paid to redistribution of land to subsistence farmers or impoverished communities in the bleak rural areas so that they could at least produce their own food.

In fact, the ANC's land negotiators were almost all urban-based, and stability and market reassurance were considered more urgent than restitution to black communities whose land had been brutally seized by the apartheid government. After a decade of democracy, many of the victims remain trapped in squalid informal settlements and slums, cut off from the economic mainstream, with no property to put up as collateral for loans they might use to start small businesses or educate their children.

As part of a market confidence-boosting measure, the ANC negotiators also agreed to repay the apartheid government's foreign debt to commercial banks, and accepted guarantor responsibility for more than $25 billion owed by parastatals. In 1994, South Africa's national debt stood at R190 billion. By March 1999, it had ballooned to R376 billion.

Of the pre-1994 debt, the so-called independent homelands were responsible for R13.9 billion, and the former regional authorities for R14.8 billion. When these structures were incorporated into the 'new' South Africa, their debt came too. About 96 per cent of the money was owed to South African creditors, and 40 per cent of the debt load was absorbed by the Public Service Pension Fund, while another 40 per cent was owed to the Public Investment Commission, which invests state pension funds. Obligations to the Public Service Pension Fund swelled from R31 billion in 1989 to R136 billion in 1996.

Mac Maharaj supports Mbeki's argument that the ANC had little choice but to accept responsibility for the debt: 'We had to be careful not to leave important people disgruntled. This would have been a source of instability, something we could not afford.' Moreover, agreeing to pay the debt would elicit a positive response from the market, and South Africa's first black government would gain enormous stature in the international community by doing what none of its counterparts elsewhere in Africa had been willing to do.

Mbeki played a key role in the agreement on local government that would see municipal elections and integration deferred until 2000. Until then, white municipalities continued to receive the lion's share of resources, while black local authorities had to make do on smaller budgets and fewer resources for larger populations. National Party negotiator Tertius Delport[29] credited Mbeki with accommodating the NP's demands for checks and balances in respect of negotiated agreements on local government.

A few weeks after the new government took office in 1994, Mandela, Mbeki and the ANC's key economic chiefs, including Manuel, Erwin and Mboweni, met with the Brenthurst Group to make final revisions to the RDP. It was already in its fifth draft, and the industrialists suggested several more changes in order to make the policy market-friendlier. These included a more overt emphasis on fiscal discipline, trade liberalisation in line with GATT, and committing the government to vigorous reduction of the accumulated national debt. One clause proposed ensuring 'a macroeconomic environment that is stable', while another stated that government should 'avoid undue inflation and balance of payments difficulties'.[30]

Even after the Brenthurst Group had signed off on the RDP, Mandela and the senior ANC leadership deliberately refrained from formally informing the SACP and COSATU of meetings with the industrialists. By now, Mandela, Mbeki and other centrists were wholly convinced that the ANC could not govern without pleasing the 'amorphous' markets, to paraphrase Trevor Manuel.

Mandela hoped that the Brenthurst Group's approval of the final RDP document would send positive signals to the market and launch a flood of new investment, on which the ANC leadership was depending to kickstart its transformation programme. Mandela contended that globalisation, particularly the integration of capital markets, made it 'impossible to decide national economic policy without regard for the likely response of the market'.[31]

After the Brenthurst meeting, he explained:

> I was present when we had a discussion with Harry Oppenheimer and other top businessmen ... and we discussed the plan very openly, very frankly, and we took down their criticisms, and accommodated them. We are now planning a second meeting with them because we are concerned that we should put before the country a plan which embraces the concern and the fears of all population groups, especially business.[32]

And, he added:

> I have not taken a single extended visit abroad without coming back and telling business what I have been doing. What I have done ... is to see heads of states, the heads of governments, the World Bank, the IMF, commercial banks and industrial organisations to say we are building a new country, we want your assistance with resources.[33]

By the time the RDP was adopted, it had been scrutinised by the World Bank, the IMF and the governments of Britain, America, France, Germany and Japan. Crucial sections of the document were revised to accommodate their suggestions.

For a party that had openly espoused nationalisation as late as 1993, submitting the centrepiece of its economic policy to the captains of South African industry and foreign governments for approval was a dramatic departure from the Freedom Charter's unambiguous call for public ownership.

There was a special irony in the fact that Mandela and Mbeki submitted the RDP to Oppenheimer for approval. Some thirty years earlier, he had turned down a request from Mandela for a donation to the ANC. At the time, Mandela said that he had an 'utmost hostility to businessmen'.[34]

At his first meeting with the Brenthurst Group after becoming president, Mandela reaffirmed his commitment to the free market:

> If there is anything I am conscious about, it is not to frighten the minorities, especially the white minority. In our economic policies – the reconstruction and development programme – there is not a single reference to national-isation, and this is not accidental. There is not a single slogan that will connect us with any Marxist ideology. We have drafted this plan five times. It emerged from people's forums and we sent it to various people in the country – business people, academics, state corporations, government departments.
>
> We can never get the support of business if we are going to have radical policies, and that is why we have put forward this perspective of a govern-ment of national unity, which may consist of [FW] De Klerk, [Constand] Viljoen, Zach de Beer, [Mangosuthu] Buthelezi, [Clarence] Makwetu, people who don't share at all in radical left policies, with the exception of the PAC. That is intended to bring about stability so we can face any threat to stability.[35]

Political and economic stability were two of the new government's most immediate concerns. They still feared that the white right wing could mount a resistance campaign or that white business would orchestrate a flight of capital. There had been dark predictions that white entrepreneurs would take their money offshore if the ANC pursued a policy of redistribution, and Mandela hoped that by including members of the opposition parties – both white and black – in his cabinet, he would appease local and foreign investors.

The first meeting of the post-apartheid cabinet was pregnant with expectation. Those present looked at one another in disbelief. After almost a century in opposition and as a liberation movement, the ANC now held the purse strings of the African continent's largest economy.

There were five fundamental problems to be addressed in the economic sphere: poverty, inequality, racism, unemployment and stagnation. Any one of them was a daunting prospect in itself. Having to tackle all five simultaneously was a staggering challenge. Reality would set in quickly. The economy the ANC government had inherited was in dire straits, far removed from the rosy picture usually portrayed to the public. Not only had the apartheid regime rushed through the privatisation of companies such as steel giant Iscor, placing it in the hands of friendly business consortiums, but billions of rands of taxpayers' money had been used to bail out struggling traditional Afrikaner banks, the forerunners of ABSA. Moreover, in the death throes of apartheid, many loyal public servants had been swiftly promoted and given pay rises, thus placing them in a more advantageous position regarding severance or pension packages.

Compared to high growth rates in the 1960s and early 1970s, the two decades from 1973 had seen a steady decline in South Africa's economic growth, decreased nett investment, rising unemployment, falling average real wage rates, and high levels of poverty and inequality. Physical and social infrastructure – housing, health, education, sanitation, water, electricity, welfare – for the majority black population was dismally inadequate.[36]

Economic growth had been declining since the early 1970s. Annual real growth of GDP averaged 5.5 per cent in the 1960s, fell to 3.3 per cent in the 1970s and fell again to 1.4 per cent in the early 1980s. Between 1989 and 1993 the economy was in recession, except for a brief recovery in the second half of 1993, when an annualised real GDP growth rate of 2 per cent was notched up. The annualised growth rate for the first quarter of 1994 showed a deficit of –3.5 per cent. The rate of job creation, which averaged more than 3 per cent in the early 1960s, had fallen to almost zero at the beginning of the 1980s, and was negative from 1986 onwards.

In its last years in office, the National Party government presided over a rapid increase in government debt as a proportion of GDP. The budget deficit rose from 0.9 per cent of GDP in 1989 to 9.2 per cent in 1992–93, and to 10.8 per cent in 1993–94. The total national debt to GDP ratio stood at 52.5 per cent in March 1994. South Africa's foreign debt to GDP ratio stood at 14.8 per cent at the end of 1993.

Through a series of debt-rescheduling agreements after South Africa's 1985 debt crisis, the country had succeeded by the end of 1993 in reducing its total foreign debt to around $16.7 billion. However, this was achieved at the expense of a decade of domestic economic and employment stagnation, as only through a recessionary domestic economic policy could the government maintain a current account surplus to service the debt. One of the biggest macroeconomic policy problems for the new government lay in the external account, from which the apartheid government had been forced since 1985 to run trade account surpluses to meet debt repayments and compensate for large nett capital outflows.

Total nett capital outflow increased to R16.3 billion in 1993, or 5 per cent of GDP, the highest since 1985. Around 90 per cent of the outflow was short term, a major proportion of it classified by the central bank as 'non-monetary private sector outflows' – essentially capital flight. In 1993 as well, nett capital outflow far exceeded the current account surplus, and led to a deep decline in gold and foreign exchange reserves. Inflation, which stood at 15 per cent in 1991, dropped to 8 per cent in 1994.

Despite being rated in 1993 as an upper middle-income economy, poverty was endemic to South Africa. Depending on the definition used, the proportion of the population classified as poor ranged from a third to almost half. Nearly 95 per cent of the poor were African, 5 per cent Coloured and less than 1 per cent white or Indian. South Africa's population breakdown at the beginning of 1994 was 71 per cent African, 10 per cent Coloured, 16 per cent white and 3 per cent Indian.

In addition to the racial bias in poverty distribution, there was also a marked gender bias, with households headed by women having a 50 per cent higher poverty rate than those headed by men. Poverty was skewed towards the rural areas, with 75 per cent of people in rural regions housing 50 per cent of the country's residents, classifiable as poor.

Income distribution became steadily eroded until it was among the worst in the world. The Gini coefficient was measured in 1993 at 0.61. This meant that the average income per capita of the richest 10 per cent of households was 125 times higher than that in the poorest 10 per cent. Disparities in personal and family wealth were huge and tended to mirror income disparities. There were also widespread disparities in access to savings, housing and land, as well as in human capital in the form of education, training and experience.

The legacy of apartheid in regard to the basic needs of the black majority was truly grim. Anglo American chairman Julian Ogilvie Thompson summed it up as follows:

> The challenges facing the country were not hard to identify ... but their magnitude and their intractability were only fully revealed as the euphoric glow of the mid-90s faded. South Africa came to occupy its true status as a middle-order nation struggling to undertake complex economic and political reforms in a highly competitive world. Though the world wished South Africa well and wanted it to succeed, no special favour could be expected, and indeed none has been forthcoming.[37]

The apartheid government had built its economy on cheap black labour. A modern South African economy would have to be constructed around a highly skilled workforce. But the vast majority of blacks had been prevented from acquiring such skills due to the inferiority of Bantu Education. Until quite late in the 1980s, special government permits were needed for blacks to study certain professions, and entrepreneurs found it all but impossible to establish anything but the simplest of township outlets, called spaza shops.

The lack of skills would be among the new government's greatest headaches, but by no means the only one.

Approximately 85 per cent of urban and 28 per cent of rural areas had access to electricity, but while almost 100 per cent of whites were linked to the national power grid, only 37 per cent of Africans were. South Africa was generating 60 per cent of Africa's electricity, yet 45 per cent of the country's own households had none.

Unemployment had been rising since the 1970s, and by 1993, 30 per cent of the economically active population was jobless. Here, too, there was a huge disparity along racial lines, with 5 per cent of whites unemployed, compared with 39 per cent of Africans. The highest incidence of unemployment, 40 per cent, was in rural areas and among the youth, with 53 per cent of those aged between sixteen and twenty-four, excluding those at school or university, not having jobs.

The deficiencies of Bantu Education would take years, if not decades, to overcome. Respected economist Francis Wilson says:

> The mean-spiritedness which underlay the philosophy of Bantu Education, the inadequacy of the funds made available throughout most of the apartheid years and the crippling effect of job reservation and the colour bar on the acquisition of skills and experience by the majority of [black] workers could almost have been designed to prevent them from being adequately prepared for the challenges of the 21st century.[38]

At the end of 1993, 38 per cent of South Africans over the age of sixteen had completed ten years of schooling, and only 20 per cent had left school with a matriculation certificate. The racial breakdown was stark. Nearly 61 per cent of whites had matriculated, while only 11 per cent, or one in nine, of Africans had done so, and even they lagged far behind in subjects such as mathematics and science, deliberately denied to them in accordance with the apartheid ideology, which reserved highly skilled jobs for whites.

In 1989 only 1 per cent of architects, less than 2 per cent of engineers and 13 per cent of computer programmers in South Africa were black. The ANC government was confronted by a desperate shortage of the professional, technical and managerial expertise required by a modern industrial economy.

As if the domestic problems were not formidable enough, the new South Africa was born at a time when the global economy was undergoing a fundamental shift that would see the gap between rich and poor widen across the world.

In April 1994, the very month in which South Africa held its first democratic elections, an international agreement signed in Marrakech, Morocco, laid the ground for establishment of the World Trade Organisation (WTO). The fall of the Berlin Wall and the collapse of the Soviet Union, the rise of the Internet on the back of a technological revolution and the founding of the WTO combined to present a whole new set of global challenges.

The advent of online trading and personal electronic banking saw a dramatic increase in the nett flow of private capital to developing countries, mostly speculative portfolio investment, which could flow out as quickly as it came in. South Africa faced the prospect of uncontrolled speculative capital flows and was under pressure to reduce tariffs. A year into democracy, speculators sowed panic when they relentlessly attacked the rand, causing it to nosedive.

High levels of crime, endemic to all societies in transition, presented another major problem, aggravated by the disintegration of the existing police structure.

According to eonomist Francis Wilson, 'People living on the protected side of the apartheid fence were not always aware of the extent of crime in the country as a whole before 1994.'[39] The incidence of violent crime rose, while new forms of crime included hijacking, fuelled by the relatively easy export to other African states of stolen vehicles across South Africa's borders, and drug-running, which exploited good air and shipping links with South America and the Far East.

Transformation of the police force was a major problem in itself, due to lack of training and experience and the fact that skilled officers were mainly deployed in historically white areas. In 1994, 75 per cent of police stations were situated in white residential and commercial precincts, only one in four detectives had received formal training, and one in ten had more than six years of experience in policing.

The ANC government was also sitting on a health time bomb. Preoccupied with the need for a political settlement, the organisation's leaders had not fully grasped the devastating dimensions of South Africa's HIV/AIDS pandemic or the threat it posed to the economy. This lack of insight would return to haunt Mbeki's administration.

Apartheid notwithstanding, South Africa had historically been an integral component of southern Africa's economy. Migrant labourers were drawn to the gold mines from neighbouring states, a functioning transport infrastructure offered portals to the rest of the continent, and South Africa offered goods, services and investment opportunities to sub-Saharan Africa.

Prior to 1994, the ANC had not dwelt on the effects of political instability in the region, but Mandela and Mbeki would both come to realise that political stability beyond South Africa's frontiers was vital for long-term development. Civil war or economic collapse in African states would threaten South Africa's export market at a time when the new democracy's neighbours were looking to the ANC government to lead the much-needed economic regeneration of the region.

The shock of discovering how fragile the economy was pushed the ANC leadership to start broadcasting that there were limits to the state's ability to deliver economic and social redistribution. When the dust of negotiations and the election settled, it became clear that despite all the overtures and compromises, the ANC did not enjoy the confidence of local or international business.

Maharaj explains: 'We discovered that the business community did not trust the black government. They thought we were a bunch of radical revolutionaries, bent on pursuing the communist policies of the Soviet Union and likely to go the same way as liberation movements that had become governments in the rest of Africa.'[40]

The investment promised by businessmen and foreign countries if the ANC eschewed nationalisation did not materialise. Industrialists demanded yet more concessions, claiming they were still not convinced of the government's commitment to a market-friendly economy. They wanted more assurances, a signal or guarantee that the SACP and COSATU could not still force nationalisation on the country. A new economic strategy focused entirely on growth would be a good starting point, the moguls suggested. By early 1995, local and international corporate leaders were asking the government: Where is your macroeconomic framework? 'We were heading for a fiscal crisis,' recalls Iraj Abedian, former chief economist at Standard Bank.[41]

The problem was threefold: the government's economic management was viewed with suspicion in the market, creating a credibility crisis; the fiscal indicators showed that a crisis was imminent, causing even more market uncertainty; and the economy was even worse than initially thought.

Something had to be done. The ANC's allies and grassroots supporters were starting to murmur about slow service delivery. Mandela panicked and banned ministers from making anti-market statements. When Manuel commented about not supporting the all-white Springbok rugby team, it caused a currency slide. Some ministers switched to traditional business suits and ties – notably Jay Naidoo – to show the government's earnestness on money matters.

As deputy president, Mbeki had assumed overall control of economic policy, and it soon became clear that he would brook no criticism from COSATU or the SACP in this regard. He had come to regard the tripartite alliance as being ANC-led rather than a union of three equal partners, a view shared by many ANC leaders, who saw left-wing attacks on the economic policy as more ammunition for the reluctant business community.

Subsequently, the RDP White Paper tabled in parliament in September 1994 lamented the shortcomings of the South African economy and the declining power of the state to restore it. The main problems were identified as falling rates of return, isolation from the global economy, excessive protection, primary product export dependence, excessive concentration of economic power, government expenditure, low exports and high imports, lack of domestic savings and investment, and lack of skills.[42] The only possible solution lay in applying internationally accepted economic policies in line with the Washington consensus. Mandela and Mbeki now had to have the new economic direction accepted by the ANC. But ANC militants were not impressed.

At the ANC's national conference in December 1994, Mbeki and the centrists packed the economics commission, while Manuel, Mboweni and Erwin ensured that the line held on budget deficit reduction and macroeconomic stabilisation. Despite fierce resistance from the left, the Mbeki-ite centrists, with the support of Mandela, managed to convince delegates that the RDP's delivery targets would not easily be achieved given the resource constraints of the new government. Leaders to the left, such as Mbhazima Shilowa, Blade Nzimande and John Gomomo, protested fiercely. Mbeki-ites started to ponder how they could secure the adoption of an orthodox, market-friendly economic blueprint without unleashing a popular grassroots rebellion.

By early 1995, the country was engulfed in strikes by students, nurses and municipal workers. By June, COSATU threatened a six-month strike to demand that the ANC take their views seriously, adopt centralised bargaining and accept their right to strike – demands the Mbeki-ites believed would portray the ANC as 'anti-market'.

In July 1995, after being in office for fifteen months, Mandela instructed his cabinet to abandon its 'obsession' with grand plans and make economic growth the top priority. Mbeki was appointed to head a special committee and come up with a growth and development strategy that would make the RDP's goals achievable.

Government officials were finding it difficult to extend services to the previously disadvantaged while detailed policy was still being developed. In addition, tension was running high between 'old-guard' public servants and their new colleagues. There was a discernible reluctance among established officialdom to share experience and technical knowledge with those destined to replace them.

Some went so far as to deliberately obstruct service delivery by burying projects in mountains of bureaucratic paperwork, safe in the knowledge that it would take a generous golden handshake to remove them.

Housing delivery suffered the most, with die-hard adherents of apartheid insisting that if the government was to stay within its budget, 'RDP houses' had to be the substandard matchbox structures found in black townships across South Africa. The sneering attitude was that the recipients should take what they got, because almost anything was better than a squatter shack.

By spring 1995 the economy was heading for a meltdown, and the ANC's critics continued to criticise the government. Having punted the RDP as a statement of principles rather than government's economic policy, Mbeki needed someone as a scapegoat for non-delivery. There was no love lost between him and Jay Naidoo, minister without portfolio in charge of the RDP, whom Mbeki suspected of being the left wing's cabinet 'mole'. The former COSATU general secretary controlled the RDP budget, made up of funds allocated by all government departments, and thus had a measure of control over social spending by the various ministries. A number of cabinet members resented what they saw as interference, and Mbeki himself thought Naidoo was becoming far too autonomous, approving or rejecting applications for RDP funding as he saw fit.

Mbeki hinted at change when he addressed the Intergovernmental Forum's development summit in November 1995. He cautioned against the RDP's 'almost biblical character',[43] and warned that its priorities would have to be subjected to realistic macroeconomic considerations. 'A [new] strategy of growth with development would underpin all RDP targets, to be streamlined into six pillars which would address poverty, employment, crime and good governance within a powerful competitive South African economy [that would] secure the wealth of the country and promote investment.'

With Mandela's approval, he began working on a new policy that would focus on macroeconomic stabilisation and inspire business confidence. Growth rather than redistribution would be the focus, and service delivery would be placed on the back burner.

Mbeki completed the draft of his national growth and development strategy in February 1996. Within the next two months the RDP office was shut down, and Naidoo redeployed as minister of posts and telecommunications.

Mbeki moved unfinished RDP business into his office, and, for the first time, had unfettered control over the government's economic planning. He was now ready to work out a new economic plan that would please the markets and boost confidence in the ANC government.

His intention was to have politically neutral mainstream economists design the new strategy so that it would be acceptable to the business community. Mbeki and his most trusted allies, including Manuel, Erwin and Netshitenzhe, hand-picked GEAR's architects.

The team was led by Iraj Abedian, with Richard Ketley, seconded by the World Bank, in close attendance. Others commissioned by Mbeki were Stephen Gelb, André le Roux, Andrew Donaldson, Brian Kahn and Ian Goldin. As a group, Mbeki saw them as economists with liberal social democratic instincts who understood the need for some kind of redistribution strategy. All were sworn to secrecy and the entire process was shrouded in deepest confidentiality lest the left wing get wind of Mbeki's plan.

The IMF and World Bank kept a close watch on progress, but Abedian discounts claims that the committee was anything but independent. 'I myself rejected the World Bank and IMF's orthodoxy,' he said. 'It could never be applied in South

Africa. I was the coordinator of the committee, and I can assure you that at no point did the committee relent under [World Bank and IMF] pressure.'[44] But Gelb, another member of the GEAR team, disagrees: 'Close affinity with the Washington consensus characterised not only the substantive policy recommendations of GEAR, but also the process through which it was formulated and presented to the public.'[45]

Abedian says the committee resisted World Bank calls for limited social spending to form part of the policy, but concedes that it took suggestions on low budget deficits to heart. He also maintains that COSATU's redistribution proposals were taken seriously, particularly in regard to social spending.

In February 1996 the rand plunged 20 per cent against the US dollar within a few weeks. Mbeki urged the GEAR committee to complete their task sooner rather than later. The finishing touches were still being put to the document at 2 a.m. on the day of its 10 a.m. release, and, by default, ended up as some kind of economic 'middle way', not unlike the Third Way economic policy proposals. In the words of Abedian, 'it was a stability pact, but a homegrown one', which differed from similar policies in its calls for social spending to be increased rather than cut.

In the end, GEAR was remarkably similar to the National Party's Normative Economic Model, released in 1993. 'The immediate aim of the GEAR strategy,' wrote Gelb, one of Mbeki's favourite local economists, 'was to signal to potential investors the government's commitment to the prevailing orthodoxy.'

The document, released in June 1996, was a dramatic departure from the foundations of the RDP.[46] Mbeki and ANC centrists had to get the policy adopted quickly by the ANC, and the left had to be prevented at all cost from trying to dilute the policy.

Even while defending GEAR as non-negotiable, Mandela admitted that he'd had no hand in its formulation.[47] The proposed strategy entailed a parcel of tough adjustments aimed at what it described as increased economic growth and greater utilisation of labour.

Joel Netshitenzhe, who had studied economics at London University's School of African and Oriental Studies, explained: 'GEAR was a structural adjustment policy, self-imposed, to stabilise the macroeconomic situation [to deal with] the realities of an unmanageable budget deficit, high interest rates and weak local and foreign investor confidence.'[48]

The crux of GEAR was:

The higher growth path depends in part on attracting foreign direct investment, but also requires a higher domestic saving effort. Greater industrial competitiveness, a tighter fiscal stance, moderation of wage increases, accelerated public investment, efficient service delivery and a major expansion of private investment are integral aspects of the strategy. An exchange rate policy consistent with improved international competitiveness, responsible monetary policies and targeted industrial incentives characterise the new policy environment. A strong export performance underpins the macroeconomic sustainability of the growth path.[49]

Alec Erwin observed that a 'fairly common package' of economic measures had worked 'for virtually all economies that have grown significantly over the last 10 to 15 years',[50] and that GEAR was based on this premise. He neglected to add that Malaysia, South Korea and Thailand were among countries that had successfully bucked the trend.

At the same time that GEAR was unveiled, Mbeki released an ANC discussion document, *The State and Social Transformation*, which argued that the state should be a 'neutral' referee between business, labour and other contesting social groups.[51] Four years later, Trevor Manuel would acknowledge: 'I want someone to tell me how the government is going to create jobs. It's a terrible admission, but governments around the world are impotent when it comes to creating jobs.'[52]

Mbeki sold GEAR to business and international financial organisations as a radical shift in the government's economic strategy compelled by a thorough reassessment of its earlier policies. Towards the end of 1996 he told business leaders: 'The policies and objectives embedded in GEAR are a pragmatic balance struck between our domestic economic demands and the realities of the international context. These policies and objectives emerged after a thorough analysis of global trends and the specific conditions in our economy.'[53]

ANC members and critics on the left were told that GEAR was a stabilisation package that the government was forced to adopt following the collapse of the rand earlier in the year. Mbeki argued that the ANC needed to secure sound economic fundamentals quickly.[54] In his political report to the ANC's 1997 national conference, Mandela blamed globalisation, especially the integration of capital markets, which 'make it impossible ... to decide national economic policy without regard for the likely response of the markets'.[55] In his State of the Nation address a few months later, Mandela said that 'there is no other route to sustainable development' than the market-friendly policies adopted by the ANC.[56]

At the public launch of GEAR, Mbeki goaded the left with his comment: 'Just call me a Thatcherite'.[57] When Manuel presented GEAR to parliament, Mbeki introduced the strategy by describing it as 'an important part of government policy ... which will guide all government actions'.[58]

The broad economic framework essentially reflects the requirements set out in the Stability Pact for countries wanting to join the European Monetary Union in terms of the Maastricht Treaty. The South African model emphasised that strict fiscal and monetary conditions, including low inflation and a 3 per cent ceiling on budget deficits, had to be applied aggressively in a developing country with immense development problems, such as a 30 per cent unemployment rate.

ANC leaders had been told only that a new economic policy was being formulated, and even the NEC was only informed about the secret process when GEAR was nearing completion, because Mandela and Mbeki feared it might be rejected before it got out of the starting blocks. 'I confess that even the ANC learned of GEAR far too late – when it was almost complete,'[59] Mandela later admitted. The drafters had planned a surprise for the markets in the form of a 20 per cent currency devaluation as a gesture of goodwill.[60] However, they were still preparing the strategy when South Africa was hit by a currency crisis that depreciated the rand by almost the same amount during the first six months of 1996.

Mbeki, Manuel and Erwin wanted the strategy unveiled and adopted by the ANC before its alliance partners or anyone else could object to the conservative economic policy and mobilise opposition. Mboweni, Manuel and Erwin were dispatched by Mbeki to inform the various ANC structures about the reasons behind adoption of GEAR and to convey the message that it was non-negotiable.

Mbeki, Mandela and Manuel briefed a small and select group of ANC, COSATU and SACP leaders. Charles Nqakula of the SACP and Mbhazima Shilowa of COSATU were shown only the section headings of the document. Some twenty 'trusted' MPs were unexpectedly invited to a meeting where Manuel announced the new policy and unveiled an outline. A few questions were allowed, but access to the full GEAR document was denied on the grounds that it could be leaked.

The briefings emphasised that GEAR would result in growth, job creation and redistribution. It would be based on fiscal and monetary discipline, reducing the budget deficit to 3 per cent of the GDP by 2000, and slashing public debt, which stood at 56 per cent of GDP in 1996. Annual growth would be increased by 4.2 per cent, 1.35 million jobs would be created by the year 2000, exports would be boosted by 8.4 per cent per annum on average through an array of supply-side measures, and social infrastructure would be drastically expanded.

GEAR recommended the complete privatisation of non-essential state-owned corporations and the partial privatisation of others. It called for wage restraints by organised labour and the introduction of regulated flexibility in the labour market. It promised lower inflation and trade liberalisation, and the removal of most tariffs and other forms of protection by 2000.

The entire strategy depended heavily on new investment, particularly from foreign sources, pouring into South Africa.

COSATU and the SACP were stunned. They were so unprepared for GEAR that it took almost a week before they issued a public response. COSATU general secretary Shilowa lambasted the strategy in a speech at the University of the Western Cape, and the left wing reserved its harshest criticism for the proposals on reduction of the budget deficit and the suggested downsizing of the public service.

Mbeki and his allies defended GEAR by insisting that South Africa had no choice but to play by the rules of the globalised economy. The same argument had been used by Brazil's former finance minister and president, Carlos Cardoso, two years earlier, when he unveiled his *Plano Real*. As Luiz Carlos Bresser-Pereira, Brazilian economist and former minister in Cardoso's cabinet, had pointed out, 'The recipe is simple. If a country completes its fiscal adjustment, if it carries out other neo-liberal reforms and if it opens up the financial sector to the world market, then it will be rewarded by an influx of foreign capital. Instead of development with debt that characterised the 1970s, it will have development with foreign savings.'

The Washington consensus, he observed, offered direct foreign investment as a panacea for all the problems of developing countries, seemingly with no cost and myriad benefits to countries that accepted it.

One of the first indications of dramatic change in the ANC's economic policy was the release in 1996 of *The State and Social Transformation*,[61] a discussion document inspired by Mbeki. It sought to explain that a cooperative relationship between business and the government was the most important precondition for success in the ANC's struggle for democracy and economic equality. Mbeki was at pains to highlight that the government had inherited massive fiscal constraints from the old order, most notably a debt that rose from R37 billion in 1985 to R280 billion in 1996, about 65 per cent of the GDP.

In a changing global environment that sees investment funds cross borders unfettered, the state's ability to implement full democracy on its own had been limited, Mbeki argued. This had led to what he called 'oscillation' within the tripartite alliance between establishment of a democratic state and 'the wish to establish a state whose distinctive feature would be the total defeat and suppression of both the national and class forces responsible for the system of national suppression and class super-exploitation epitomised by apartheid'.[62]

Although the ANC had abandoned its socialist pretensions as early as 1994 in favour of a pragmatic social democratic approach to economics, no leader had previously spelt out that the economic phase of the struggle could succeed only if it was based on a mutually beneficial relationship between the public and private sectors. Invoking struggle rhetoric, Mbeki called for a dialectical relationship with private capital as a partner for development and social progress.

Despite being slammed by the ANC's left-wing alliance partners, the adoption of GEAR and Mbeki's views on economics bolstered his standing within the party and sealed his claim for the presidency. While his potential rivals wrestled with provincial governance or constitutional issues, he had boldly fashioned a vision for South Africa, even if the result was not popular with some. Mbeki and his allies pushed successfully for GEAR to be accepted by the ANC's 1997 national conference in Mafikeng against fierce resistance from the ANC's left.

Through patronage and promises of high office, Mbeki had patiently lured key COSATU and SACP leaders into accepting GEAR ahead of the conference. He drew both Nqakula and Shilowa into his camp, and although initially opposed to GEAR, they later became loyal defenders of the policy. Both were richly rewarded: Shilowa became premier of Gauteng, and Nqakula was appointed to Mbeki's cabinet as safety and security minister.

Prior to the 1997 ANC conference, Mbeki-ites had identified SACP members who could be expected to block GEAR 's passage. Given an ultimatum to either recant or face harsh sanction, those who didn't were subjected to disciplinary hearings and some were stripped of their positions in the party. Others had their routes of advancement in the ANC blocked. Not surprisingly, the private sector hailed GEAR as business-friendly, praising it for responding to many of the concerns that had been expressed, but real private investment and foreign direct investment plunged. Among GEAR 's obvious shortcomings was its failure to attract investment, slash unemployment or raise growth to the same levels as those of other emerging countries. Moreover, the strategy paid scant attention to the relationship between GEAR and industrial policy.

For all the buoyancy generated by the new market-friendly policy, GEAR offered no insurance against the devastating Asian financial contagion that wrought havoc on South Africa's financial markets and currency in 1997 and 1998. Nervous ANC leaders, already suspicious of GEAR, were forcefully reassured by Mbeki that if not for GEAR, the Asian crisis would have been far more damaging to the South African economy. From May to August 1998 the rand lost 16 per cent of its value on average against major foreign currencies. The doomsday prophets on the white right dusted off their predictions of a bleak future under a black government.

Mbeki and his chief economic mandarins, Manuel, Erwin, Mboweni and Netshitenzhe, calmed the fears of ANC leaders with assurances that the crisis had nothing to do with government policy, which was sound, and blamed greedy currency speculators for scavenging on developing economies. The solution, he suggested, was to change the international financial system, which was stacked against developing nations. Globalisation carried the inherent danger of contagion or 'spillover' anywhere in the developing world, affecting even a sound economy such as South Africa's, he maintained, and the best the country could do was step up marketing to show the world that its economy was far better managed than any of the emerging models.

He insisted that economic policy should be left untouched while South Africa rode the storm and prepared to take on an unequal world. The government spurned a suggestion by Malaysian leader Mahathir Mohamed that capital controls be reintroduced in tandem with his country. The issue was debated by the ANC's National Working Committee, but Manuel, Erwin and Mbeki argued against it.

Malaysia went ahead and secured an enormous amount in savings. The South African government steadfastly refused to entertain capital controls, even though Chile and Malaysia applied them with success. The ANC feared that such a move would signal to the market that it was, after all, a closet communist regime, and lead to an even bigger backlash.

The fallout between the World Bank and the IMF over who was to blame for the Asian financial crisis opened up space for developing countries to pursue alternative strategies, but South Africa remained cautious. Former World Bank chief economist Joseph Stiglitz was fired after joining experts who publicly criticised the international financial organisations' response. Ravi Kanbur, erstwhile chief author of the *World Development Report*, resigned in disgust after he objected to attempts by former US Treasury head Lawrence Summers to rewrite his criticism of the World Bank and IMF reaction to the Asian crisis and the way they dealt with poverty in developing countries.

A year after the crisis, Mandela had some leading questions for the heads of state and multinational corporations gathered at Davos to debate whether or not global capitalism was delivering the goods: 'Is globalisation only to benefit the powerful and the speculators? Does it offer nothing to men, women, and children who are ravaged by poverty?'[63]

Mbeki told the September 1998[64] summit of the Non-Aligned Movement: 'The free market path of development ... has failed to live up to the expectations of the people of the south.' Shortly afterwards, he urged South Africa to 'be at the forefront in challenging the notion of the market as a modern God, a supernatural phenomenon to whose dictates everything human must bow in a spirit of powerlessness'.[65]

The run on the currency, continuing low growth, sluggish investment and high unemployment meant that Mbeki had his hands full defending GEAR. Some ANC leaders suggested that the policy be abandoned, while criticism from the alliance partners became more strident than ever.

Mbeki increasingly sought to distance himself from COSATU and the SACP to show the market that the government was not being held hostage by the left. As the disillusionment of devaluation set in among the ANC faithful, SACP and COSATU leaders such as Jeremy Cronin, Blade Nzimande, Gwede Mantashe,

Zwelinzima Vavi and Willie Madisha all pointed to the failure of GEAR, and as the pain of the reforms began to bite, critics found eager ears among the ANC's grassroots supporters. With the currency continuing its downward slide and investors remaining conspicuous by their absence, business leaders blamed COSATU and the SACP for the market's lack of confidence in the government.

Mbeki went on the offensive, slamming the communists for criticising the official economic policy and threatening that they could be denied their privileged access to government unless they changed tack. Mandela had already conveyed the same tough message to COSATU 's national leadership conference.

In June 1998 Mbeki launched a patronising attack on COSATU 's central committee, saying they were being misled and misinformed by forces opposed to change. A month later, he lambasted delegates at the SACP's annual conference for their ignorance and criticism of government policies, and vowed that Pretoria would not deviate from its chosen economic path.

While it is true that GEAR allowed the government to achieve macro-stability, the real economy was spectacularly off the mark. Fiscal restraint, tariff reduction and inflation control succeeded, but growth and employment sputtered and real interest rates remained high. Even as GEAR was failing to deliver on jobs and growth, Mbeki's strategy was to continue holding out the promise that delivery was just around the bend.

In hindsight, the government had more than enough opportunity to come up with alternatives. A more differentiated and strategic approach to South African business would have found a significant real economy bloc of industrialists, and those involved in construction, civil engineering and infrastructure, quite prepared to support a sensible expansionary approach.[66] In a sense, the ANC's policy was dictated by the financial bloc of the South African economy, which favoured stabilisation over any prioritisation of social development.

Moreover, the government erred on the side of caution in choosing financial stabilisation over economic transformation. For the government, the threat of short-term financial instability loomed larger than any risk of social or political instability, and in this sense the government was perceived, especially by the Mbeki-ites, to have made a rational policy choice.

But this approach severely restricted key elements of local capital that would have benefited from a more robustly implemented redistribution and could have assisted in developing a consensus bloc around social transformation. For example, instead of cutting taxes by about R72 billion in the first ten years, that amount could have been used to address the housing problem. The direct investment in infrastructure would surely have spun off into a wide range of increased economic activity and indirect job creation, while at the same time generating increased tax revenues to compensate the fiscus.

Though Mbeki and his allies acknowledged in private that GEAR did not deliver, they refused to change tack, arguing that to do so would trigger an even bigger backlash from the market. The social cost to the ANC's bedrock constituency – the black poor majority – was devastating, but in October 1997 Mbeki's advice was, 'We can't sustain the high deficit, we have got to bring it down. It carries with it certain pain. It has got to be done.'[67]

The brunt of the pain would be borne by the ANC's grassroots supporters, but the realisation that the ANC was out-negotiated economically at the World Trade Centre came to permeate all levels of the organisation.

The tragedy is that those who suffered the worst deprivation under apartheid also ended up paying the highest price for democracy. The legacy of apartheid, the ANC's compromises and wrong economic choices would all combine to prevent the ANC from fulfilling its promise of a better life for those who need it most. A decade into democracy, the poorest of the poor, with laudable exceptions, remain mired in gut-wrenching misery.

# — 5 —

# Economics
# for the Poor

In politics we will have equality and in social and economic life we will have inequality. In politics we will be recognising the principle of one man, one vote and one vote, one value. In our social and economic life we shall, by reason of our social and economic structure, continue to deny the principle of one man, one value. How long shall we continue to live this life of contradictions? How long shall we continue to deny equality in our social and economic life? If we continue to deny it for long, we do so only by putting our political democracy in peril.
– BR Ambedkar, leader of India's 'Untouchables', 1949[1]

CAN SOUTH AFRICA TURN ITS POLITICAL MIRACLE INTO AN ECONOMIC ONE? It is indeed not only possible, but urgently desirable. The foundations are there, but what's needed are determined changes that go far beyond mere tinkering on the fringes of the economy.

Much progress was made in the first ten years of democracy. Since 1994, almost 8.4 million people gained access to clean water, 3.8 million to electricity, 1.5 million to housing and 6.4 million to sanitation. However, inequality is more prevalent than ever, with the poor truly having become more impoverished, while the rich amassed even greater fortunes.

Taxation rates are lower, but efficient collection and a broader tax base have boosted government revenue. Certainly blacks have joined the moneyed class, but the gap between the white rich and their wealthy new black cousins and the overwhelmingly black poor majority has become a chasm. Still fragile after the trauma of protracted internal conflict, South Africa's social fabric has been damaged even more by a decade of aggressive and painful economic reform that has forced hundreds of thousands of lowly and unskilled blacks to the streets. Little wonder that high crime levels have been such a problem.

The degree of racial segregation in residential areas, schools, lifestyle, clubs, the workplace, even something as mundane as music preference, is disturbing. Only in the gaudy shopping malls that have sprung up like giant mushrooms in every city do the races mingle, it seems. Consumerism could well go down in history as the key to unity between black and white South Africans.

Shopping, however, is hardly a solid foundation for the social cohesion needed to build a secure future. One observer says the ANC government has a patchy record of brilliant achievement and shabby compromise.[2]

Self-congratulation sits somewhat awkwardly with the new elite. Almost a third of first-time water, electricity and telephone consumers have seen the services suspended, as they are unable to pay for them. In the first ten years of democracy, an estimated 12 million people turned to cellular phones as a more affordable alternative to the single fixed-line service. The so-called RDP houses are tiny, unhealthy matchboxes on the urban periphery, far from the workplace and often inaccessible to public transport. Just as under apartheid, they have by and large been constructed on barren stretches of land in areas devoid of public libraries, parks or community centres.

Instead of using imaginative indigenous designs and bright colours to make the housing estates more attractive, the apartheid model has been copied to create impersonal ghettos, though since 2000 there has been an attempt to be more creative, for example in the township of Alexandra, adjacent to ultra-wealthy Sandton, north of Johannesburg.

Costs are routinely cited as the reason for these fields of unimaginative structures, but the government has had access to a wide range of cheaper building material that could have been produced by the unemployed. Examples of creative mass housing abound in densely populated countries such as China or India, and South African entrepreneurs have offered dozens of homegrown examples shunned by the government.

The country's economy is undeniably more robust than when the ANC came to power in 1994, and Mbeki's vision of establishing the ANC's reputation as that of an African government capable of prudent economic management has largely been realised. This in itself is a notable achievement, since the ANC faced much the same dilemma as Britain's Labour Party, painted for years by the Conservative Party as being unable to manage the economy. New Labour leader Tony Blair and his chancellor Gordon Brown set out to prove the opposite in the United Kingdom, and the Mbeki-ites in South Africa did the same.

The first decade saw an aggressive makeover of the South African economy into a modern manufacturing economy, reinforcing the country's position as a competitive trading partner. But rapid modernisation within a short time frame came at great cost to the victims of apartheid's grotesque social engineering.

From an individual standpoint, South Africans grew wealthier at an average rate of slightly less than 1 per cent a year since 1994,[3] an unspectacular performance compared with most developing economies.

Governance is essentially about weighing trade-offs and making choices. Compared to apartheid, the government has done well in all respects, but as political scientist Adam Habib rightly asks: Should we be using the apartheid government as a yardstick for the ANC's success? The answer, of course, is no. Mbeki has often referred to South Africa as being two nations with two economies – one rich, the other poor; one First World, the other Third World – and the urgent need to change this. The rich are still predominantly white, though a small percentage of blacks have been elevated to this level, while the poor remain almost exclusively black.

Inevitably, some have lost hope that change will ever come, but many continue to dream of the better life they were promised. During the ANC's 2004 election campaign, the dream was fuelled, albeit briefly, by Mbeki himself admitting on the hustings that the party had failed its grassroots supporters, but promising anew that the elusive dream would finally come true during his second term in office.

For ten years, government focus on the 'first' economy saw professionals and entrepreneurs of all racial groups benefit enormously, but now it is time to concentrate on the 'second' nation and devise policies to uplift the poor and marginalised black majority.

In pursuing a mixed bag of praiseworthy policies, the government has made some really appalling choices, as with social spending. Since 1992/93, expenditure on social services increased from 44.4 per cent of the budget to 56.7 per cent in 2002/03. But when inflation is taken into account, this actually represents a decline, which is mind-boggling in a country faced with such grinding poverty. Since many of South Africa's problems are structural, orthodox measures that might work in developed countries, or those with less inequality, will not suffice. Historian Colin Bundy makes the point that 'to persist with timid orthodox changes and imagine that South Africa can somehow absolve its economic history and enter a future like that of Sweden or Taiwan – now that really requires a leap of faith'.[4]

Measured against most international benchmarks, the competitiveness of South Africa's economy has improved since the early 1990s,[5] and the country has achieved a level of macroeconomic stability not seen for forty years. The ANC has cut budget deficits to less than 3 per cent of GDP, reduced inflation and slashed the cost of government. The budget deficit declined from 9.5 per cent of GDP in 1993/94 to just over 1 per cent for the 2002/03 financial year. So great was the government's commitment to its chosen economic strategy that even in 1999, an election year in the middle of a recession, the budget deficit fell.

But do low budget deficits make any sense in a country faced with such huge development and poverty challenges? The US and most of Western Europe have higher budget deficits, yet they do not have the same mountain of development problems as South Africa.

Our economy needs to grow by at least 5 to 6 per cent a year in order to absorb the unemployed and start dealing with the crippling inequalities created by apartheid. From 1977 to 1992, economic growth averaged 1.56 per cent a year. For the period 1995 to 2002, the figure was 2.8 per cent, a significant improvement, but not nearly enough, nor even as much as had been projected.

The market-friendly GEAR policy was supposed to boost the growth rate to 6 per cent of GDP a year by 2000. It failed. Finance minister Trevor Manuel woefully laments that South Africa, and most other African governments, followed the advice of the World Bank and the IMF to cut deficits from above the 7 per cent of GDP range in 1992 to around 2.6 per cent in 2000. The result has been stagnation of economic growth and a decline in per capita income.

GEAR projected that for the economy to achieve a 3 per cent growth rate, total fixed investments (private, foreign and public) needed to represent at least 25 per cent of GDP.[6] Foreign investment – one of the bedrocks of economic policy since 1996 – has remained a trickle, much of it in the form of short-term flows. Investment as a percentage of GDP has averaged around 16 to 17 per cent, low by the standards of successful developing countries.[7] Relatively little of the paltry investment received has gone into major new projects or plants.

Government often blames the country's skills base, volatility of the exchange and interest rates, the cost of inputs, such as transport and telecommunications, lack of competition in the domestic market, and poor perceptions of Africa as a whole and the southern region in particular, for sluggish investment. It also points to the low savings rate of South Africans. Increasingly, however, there is a tendency to trot out subjective reasons – Afro-pessimism, negative perceptions about Africa and developing markets in general, inadequate marketing – to explain the lack of investment.

Obviously, there is some basis for these claims. Many foreigners do look at Africa as one dark, conflict-ridden mass, and certain sectors of South Africa's population have still not come to terms with a black government, expressing their racist views by denigrating the changes brought by democracy and showing up real or perceived failure at every turn.

But the government is not blameless. Mbeki's controversial stance on HIV/AIDS, for example, feeds into the anti-African psyche, yet negative perceptions and human rights abuses do not prevent a flood of FDI to countries such as China.

More damaging, however, has been government's reluctance to invest in the economy itself.[8] New government investment in large plants or stock has effectively been frozen, and the squeeze was put on capital expenditure until 1999, when it stood at 5.3 per cent of public expenditure. The 2002/03 financial year saw a welcome rise to 9.3 per cent, but this is still well below what is required.

If neither government nor local investors show confidence in the economy, how can foreign investors be expected to pour money into the country?

Sluggish investment has gone hand in hand with an extraordinary rise in unemployment among the ANC's base constituency – the black majority. Indeed, not since the Great Depression has any developed country made so many jobs redundant over a seven-year period. On a per-job ratio, South Africa has wiped out more employment opportunities than any other developing country in history.

Between 1993 and 2000, the country's gross national income rose at an average annual rate, in real terms, of 2.5 per cent. During the same period, however, employment in the non-agricultural, private and public sectors fell each year (with the exception of 1995) by 1.7 per cent on average.

Since 1994, the economy has shed almost one million jobs, chiefly in the mining, agricultural and manufacturing sectors. In commercial agriculture, excluding subsistence farming in the former homelands, unemployment has gone into free-fall. Between 1993 and 1998, agriculture is estimated to have lost around 46 000 jobs, at a rate of just under 1 per cent a year.

Aggressive modernisation of the economy, including lifting trade tariffs higher than required by the WTO, has left many sectors out on a limb. Indeed, government's policy of unbundling tariffs much faster than required by the WTO – to prove acceptance of free trade – is absolute folly. Furthermore, the restructuring of agriculture and mining (including the withdrawing of state subsidies for farmers and increased mechanisation in mining) to make these sectors more competitive, added significantly to the devastating shedding of jobs. Technological innovation, which has seen various industries and whole sectors transforming skills requirements, and the culling of public service jobs are also major culprits.

Government counters that 1.6 million new jobs were created between 1995 and 2002,[9] but readily admits that the number of people defining themselves as unemployed has increased by 2.3 million. 'We [had to] change the structure of the South African economy – some people's jobs may be lost,' explains Alec Erwin, former trade and industry minister. 'It had to be a choice of government, it was a difficult and hard choice.[10] We have debated [GEAR] again in the ANC's National Working Committee [and] we accepted that yes, GEAR has given us problems, but let's stick to it.'[11]

Significantly, employment has increased only in the informal sector, but members eke out a miserable existence, most living far below the breadline. Not surprisingly, the level of unemployment is heavily disputed and, depending on which research agency is cited, ranges from 30 to 40 per cent. Many no longer even bother to look for a job.

Continuous job losses and the movement of more and more people into the informal sector have ensured an ever-wider gap between the haves and the have-nots. One of the key contributors to rising unemployment has been a shift towards the tertiary sector or services. Mining, agriculture and fishing contribute less than 10 per cent of the national income, while public service cuts, trade reforms and the fall in gold reserves have all played a role. The economy has become skills intensive and those with the appropriate qualifications are in great demand, but South Africa has an entire generation equipped with skills that are redundant in the changing economy. Says Manuel: 'We have lots of people but we don't have sufficient skills.'[12]

South Africa's large companies have been responsible for more than half of GDP growth, but only 46 per cent of new employment opportunities. Conventional wisdom has it that a high economic growth rate would automatically solve the problems of both unemployment and poverty, but conventional measures to deal with the crisis are not enough.

The economy needs to break through the 3 per cent growth ceiling just to prevent unemployment from rising even more, but fundamental shifts in the structure of the economy call for radical shifts in policy direction. The most pressing need is finding ways to plug the skills gap. The vast majority of the unemployed are unskilled, and in the past thirty years black youth and women have added steadily to their numbers. The government needs to address this problem just as urgently as it must push through a long-term change in the structure of the labour force.

A vast amount of money would have to be invested in a skills programme, and it is foolhardy of ANC policy-makers to insist that increased growth and foreign investment would be sufficient. The problem predates the new democracy by decades, with a steady decline in the demand for unskilled labour since the 1970s.

South Africa's primary economic sector – mining and agriculture – has become less significant, the industrial sector's contribution to the national output has tapered off since the 1980s, and there has been a dramatic rise in the services sector to the point where it currently represents 65 per cent of national income.

The need for highly skilled labour by the services sector has almost doubled, from 15.5 to 28.6 per cent, and in the wholesale and retail trades it has risen from 7.5 to 14.5 per cent, while unskilled labour demand has dropped from 36.9 to 24.5 per cent.[13] The faster the economy grows, the more jobs will be created for the highly skilled, so the desperately needed higher growth rate is a double-edged sword.

Government will need to identify where the skills shortages are and focus on increasing the labour supply accordingly. An employment subsidy scheme could be used to reward companies for providing training. Incredibly, there has been no attempt to attract skilled foreigners, though prevailing global conditions are ideal to draw qualified immigrants from the black diaspora and other sources. Since the terror attacks in America on 11 September 2001, it has become increasingly difficult for aliens to gain a foothold there, and South Africa should be able to lure many talented entrepreneurs and professionals.

Most importantly, the economy has to be transformed quickly into one that beneficiates rather than relying on production of primary commodities for the world markets. Changing South Africa's mineral industry from extraction to beneficiation could offer numerous opportunities for disadvantaged communities to acquire skills. As economist Francis Wilson[14] points out, the demand for gold comes not from central bankers, but from their wives and children who want to wear jewellery. The automotive industry has already successfully shifted in this direction with its change of focus from import substitution to export promotion.

The agricultural sector cries out for creation of a corps of small-scale farmers in the rural areas who can produce food for their immediate environs, yet key economic reformers show no enthusiasm for such projects. Incredibly, Manuel claims that black South Africans are not much interested in farming, finding the glitter of cities more attractive for the most part. Mbeki did announce a rural development plan in 2000 – almost six years after the ANC came to power – but it has yet to bear fruit.

If South Africa is serious about reducing the number of people who live in poverty, at least 6 million of them have to be brought above the breadline. This would require the creation of 3.5 million new jobs in the second decade of democracy – not an impossible target, given that China lifted 150 million people from the mire of poverty over a fifty-year period from the mid-1950s. Small, medium and micro enterprises (SMMEs) should contribute at least 60 per cent of GDP and be responsible for 80 per cent of new jobs if South Africa wants to slay the poverty dragon.

Thankfully, 2004 saw South Africa's aggressive economic restructuring to modernise the economy, which caused most of the job haemorrhage, coming to an end – unfortunately, too late for many. At the same time, population growth showed a dramatic decrease, but the government had yet to show that it has the political will to attack poverty in earnest. Unemployment remains the yardstick by which the majority of the ANC's constituency measures the government's performance, and the prognosis is not good.

The Reserve Bank's constitutional mandate is to deliver on price stability, just as it was during the apartheid era. Clearly, this needs to be reviewed in order to make job creation an aim of monetary policy. One of the cornerstones of the US

Federal Reserve is job creation, and extending the South African Reserve Bank's mandate would place the problem at the forefront of central bank thinking. However, this does not appear to be on the horizon, and, in fact, Mbeki has made it clear that he will not meddle with Reserve Bank policy.

Controversially, the government introduced inflation targeting in 2002. The aim was to reach a figure in a band of 3 to 6 per cent by 2005 in order to bring South Africa in line with its major trading partners, the European Union, Japan and the US.

The notion is somewhat misplaced. South Africa is not comparable, and any crude convergence is only likely to hurt the economy. Worse, inflation is often overstated in South Africa, as in many other countries, because indices do not account for the shift in consumer habits in good times or changing tastes. Furthermore, inflation targets needlessly curb growth by having the central bank keep interest rates higher than necessary.

Another reason for the pursuit of inflation targets was to build credibility in the markets for the first black central banker, but Reserve Bank governor Tito Mboweni has gone to the other extreme and opted for a chokingly low target. This has unquestionably been good for his credentials as a conservative and trusted central banker, but his image enhancement has come at a price. Obviously, raising the inflation target band would undermine the bank's credibility, but the economic mandarins should certainly not lower the current range any further. Mboweni needs to wait until South Africans have adjusted to a low inflationary environment, and the productivity gap between the country and its main trading partners has narrowed.

What we need is a more balanced approach towards monetary policy. The central bank's prevailing strategy is to use the blunt monetary tool of high interest rates to fight inflation, regardless of the restrictive effect this has on growth and investment. High interest rates are never good for an economy, but Mboweni, consistent with government's overcautious approach, has defied calls for bigger interest rates cuts, opting to bring the figures down in small increments. If investment is to be kick-started, interest rates need to come down quickly and significantly.

Since the panic over depreciation of the rand at the height of the 1998 Asian financial crisis, the currency has seen a spectacular rebound. The gains are attributed largely to the appeal of South Africa's high returns for global investors, but the volatile unit has remained resilient. By September 2003 the central bank had cut interest rates by 350 basis points to 10 per cent, and the rand had recovered 30 per cent against the US dollar since the start of the year. Exporters and organised labour began clamouring for a weaker currency.

COSATU demanded a foreign exchange rate of R9 or R10 to the dollar in order to create jobs and boost sluggish economic growth. Many of the country's top firms warned that the strength of the rand was undermining their export earnings and could lead to hefty job losses. Mining companies warned that 125 000 jobs were at risk in this sector alone, and some mining houses began trimming their labour force, blaming the strong rand.

Curiously, at the height of the resources boom, very few mining companies carried over their profits to their workers or invested in new plants. South African mining houses creamed the profits without making any significant new local investments. Government needs to take a strong stand on companies that grab conveniently handy excuses – in this case a strong rand – to retrench workers, without first exploring alternatives.

Various cabinet ministers have raised eyebrows by suggesting the stronger rand is proof of a robustly healthy economy. On a trip to Sweden in September 2003, deputy president Jacob Zuma was one of those who did so, and almost all the Mbeki-ites point to the strengthening of the currency as evidence of a black government's capable management of the economy. Conversely, old-guard whites never pass up a chance to finger a weakening of the currency as proof of the same black government's incompetence.

Unfortunately, it seems Mbeki and his supporters have taken the bait and are determined to maintain a strong rand, regardless of the economic consequences for the poor. It's a specious exercise, since no healthy economy sheds jobs at the rate South Africa does.[15]

Privatisation of state-owned enterprises lies at the very core of the country's economic blueprint. Hawkish reformers like Mbeki, Manuel and Erwin urge privatisation as the way to slash government debt, provide more efficient service, and attract foreign capital and skills. Failure to attract foreign investment through other measures had led the economic mandarins to double their efforts to do so via privatisation.

But what is referred to in South Africa as 'the P word', because government ministers are afraid to utter it in public, has also been the driving force behind Mbeki's determination to create a big black business class. Like any embarrassing activity, privatisation has its own euphemism in South Africa – restructuring – and a report commissioned by the government to survey the first ten years of democracy[16] asserts that one of the successes of state restructuring has been a R24-billion reduction of public sector debt.

In 1995, the government spelt out that restructuring was needed 'to facilitate economic growth, fund the RDP, create wider ownership in the South African economy, mobilise private sector capital, reduce state debt, enhance competitiveness of state enterprises, promote fair competition, finance growth and the requirements for competitiveness'.[17] In addition, a pillar of privatisation is to secure global financial approval for the government and to win over foreign investment.

Jeff Radebe, the responsible minister at the time, made it clear that restructured parastatals would be expected to 'promote good governance, sound financial management and ethical probity. They must serve public needs and provide quality services.'[18] Simultaneously, they had to become globally competitive, hence the entry of strategic minority equity holders to ailing state-owned enterprises at the government's invitation. At Telkom, for example, the newcomers could inject new technology and expertise.

Privatisation is focused on South Africa's big four: defence firm Denel, telecoms utility Telkom, power utility Eskom and transport group Transnet, which have a combined asset value of R150 billion. These four corporations lie at the core of the privatisation programme and represent 91 per cent of total state assets, 94 per cent of nett income and 77 per cent of all public sector employees. According to Manuel, the partial privatisation programme could rake in more than the budgeted R21 billion in revenue.

But the restructuring programme is in desperate need of success. The best performer to date is the South African National Roads Agency, established in 1998 as a commercially driven company with the minister of transport as the sole shareholder. It quickly acquired substantial resources through the efficient management of toll roads, and also began to assist provincial governments with road maintenance.

But setbacks have plagued the programme in general. The planned 20 per cent listing of telecommunications utility Telkom, scheduled for 2001, had to be postponed because of a weak telecoms market. Government also had to postpone the sale of 20 per cent of M-Cell, South Africa's second largest mobile operator, to 2002/03, because of weak market conditions.

The massive potential for corruption when privatisation is used to promote black economic empowerment (BEE) was underscored when state forests in Komatiland worth R335 million were sold to Zama Resources in 2002. Zama CEO Mcebisi Mlonzi allegedly paid R55 000 to public enterprises chief director Andile Nkuhlu – subsequently suspended – as a sweetener for the deal.

In 2001, South African Airways was hit by a corporate governance controversy when former CEO Coleman Andrews was paid nearly R220 million for his two-year tenure. Following financial difficulties in its partnership with Swissair, SAA had to be renationalised. The smaller SunAir went belly-up after privatisation, with airline executives blaming dirty tricks by SAA. Public entities placed under management contracts, such as state diamond mine Alexkor and the Post Office, have not performed.

But Mbeki is determined to ram through his privatisation efforts, even in the face of widespread popular resistance because of the inherent threat of job losses. COSATU, supported by the SACP and civil society groups, staged national strikes over the rising cost of basic services, unemployment caused by cost recovery methods and outsourcing applied by new partially privatised concerns. Clouding the issue even more are confusion over policy and disputes over contentious matters within state departments, industry and regulators. Restructuring is a complex exercise involving several arms of government, and the reality is that they do not proceed at the same pace, and, at times, policy conflicts with the public enterprise department's vision.

So, what is the future of the government's privatisation initiative? Staff morale in the department that runs the programme plummeted following a series of setbacks, such as those listed above. 'We desperately need a privatisation success story,'[19] says a senior official. 'Either a process that delivers a substantial amount to the Treasury or that allows people to clearly see the benefits of privatisation.'[20]

In what was seen as a vote of no confidence, public enterprises minister Jeff Radebe was moved to transport and replaced by Erwin, former minister of trade and industry. Disappointed by Radebe's style of close consultation with trade unions, which he blamed for the slow pace of reconstruction, Mbeki gave Erwin a brief to push privatisation more vigorously via black economic empowerment.

Government has come under fire on two fronts over privatisation. On the one hand, the market, economic pundits and white opposition parties, such as the Democratic Alliance, have urged that privatisation of state-owned enterprises should proceed at full steam, with some business people, for example, erroneously blaming delays as one of the reasons for the rand's decline in 2001.

According to Kevin Wakeford, the former CEO of the South African Chamber of Business (SACOB), 'The South African Chamber of Business calls for an urgent privatisation programme of substance, coupled with more competition, by allowing other operators to enter these markets. This could lock in much needed foreign capital that could further strengthen the rand, enhance productivity and drive down prices through competition.'[21]

On the other hand, mainstream ANC opponents, civil society groups, churches and the left urge government to go slow on privatisation, as the social cost in terms of people losing their jobs and increases in tariffs associated with the new profit motive for restructured parastatals is simply too high.

The point that often gets lost is that COSATU and the SACP are not entirely opposed to privatisation, but argue that seeking private sector partners or borrowing from banks is more acceptable. COSATU general secretary Zwelinzima Vavi advocates a case-by-case approach, while a document presented at the SACP's congress in July 2002 stated: 'Privatisation is not necessarily wrong.' Indeed, the issue is a case study of how economic debate in South Africa has been wilfully distorted to the detriment of sustainable policies that would secure wide buy-in.

Those opposed to privatisation are likely to be labelled Soviet-style communists, while those in favour are berated as heartless capitalists. The truth is most likely something in between.

It would be inaccurate to say that privatisation has been slow. From March 1997 to 2004, the government privatised eighteen state-owned enterprises, ranging from radio stations to SAA, raising about R26.8 billion, of which some R12 billion was used to service the national debt. In addition, but frequently overlooked, were numerous instances at municipal level of services being outsourced or public–private partnerships being formed.

Wholesale disposal of state-owned assets in developing countries, as advocated by the World Bank, could never work in South Africa and should not be allowed. Irrespective of the arguments made by Western pundits, the road to ruin for many African countries has been mapped by limited control over their own resources. In oil-rich African states, for example, production is mostly controlled by outsiders – with the help of corrupt locals – who invest their vast profits in the industrial countries from whence they come. In sharp contrast, Norway, for example, has retained ownership of its rich oil fields and ploughed the revenue back into domestic development.

The shrill cries of the DA in support of wholesale privatisation is very much out of kilter with black society as a whole, except for those black business people who favour privatisation because it allows the transfer of major assets into their hands.

Government has an obligation to extend basic services such as electricity, transport and postal services across the country. The state remains one of the few vehicles for redistribution in a country where most business people do not accept that they have a social responsibility, despite most of the large corporations having made their fortunes on the back of cheap black labour and apartheid policies that saw black-owned land, with its mineral deposits and fertile soil, forcibly expropriated for white use.

In meeting its responsibility to ensure the provision of social services, government should not allow competition to be an end in itself, but rather a means to achieve development and improved efficiency. There is more than enough evidence in industrial countries that privatisation does not necessarily guarantee competence. Trains are neither safer nor more punctual since British Rail was placed in private hands.

But Mbeki is determined to bring blacks into the economy by getting them to buy into privatised or partially restructured state-owned companies, but it would be foolish to do so only via big business rather than through broad-based poor communities, or cooperatives formed by such communities.

Government's privatisation strategy is four-pronged. State-owned companies that are non-core, such as the holiday resort group Aventura, qualify for full privatisation. Those that are of strategic importance, such as the so-called 'big four' of Transnet, Denel, Eskom and Telkom, are restructured and partially sold in the interest of competition and efficiency. Port and rail services are run by means of operating concessions, and public–private partnerships are formed to deliver essential services, especially at municipal level.

The privatisation of Telkom, in which 20 per cent of South Africa's fixed-line communications company was listed in 2003, was the biggest sell-off. A 30 per cent stake in Telkom had been sold to American company SBC and Telkom Malaysia for R5.6 billion in May 1997, and in the 2002 financial year Telkom saw a rise in profits, with annual earnings increasing by 17 per cent to R1.915 billion. Mbeki-ites used the Telkom restructuring to make privatisation 'popular' among sceptical ANC supporters. The 2003 Telkom privatisation was a kind of *volkskapitalisme*, where poor people could secure shares at low costs in the authority. Mbeki is keen on using privatisation to create a new black class of shareholders. However, since 1998 Telkom has reduced its workforce by more than a third and raised its tariffs to a level that required it to report in the 2001/02 financial results that only 667 039 of the 2.67 million lines installed in poor and rural areas were still in service. The rest had been disconnected due to the inability of subscribers to pay.

In 1998, government sold 20 per cent of the Airports Company of South Africa (ACSA) to Aeroporti di Roma. Radebe had hoped to list ACSA in 2004, but, before he died, former transport minister Dullah Omar insisted that no decision had been made to list ACSA. 'Our agreement with Aeroporti di Roma is only to consider a listing, but we are not compelled to list,' he said.[22]

Government forged ahead with the controversial restructuring of Eskom, the energy utility, which will see its generation, supply and transmission components incorporated as separate business divisions. The state plans to sell about 30 per cent of Eskom by 2008, when the utility will no longer have an overcapacity. In 2002, Eskom was converted from a public enterprise, led by an electricity council, to a public company with share capital. Management consultants predicted that households could expect tariff increases of 'between 22% and 50%'[23] from a privatised Eskom. In a move to ensure that users buy only what they can afford and do not default on payments, the introduction of prepaid electricity services has become widespread.

Radebe has kept the privatisation programme on track by means of a delicate balancing act, vigorously consulting with trade unions while at the same time trying to move quickly. But while the pace has been too rapid for COSATU and the SACP, progress has been too slow for Mbeki's liking. Labour's ire has been raised by large tariff increases by many of the restructured parastatals. For example,

Spoornet increased tariffs for the transport of certain foodstuffs by between 12 and 67 per cent in 2001, causing upward pressure on food prices.

Outsourcing of basic services has not gone smoothly. Soon after international companies were awarded contracts to supply household water in KwaZulu-Natal and Mpumalanga, already hard-pressed consumers were unable to pay the tariffs. Their supplies were suspended, forcing them to drink water from nearby rivers and streams, which resulted in a major cholera outbreak.[24]

The stock market route, such as the Telkom IPO (initial public offering), is probably the least favourable, as it is difficult to hold companies to account for social responsibility. Concessions in the rail sector, for example, are problematic, since investors tend to be interested only in specific operations, such as the high-density Coallink or Orex lines, rather than the entire Spoornet network.

Some ventures have been successful because trade unions and government have struck amicable privatisation deals. The R45-million sale of the Eastern Cape North forestry package to Singisi Forest Products in 2000 gave local communities a stake in the forestry industry for the first time. Trade unions ensured that Singalanga Trust, representing 163 communities, would hold 10 per cent of the equity, and interim job security was achieved through negotiations between government and the buyers, which placed a three-year moratorium on retrenchments.

In 1999, Radebe halted a Spoornet plan to retrench 27 000 workers by embarking on discussions with management and the South African Transport and Allied Workers Union (SATAWU). In a fine example of how the privatisation impasse can be overcome, the combination of new management and union cooperation subsequently saw a profit of R605 million being posted and a turnaround plan being put in place that looked sound and showed hope for further efficiency gains.

There is no question that the social cost of privatisation has been huge. Thousands of jobs have been lost in an economy that can ill afford more un-employment. Radebe concedes: 'It is generally agreed that the immediate impact of restructuring may involve some employment losses.' South Africa's state sector offers an income to about 1.1 million employees, and the government bargains on a social plan being able to cushion job losses. But what about the future? Any social plan is necessarily short term, and it is unrealistic to expect that retrenched workers will be able to find jobs in other sectors, as might be the case in developed countries.

Even so, government has yet to come up with a comprehensive plan to cushion job losses where restructuring takes place. Moreover, government strategy should encourage foreigners to invest in greenfield projects – building new factories, and so on – rather than buying existing state, or, for that matter, private assets.

While South Africa has shed one in eight jobs since 1994, productivity has grown at twice the rate in the US. Though still only about half as productive as its American counterpart, the South African labour force is four times as productive as China's, five times more than India's and better than most East Asian developing countries, excluding Singapore, Taiwan and Korea.

The dramatic rise in productivity – 33.6 per cent from 1990 to 1999 – is one of the biggest successes of the first decade of democracy, but the key to sustained high productivity lies as much with management as with blue-collar workers. Clearly, the productivity and efficiency of South Africa's management echelon is not up to par, and if unions are compelled to make adjustments in order to increase productivity, outdated management practices should similarly be discarded.

South Africa's R43.8 billion strategic arms procurement package is likely to punch holes in government's attempts to keep a tight rein on public finances. Approved by parliament in April 1998, a defence review led to a cabinet announce- ment in September 1999 that it had decided to purchase armaments worth R21.8 billion over the next eight years, with an option for further procurement over an additional four years. However, the real costs have ballooned due to fluctuations in the foreign exchange rate since the contracts were signed, and it is impossible to calculate the final cost to taxpayers. The deal has been widely and justifiably criticised. South Africa should hardly be spending billions on sophisticated military hardware instead of on poverty alleviation and social upliftment. Certainly, no further arms should be procured, and the whole deal must be stringently monitored to ensure that at least the promises of counter-trade benefits are realised and that corruption does not taint the transactions.

In two successive budgets, Manuel gave back huge sums to taxpayers. In 2001, tax cuts totalled R8 billion, while the following year the figure was R15 billion. Nothing wrong with that, except that the chief beneficiary was the mostly privileged middle class, black and white, and the government lost a great opportunity to assist the poor. Manuel argued that this was a means of rewarding diligent taxpayers, but instead of boosting the coffers of those already well off, the government could have diverted the funds to a basic income grant or an extended social welfare net.

Failure to use the tax system to redistribute wealth must rank as one of the great disappointments of democracy. The feeling in some ANC alliance quarters is that South Africa's black and mostly impoverished majority has borne the brunt of freedom's price. There is no clear correlation between the increase of disposable income through reduced income tax and more labour-intensive investment and economic growth.

Astonishingly, rollovers abound in government departments, where unspent funds are carried over into the next financial year. Even more astonishingly, Manuel sees the country's biggest problem as the incapacity to distribute money. However, the government's inability to get money to those who need it most serves to underline the folly of culling the public service merely for the sake of doing so, rather than ensuring that the best people remain on the payroll while those at the lower levels learn the skills they need.

Slashing public service jobs without taking into account service delivery targets or improved work performance is a recipe for disaster. There are about 1.1 million public servants, a ratio of one to every 36 citizens, which is consistent with international norms. In spite of a 13 per cent drop in the number of public servants in 1995, government's wage bill continued to rise[25] due to non-wage benefits like pension and medical aid contributions, thirteenth cheques, retrenchment packages, an elite layer of highly paid technocrats, above-inflation increases won by rank-and-file public servants, and consultancy fees. Spending huge amounts to retain the expertise of former employees as 'consultants' makes no sense at all, yet this has become accepted practice in the public service.

Instead of downsizing, the government should be rightsizing. In the case of teachers, for example, this would see expenditure guided by targeted teacher–pupil ratios, rather than ratios being determined by available funds. In the short term, increased resources for such a policy could come from a restructuring of public sector pension funds.

Under Mbeki, government departments with the greatest technical proficiency and the most political clout have the advantage of securing allocations for their specific reconstruction programmes rather than allocations being made on the basis of need and ability to deliver. This means that many social delivery departments often lose out against those whose ministers are members of Mbeki's inner circle.

South Africa's land reform programme has been mixed. The three-pronged strategy revolves around restitution, redistribution and tenure. Of 64 000 claims for restitution, only 46 727 had been settled by 2004. A decade into the new dispensation, whites still owned 70 per cent of available land in South Africa. Examples of successful economic development on the basis of effective land reform[26] abound, especially in Asia, but cooperatives, for example, appear to be way down on the South African government's agenda. Yet they have been extremely successful in Israel, and, closer to home, helped lift Afrikaners out of poverty. The KWV wine cooperative and the Koo brand offer proof that cooperatives have enormous potential for upliftment, ranging from poor black farming communities to urban home ownership.

Government has also shown appalling neglect regarding attendance of pre-schools by black toddlers. Consequently, many black children lag far behind their white counterparts when they start school. Apart from the obvious disadvantage to the children, numerous employment opportunities are being lost by failure to set up state-funded pre-schools in communities that need them most. Today's children are the foundations on which South Africa's future prosperity will be built, and it is at the highly unfashionable grassroots level that black economic empowerment must happen and will make a lasting impact on the nation.

Government has also not actively intervened to stop another generation from leaving school ill equipped to be economically active due to being offered soft subjects like Bible studies at underfunded black rural and township schools. Science, commerce and technical subjects are what the economy needs and what pupils should be focusing on, and it is up to the government to make sure that this happens. Despite the introduction of new syllabuses, however, these subjects are still being taken by an alarmingly low number of black pupils.

Just as government departments are expected to run on business lines, higher education is being nudged in that direction, putting academic qualifications and skills even further out of the reach of those who need them most. At a time when South Africa needs all the skills it can get, potential students are being turned away in droves because they cannot afford to pay for tuition. Black students still account for only 30 per cent of all enrolments for master's degrees and doctorates. Government's blueprint for the restructuring of higher education does not inspire confidence.[27] It has seen historically white institutions, such as the universities of Cape Town, Stellenbosch, Pretoria, Natal, Witwatersrand and Rand Afrikaans, largely unaffected, while historically black universities and technikons have either been merged or closed down. Instead, a new apartheid is created: capable, effective white universities, and poor, low-quality black universities.

Education policies have not included proposals to redress funding inequities left over from apartheid, improve black access to tertiary institutions or bridge the rural–urban divide. How can it possibly make sense to shut down or cut back on a university or technikon in rural Transkei or Zululand, for example, when entire communities depend on the jobs they offer? Would it not make more economic sense to refocus institutions to become relevant to the communities they serve by educating a new generation of technicians, entrepreneurs and farmers?

Even as it was planning political reforms, the last apartheid government took a decision that would place a massive burden on democratic South Africa. In 1990, the public service pension fund was restructured in such a way that it inflated government debt from about R90 billion at the time to close on R400 billion in 2004.[28]

Reluctant to scrap the debt incurred by the apartheid government lest it lose business confidence, the Mbeki government used the debt not only to justify cutbacks in spending on social services, but also to retrench the very public servants in whose name this unilateral action was taken. Public sector debt fell from 64 per cent of GDP in 1993/94 to 50 per cent in the 2002/03 financial year. If the debt is to be paid, it would have been more practical to structure repayment over a longer period, and set aside additional funds for social spending and development of infrastructure. More importantly, it would have done much for reconciliation if companies that oiled the wheels of apartheid and who are now being repaid by the democratic government for doing just that, had cancelled the debt or allocated it to programmes that would uplift South Africa's disadvantaged communities.

Another important area that should be revisited, and which could unlock up to R50 billion for social investment, is the potential of prescribed assets on retirement funds,[29] requiring them to invest a stipulated percentage of income in bonds dedicated to social investment and employment creation. Prescribed assets were extensively used by the apartheid regime to finance entities like the Armaments Corporation, among others, but this practice was abolished prior to democratisation. Mbeki has rejected a revision of the policy, fearing objections by white business and a possible backlash from the market.

A 'solidarity tax' levied on wealthier South Africans – black and white – is a short-term measure that might be considered to deal with the backlogs created by apartheid. The TRC recommended that in order to empower the poor, business should contribute to a wealth tax – a once-off levy on corporate income or a donation by listed companies of 1 per cent of their market capitalisation. For the sake of social justice and reconciliation, such a move is still urgently needed.

The government's view is that the state should step in only where markets fail, and should play no role in directing industrial policy. Former World Bank chief economist Joseph Stiglitz says:

> I do not believe in blanket statements like 'government is worse than markets'. Government has an important role to play in responding to market failures, which are a general feature of any economy with imperfect information and incomplete markets. The implication of this view is that the task of making the state more effective is considerably more complex than just shrinking its size. The state has an important role to play in appropriate regulation, industrial policy, social protection and welfare. The choice should not be whether the state should or should not be involved. Instead it is often a matter of how it gets involved.[30]

Industrial policy measures should be designed to include incentives for employment creation and penalties for the favouring of capital over labour intensiveness, and 'employment audits' should form an integral part of mid-term and final reviews of investment promotion programmes. It is vital that investment-promoting measures, such as spatial development initiatives and tax holiday concessions, are employment sensitive.

While many agree that South Africa should aim at becoming an internationally competitive economy, there should be greater emphasis on achieving this through properly sequenced introduction of supply-side measures, including increased skills training and policies promoting research and development, rather than simply reducing tariffs in order to expose enterprises to the chill winds of competition. Indeed, there should be a close analysis of the effect of accelerated tariff reduction on employment levels in key sectors, such as clothing, with the possibility that it will be eased in critical sectors. There also needs to be ongoing improvement of effective customs control and anti-dumping prosecution in order to protect jobs from the effects of illegal imports.

Terms of reference for the Industrial Development Corporation (IDC) and Development Bank of Southern Africa (DBSA) should be explicitly altered to reward labour intensity and employment creation, and success should guide the resourcing of these institutions. Government procurement policy should be designed specifically to favour goods that are produced by labour-intensive methods. Given South Africa's unemployment crisis, it is important that industry's one-sided emphasis on competitiveness, which is necessary for sustainability and efficiency, is adjusted to include a renewed focus on job creation.

It is critical that mechanisms be put in place to stem the shedding of existing jobs. For example, retrenchments should be more tightly regulated, and the impact on employment should be taken into account more seriously before company mergers are approved. Measures should also be put in place to ensure that social plan procedures, aimed at re-skilling and alleviating the problems associated with industries in decline, do not become standard justifications during retrenchment proceedings.

Investment presupposes that there is a market that will buy products, and this generally means a sizeable population with sufficient disposable income. Investment also requires stability and productivity, which are facilitated rather than undermined by a well-regulated standards-based labour market. Other societies have made bold decisions at critical stages in their development to build their economies on a stable foundation of worker and social rights.

By the end of 2000, the Mbeki camp began conceding that some adjustments had to be made to economic policy. Despite tweaking and tinkering, grinding poverty, inequality and unemployment persisted. However, Mbeki was loath to publicly admit large-scale failure, and instead sold the shift in direction on the basis that success in certain areas had created a climate for adoption of more expansionist policies. In his State of the Nation address in 2001, Mbeki hinted at a switch from macro- to microeconomics.

There is a growing consensus in the tripartite alliance that it has not been as effective as it could be to lever business capacity and to use state power to achieve its objectives of reducing poverty, unemployment, underdevelopment and inequality in partnership with the private sector. Joel Netshitenzhe says there has been 'a GEAR shift'. He explains: 'The principles of macroeconomic stability remain. But because such stability has essentially been attained, there is more space for massive social and economic interventions by the government. In that sense, we are in a post-stabilisation phase, a post-GEAR period.'

Certainly the biggest shift in both the government and local business sector has been the move away from the belief that foreign investment is the panacea for all the country's problems. There is a growing realisation that investment must come from within, and the only thing that government and the private sector now have to do is start making the investments!

One of the first changes in economic policy was that government began investing in infrastructure development incrementally from 1999. But at least R45 billion was needed to boost short- to medium-term local demand and stimulate growth.

In 2003, Manuel announced that he would allow a budget deficit of more than the 3 per cent prescribed by GEAR – 3.2 per cent in 2004 and 3.1 per cent in 2005 – in order to make extra funding available for poverty alleviation and redistribution. This is a change from the well-trodden path of balancing the budget and controlling inflation in preference to creating jobs. Mbeki argues that fiscal prudence since 1994 allowed the ANC to get ready to embark on bolder wealth redistribution, but the initial offerings are far too timid.

South Africa urgently needs a national accord or understanding between business, labour, government and community organisations to establish its own New Deal. This could take the form of a national agreement binding key constituencies to a social and economic accord that would prevent the explosive mix of poverty and economic imbalance from developing into a crisis, such as that in Zimbabwe, where neglect of land and racial inequalities over two decades resulted in lawlessness and a threat to destabilise the regional economy.

South Africa's poverty levels resemble those of Europe in the aftermath of the Second World War. In many of the worst-affected countries, social accords were struck between the major role players, holding them to trade-offs that contributed to social and economic upliftment. Such an accord was mooted by South Africa's Labour Market Commission, which looked into the modernisation of the labour market, but it fell flat when it was overtaken by GEAR.

Kevin Wakeford says: 'At the moment, those feeling the pain are society's voiceless: the poor and the unemployed. But employers and the well off will bear more and more of the social cost associated with increasing poverty and joblessness through increased costs for security and crime prevention.'

A social accord would demand substantial compromises from different groups that traditionally have strong interests to protect. The private sector would have to give a commitment that it would invest in certain areas in order to create jobs, and banks, for example, would have to devise more innovative ways of lending to the poor, unemployed and small business. But such loans would certainly be more feasible if the state provided collateral.

Likewise, organised labour has to become more flexible about working hours, wages and productivity. Government should be less dogmatic about economic policy and more flexible on questions about the extent of state spending on social services. Investment should increase without scrambling budget-deficit targets, government should occasionally intervene to correct market distortions and look anew at what sorts of incentives are offered to investors.

The Growth and Development Summit held in Johannesburg in 2003 could be the basis of such an accord, provided contentious issues are not skirted. The summit's mission was to reach consensus on an economic blueprint for the country, which would offer solutions to unemployment, inequality and poverty.

However, ahead of the meeting, Mbeki warned that this should be done without tampering with GEAR – a tall order. The injunction dramatically reduced the summit's scope for negotiation and compromise. One of the summit's major failings was its inability to come up with a strategy to deal with the potentially devastating economic impact of HIV/AIDS, a reality that has to be factored into any plan aimed at rejuvenating the economy.

The first attempt to negotiate a consensus for economic development and job creation, the Presidential Jobs Summit in 1998, failed spectacularly, precisely because of government's sensitivity about GEAR. It would have served no purpose for the growth summit to try to ram non-negotiable economic policies down distrusting throats, and there was the additional pressure of a forthcoming election. Mbeki had at least to pretend that he would take the concerns of the ANC's angry partners, COSATU and the SACP, seriously.[31]

The dialogue stimulated by the growth summit seemed to have helped change the tone of South Africa's economic debate, and to draw social partners closer on a range of important policy questions. In a sense, it also provided an opportunity for government departments to come together and generate a measure of synergy between their various development and employment stimulation programmes. As a result, there is greater consensus on job creation and coordination, and consensus within government has been encouraged.

The growth summit reached broad agreement on two key initiatives: an expanded public works programme and internships. These will focus on delivering training and experience to those struggling to find jobs. Soon afterwards, Mbeki outlined a public works programme that was the biggest, most precise and most expensive pledge the government had made since coming to power in 1994. A million job opportunities would be created over five years at a cost of R20 billion. Obviously, with the 2004 election lying ahead, there was a whiff of electioneering, but however belatedly, jobs seemed to be at the apex of the government's economic policy.

Public works are necessary for a society where a proportion of the labour force is marginalised, something that the government had been reluctant to accept. The programme announced in 2003 aims at providing a safety net while high-growth industries (such as motor manufacturing, clothing and tourism) come into their own and create jobs. It is also meant to help bring poor, unskilled and unemployed workers into South Africa's formal economy by linking skills training to every job. The unskilled will be employed to build low-volume roads and dig trenches for electricity, sanitation, and water pipelines and stormwater drains. Over a five-year period, R15 billion will be spent on public works infrastructure, disbursed through and managed by provinces and local councils.

Another R4 billion will go into environmental programmes, such as Working for Water, while an initial R600 million will go to the community sector to fund a corps of development workers likely to be deployed in providing home-based care for people living with AIDS and early childhood development. Every public works participant will receive at least two days of training a month in formal economic skills.

However, public works should not detract from formal sector employment strategies. The lesson of the past is that growth does not necessarily lead to large-scale employment. Capacity also needs to be spread across the country, or South Africa's plan could go the way of India's, where spots of success led to migration, defeating the purpose when certain areas were swamped. Most importantly, the public works programme cannot replace the desperate need for a comprehensive social safety net for the many destitute who would not even qualify for the programme.

The sometimes amazing short-sightedness of South African business was much in evidence at the growth summit. The business sector promised to commit to 72 000 internships over the following two years – clearly hugely inadequate even to make a dent in unemployment. As Standard Bank's former chief economist Iraj Abedian said, neither was it visionary in terms of the sheer self-interest of the business sector, since government carries almost all the financial costs incurred by participants. South Africa has more than 200 000 registered companies. If only 10 000 participated in a national scheme to reduce unemployment, taking on 50 interns on average, at least 500 000 positions could be created in a relatively short time for those who would otherwise have little or no chance of exposure to a formal working environment. Abedian is of the opinion that the wholesale industry, retail and major banks could easily take on between 500 and 1 000 learners each. The multiple impact on broad empowerment, economic growth, poverty reduction and development would be phenomenal.

South African business urgently needs leadership interventions, such as those by Nicky Oppenheimer,[32] who suggested that the family empire was prepared to do more to bring blacks into the economy. Though his suggestions fell well short of real demands, the underlying sentiment was important. At the same time, government will have to reward companies and businesses that throw off the shackles of inertia and positively contribute to change. The amount of reconciliation and goodwill that could be engendered by South African businesses voluntarily investing in black upliftment would be enormous. That is the great challenge for white South African business.

Among the reasons for lack of investment given by the ten-year review, for example, are that the South African and regional markets are neither large enough nor growing fast enough. Though this is not as overriding a factor as Mbeki believes, it is important, because in reality many foreign investors have a poor understanding of democratic South Africa. Indeed, South African policy-makers place great emphasis on combating negative perceptions.

The government established an international marketing council to fight negative images and perceptions of the country. The image of Mandela, attached to the 'miracle' of South Africa's transition, helped give the country an advantage over similar developing economies. However, as Netshitenzhe concedes: 'The mistake was to assume that it [the Mandela brand and miracle phenomenon] will sustain itself.'

Policy-makers have tried to develop a market identity for the country that is less dependent on the icon of Mandela, but this may be government's Achilles heel. It has dealt with the symptoms rather than the substance of the problem. Blaming the media for creating negative perceptions, which Mbeki frequently does, shows another weakness. It is easier to find scapegoats than to tackle the tasks at hand: devising and implementing policies that will deal with the country's deep-seated problems.

The ANC has been reluctant to consider providing a basic social safety net, such as a basic income grant, for those left hopelessly destitute as the government aggressively liberalises the economy. As government embarks on its radical reforms, it is the poor who are the worst affected, who need most to buy into the reforms.

The current welfare system covers no one between the ages of eight and sixty-five – though there are plans to raise the lower age limit to fourteen – and reduces the poverty rate by only 25 per cent. Calculations have shown that a monthly basic income grant of R100 to the destitute, including children, would offer relief to 75 per cent of those who currently fall through the cracks. This alone would promote 6 million people above the breadline, if that figure is R400 a month. It would help families with basic food, keep children in school and generate savings in other areas, such as healthcare and law enforcement.

Michael Samson of the University of Cape Town's Economic Policy Research Institute, reckons:

> The positive growth effects of social security reform are likely to more than offset any negative impact of higher taxes. The grant will nearly triple the average per capita transfer to poor households, reducing the poverty gap by more than 80 per cent. Payment could be through the post office or public institutions. It could be funded by only marginally increasing the tax rate of middle and high-income earners, without reducing the international competitiveness and economic growth of the country. This could be one form of wealth redistribution.

Mbeki, Manuel and other centrist economic managers continue to disdainfully dismiss calls for extended basic income grants as populist and fiscally unsustainable. Manuel says the country cannot afford to finance a culture of dependency or entitlement, to which Archbishop Desmond Tutu responds that one can hardly speak of entitlement when a minority becomes disproportionately rich through black economic empowerment.

Paying out a social grant to the poor could be the basis of a new consensus, based on the economic justice the TRC urged was needed if real reconciliation was ever to take place between black and white in South Africa. The government needs to urgently provide interim social security for those waiting for economic growth to trickle down to them. Even if robust economic growth finally arrives, it is unlikely to significantly narrow the gap between the rich and the poor. If government does not provide a social safety net, its market-orientated reforms will run up against a wall of dissatisfaction.

South Africa can translate its political miracle into the economic and social arenas, provided that government, business and civil society, including labour, share responsibility for negotiating and making the required changes. The crippling extent of poverty, inequality and unemployment among the black majority is a huge crisis that calls for drastic steps before a political and social explosion can occur.

The problem in South Africa is also one of mindset. People need to accept that it is in their own best interest to do away with inequality. Although the sacrifice seems huge, it is actually tiny compared to the potential gains for the country and individuals.

Neither whites nor newly rich blacks are expected to share everything they have, but vast differences can be made by small sacrifices, such as sponsoring the education of a disadvantaged child. Government, for its part, could introduce loans for impoverished students at tertiary institutions, which can be paid back once the recipients start working.

The ANC needs to adopt greater flexibility in its macroeconomic policy. More appropriate and developmentally orientated macro-policies should be adopted. The consensus around a commitment to fiscal discipline should not have the effect of neutralising fiscal policy. As in times of downturn, state expenditure should be used more effectively as a counter-cyclical tool.

Government's current premise, that growth must be achieved before redistribution, is misdirected. The two should be pursued in tandem. Incredibly, there is still no overall framework to eradicate poverty. Government's anti-poverty programmes remain disjointed and uncoordinated, and this has to change.

Moreover, there needs to be a relaxing of inflation and budget deficit targets to release funds for public infrastructure and social services. More flexible budget deficit targets should be linked to different stages of the business cycle, to levels of private sector investment and to GDP growth. Adjustments are definitely called for in monetary policy, including a much deeper lowering of interest rates. This should be combined with more flexible fiscal and trade policies, which offer some protection against imports for the domestic market. Government should tighten its capital control policy by closing loopholes such as transfer pricing and double invoicing, through which many South African businesses export capital.

Sustainable job creation requires overarching policies that will move the economy onto a new growth and development path: a genuine commitment to human resource development by both the private and public sectors; national consensus on a bedrock of acceptable labour standards upon which we plan to build the economy; a commitment to contra-cyclical job-creating public sector investment, particularly in infrastructure; employment-sensitive industrial policy measures; and creative trade unions and strong civil society groupings capable of effectively representing and articulating the interests and needs of marginal and disadvantaged communities.

It is clear that South Africa is not going to deal with unemployment and poverty overnight. According to some estimates, 45 per cent of the population lives in poverty.[33] This means that another generation will know nothing else. How are they going to get through school in a poverty-stricken environment, with low nutrition and parents unable to pay for basic health needs? What about the social costs – school dropouts, more jobless youth unprepared for the job market? In South Africa, the crime rate is almost never associated with the huge apartheid-induced inequalities that persist ten years after democracy. The government must try to break the cycle of poverty and despair that frequently results in crime.

Look no further than the widespread dissatisfaction among the populace of Latin America after their countries pursued market-orientated reforms in the 1980s without paying much attention to providing social insurance and safety nets. Even if the South African economy reaches the 6 per cent growth rate and the spurt of investment needed, there will remain the issue of the large unemployed sector with no or inadequate skills for a modern economy.

So far, the economic cost of South Africa's transition has fallen disproportionately on those it was supposed to benefit most – the millions of black poor. Clearly, even if growth and investment rise rapidly, it is unlikely to trickle down to them immediately. What is urgently needed is a welfare net to soften the blow, coupled with a huge re-skilling programme, starting with basic literacy and public works, and the transfer of land and skills in the rural areas.

Unless the economy delivers to the country's poor, South Africa's democratic miracle could unravel.

# — 6 —

# The CEO

Socialism can come later when I have discovered it.　　　　　　 – Joe Slovo, 1994[1]

The ANC is not a socialist party. It has never pretended to be one, it has never said it was, and it is not trying to be. It will not become one by decree for the purpose of pleasing its 'left' critics.　　　　　　 – Thabo Mbeki, 1984[2]

F OR THABO MBEKI TO PUSH THROUGH HIS AMBITIOUS CONSERVATIVE economic and social reform agenda, he had to capture full control of the ANC as a party, secure the commanding leadership positions for like-minded trusted allies and tightly police internal opposition.

The scene of his spectacular victory was the ANC's national conference at Mafikeng in 1997, where a majority of pro-Mbeki leaders were elected to the National Executive Committee. Afterwards, the battle was to maintain their dominance of the party, especially once the strict macroeconomic and social policies started to bite and rebellion mounted.

Mbeki handled the situation masterfully, despite the odd scare when the left wing made a determined surge, only to be pushed back firmly by Mbeki's centrists.

By the time South Africa celebrated its tenth year of democracy, most of the ANC's leadership structures were packed with pro-Mbeki centrists: the NEC, internal party commissions and committees, parliament and its important committees, cabinet, the provincial organs, the Youth and Women's Leagues. The powerful National Working Committee, which makes decisions from one national conference to the next and comprises NEC members, was filled with Mbeki's most loyal supporters.

With control of the party firmly under his heel, Mbeki moved quickly to mould the movement in his image. His strategists called it 'modernising' the

ANC from a broad-based liberation movement to a governing political party, with centrist political, social and economic policies firmly orientated towards the market. Ideologically, the ANC is a broad church, sheltering under its umbrella myriad political hues: liberals, Christian democrats, communists, socialists, social democrats, African nationalists and Africanists.

The bedrock of the ANC under Mbeki has been liberal social democratic. He has drawn influential leaders from the disparate ideological strands into a close-knit alliance – the Mbeki-ites – to take the ANC down its new centrist path. But within this group, many former communists and capitalist African nationalists, including pure Africanists, are in the ascendancy. The presidency resembles a royal court, with minions jockeying for position and jostling one another to gain access to the king. Keeping watch are the gatekeepers, Essop Pahad (in government) and Lulama 'Smuts' Ngonyama (inside the party).

Some of the changes in the ANC happened so quickly that many members were not even aware they had taken place or grasped their significance. Mbeki was determined to remake the ANC into a modern African party with a social democratic orientation, something of a mix between the Swedish Social Democratic Party, the German Social Democratic Party and Britain's New Labour Party, adapted to the demands of Africa and run efficiently along business lines.[3] The oldest liberation movement in Africa was to become a hybrid that appealed to both business and the poor, all the while holding on to its large mass base.

One of Mbeki's most trusted allies and a key architect of the new ANC, Joel Netshitenzhe, argued in the influential June 2000 discussion paper, *ANC – People's Movement and Agent for Change*, that it was necessary to 'examine the challenge of the modernisation of the ANC as both a concept and in its practical application.'[4]

Netshitenzhe, the quintessential back-room workhorse, cut his political teeth in the Black Consciousness Movement. He is a protégé of Mbeki, who recognised his prodigious talent and snapped him up to work in the propaganda arm of the ANC in exile, where his *nom de guerre* was Peter Mayibuye. Born in Sibasa, deep in the Northern Province, the quiet but sharp political strategist has been with Mbeki ever since, and the two men speak almost daily.

Smuts Ngonyama, head of the presidency in the ANC, is one of Mbeki's most trusted lieutenants, whose job is to ensure that nothing prises open Mbeki's iron grip on the party. Ngonyama's almost priestly appearance masks a core of steel. In the former Ciskei bantustan, the apartheid security police had tried repeatedly to silence him, and at one point he was obliged to send his family to safety elsewhere after their home was riddled with machine-gun fire. Yet he unfailingly offered the security police a cup of coffee each time they came to detain him.

As Mbeki's chief strategic advisor, he willingly cracks the whip to flay errant party leaders into submission.

At the ANC's December 2002 national conference, Mbeki elevated another trusted acolyte, Sankie Mahanyele-Mthembi, to the post of deputy secretary general as additional insurance against any attempt to push the reform project off course. The former housing minister and budding poet is one of an array of influential women appointed to key posts by Mbeki.

Other powerful figures in Mbeki's inner circle are ministers Essop Pahad (office of the presidency), Sydney Mufamadi (provincial and local government), Nkosazana Dlamini-Zuma (foreign affairs), Trevor Manuel (finance), Jabu Moleketi (Manuel's deputy), Geraldine Fraser-Moleketi (public service and administration), Alec Erwin (public enterprises), Phumzile Mlambo-Ngcuka (minerals and energy), Malusi Gigaba (home affairs deputy) and Lindiwe Sisulu (housing). They represent different political generations, temperament and upbringing, but they share a fierce loyalty to the president and his vision for the ANC.

As mentioned, Mbeki aligns himself ideologically with British prime minister Tony Blair, German chancellor Gerhard Schroeder and Swedish Social Democratic leader Göran Persson. They embrace a common theme, known as the Third Way. It amounts to less government, using the market to deliver, distancing themselves from the unions and moving closer to business. They keep a tight rein on their parties.

Originally a British–American venture, Blair and Schroeder co-authored a document, *Third Way/Neue Witte*,[5] which argues the merits of flexible labour markets and identifies high public spending as the road to ruin. Schroeder based the modernisation of the German Social Democrats on the concept, while Blair used it to turn his party away from its overtly leftist orientation and into a party of the political centre and the market.[6]

Stan Greenberg and Phillip Gould, major adherents of the Third Way, argue that the future of social democratic parties lies in shedding the political baggage of rigid ideology. Like Blair's favourite theorist, former London School of Economics head and sociologist Anthony Giddens, they believe that social democratic parties should reinvent what Giddens calls the 'radical centre', or the end of party ideology as we know it.[7] This has been Mbeki's mantra.

His problem has been how to get the mix accepted by a constituency that, not surprisingly, looks to the state for speedy social delivery, much as the National Party lifted Afrikaners to prosperity after 1948. Mbeki and the ANC chiefs have taken a lesson from Blair and Schroeder in how to market unpopular party policies to their constituencies.

The modernisers increasingly talk 'left' to the ANC membership, but act 'right' as government.[8] In order to keep the tripartite alliance from coming unstuck, party leaders often talk of a 'national democratic revolution' to describe essentially liberal democratic changes. Respected South African sociologist Sakhela Buhlungu puts it succinctly: 'Today the rhetoric about the "national democratic revolution" and "delivery" often creates the impression that what we are witnessing are unprecedented revolutionary changes.'[9]

Mbeki and many of his cabinet ministers increasingly use the same media sound bites and savvy pioneered by Blair's New Labour and the German Social Democrats. Blair famously adapted the US Democrat slogan 'Tough on crime, tough on the causes of crime'. Mbeki-ites such as Manuel trot out catchphrases like 'It's a budget for the poor', 'You never had it so good' and 'Hunger is in danger'.[10]

Mbeki greatly admires the changes in New Labour under Blair, but then he has always been a fan of Britain's Labour Party. In the 1960s, when he was in his late teens and twenties, he was a keen supporter of Labour leader Harold Wilson,[11] so it's hardly surprising that he would look to Blair's brand of liberal social democracy.

A priority for Mbeki and the centrist modernisers was to transform the ANC from a bloated liberation movement to a lean and mean election machine. This would also bring change to the way the party conducts election campaigns.

The goal is a more efficient structure, streamlined to wind down between elections and ratchet up at ballot time. With a view to the ANC having a permanent election apparatus for the first time,[12] Mbeki created the full-time position of elections coordinator at the party's Albert Luthuli Headquarters in downtown Johannesburg.

Peter Mokaba, former deputy minister of tourism and environment, was the first to hold this powerful post. Northern Cape premier Manne Dipico was temporarily installed to replace Mokaba for the 2004 elections. The capable Dipico had run a well-oiled campaign, based on personal neighbourhood canvassing, to capture the far-flung province that had been widely accepted as an impenetrable National Party stronghold. Mbeki would use the same tactics during the 2004 national campaign.

In 2000, the ANC moved from its sprawling offices overlooking Johannesburg's Joubert Park to smaller offices in Sauer Street. In keeping with the 'modern' and urbane ANC, secretary general Kgalema Motlanthe proposed issuing new electronic smart cards[13] to party members. Such has been the change within the ANC that donations from corporate benefactors, black and white, now count for more than membership subscriptions. Inevitably, this presents the danger of affluent donors having greater access to the party and its leaders than ordinary supporters.

Mbeki wants to adjust the ANC's focus away from the provinces to six newly designated metropolitan areas, or mega-cities. This has entailed a reduction in the number of branches from more than 1 500 to 365 and fewer municipalities, introduced during the local government elections in December 2000.

The result has been a sea change in the way the ANC operates. Branches used to be the heartbeat of the party, serving roles not unlike those of community organisations or churches. Members could secure support for anything from funerals to administrative headaches, such as registering a birth, or just enjoy the warmth of human solidarity. Now most of that has changed, and the top echelon of the party has adopted the cold formalism of a business operation. Appointments must be made, ID documents produced. Often the leaders are too busy with 'national concerns' to spend time with members. The identity of the old ANC is changing fast and its soul is becoming harder to locate.

Mbeki and other ANC chiefs have used other New Labour techniques, even the same advisors, to sell the party's makeover, engaging the services of US election campaign guru Stan Greenberg, who runs a London-based public opinion consultancy, and UK Labour Party election expert Philip Gould.[14] Both were instrumental in changing the image of the US Democrats to a party of fiscal discipline before turning their magic on Britain's Labour Party, then rebranding the ANC.

Greenberg is a proponent of progressive parties bypassing their traditional trade union allies: 'The institutions [trade unions] that used to be effective in mediating popular sentiment have atrophied, and have lost their ability to articulate. So the trade unions, for example, just don't have the kind of base that they used to have.'[15]

Greenberg was used in both the 1994 and 1999 elections, and Mbeki was instrumental in securing the services of former US president Bill Clinton's chief poll-taker and architect of his winning pitch in 1992. Ahead of the 1994 elections in South Africa, Greenberg spent nine months at the heart of the ANC's election team, commuting to South Africa to conduct opinion surveys and help shape the party's message.

Greenberg's insights into the 1994 campaign are fascinating. Most of the ANC leaders wanted to use the slogan 'Now is the time', but Greenberg's focus groups and other researchers found this 'threatening ... beyond the core supporters of the ANC'.[16] Although the slogan stuck, it was finally decided that the official campaign would be built around the promise of 'A better future for all'.[17]

Since then, the ANC has increasingly made use of professional pollsters, surveys and outside consultants to guide policy. Mbeki relies extensively on outside advisors, and consults with his presidential working groups and councils – big business, labour, agriculture and the international investment advisory council[18] – which he has set up. The use of counsel from party leaders is rare.

The 2004 campaign saw Mbeki reinvented by his PR machine, headed by Ogilvy & Mather, as a warm, hands-on president, prepared to listen to the voice of the people. There was no need to use outside consultants, because ANC insiders had learnt their craft during the 1994 and 1999 campaigns. The difference was obvious to all. Mbeki, widely seen as an aloof and stubborn intellectual, campaigned door to door around the country – smiling, dancing and meeting the people, rather than holding the mass rallies of old. He did so tirelessly, and the ANC's landslide victory, at a time when surveys claimed a high level of dissillusionment among blacks over slow delivery, was more than a little due to deft electioneering.

The president, usually averse to baby-kissing, was photographed handing out pamphlets and wearing casual shoes, going door to door, listening to voter concerns. Voters responded warmly. Arriving unannounced at the home of forty-nine-year-old Regina Pikosi, a two-roomed tin shack in the N2 squatter camp near Port Elizabeth, Mbeki was told: 'We do not have water here, we live in tin houses and they leak.' Nevertheless, she was delighted that the president had made the effort to call, and felt he was 'a good man'.[19]

During the 1999 campaign, Greenberg's team[20] had also advised Mbeki to loosen up and to appear often on the same platform as Mandela in order to emphasise continuity and impress on a sceptical ANC membership that he had Mandela's blessing. Election posters showed photographs of a noticeably greyer Mbeki to promote the image of an older, wise leader, capable of following in Mandela's footsteps. By 2004, Mbeki had moved out of Mandela's shadow; their relationship had become strained and he preferred to stomp the campaign trail alone, underscoring that he had become his own man.

The ANC's shift to the centre has not left its closest allies untouched. COSATU and the SACP have been forced to contemplate either moving further to the left – and risk being ridiculed as 'ultra-left' – or be pragmatic and adopt more centrist policies, possibly facing a leftist rebellion from within. In *Advancing Social Transformation in the Era of Globalisation*,[21] a document adopted by COSATU's central committee in October 2000, the trade union movement warned that the ANC's new business style of party management could lead to 'low intensity democracy, where the people are reduced to electing leaders every five years or so'.

Even opposition parties have been caught embarrassingly off guard. Those that traditionally occupied the political centre have, suicidally, not come to terms with the ANC's dramatic repositioning. The ANC has become a party with more liberal values than the Democratic Alliance, even if this fact irks the DA and is fiercely contested by the ANC leadership.

The Mbeki-ites worked strenuously to place sole control of the policy-making apparatus of the ANC alliance in the hands of the centrists. Mbeki acolytes such as Essop Pahad and Joel Netshitenzhe frequently argue that this is in the interest of more efficient policy implementation.

But the Mbeki-ites are vigilant to the threat of the left, trade union groups or socialists influencing policy (except for the odd concession) or derailing their reforms. In order to circumvent potential resistance, decisions on policy have been removed from the ANC's mass membership and entrusted to a few hand-picked insiders. Even the party machine has been taken out of the policy-making loop to avoid possible dilution of policies.

Officially, ANC structures such as local branches, provinces or the NEC make policy, which is then turned into legislation by parliament and implemented by the government. The reality is different, however. Policy-making is much more top-down, originating in government and often formulated by outside experts and consultants. The process rests squarely with the presidency, cabinet and government, and the presidency has the final veto.

Mbeki's presidency and cabinet have been based on the three Cs: control, coordination and centralisation.[22] The presidency consists of four central components: the offices of the president, the deputy president, the minister in the presidency and the director-general, who does double duty as the cabinet secretary. After the 2004 election, the incumbents were Mbeki, Jacob Zuma, Essop Pahad and Frank Chikane.

Pahad's position at the heart of power in the first tier of the enlarged presidency is that of a super-minister or premier.[23] The organogram of the presidency places the deputy president above the minister in the office of the presidency, but in truth, Pahad, not Zuma, takes charge of most presidential projects and has a hand in the executive management of the cabinet.

Mbeki, Pahad and Zuma formed a close political troika[24] until Zuma fell out of favour around New Year 2001, when Mbeki suspected that he was being punted by internal opponents as his possible successor, following policy failures over Zimbabwe and AIDS.

Chikane, the director-general, is also a powerful figure. He retained the same title as Jakes Gerwel, his predecessor in Mandela's administration, but has additional responsibility for the public service, and is in charge of transformation in that sector.

Chikane also oversees the directors-general of the various departments, with whom he frequently meets under the auspices of the Federation of South African Directors-General. Under Mandela, DGs reported to their ministers, but Mbeki took to appointing all directors-general himself, and, through Chikane, he thus has control of every government department. Indeed, there is not a single aspect of the administration that does not give the Mbeki presidency greater control over the executive than Mandela ever had.[25]

The next tier in the presidency is the cabinet office, beefed up by Mbeki along the lines of its British counterpart and consisting of three sections: research, operations, and a secretariat that oversees and coordinates the implementation of policies by the various ministers. The cabinet secretariat is the presidency's 'thinking machine'. It vets policy proposals from and recommends policy to the cabinet.[26]

Netshitenzhe was appointed as head of policy coordination and advisory services in late 2001, making him Mbeki's primary policy czar. He already was the government's chief spinmeister as head of the Government Communication and Information System (GCIS). Ministers are required to submit all new policy documents and draft laws to the presidency for scrutiny, and they all go through Netshitenzhe, who decides whether or not proposals are in accordance with government's policy goals. In mid-2001, Mbeki raised eyebrows when he established an intelligence support unit within the presidency to serve as his 'eyes and ears'.[27] Fears were legitimately raised that the president had his own spy network.

In August 2001, COSATU's central executive committee resolved to embark on a new strategy to influence policy-making by exerting pressure on the presidency. The tactic, according to COSATU chief Willie Madisha, was based on a political assessment by the leadership that the locus of policy-making rests firmly with the presidency.[28]

'It is certainly true that the capacity of the presidency has increased and that certain aspects of policy coordination have become centralised,' said a worried COSATU strategist Neil Coleman. 'A useful debate would be whether it is the appropriate issues which are being centralised and whether this is being done in the right way.'[29]

Essentially, Mbeki and his key strategists see the president as the joint CEO of SA Inc. and ANC Ltd, but this has major implications for democratic decision-making. The ordinary employee in a large firm has no say in the tight hierarchical lines on which businesses are run, and the grassroots ANC member has been relegated to a similar position. Herein lies the danger to democracy – ordinary people feel increasingly excluded from influencing policies.

Mbeki also runs his cabinet according to business principles. Whereas the cabinet secretariat in the Mandela administration was little more than a secretarial pool,[30] Mbeki has created a 'super-cabinet', comprising the cabinet proper, a coordination unit and a stronger secretariat to run the country. The nerve centre is the secretariat, headed by Chikane, and, like Britain's cabinet office, this is where policy implementation is planned and obstacles are dealt with.[31]

A coordination and implementation unit serves as the cabinet management team. Cabinet committees have assumed far greater importance than under Mandela,[32] and Mbeki has introduced clusters to tackle national priorities. Cabinet ministers whose functions overlap are grouped together and work cooperatively, but the clusters actually allow Mbeki to exercise personal control over individual ministries.

The key clusters are: efficient governance, investment and employment, human resource development, poverty eradication, international affairs and overall development. Mbeki keeps a tight rein on the running of individual departments,[33] with DGs signing employment contracts with the presidency rather than with the ministers under whom they serve.

In theory, the ANC's policy-making mechanisms consist of three sets of processes: those focused on the NEC's subcommittees; those based in the ANC's parliamentary study groups; and the permanent professionally staffed departments at Luthuli House. In practice, though, the policy-makers are cabinet ministers and their deputies (who constitute more than half of the NEC), their directors-general, and certain ANC caucus study groups and portfolio committee chairs.[34]

SACP stalwart Jeremy Cronin[35] emphasises that policies are now made mostly in government, meaning the ANC mass membership's ability to impact on policy-making has been severely curtailed. Even the 1997 national conference noted that 'since 1994, the point of gravity as regards policy development appears to have shifted to government and away from ANC constitutional structures'.[36] The left wing pushed hard at the conference for a resolution to shift the policy-making nexus from the state to Luthuli House, hoping that this would allow ordinary ANC members to exert at least some influence on policy-making. They won a rare victory.

The conference resolved: 'Whereas the ANC policy process should not attempt to cover the finer detail that government departments need to deal with, the ANC should build and maintain sufficient capacity to take the lead in the development of ANC policy to be implemented in the central, provincial and local spheres.'[37]

However, policy-making was not democratised, which has caused considerable tension between the ANC and its alliance partners ever since. The alliance partners have become increasingly marginalised in policy-making, notwithstanding reminders by angry COSATU affiliates that the trade union federation pegged its support for the ANC's 1999 election effort to an agreement on a pact that set out COSATU's minimum demands.

Most controversially, the 1997 ANC conference adopted a Mbeki-inspired proposal to lengthen the period between party conferences from three to five years, in line with government's term of office. The Mbeki-ites argued that this would streamline[38] policy-making. However, the implications were massive. Once policy has been decided on at the five-yearly conference, it is all but impossible to change it. Lengthening the period between national conferences from three to five years removed a key mechanism for ordinary members to change or throw out policies they were unhappy with.

The national general councils still meet between national conferences, but they have no power to amend policies. By contrast with the 'new' ANC, most other parties hold their national conferences annually or every two years, when policies are extensively debated and can be rejected midstream.

When the ANC's national general council met in Port Elizabeth in July 2000, the National Working Committee made it clear that policy, particularly economic policy, was not up for debate.[39] There seemed little point in meeting, then, and indeed the council did not discuss any economic policies, though this is one of the biggest bones of contention within the party.

Disgruntled members murmured that the general council had been reduced to a 'rubber stamp'.[40] If policies could not be changed between national conferences, what other vehicle is available? The appeal of the lower structures has been severely restricted in the restructured ANC.

Additionally, plans have been mooted to set up a national policy think tank, where ANC policy will be formulated before being disseminated to the rank and file.[41] Based on the German Social Democratic Party's Friedrich Ebert Foundation,[42] Motlanthe says the think tank would strengthen the ANC's policy-making capacity.[43]

However, critics argue that it would distance the leadership even further from the grassroots and alliance partners. Amid talk of ANC intellectual and socialist Pallo Jordan being appointed to head up the proposed think tank, Mbeki-ites delayed its formation rather than risk having a leftist at the helm.

The five-yearly national conference has ceased to be a forum for debate and decision-making. Ahead of the December 2002 conference, ANC leaders[44] stated there would be no policy changes, although in terms of the ANC constitution the national conference has the power to review or endorse policies.

The gathering has become nothing more than a jamboree, where the delegates network and leaders show off their newfound wealth. Those who attend are carefully screened at branch level in advance to weed out potential rebels and dissenters, draft policies are prepared beforehand, candidates for office are presented to delegates by the leadership, and all that remains is for decisions to be rubber-stamped.

After ten years as a governing party, the ANC bore scant resemblance to the liberation movement that had endured three decades of vilification and suppression by the apartheid regime, but if there is a single defining event in the battle for the organisation's soul, it must be the internal struggle over economic policy.

When the ANC came to power in 1994, its basic policy platform was the Reconstruction and Development Programme (RDP). Despite many shortcomings, the RDP drew wide support from both the tripartite alliance and various other mass-based political organisations that were signatories to the document. Started on the initiative of COSATU, the RDP represented a consensus policy, supported by most of the ANC's constituencies, which mapped out a post-apartheid development path.[45] The document encapsulated the spirit in which policy-making in the new democracy was envisaged.

The policy rested on six principles: an integrated and sustainable programme; a people-driven process; peace and security; nation-building; reconstruction and development; and democratisation.[46] The latter was defined as follows:

The RDP requires fundamental changes in the way that policy and programmes are implemented. Above all, the people affected must participate in the decision-making. Democratisation must begin to transform both the state and civil society. Democracy is not confined to periodic elections. It is, rather, an active process enabling everyone to contribute to reconstruction and development.[47]

The RDP aimed at growth through redistribution, building a mixed economy with an active and major developmental state, and using a people-driven approach to policy-making.[48] The inclusiveness of the RDP's evolution also resulted in a wish list that did not prioritise policy goals or clear strategies for implementation.[49]

After little more than a year in power, the ANC leadership was told by Mbeki that he feared the expansionist RDP was not inspiring market confidence. A new, market-friendly policy of growth before redistribution was needed to dispel apprehension that the ANC was in thrall Eastern European-style socialism. Moreover, Mbeki believed the RDP was under control of the left, which, he contended, aggravated the lack of market confidence in the ANC's policies. What was needed, Mbeki told his allies, was a new economic policy framework that was to be entrusted to the centrists. The first priority was that the RDP ministry and its leftist leader had to go. His allies, Netshitenzhe, the Pahad brothers, Zuma and Erwin, agreed.

Mbeki blamed bottlenecks in the RDP office[50] for government's failure to spend more than one third of the RDP fund since 1994, and claimed that the existence of a separate administrative department risked marginalisation of the RDP. What he really wanted, however,[51] was to bring economic planning fully into his own ambit and out of the hands of any influence from the left.

RDP minister Jay Naidoo was duly transferred to posts, telecommunications and broadcasting after Jordan was sacked for criticising Mandela, and the RDP office was placed under the control of Mbeki, then deputy president, the finance ministry and line departments.

In June 1996, the market-friendly Growth, Employment and Redistribution (GEAR) strategy replaced the RDP. Mbeki closely guarded the formulation of GEAR and trusted only his closest allies, such as Netshitenzhe, the Pahads, Manuel, Erwin and Mboweni. Significantly, GEAR dropped the RDP's bedrock strategy of growth through redistribution in favour of growth before redistribution.[52]

GEAR was presented to parliament as non-negotiable,[53] and even the National Economic Development and Labour Council (NEDLAC), established in 1995 to build consensus between government, labour, business and civil society on social and economic issues, was bypassed.[54]

Not surprisingly, many complained about not being consulted, and some still wonder how the decision to dump the RDP was made and how GEAR was adopted. At the time, COSATU general secretary Mbhazima Shilowa fumed: 'The mass-driven character of the RDP is at this stage a total myth. Involvement of the people in the process is spontaneous, and where it happens, it is by accident rather than design.'[55] Since then, Shilowa has changed his tune.

Similarly, the government's 1995 decision to pursue its privatisation strategy was taken by a select few in Mbeki's inner circle of economic managers. Mandela declared that privatisation was 'the fundamental policy of the ANC', and, like GEAR, was not open to negotiation.[56] In December 1995, Mbeki announced plans for the full or partial privatisation of parastatals, including Eskom, Telkom, SAA and SunAir, without consulting either the NEC or the leadership of alliance partners. The subsequent outcry, including a twenty-four-hour strike by COSATU, forced Mandela and Mbeki to agree to negotiations with the unions. These led to conclusion of the National Framework Agreement on 1 February 1996, which set the parameters for privatisation or restructuring.[57]

The agreement, which came into effect on 27 April, committed the government to negotiating details of the sale of public companies with the unions through a strategic implementation committee.

COSATU accepted restructuring on the basis that the state, in each case, remained the majority shareholder and that essential services would not be privatised.[58] However, COSATU and the SACP made no headway in forcing government to put a brake on privatisation.

The way in which Mbeki's biggest foreign policy success, the New Partnership for Africa's Development (NEPAD),[59] was cobbled together elicited great criticism from within the ANC and allied civil society groups. Many felt that the programme, dubbed a Marshall Plan for Africa, was much needed, but were unhappy that it had not been formulated through customary policy-making processes. Few ANC leaders were involved in drawing up the plan and fewer still even knew who they were.

Even the NEC was kept in the dark, due to Mbeki's fear that his blueprint could be watered down.[60] His closest aides told senior ANC leaders that the document had to be perused by a host of African leaders before it could be released. When trade unionists complained that they had been kept in the dark on NEPAD, Mbeki despatched his most trusted policy managers, including Erwin and Netshitenzhe, to present the key points of the plan to COSATU 's top leadership.

The growing unhappiness that policy-making had shifted from ordinary members, the ANC as a party and its alliance partners was acknowledged at the 1997 national conference, when the ANC conceded that it did not have control over this important area. In a document titled *Accelerating Change*, the party says:

Too often, government departments pursue closed agendas that date back to before 1994. Some have policies contrary to the ANC's overall strategy or other departments' aims. The structures of the bureaucracy remain hostile to public participation and pressure. Policy processes often remain secretive and closed to the influence of alliance partners and the broader public, leading to mistaken and unpopular measures in some cases. People's organisations have only limited routes to participate in governance.[61]

Increasingly, policy is formed by directors general of government departments and their senior management, or even worse still, by external and very often private sector consultants from the EU or North America or whatever. So lots of policy is formed in this way.[62]

At the same time, the lack of people-driven policy-making is laid at the door of lack of expertise:

The extent to which the democratic movement had clearly defined policy is [limited in part because] of uneven policy expertise and because of uneven priority.

The formal structures of the ANC are weak when it comes to policy making. In common with many other political parties in government, ANC policy is now predominantly made by ministers and their departments. The role of head office and the party branches in formulating, evaluating, or amending policy is minimal.[63]

Motlanthe readily admits to limited ANC involvement in policy-making, saying the party lacks capacity and resources to come up with policies or to effectively monitor them. COSATU and the SACP are similarly affected.

'The ANC and its cadreship, never mind the broader alliance, are very often distant from key policy formation, partly reflecting our own weaknesses, but also partly reflecting the capacities and energy and the sense in key places that there aren't any alternatives and that the Americans know best or the World Bank knows best,' says Jeremy Cronin.[64]

Mbeki-ites responded with derision to COSATU's call for increased participation by trade unions in policy-making. Manuel warned that 'trade unions will have limited ability to influence macroeconomic policies'.[65] Mbeki called for a new breed of worker that would restrict itself to shop floor matters rather than broader political and macroeconomic affairs. Limpopo premier Ngoako Ramatlhodi argued in a discussion paper that unions should stick to shop floor matters.[66] NUM general secretary Gwede Mantashe angrily responded that trade unions had a right to be involved in the broader policy-making process.

When Cronin conceded that the left lacked the capacity to influence government policy-making, COSATU tried to rectify the situation by putting Neva Makgetla in charge of the trade union federation's fiscal and monetary policy in 2000. However, the ability to quickly produce alternatives to policies presented by Mbeki's consultants was lacking.

For most ANC members, policies might as well fall from the sky. They resent their lack of ownership over government policy, and party leaders increasingly don't even bother to explain the rationale behind decisions, creating an impression of arrogance and disdain for ordinary members.

The masses assume importance only during election campaigns. When their votes are not needed, the leadership is barely interested in party members' views. Internal democracy has given way to control.

As the Mbeki-ites stepped up their bid for command of all the ANC's power levers, they resorted to stealth to take control of the party's noisy parliamentary wing. The ANC in parliament is a virtual case study of how democratic institutions can increasingly be excluded from policy-making. The debate revolves around whether power should lie with parliament or with the executive branch of government. COSATU's parliamentary chief, Neil Coleman, noted in 2000: 'During the early days of the democratic parliament, members played a fairly active oversight role over the executive.'[67]

During the first three years, many ANC members of parliament were prepared to take the leadership to task and block policies they felt had not arisen from democratic debate. The parliamentarians were especially angry that GEAR had been adopted at the cost of redistribution, which the majority favoured.

Attempts to neutralise the parliamentary wing were initially fiercely resisted by most MPs. Mandela was routinely grilled by MPs who were adamant that, as elected representatives, they fully intended holding the executive to account. The ANC's parliamentary caucus went so far as to lobby the 1997 national conference to adopt a resolution giving the parliamentary wing constitutional power, but the bid was blocked by those alert to the danger that any grouping not firmly under the heel of the centrists could derail their economic and social transformation plans.

Immediately after the conference, Mbeki moved to discipline the caucus and make it plain that internal revolt against the ANC leadership would not be tolerated. It worked. The caucus became wary of taking on the executive and the president, while the parliamentary committees bridled their criticism of Mbeki and the executive. COSATU leader Neil Coleman observed:

> Towards the latter half of the first term of governance, some [parliamentary] committees became increasingly reluctant to take independent positions from the executive. The members of parliament are not involved in shaping policies and are invariably confronted with a fait accompli.[68]

This is not in itself exceptional – it becomes a problem when the legislative and policy role of parliament is emasculated by a culture which says that you don't question your minister. The passivity of some MPs is exacerbated by the absence of adequate mechanisms for MPs to feed into political decision-making in the caucus, the constitutional structures of the party, as well as the alliance processes.[69]

Coleman and other COSATU leaders indicated that anxiety about losing patronage and lack of security of tenure were some of the main reasons why ANC MPs feared rocking the boat.

Mbeki adopted what many backbenchers interpreted as a disdainful and contemptuous attitude towards parliament. He has often been accused of by-passing parliament and rarely appears in the assembly to answer questions, relying on the fact that the Constitution allows him to operate from outside the institution.[70] One unfortunate consequence has been that the ANC's parliamentary wing increasingly reverted to the exile style of politics, based on secrecy and loyalty, instead of coming to grips with the new demands of transparency and public accountability, as required by the Constitution.

The problem is compounded by the fact that opposition parties fare no better. Their leaders lash dissenters as much, if not more. A case in point is DA member of parliament Raenette Taljaard's questioning of party leader Tony Leon over policy. Such was the drubbing she received that she quit.

The blocking of legislation by Mbeki and Manuel that would enable parliament to initiate and amend money bills, as required by the Constitution, has become the symbol of the executive's reluctance to cede power to the legislature. Indeed, who decides on the budget priorities has been a major source of bitterness among ANC MPs, who feel they are left out of the process and required only to rubber-stamp the end product.[71]

Ever since it was introduced, GEAR as economic policy has been sacrosanct. Those who criticise it do so at their peril, and MPs generally endorse government policy without fundamental change.[72] For instance, parliament was not involved in the government's proposals to the World Trade Organisation, which resulted in the lifting of trade barriers at a much faster pace than even the WTO demanded, causing rampant hardship when numerous factories in the textile industry, for example, were forced to close under the pressure of cheap products flooding the market.

Calls from within the ANC alliance to make the budget more of a tool for redistribution have been dismissed with contempt. COSATU has been so incensed at the government's failure to consult with it when the annual budget is drawn up that the trade union federation has boycotted budget hearings since 1998.

Parliament was also bypassed with regard to South Africa's controversial multibillion-rand arms acquisition programme. Many ANC leaders, such as Pregs Govender and Joe Slovo, loudly bemoaned the fact that the decision was taken undemocratically, veiled in secrecy until being presented to parliament as a fait accompli. The presidency made the final decision to go ahead with the deal.

What made the arms deal especially sensitive was that it was at variance with the moral convictions of many ANC members. The party came to power pledging drastic cuts to the defence spending that characterised the apartheid era, in favour of social services. And for the first few years in power, this was indeed the policy followed.

But even before the ANC formed a government, senior military commanders, anxious about expected defence cuts, approached ANC securocrats such as now deceased former MK commander Joe Modise, who would be Mandela's defence minister, and MK's former intelligence chief Ronnie Kasrils, with warnings that the South African National Defence Force (SANDF), and especially the navy and air force, urgently needed refurbishing and rearmament.

The old guard dusted off a pre-democracy document, which became the basis of the Defence Review used by the government to justify the arms acquisition programme.

With not an enemy in sight, Kasrils revelled in his role as deputy defence minister under Mandela, arguing: 'International crises can break out at amazing speed, and every time they surprise us. We're living in a world where there's greater competition for scarce resources – and that's a major cause of war. Two weeks ago, Spain and Canada had a flare-up over fish. We've got a billion rand fishing industry providing thousands of jobs and this will grow because our seas are rich.'[73]

Modise, Kasrils, and South African National Defence Force chief Siphiwe Nyanda were accurately described by Gillian Slovo, daughter of Joe, as 'Boys' Own personalities'. The men had previously punted an MK guerrilla army so large and powerful that it would strike fear and awe into the apartheid government, and they lobbied equally hard for a post-apartheid defence force that would do likewise. Ironically, their thinking dovetailed neatly with that of those apartheid generals whose dominance of the security forces extended into the democratic era.

Initially, the head of parliament's defence committee, Tony Yengeni, was bitterly opposed to the arms deal and scored major points among MPs by challenging the proposed defence expenditure at the cost of social spending. But the unseen pressure groups went to work on Yengeni, and when the time came for the ANC's parliamentary caucus to bare its teeth to block the deal, he had been tamed.

Following Yengeni, Govender and other ANC MPs' opposition, Modise and Kasrils had taken the matter straight to the cabinet, where senior ANC leaders, like Manuel and Erwin, rejected it. In a compromise, they persuaded cabinet to ask the defence force for a detailed needs assessment. At the same time they started lobbying Mbeki.

It was not a universally popular decision. Joe Slovo, for example, vigorously opposed the military proposal, pointing out: 'We can certainly ensure that this bird [the arms deal] does not change into an albatross around the neck of the RDP in the next budget. There can be little doubt in my mind that South Africa's greatest defence will be a satisfied population. We need to ensure we can deliver better housing, healthcare and education, because then we can be secure in the knowledge that any aggressor trying anything in South Africa will be unsuccessful.'[74] The SACP, COSATU and civil society groups aligned to the ANC heavily opposed the arms deal.

As debate raged over the spin-offs of the deal, ranging from job creation and establishment of technology-based industry to massive counter-trade benefits, the argument that swayed Mbeki was the importance of an upgraded defence force if South Africa was to play a leading role in the proposed African Renaissance as a continental peacekeeper and resolver of conflict. But he was canny enough to commission an investigation, led by former NEDLAC director Jayendra Naidoo, which would defend the rationale behind the deal.

From a moral standpoint, the deal was always indefensible, and it has been mired in allegations of corruption and irregularities. Having slashed social spending and claimed there were no funds to make anti-AIDS drugs available to patients at state hospitals, having resisted payment of basic income grants to the poorest of the poor on the grounds that such measures would play havoc with its commitment to fiscal rectitude, the government has seen the bill for its sophisticated new weaponry balloon due to currency fluctuations. Even worse, perhaps, is that nothing so clearly illustrates the emasculation of the ANC's parliamentary wing as the controversial and exorbitantly expensive arms deal.

Following its failure to be included in the budget-making process and having been sidelined on the arms deal, a frustrated COSATU contemplated recalling unionists deployed as ANC members of parliament but who did nothing to defend the principles of the trade unions. 'Many COSATU leaders hold senior positions in government, parliament, the public service and in the ANC, yet this has little impact on government programmes,'[75] observed a despondent COSATU central executive committee. 'The tensions between the ANC alliance and government point to the need to assess COSATU's deployment strategy.'[76]

Astonishingly, despite having been ridden roughshod by the executive, there was still some fight left within the belly of the ANC's parliamentary caucus. After the 1999 elections, a new crop of younger ANC MPs reignited the debate to secure more power for the parliamentary wing. In the middle of 2000 and in the spirit of this new robustness, Jordan – fresh from being unceremoniously relegated to the backbenches after criticising Mbeki and his acolytes – tabled a resolution slamming Zimbabwean strongman Robert Mugabe's disregard for the rule of law. Read on behalf of the ANC's parliamentary caucus, the resolution pointed out that harassment of ordinary citizens by Mugabe's regime was so horrendous that any elections in the neighbouring state would be a sham.

The statement mirrored all the frustration of ANC MPs over Mbeki's policy of 'quiet diplomacy' in dealing with the Mugabe regime. While Jordan was tabling his resolution in the National Assembly, Mbeki was telling an audience on the other side of the Atlantic the exact opposite. While on a visit to America, he said that the situation in Zimbabwe was nowhere near so bad that free and fair elections could not take place. The contradiction angered ANC headquarters, and chief whip Tony Yengeni was forced by the leadership to issue a rather ridiculous and embarrassing statement saying Jordan's resolution should not be seen as contrary to Mbeki's view. This, in turn, angered the ANC's MPs, but they were powerless to do anything more.

The next incident that rattled the ANC leadership was ANC MP Andrew Feinstein's attack on the party's handling of the probe into allegations of corruption in the arms deal. Mbeki had apparently reached the end of his tether over the sustained 'rebellion' by MPs, and at a special meeting of the ANC's parliamentary caucus, he slammed their criticism of the government's policies.[77] He accused the 'rebels' of being in cahoots with a conspiracy by Western governments, intelligence agencies and pharmaceutical companies to undermine his campaign for an equitable global financial architecture and trading system.

The situation was volatile. Public and private criticism by MPs of the ANC government's arms deal and the HIV/AIDS policy coincided with various incidents of provincial and local ANC leaders voting against official party positions, and had the Mbeki-ites gnashing their teeth. Discipline had to be restored as quickly as possible.[78] The culprits needed to be shown, if they had forgotten, that Mbeki was still firmly in charge. By mid-2001, Mbeki and the ANC leadership were ready to crack the whip.

A special caucus meeting was called for June in Cape Town, to be attended by all the ANC's parliamentary representatives. No agenda or reason was given, just a stern warning that attendance was mandatory. Mbeki, Zuma, ANC national chairman Mosiuoa Lekota, Motlanthe, Essop Pahad and Netshitenzhe were all in attendance, and before the meeting began, Ngonyama – one of Mbeki's most loyal lieutenants – warned MPs that they, 'like all other members, had to respect the party's oath of allegiance'.[79]

A stony-faced Mbeki made it clear that the parliamentary wing's call for greater constitutional power would come to nought as long as he was president. Zuma told the MPs it was folly to go against the party line.

A few weeks earlier, parliamentary caucus leader Thabang Makwetla,[80] a vocal proponent of greater powers for the caucus, had been redeployed as a lowly member of the executive council in the Mpumalanga provincial legislature. His successor was Nathi Nhleko, who had strict instructions to maintain a tough line on ill discipline.

The ANC leadership also appointed a political committee to oversee the party's work in parliament. Few MPs doubted that the sole purpose of the committee, chaired by Zuma, was to beat discipline into wayward parliamentarians and reassert the leadership's control.

Ngonyama vehemently denied that MPs were being muzzled, saying: 'The committee will help to enrich the relationship between parliament and the executive. They can inform each other, it creates a very smooth relationship ...'[81] But it was clear for all to see that ANC MPs were being turned into rubber stamps and deprived of their constitutional role as watchdogs, no matter how grave the implications for South Africa's infant democracy.

South Africa's electoral process discourages dissent in party ranks, as members of parliament are appointed from party lists rather than being elected on an individual basis. This strengthens Mbeki's hand in maintaining party discipline, as he can strike names off the list at will or redeploy fractious MPs. In an internal discussion paper entitled *Good Governance Needs An Effective Parliament*,[82] and released ahead of the ANC's 2000 national conference, Firoz Cachalia, speaker of the Gauteng legislature, expressed the anxieties of some MPs in averring that parliament's hand needed to be strengthened as a matter of some urgency.

But it was already too late. With the exception of Mbeki's cheerleaders, MPs have been marginalised or cowed by the executive, and democracy is the victim.

Mbeki increasingly hand-picks like-minded colleagues for senior positions in the ANC, government and parastatals to ensure that centrally made policies are applied to the letter. Those who resist are simply sidelined. The primary reason for Mbeki keeping a firm hand on the tiller of both the ANC and government is to smother internal resistance. He has surrounded himself with partisan cabinet ministers, though his 2004 appointments offered some surprising and refreshing choices. He continues to protect health minister Manto Tshabalala-Msimang, but at Motlanthe's suggestion, he rehabilitated 'old enemies' Pallo Jordan and Derek Hanekom, who served as Mandela's minister of land and agriculture.

Through his Premiers' Council, Mbeki's vigilance extends to provincial dissidence, and thanks to the redeployment committee set up in 1999 and headed by the ever-faithful Zuma, only those prepared to defer to the president and accept government's policy stances get plum postings.

Leaders critical of central government policies or Mbeki's 'new deal' have been systematically neutralised, and since the ANC does not have a policy of competitive election of leaders, internal democracy has effectively been snuffed out.

In 1991, at the ANC's first national conference since its unbanning, Walter Sisulu had been nominated as national chairman. His election was a foregone conclusion until, at the last moment, KwaZulu-Natal leader Harry Gwala announced that he was available for the post. Delegates were stunned and the entire process was thrown into disarray.

Asked later why he had taken the unprecedented step of standing against Sisulu, knowing that consensus had already been reached on the national chairmanship, Gwala replied, 'This is the ANC's first legal conference inside South Africa after thirty years as a clandestine operation. I stood to reassert the principle that there should be competitive elections for leadership positions.'[83]

Gwala's position would not find favour with an ANC under Mbeki. The controversy that surrounded his own elevation to heir apparent under Mandela was one of the first, and most visible, central interventions in leadership elections. Even though Mandela admitted afterwards that he had favoured Cyril Ramaphosa, he bowed to the consensus of the senior leaders and specifically instructed potential rivals for the job not to challenge Mbeki, in the interest of party unity.

Mbeki has been particularly aggressive in marginalising provincial leaders whom he perceives as rivals or having the potential to build a mass following that could be used to take on the centrists. In 1996, the ANC's national leadership intervened in the power struggle between Free State premier Mosiuoa Lekota and provincial party chairman Ace Magashule. Lekota had used his constitutional powers and prerogative to hire and fire MECs unilaterally to sack Magashule and two other high-ranking provincial party officials following allegations of corruption. A bitter struggle was unleashed between the premier and the party provincial chairman. Mbeki saw Lekota as a threat, and the national leadership promptly redeployed him to the National Council of Provinces, sending Magashule and Pat Matosa to the National Assembly as MPs.

The national leadership appointed a more pliant Winkie Direko, without even consulting her constituents. One local branch member launched a last-ditch court challenge to have the appointment declared unconstitutional, and lost. An independent inquiry and investigation by the Auditor-General later vindicated Lekota, but this did not stop Zuma from warning him, and other ANC leaders, against regarding the country's Constitution as more important than the ANC. 'Once you begin to feel you are above the ANC you are in trouble,' Zuma pointedly reminded them.[84]

In the same year, Western Cape MEC Ebrahim Rasool received a fax from Manuel, warning him that it would be considered 'uncomradely' if he stood against then justice minister Dullah Omar for the party's provincial leadership.[85] Rasool withdrew, and his meek acceptance of the party line was well rewarded when Mbeki made him premier of the Western Cape in 2004.

In 1996, SACP stalwart and former Rivonia trialist Raymond Mhlaba was pushed out by the national leadership as premier of the Eastern Cape and replaced by Makhenkesi Arnold Stofile. Mhlaba counted both Mandela and Mbeki's father, Govan, among his close friends, and they had been imprisoned together on Robben Island for many years. Like the elder Mbeki, Mhlaba was an uncompromising leftist.

But a report secretly commissioned by Mandela and his deputy president into the affairs of the Eastern Cape provincial government recommended a complete overhaul of the political leadership in the traditional ANC stronghold, including the axing of Mhlaba. Some of his supporters, such as former Transkei strongman Bantu Holomisa, protested against Mhlaba's removal before his five-year tenure was up, pointing out that he had made great strides in uniting the various factions in the province. This was unquestionably true, but Mhlaba, the hard-core communist, had become a liability at the time when the government was throwing its weight behind GEAR.

Ironically, Stofile, in turn, found himself out in the cold in 2004, Mbeki having perceived that he was giving the left too much of a free hand in the province.

Also in 1996, Ramatlhodi, a staunch Mbeki ally, was ousted by SACP stalwart and Stalinist George Mashamba as provincial chairman of the ANC in the then Northern Province. However, the national leadership intervened and blocked Mashamba from becoming premier. Three years later, Ramatlhodi faced a new challenge from former provincial MECs Collins Chabane and Joe Phaahla. Predictably, the national leadership intervened again, and Phaahla was redeployed to the South African Sports Commission.

When Gauteng premier Tokyo Sexwale quit in 1997, Mathole Motshekga and Frank Chikane emerged as rivals for the top post in the country's richest province. Eyebrows were raised when the ANC's national leadership openly declared its preference for former UDF stalwart and Mbeki ally Chikane. As insurance, a commission of inquiry was set up to probe allegations that the popular Motshekga had abused donor funds while he was head of a legal non-governmental organisation in the late 1980s, and of mismanagement during his term of office in the Gauteng provincial legislature. The National Intelligence Agency was also instructed to investigate rumoured links between Motshekga and controversial figures such as University of South Africa professor Andre Thomashausen, a former counsellor to the apartheid-backed Mozambican rebel army, Renamo.

Motshekga was cleared on all charges and, in defiance of the national guidelines, duly elected by his large grassroots support base.[86] His only public comment on the controversy surrounding his bid was: 'My experience is that the ANC branch leadership is the body that decides on the question of leadership. They are so mature and developed that they know who will be the right person at the right time.'[87]

Mbeki had lost the round, but Motshekga's victory was short-lived. In 1999, Mbeki invoked a new rule giving the president the power to appoint provincial premiers in consultation with the NEC, and did not extend Motshekga's appointment. Former COSATU general secretary Mbhazima Shilowa was given the plum position instead.

Similarly, Mbeki clipped the wings of Mpumalanga premier Mathews Phosa in 1997, when the provincial branch and Youth League nominated him as deputy president of the ANC. The leadership had already warned possible contenders that the position was being reserved for Jacob Zuma, and Phosa was instructed to decline the nomination.

He defiantly refused, stating: 'Let me put the record straight. Nobody has yet asked me not to stand. In any case, individual members and groups within the ANC have a right to lobby support for a particular person. However, they cannot decide who should be kings, or stage-manage the election process. They have particular preferences, but they have no right to manipulate who gets what position. What is the purpose of democracy if the leadership appoints and anoints its own candidates?'[88]

But under extreme pressure, Phosa eventually turned down the nomination and was sacked as premier to boot. His successor was former Bantustan leader Ndaweni Mahlangu, who scandalised the ANC by asking publicly: 'What's wrong with politicians lying to the public? Even [former US president Bill] Clinton does it.'

ANC Women's League president Winnie Madikizela-Mandela similarly outraged the national leadership when she insisted on contesting the deputy presidency in the same year. Mbeki and the leaders tried everything to thwart her, but it was not until moments before the vote was called that she finally wilted in the face of a well-orchestrated campaign to keep her out of office.

At the Mafikeng conference, the national leadership tried to prevent Lekota from becoming the ANC's chairman. Mbeki loyalist Steve Tshwete had been punted for the job, but Lekota went against the party line and stood for election, securing a clear victory, much to the chagrin of the national leadership.[89] He has been a marked man ever since.

The election of ANC office-bearers at the 1997 conference was marked throughout by manipulation on the part of the national leadership to ensure that the 'right' people became the party stewards. For example, only two ballots were held for NEC positions, and lobbying behind the scenes ensured that only approved candidates stood for the other positions. Lekota's victory was one of a handful of setbacks.

Early in 1999 the NEC separated the positions of premiers and provincial chairmen, and endorsed a proposal that in future the president, in consultation with the NEC, would appoint all provincial premiers. The leadership argued that this would prevent ambitious contenders from embarking on brutal contests for the provincial chairmanships in order to automatically become premiers.[90]

Mbeki also proposed a super leadership structure that could act as an early warning system against party rebels and select the most suitable candidates for jobs in government, parastatals and the party. His loyal lieutenant, Zuma, was put in charge of the new apparatus. The deployment committee screened all but the upper quadrant of election lists to ensure that candidates offered the desired mix of experience and new blood, ethnic, gender and regional considerations. In practice, it was a centralised mechanism that gave the party hierarchy extraordinary influence over the appointment of ANC members to government and party jobs at all levels, with the exception of the cabinet.

Appointments extended to the chairmen of executive and local councils. The national deployment committee appointed the six executive 'super-mayors' of South Africa's biggest metropoles ahead of the 1999 elections, including the dour Amos Masondo, despite his lack of popularity among Johannesburg's grassroots ANC membership.

A secret internal investigation in 2000 showed that many ANC members viewed the national deployment committee with deep suspicion, and concluded that 'The composition and work of the deployment committee is viewed with suspicion and as jobs for pals [by many ANC members in the provinces].'[91]

Not surprisingly, there was huge controversy when the committee compiled the ANC list for the December 2000 local government elections and excluded candidates nominated by local branches, as well as serving councillors known to have voted against party policies.

Local leaders were in uproar, and Zuma was obliged to revise the list several times. Some ANC members who did not make it to the final list stood as independents.

South African National Civic Organisation leaders were particularly aggrieved. Several branches complained to the ANC national leadership that they had been struck off the list or moved to the bottom, thus reducing their chances of serving, because they had been too critical of government's economic and social policies. Said an outraged Mzwandile Buzani, a SANCO leader at Mdantsane in the Eastern Cape: 'We totally reject the ANC election manual clause which empowers the [deployment] committee to eliminate the community-chosen candidate if it sees fit to do so. It's totally undemocratic.'[92]

Angry COSATU delegates adopted a resolution at their 2000 conference that read: 'Deployment must be a collective decision, and not left to individuals. The tripartite alliance must develop procedures that limit patronage by curbing the power of the individual leaders to decide on employment and promotion.'[93]

As the storm of outrage grew against the manipulation of elections, jobs for pals and deep suspicion that the committee was being used to sideline those seen as independent-minded, the committee was suspended and then disbanded at the ANC's 2002 national conference in Stellenbosch.

Rebellion against the national leadership's appointment of provincial premiers was also mounting. In 2002, Mahlangu lost the battle for chairmanship of the ANC in Mpumalanga to a rank outsider, Fish Mahlalela, despite Mbeki having sent Tshwete, one of his most trusted troubleshooters, to the province to shore up support for Mahlangu.

Soon afterwards, the national leadership's choice as Free State provincial chair, premier Winkie Direko, was defeated by another outsider, Ace Magashule, even though Luthuli House had despatched a high-powered support team led by public enterprises minister Jeff Radebe to bolster their candidate.

ANC MP Thandi Modise, perceived at branch level as being a lackey of Mbeki and the national leadership, suffered the indignity of being booed when she stood for the provincial leadership of North West against the incumbent premier, Popo Molefe. On that occasion, Mbeki got the message, and in 2004 he appointed former trade unionist Edna Molewa as premier. Although, or possibly because, she was an outsider, she was grudgingly accepted as not being an obvious front for Mbeki.

The ANC's alliance partners did not escape manipulation either. In 1998, the general secretary of the National Union of Metalworkers of South Africa, Enoch Godongwana, was redeployed as an Eastern Cape MEC after being nominated by disgruntled trade unionists to challenge Shilowa at the trade union federation's national conference.

Godongwana had huge support within COSATU, whereas Shilowa's purported closeness to Mbeki aroused resentment and suspicion that his opposition to government's conservative economic policies was little more than lip service.[94] Godongwana, a fiery critic of GEAR, had been expected to spearhead far tougher and more militant opposition.[95]

Despite the earlier opposition to centrally appointed provincial premiers, Mbeki did not deviate from the practice following the 2004 elections. In the Eastern Cape, ANC leaders lodged strong objections to Mbeki's choice as premier, the flamboyant Nosimo Balindlela, who had taken to dressing in school uniform while the province's education minister. Stofile had fired her from that post for poor performance and dismal matric results, and her more senior appointment was not well received.

'Why reward non-performance?' one prominent activist asked.[96]

The revolt was not long in coming. Local ANC leaders publicly slammed Balindlela for not consulting them on her cabinet appointments. She dismissed their criticism on the grounds that ANC headquarters had already briefed her on whom to appoint.

It was the same in the Free State, where Mbeki's choice of Beatrice Marshoff as premier over the heads of the most popular provincial leaders sparked outrage. Ahead of the 2004 elections, local leaders had threatened to boycott the process if Mbeki appointed an outsider as premier without first consulting them. He gave the job to a political novice anyway. When Marshoff, a former nurse, announced her cabinet, as approved by Mbeki, the inauguration had to be postponed, because some of those selected had never considered themselves in the running and were not immediately available.

Clearly, Mbeki's plans for his last term as president included control not only of the provincial premiers, but also of their cabinets. In Mpumalanga, the quiet but capable Thabang Makwetla would face an uphill battle against local party boss Fish Mahlalela, who had been sidelined by Mbeki. In the Northern Cape, Mbeki appointed former social worker Dipuo Peters in the face of overwhelming support for John Block, who was facing corruption allegations at the time but has since been rehabilitated.

In KwaZulu-Natal, one of Mbeki's staunchest supporters, Sibusiso (S'bu) Ndebele, was propelled into the premier's seat despite the fact that many ANC leaders would have preferred someone less closely involved in the acrimonious power battle against the IFP.

The Mbeki-ites also moved to consolidate control of the Women's and Youth Leagues. The president backed yuppie politician Malusi Gigaba as head of the ANCYL, when he was challenged by hard-working trade unionist David Makhura. Under Gigaba, the organisation was beset by internal strife, moved financially into the red and was, for the most part, wholly ineffective.

In the 1940s and 1950s, the Youth League, led by men of Mandela's stature, spearheaded the radicalisation of the ANC. Those days are long gone, and the ANCYL has become the playground of yuppie politicians who drive smart cars and live the high life, using the league as nothing more than an entry point to big business and national politics. As happened with the youth league of India's Congress Party under the wayward leadership of Indira Gandhi, the ANCYL has become a doorway to central government. Under Gigaba, the league was at Mbeki's bidding when it came to unsavoury tasks such as public attacks on critics and smear campaigns against dissenters. For his reward, Gigaba was appointed deputy minister of home affairs.

The new ANCYL leader, Fikile Mbalula, took up where Gigaba left off. Despite threats by the Young Communist League to nominate candidates for the top five ANCYL jobs, Mbalula was elected unopposed after the ANC leadership warned opponents not to stand against him. Shortly afterwards, he showed why he had been the favourite when he launched a scathing personal attack on COSATU general secretary Zwelinzima Vavi over public criticism of Mbeki's quiet diplomacy on Zimbabwe.

The once powerful Women's League has been removed from the control of the strident Madikizela-Mandela and her vociferous complaints about the government's failure to deliver.

Through all these machinations, Mbeki and the ANC leadership have gained unprecedented control of both the party and the government, concentrating enormous powers of patronage in the hands of the party bosses. The changes have been wrought in the name of more efficient governance and delivery, but they have worrying implications for internal debate and democracy.

The climate of fear instilled by the party bosses, and the self-censorship it breeds, spills into broader society, because the ANC is such a dominant party. Thus is the quality of the democracy undermined.

# — 7 —

# Mbeki's AIDS Denial – Grace or Folly?

For too long we have closed our eyes as a nation, hoping the truth was not so real. For many years, we have allowed the HI virus to spread, and at a rate in our country which is one of the fastest in the world.    — **Thabo Mbeki, 9 October 1998**

Now ... the poor on our continent, will again carry a disproportionate burden of this scourge – would if anyone cared to ask their opinions, wish that the dispute about the primacy of politics or science be put on the backburner and that we proceed to address the needs and concerns of those suffering and dying.
                                          — **Nelson Mandela, 13 July 2000**

It is important that we recognise that we are facing a major crisis and that we want to invest as many resources as we did when we fought against apartheid. This is not a state of emergency but it is a national emergency.
                                   — **Archbishop Desmond Tutu, 30 November 2001**

A S HIS INTERNATIONAL AIDS ADVISORY COUNCIL MET FOR THE FIRST TIME, Thabo Mbeki mulled over the words of Irish poet Patrick Henry Pearse: 'Is it folly or grace?'

Notwithstanding the conclusions of mainstream scientists almost a decade before, Mbeki set up the council to examine both the cause and most effective way of treating acquired immune deficiency syndrome (AIDS) in developing countries.

His 'folly' in reopening the debate on what causes AIDS rather than focusing on practical ways to curb the pandemic sweeping Africa was roundly condemned. 'Stop fiddling while Rome burns,'[1] chided Desmond Tutu, former Archbishop of Cape Town. But AIDS denial is not the exclusive province of presidents. Mbeki's controversial health minister, Manto Tshabalala-Msimang, enthusiastically prescribed an alternative therapy that sounded more like a salad dressing than treatment for a sexually transmitted disease that kills around 600 South Africans a day.[2]

After years of foot-dragging and obfuscation, the South African government finally rolled out anti-retroviral drugs that could save the lives of millions at state hospitals two weeks before voters went to the polls in April 2004. The long-awaited plan to distribute ARVs to an estimated 5 million people had been approved in November 2003, but due to what officials claimed were 'capacity constraints', patients had to wait another five months for the first drugs to reach them.

Few were surprised when AIDS activists questioned the government's timing and motives. 'Even though we welcome the roll-out plan, we have mixed feelings about whether the government reached a turning point because of elections,' said Tembeka Majali of the Treatment Action Campaign (TAC), the country's most vocal and visible AIDS activist group.

Before the limited public roll-out, fewer than 20 000 South Africans were taking ARVs, as only those with expensive private medical insurance could afford them. Zackie Achmat, head of the TAC and the country's best-known AIDS activist, only started taking ARVs towards the end of 2003 after refusing for years to avail himself of the life-giving drugs until the government agreed to offer treatment through the public health system.

Achmat's friend Simon Nkoli died in 1998 after contracting AIDS-related thrush. He was among the millions who could not afford the drugs, and at his funeral Achmat announced that he was launching a campaign to make ARVs available to poor South Africans. He had learnt that the generic version of fluconazole, used to treat thrush but not sold in South Africa because of international patent laws, cost just 80 cents a day.

Government blamed lack of efficacy, potential toxicity and costs for ARVs not being made available at state expense, but scientific evidence indicates that the drugs are highly effective against mother-to-child transmission of HIV and, at least in the short term, the benefits appear to outweigh the risks.

In Europe, North America and Brazil, ARVs have reduced mortality due to HIV/AIDS by between 50 and 80 per cent. In South Africa, two critical barriers remain to the widespread availability of these life-saving medicines and a possible nett saving on the health budget in the long run: lack of political will, and resistance on the part of patent holders to generic competition.

Pharmaceutical companies are protected by intellectual property rights policed by the World Trade Organisation from the manufacture or import of cheaper versions of their drugs. The corporate view is that high prices are necessary to recoup research and development costs.

However, generic anti-AIDS drugs are sold in India for a quarter of the price charged by the big pharmaceutical companies, and have the added advantage of combining three drugs in a single pill that has to be taken twice a day. The Western ARV protocol requires patients to take up to twelve pills – all produced by different companies – a day, at different times, some with water, some without. Despite the obvious advantages of a simplified regimen, South Africa succumbed to pressure from the West and opted for the more expensive and complex therapy in its limited ARV roll-out.[3]

Private healthcare in South Africa makes up around 70 per cent of the total national budget, yet only about 7 million of the country's 44 million citizens can afford private health insurance. The rest depend on government services. Until 1999, medical aid funds were allowed to cherry-pick their paying members and typically accepted young, healthy, low-risk candidates.

The poor and unemployed were generally excluded due to the high premiums and relied on the state for healthcare. An Act of Parliament put a stop to the rejection of certain candidates by insurance carriers, but most South Africans still cannot afford the astronomical costs of private care.

Drug costs are a significant factor in the national health budget. Only medication that is included on a list of essential drugs is available within the state system, and generics are encouraged where possible. When no generics exist, the health department buys in bulk from the pharmaceutical industry via a tender system. Drug companies have fiercely resisted parallel imports of cheaper generics, insisting that their patents be respected.

The social, economic and health consequences of AIDS for South Africa are devastating. Particularly harrowing has been the rise in the number of orphans and the emotional impact on millions of children who will grow up without parents. Not only are crime and social instability destined to follow in the wake of the pandemic, but current and future demands on the state coffers are astronomical.

In alliance with COSATU, the SACP, churches and social organisations, the TAC has been at the forefront of attempts to shift government's head-in-the-sand AIDS policies. The cabinet plan released in November 2003 promised that government would establish a network of centres for distribution of ARVs, beef up efforts to prevent transmission of the virus and increase support for families affected by HIV/AIDS.

The cost of offering treatment to all South Africans with AIDS by 2010 was estimated at between $2.4 billion and $3 billion a year. The cabinet cited the lower costs of ARVs as a major factor in the decision to go ahead with the roll-out, noting: 'New developments pertaining to prices of drugs, the growing body of knowledge on this issue, wide appreciation of the role of nutrition and availability of budgetary resources [had] allowed government to make an enhanced response to AIDS.'[4]

But why had it taken so long to reach this point?

In the heady days following the ANC's unbanning, little attention was given to AIDS. Although alarm bells were ringing, South Africa's collective political focus was on the delicate and engrossing negotiations for a democratic dispensation. The apartheid regime had been deaf to calls for action, seeing AIDS largely as a disease that affected gays and blacks, constituencies the previous government was not particularly interested in, and was most prevalent among migrant workers from the southern African region.

AIDS was not high on the first democratic government's 'to-do' list either. The ANC alliance's priority was trying to hold the fractured country together while getting to grips with governance, delivery and the economy. AIDS was one among many seemingly less urgent problems.

Given South Africa's combustible social mix – a large migrant population, people displaced because of apartheid, the breakdown of traditional family bonds, a labour system that keeps men away from home for most of the year – it is hardly surprising that AIDS struck with such devastation. But when the full realisation sank in, there was first denial, then perplexity, and finally escapism, as confronting the situation became mired in foolish debate over what caused the pandemic in the first place.

During his term of office, Nelson Mandela effectively ignored AIDS, avoiding the subject on the grounds that, in his culture, an elder did not publicly discuss sexual issues. Since then, he has recognised the severity of the problem and become deeply involved in efforts to stop the spread of AIDS.

While Mandela was president, SACP general secretary Chris Hani and health minister Nkosazana Dlamini-Zuma were the ANC's most vocal harbingers of a looming crisis.[5] As deputy president, Mbeki barely mentioned AIDS, except for allusions in a couple of speeches to the disease being as great a threat as poverty in the new South Africa.

In fact, the AIDS time bomb threatened to decimate the world's youngest democracy unless vast resources were made available to defuse it, but the initial response of the ruling elite was 'this isn't happening to us … it cannot be as bad as people say'.[6]

But it was.

The ANC in exile had held a number of meetings on HIV/AIDS, and the first paper on the disease published in South Africa in 1985 forecast that it would remain largely confined to male homosexuals, as had been the case in America and Europe up to that time. In the same year, the government appointed an AIDS advisory group, followed six years later by a network of training, information and counselling centres.

In 1992, the ANC's health secretariat, the government, non-governmental organisations, AIDS service organisations, representatives from business, trade unions and churches, and a diverse group of concerned individuals set up the National AIDS Coordinating Committee of South Africa (NACOSA). In the spirit of the CODESA talks, it was instructed to reach consensus on a national AIDS strategy for the new South Africa.

Their plan, adopted in July 1994, recommended the pooling of large amounts of money from government and donor organisations for expenditure on countrywide education and prevention programmes.

First, however, an AIDS infrastructure had to be established. The centrepiece was a special directorate in the department of health, and the government also appointed a ministerial AIDS task team, headed by Mbeki. Awareness campaigns and support for an HIV vaccine initiative followed.

By early 1996, it became apparent that the plan was full of holes. Much of the intended funding was diverted by the Treasury to more pressing needs, while money that was allocated to the health department remained unspent as the AIDS plan was buried by competing priorities in a health system in transition. Many of the AIDS policy targets were never attained.

Public controversy followed revelations that a hefty chunk of the AIDS budget – R14.27 million – had been spent on *Sarafina II*. The musical production by acclaimed playwright Mbongeni Ngema was designed to raise AIDS awareness among African youth, but the critics panned it as an ineffective and costly failure in terms of relaying the anti-AIDS message. Worse, it emerged that normal tendering procedures had been bypassed in awarding Ngema the funds, and the production was scrapped in midstream.

The resulting scandal strained the bond between government and AIDS activists. Opposition parties, the media and many NGOs unleashed a barrage of attacks on the health minister, who withdrew into a defensive shell. Government and Ngema claimed the criticisms were anti-government, anti-black and racially inspired, and on the eve of World AIDS Day in 1996, activists and health workers denounced the entire National AIDS Plan as a shambles, greatly angering both Dlamini-Zuma and Mbeki.

The furore erupted just as the gloss of freedom was starting to give way to grassroots anger over non-delivery and thwarted expectations. Acutely sensitive to criticism, especially when it emanated from the ANC camp, political home to most of the AIDS activists, the government lashed out in anger. At the party's national conference that year, President Mandela railed against NGOs that stood in judgement of government.

The dust had hardly settled when a new AIDS scandal broke out. In the spring of 1996, a group of academics from Pretoria University, representing a biomedical company called Cryopreservation Technologies, claimed they had found an AIDS cure. Some months before, South Africa's Medicines Control Council (MCC), which regulates the legal drug market, had refused to issue the group with a licence to manufacture their product, Virodene, and slammed it as ineffective and dangerous.

The researchers turned to Dlamini-Zuma and Mbeki for support, pointing out that not only was Virodene a fraction cheaper than alternatives available on the international market, but it was also a homegrown product.

Mbeki was a staunch advocate of Africa finding solutions to its problems and hated what he saw as the West's meddling in the affairs of the continent. In common with other black leaders of his generation, Mbeki detests the stereotype of Africa holding out the begging bowl, and the notion that South Africa had beaten the international scientific community to the draw in finding an AIDS cure was irresistible. He had just started to mull over an ambitious plan to lift the continent out of stagnation and decline, and Virodene would be the perfect platform from which to launch his vision of an African Renaissance, led by South Africa.

At his invitation, the Virodene team addressed a special cabinet meeting in early 1997. An excited Mbeki had primed his colleagues well, and as the researchers and a small group of their 'patients' movingly related tales of miracle cures, the cabinet ministers were overwhelmed by 'awe and pride', according to secretary Jakes Gerwel. Basking in the glow of South Africa's singular achievement, the ministers readily accepted the researchers' complaint that the MCC had rejected Virodene because it was in cahoots with international pharmaceutical companies, which stood to lose billions when the wonder drug hit the market.

Mbeki became the chief patron of Virodene, and, at his urging, Dlamini-Zuma tried to fast-track production, riding roughshod over loud objections from the MCC. She publicly accused the MCC of being in league with the big drug companies, and soon afterwards the obdurate MCC chief, Professor Peter Folb, was removed from his position.

Then the bubble burst. An independent review panel led by the South African Medical Research Council found that Virodene had been tested on humans without first going through the usual rigorous and lengthy process of demonstrating its efficacy and safety on animals and in the laboratory. Far from being effective, the panel found, Virodene was in fact highly toxic. The main ingredient, dimethylformamide, was an industrial solvent known to cause severe liver damage.

The media and opposition political parties pounced. The *Sunday Times* derisively claimed that the cabinet's 'combined technical knowledge of the HIV virus would fit on the back of a postcard'.[7] Democratic Alliance leader Tony Leon accused Mbeki of being obsessed with 'finding African solutions to every problem',[8] even if this meant resorting to 'snake-oil cures and quackery'. It stung, and Mbeki would never get over his deep personal distaste for Leon that the attack provoked.

Desperate to prove that South Africa was the exception in a world that routinely condemned black governments to failure, Mbeki and his allies dismissed the criticism as racist and refused to admit they had erred. Mbeki warned that the ANC would not be cowed by 'racists hankering for an apartheid past' or those who 'wanted to see a black government fail to prove their own beliefs that blacks cannot govern efficiently'.[9] Dlamini-Zuma spewed vitriol on the DA, saying 'if they had their way, we would all die of AIDS'.[10]

It is a sad reflection on the government's handling of the killer disease that, however dubious these early forays into the field were, they were at least based on acceptance of HIV as the cause of AIDS.

But from this point on, the AIDS issue became racially charged in South Africa, and it has remained so ever since. All future responses to the crisis would be coloured by race, as had already happened in some parts of greater Africa and even among some Afro-American groups who gave credence to the urban legend that the deadly virus had been brewed in a laboratory as part of a covert Western intelligence plot to decimate blacks – the CIA's 'final solution'.

Bizarre as they were, such rumours were fuelled by revelations from the mid-1990s that the apartheid defence force had run a top-secret germ warfare programme, which included experiments on ethnic-specific killer bugs. The Truth and Reconciliation Commission heard senior former security policemen confess that HIV-positive agents had been instructed to have unprotected sex with black prostitutes as part of a diabolical state-sponsored plan to spread the infection.

In 1995, the South African government launched a battle against international tobacco companies by instituting stringent anti-smoking laws, and with the pharmaceutical giants over the high price of essential medicines.

The ANC had worked hard to make medication more accessible and more affordable to the majority black population. This led to repeated skirmishes with drug manufacturers, and a protracted trade dispute with America and various countries in the European Union. At the heart of the matter was an amendment to the Medicines and Related Substances Control Act, which gave government the power to fast-track compulsory licensing and parallel imports of medicines.

The government argued, correctly, that this was consistent with the World Trade Organisation's Trade Related Intellectual Property Rights Agreement (TRIPS), which stipulates certain exceptions to normally strict commercial regulations. In times of health emergencies, for example, poor countries are allowed to circumvent patent laws in order to produce cheaper generic versions of desperately needed drugs. Compulsory licensing allows a country to manufacture a drug in such circumstances without the permission of the patent holder, provided that 'adequate remuneration' is paid to the company. Parallel importing permits a country to buy a drug from the lowest bidder without the consent of the patent holder. But there is huge resistance from developed countries and pharmaceutical companies to these concessions, and South Africa was placed on an American 'watch list' of potential offending countries. The drug manufacturers exerted enormous pressure, both directly and indirectly, on the South African government, outraging Mbeki, Dlamini-Zuma and the ANC leadership.[11]

The pharmaceutical industry in the US lobbied the Clinton administration, which threatened sanctions if South Africa went ahead with plans to push through legislation to facilitate the import of cheaper generics. American vice-president Al Gore found support in the South African media and with opposition parties for his demand that the amendment be repealed.

It was particularly galling for Mbeki, his policy guru Joel Netshitenzhe, his 'enforcer' Essop Pahad and his trusted ally Nkosazana Dlamini-Zuma to have their political opponents and the predominantly white-owned media support foreign opinion against what they saw as South Africa's interests.[12]

The tussle ended when thirty-nine companies joined forces under the banner of the Pharmaceutical Manufacturers' Association of South Africa and took the government to court. They poured millions into their campaign, which was vigorously opposed by the government and, importantly, the TAC and several trade unions.

Dlamini-Zuma told the TAC: 'If you want to fight for affordable treatment, then I will be with you all the way.'[13] In a joint statement, the government and the TAC called on business, labour and civil society to increase pressure on GlaxoSmithKline, one of the world's largest pharmaceutical companies, to lower the price of the primary anti-AIDS drug, AZT. Mbeki accused the pharmaceutical companies of profiteering, pointing out that 'as long as [AZT] is only available at exorbitant prices, it is impossible for the government to make it available to ordinary people'.[14]

In the face of local and international protests organised by the TAC, the pharmaceutical companies reached an out of court compromise with the government and withdrew their legal action. By that time, the amendment to the Medicines Act, which applied to all drugs, not just ARVs, had become law.

Finally, government seemed to have awakened to the gravity of the AIDS crisis. Billboards had been erected, condom distribution increased and the ABC (Abstain, Beware, Condomise) campaign was in place. Yet, despite what amounted to a victory against the pharmaceutical companies, the government still refused to make ARVs available to the masses.

Activists were enraged when the health department announced that AZT would not even be given to pregnant women as a matter of course. There was ample evidence that the drug greatly reduced the risk of foetal HIV infection, but the government stuck to its claim that AZT was both toxic and unaffordable.

In December 1998, Zackie Achmat announced that he would go on a hunger strike until ordinary South Africans could be given ARVs at state hospitals. 'On principle, I won't take ARVs until they are freely available to the poorest,'[15] he said. His decision coincided with the TAC's launch of a campaign to prevent mother-to-child infection. By 1999, an estimated 40 000 babies were being born with HIV in South Africa annually, their mothers too poor to pay $75 for a short course of AZT, which would lower the risk of transferral by half. The TAC would maintain its relentless pressure on the pharmaceutical companies for the best part of a year, with NGOs in America staging solidarity protests at various points on US vice-president Al Gore's campaign trail until the threat of sanctions was withdrawn.

The TAC's sustained efforts to shame Western governments and highlight their indifference to the plight of AIDS victims in South Africa compelled President Bill Clinton to pledge in 2000 that the US would ensure that 'people from the poorest countries won't have to go without medicines'. His announcement came as the United Nations revealed that it had negotiated a deal with five multinational pharmaceutical companies to reduce the price of AIDS drugs in the developing world.

The South African government's response was guarded. Mbeki, Pahad, Netshitenzhe, Tshabalala-Msimang, and trade and industry minister Alec Erwin now argued that price reductions negotiated with manufacturers were neither substantive nor a permanent solution. If costs could not be decreased any further, it would be better to obtain the drugs through local generic production or parallel importation from Brazil, Thailand or India, where they were successfully being made at a fraction of even the discount price.

In the event, it soon became clear that the high-profile offers of cheaper drugs from the US administration came with punishing strings attached. South Africa could avail itself of some $1.5 billion in the form of export–import loans, at commercial interest rates, to buy American drugs at market prices. In addition, by May 2001, five of the world's biggest pharmaceutical companies had agreed to enter talks with African nations on reduced prices, provided the countries concerned agreed to health action plans being drawn up by McKinsey, a leading business consultancy!

The offers were turned down, but they had reinforced suspicions that Western governments and the drug manufacturers were locked in a conspiracy against Africa.

As Mbeki's views hardened, the relentless pressure applied by the TAC and various NGOs was starting to pay dividends. Drug companies squirmed under accusations of greed, and some began privately to offer significant discounts on their products. By mid-2001, Boehringer Ingelheim was offering Nevirapine, a drug commonly used by HIV/AIDS sufferers, free for a limited period to pregnant women in South Africa. Glaxo offered AZT at 30 per cent of the average international price.

But government still refused to buy the drugs, claiming they were toxic. According to some of Mbeki's close advisors, the offers were seen as a piecemeal strategy to stave off production of cheaper generics. Yet no moves were made to launch local production or import generics. In fact, keen to play a leading role in the global economy and to be seen as playing by the market rules, the government started back-pedalling on earlier threats to import generics.

In November 2001, British trade minister Richard Caborn wrote to the London-based Action for Southern Africa, an organisation that campaigns for peace, democracy and development across the region: 'I don't believe that this or related measures such as parallel importing are the answer here.'[16]

South Africa had the option all along of circumventing TRIPS by citing 'national emergency', but Mbeki had come to believe that the pharmaceutical companies were greatly inflating the AIDS threat in order to exploit developing markets.

What made Mbeki turn to the AIDS dissidents? In July 1999, Anthony Brink, an advocate and the author of the online book *Debating AZT*, had given him and senior health department officials copies of his book, which argued that the so-called life-giving drug was highly toxic. His interest aroused, Mbeki began doing further research on his own, via the Internet.

While surfing the Net, he stumbled on virusmyth.net, a website favoured by the international dissident community. On 20 October 1999, Mbeki told the National Council of Provinces that he had examined 'a large volume of scientific literature', which showed that AZT was dangerous.[17]

The orthodox scientific community has never claimed that AZT is not toxic, but makes the point that *all* drugs have side effects, and that those known to be caused by AZT were far outweighed by its benefits to AIDS patients.

But Mbeki had been seduced, and before long his meanders along the information highway led him to question whether HIV caused AIDS and whether the virus was sexually transmitted. The dissidents argued that HIV was a benign 'passenger virus', and that AIDS was a lifestyle disease caused by poverty, malnutrition and narcotic abuse by homosexuals. They claimed that, far from helping the infected, ARVs caused even greater damage to their compromised immune systems.[18]

The World Health Organisation and the MCC had classified AZT safe, but Mbeki, newly installed as South Africa's president, decided that his health minister, Manto Tshabalala-Msimang, would be entrusted with determining the 'truth' about the disease and its treatment once and for all. On 2 December

1999 she met with AIDS dissident Charles Geshekter, and came away from their discussions convinced that the president was right to question views that had already gained wide international acceptance.

In his nocturnal online research, Mbeki also found the writings of American biochemist David Rasnick, a leading rebel against the conventional premise that AIDS stems from HIV. Mbeki contacted him by fax and spoke to him at length by phone, and soon the two were in regular e-mail contact. Rasnick enthusiastically agreed to support Mbeki's quest for the 'truth'. The president also made contact with another prominent AIDS dissident, Peter Duesberg, a professor of molecular and cell biology at the University of California in Berkeley.

There was a major stir when a South African newspaper published Rasnick's assertions that 'condoms don't prevent AIDS because AIDS isn't a sexually transmitted disease. In fact it isn't contagious at all. AIDS in Africa is just a new name for the diseases of poverty caused by malnutrition, poor sanitation, bad water, parasites and so on. Using condoms to prevent the diseases of poverty is the leading obscenity of our time.'[19]

Mbeki is sincere in challenging mainstream science and in his support of AIDS dissidents. He stoically believes that he is a modern-day Copernicus who will ultimately be vindicated, even if posthumously. Needless to say, the dissidents, long banished to the scientific wilderness, latched on to the new legitimacy that the president provided, and it would prove all but impossible for Mbeki to dissociate himself from them later.

His next mission was to persuade unsuspecting world leaders of the dangers of treating AIDS with conventional methods. In a brazen and bizarre letter to Bill Clinton and UN secretary general Kofi Annan dated 3 April 2000, South Africa's head of state defended an alternative approach to dealing with AIDS. In the five-page document, Mbeki passionately defended Duesberg and the other dissidents, and suggested that factors other than HIV could be the cause of AIDS in Africa. He called for a uniquely 'African solution'[20] to the problem, as AIDS seemed to affect Africans differently to those who live in the developed world.

He also defended his right to consult dissident scientists, and accused unnamed foreign critics of waging a 'campaign of intellectual intimidation and terrorism' akin to 'the racist apartheid tyranny we opposed'. In an earlier period in human history, Mbeki wrote, Duesberg and his followers 'would be the heretics that would be burnt at the stake. The day may not be far off when we will, once again, see books burnt and their authors immolated by fire by those who believe that they have a duty to conduct a holy crusade against the infidels.'[21]

The letter, copies of which were delivered by hand to Clinton and Annan, concluded: 'It would constitute a criminal betrayal of our responsibility to our own people to mimic foreign approaches to treating HIV/AIDS.'[22]

The Clinton administration initially thought the letter was a hoax. Upon realising it was genuine, the contents were leaked to the Washington media. Mbeki was suitably embarrassed, and furious, convinced more than ever that Western leaders were conspiring against their African counterparts.

Bolstered by the counsel of the AIDS dissidents, Mbeki and Tshabalala-Msimang reiterated that the government would not provide ARVs through the public health system, adding the inability of existing infrastructure to implement the drug protocols to their earlier claims of toxicity and cost. Tshabalala-Msimang now argued that anti-AIDS drugs alone would have scant effect, and that the state simply did not have the money to simultaneously offer recipients clean water, sanitation, nutritional food and adequate housing.

When Mbeki opened an international conference on AIDS in Durban in 2000, he accused activists of being willing 'to sacrifice all intellectual integrity to act as salespersons of the product of one pharmaceutical company'.[23] He blocked every effort by civil society and private organisations to set up AIDS treatment projects involving ARVs, prompting Desmond Tutu to comment: 'In South Africa we have to introduce a vibrant and lively education for the people. Churches and religious communities are already playing a role but are hamstrung by the constant worry about what government will say, when they ought to be on the same side.'[24]

Mbeki has consistently placed poverty at the heart of all South Africa's health problems, and few disagree with him, in general. But he found no broad support for his insistence that AIDS should be treated as just another disease, like malaria or TB. The scariest realisation for many people was that Mbeki genuinely believed that a number of factors, including poverty, caused rather than exacerbated AIDS, and that HIV was not to blame.

Tshabalala-Msimang drew hoots of derision when she famously announced that people with AIDS should preserve their health not with drugs, but with a diet of garlic, lemon, olive oil and the African potato.[25] In March 2003, her credibility took another dive when she appointed Roberto Giraldo, a leading AIDS dissident and one of the most vocal naysayers regarding the link between HIV and AIDS, as a consultant on nutrition.

Amid mounting evidence of AZT's effectivity and growing criticism of the government's opposition to ARV distribution, the Mbeki-ites began searching for compliant scientists who would support them.

In October 1999, Tshabalala-Msimang had rejected a report favouring the use of AZT by South Africa's MCC on the grounds that it had not been subject to a satisfactory review process. A month later, she commissioned the Cochrane Centre, an international healthcare NGO that reviews clinical trials on new drugs and has branches all over the world, to research the risks of ARVs, especially AZT. Their preliminary study found strong evidence that both an intensive or shorter course of AZT was effective in decreasing the risk of mother-to-child transmission of HIV, even in breastfed babies. The most serious adverse effect the researchers identified was anaemia, but this condition tended to disappear once the full course of drugs had been concluded. Nevirapine, less expensive than AZT, was found to be both safe and effective.

These findings were given to the health minister in December. She filed the report and allowed it to gather dust while she turned to the National AIDS Council for an outcome more in line with dissident opinion, as well as her own. Tshabalala-Msimang appointed new members, renamed the former AIDS Advisory Council the Presidential AIDS Advisory Council, and extended the council's influence to sectors not previously involved in AIDS programmes.

Activists saw through the ploy and criticised the council as just another attempt by Mbeki and his health minister to muzzle and marginalise those with a different viewpoint. In due course, the council would issue a report that did nothing but reiterate both the orthodox and dissident views on AIDS, without attaching particular weight to one or the other.

In a new affront to activists, government revealed that in the 1999/2000 financial year, 40 per cent of the AIDS budget had gone unspent. Worse, it announced that funding of AIDS service organisations was to be cut by 43 per cent the following year. Dismayed by government's persistent obfuscation and continuous flirting with AIDS dissidents, Judge Edwin Cameron and concerned activists wrote a personal letter to Mbeki in March 2000, defending the use of AZT and expressing anxiety over government's stance.

Mbeki responded by fax a few days later, questioning available evidence that argued AZT was safe and recalling that similar consensus had existed within the medical community over the use of thalidomide, a drug formerly used as a sedative, but found to cause fetal malformation when taken in early pregnancy, in the early 1960s.

Throughout all the polemic, Mbeki was telling senior ANC leaders that the magnitude of the AIDS crisis in South Africa had been exaggerated to serve the interests of the drug giants and NGOs. Unfortunately, South African AIDS statistics have been the subject of dispute for several years, but it remains the only country in Africa that has even remotely reliable figures, even though, as author Rian Malan[26] points out, they are computer projections based on surveys on antenatal clinics.

The situation has not been helped by international studies of dubious credibility. As recently as 2003, the World Bank warned in a report that South Africa faced imminent economic collapse as a result of HIV/AIDS, and, even though respected local experts such as Standard Bank chief economist Iraj Abedian and the South African Business Coalition dismissed the report as inaccurate and unreliable, Mbeki grasped at hyperbole to defend his claims that the figures were inflated.

But the first extensive and broadly credible surveys on the incidence of HIV/AIDS, conducted independently by the South African Medical Research Council and Statistics SA in 2000 and 2001, painted a picture that was bleak. They estimated that 5.3 million South Africans would be infected with the virus by the end of 2002 and that it would be killing 600 people a day.[27] A government report leaked in late March 2004 said 100 000 public servants were HIV positive, presenting a very real threat to normal government administration.

In August 2001, the government was back in court as the TAC and various NGOs claimed it was acting unconstitutionally by refusing to make ARVs available at state hospitals. In its March 2002 judgment, the Constitutional Court agreed, ordering that pregnant women should start receiving the drugs immediately. Still the government prevaricated, claiming that state hospitals did not have the infrastructure necessary to administer ARVs. It was not until seven months later that Nevirapine became available at some urban hospitals as part of a pilot scheme, and not until the eve of the 2004 election that distribution was extended.

Costs have unquestionably played a role in the government's response to the AIDS crisis. GEAR, the economic policy adopted in June 1996, calls for economic austerity and financial prudence, and structural adjustment programmes have seen jobs frozen and public service cuts. In 2000, finance minister Trevor Manuel and Manto Tshabalala-Msimang sketched a gloomy picture for Mbeki of the costs involved in the proposed ARV roll-out, and the government concluded that it was not financially feasible to make the drugs available to all HIV-positive patients at state cost.

Thenjiwe Mtintso, assistant secretary general of the ANC at the time, pointed out: 'Making anti-retroviral drugs available is only one side of the story; the state will have to take responsibility for all the costs of AIDS-infected individuals. The state doesn't have that kind of capacity or resources.'[28] Manuel was more blunt: 'The rhetoric about the effectiveness of ARVs is a lot of voodoo and buying them would be a waste of limited resources.'[29]

Underlying the decision was an unspoken belief among Mbeki's inner circle that spending money on ARVs would be futile, since the real problem lay with the reasons for South Africa's masses being particularly vulnerable to AIDS. At its most cynical, the view suggests that the exchequer was to be spared the cost of subsidising treatment for the poor and unemployed, who were a drain on resources rather than contributors to the state coffers. It suggests that in the long term, resources would be better utilised by creating jobs, educating people, and fighting poverty and malnutrition.

Manuel said as much at a closed hearing of the committee that investigated the feasibility of a basic income grant: 'It does not make financial sense to spend money on people dying anyway, who are not even productive in the first place.'[30] He apologised when he realised that the commissioners were shocked by his comments, but, far from being an isolated aberration, such sentiments were the driving spirit behind the economic mandarins' response to the pandemic. The tendency to focus on the healthy has been the overriding objective of government's financial managers.

In June 2003, Mbeki's media spokesman, Parks Mankahlana, asked in an interview with *Science* magazine: 'Who is going to look after the orphans of AIDS mothers, the state?'[31] The clear implication was that prevention of mother-to-child transmission of HIV would be counterproductive, since the children saved would end up as welfare cases in any event.

Of course, no one in government could say this publicly – it would simply be too cold-hearted. But Tshabalala-Msimang apparently had no qualms about allegedly telling London's *Guardian* in 2002 that South Africa could not afford AIDS drugs because it needed submarines to deter US aggression, though she later denied saying anything of the kind.

Mbeki's attitude to the AIDS problem was almost certainly strongly influenced by his great personal distaste for the stereotypical Western portrayal of black sexuality, which he condemns as racist and neo-colonial. In his mind, this viewpoint extended to scientific postulations that AIDS originated in the African jungle and was primarily spread through sexual transmission. Many share these views.

In a lecture at Fort Hare University in 2001, Mbeki said: 'And thus it happens that others who consider themselves to be our leaders take to the streets carrying their placards ... convinced that we are but natural born, promiscuous carriers of germs, unique in the world, they proclaim that our continent is doomed to an inevitable mortal end because of our unconquerable devotion to the sin of lust.'[32]

The argument found support among many ANC leaders and intellectuals outside the party. Tshabalala-Msimang is a great believer in this precept, to which Achmat responds: 'The president doesn't want to believe that people in Africa have a lot of sex.'[33]

In autumn 2002, Mbeki sent an e-mail to members of his cabinet, expanding on this thesis. A 114-page document, chiefly authored by former ANCYL head Peter Mokaba, virulently attacked pharmaceutical companies, ARVs and mainstream opinions on HIV. The sarcastic monologue lashed out at the bigotry that equates blacks with promiscuity and portrays Africans as diseased and poor, and always running to the West for aid:

Yes, we are sex crazy! Yes, we are diseased! Yes, we spread the deadly HIV through uncontrolled heterosexual sex! In this regard, yes, we are different from the US and Western Europe! Yes, we, the men, abuse women and the girl-child with gay abandon! Yes, among us rape is endemic because of our culture! Yes, we do believe that sleeping with young virgins will cure us of AIDS! Yes, as a result of all this, we are threatened with destruction by the HIV/AIDS pandemic! Yes, what we need, and cannot afford because we are poor, are condoms and anti-retroviral drugs! Help![34]

Within weeks of writing the paper, Mokaba, like Parks Mankahlana, died from what is widely believed to be an AIDS-related disease, though their families persistently denied this. It was around this time that Mbeki announced that he would launch an international advisory council to investigate the high incidence of heterosexual infection in southern Africa and assess drug-based responses. Renowned medical scientist Jerry Coovadia urged him to leave science to the scientists.

Mbeki's stubborn AIDS denial epitomised the ANC's battle to keep its traditions of internal democracy alive as it underwent transformation from a liberation movement to a governing political party. The debate split the tripartite alliance down the middle, with COSATU and the SACP siding with the TAC, as did two of the great post-apartheid moralists, Nelson Mandela and Desmond Tutu.

COSATU president Willie Madisha accused Mbeki of wasting his time on scientific speculation and hindering the fight against the disease. 'The current public debate on the causal link between HIV and AIDS is confusing,'[35] Madisha worried publicly.

Privately, government officials warned that Mbeki's intellectual approach was preventing the government from getting across the message that people should use condoms. Indeed, AIDS educationists frequently encountered resistance based on the argument that if the president did not believe there was a link between HIV and AIDS, unprotected sex posed no danger of infection.

A disturbingly high number of ordinary South Africans saw Mbeki's views as an endorsement that, since AIDS was not sexually transferable, they had no reason to alter or modify their sexual behaviour.

The health department was as divided on the issue as the general public, with individuals having to battle their own consciences and decide whether they should administer ARVs and risk being fired, or follow orders. Many senior health officials at national and provincial level supported ARV distribution, and though he refused to talk publicly about the reasons for his departure, Tshabalala-Msimang's director-general, Dr Ayanda Ntsaluba, quit and went to work for foreign affairs, allegedly because of his inability to reconcile his own beliefs with those of the minister and president.

Health professionals at state hospitals were also confused. Should they administer life-saving ARVs or not? If they did, would they be punished? At grassroots level, healthcare workers were dealing almost daily with the fatal consequences of confusion over government's policy, which led the uninformed to believe that the disease was not transmitted sexually.

The greatest tragedy was that Mbeki failed to see that his refusal to acknowledge the effectivity of ARV treatment was undermining the entire AIDS education programme. It had been designed around the premise that HIV causes AIDS, and condom use was a mainstay of the government campaign that was being waged through awareness projects, educational television, radio, posters and in classrooms throughout the country.

For COSATU, the link between HIV and AIDS was irrefutable. General secretary Zwelinzima Vavi[36] pointed to the success of Brazil, a country with similar income disparities to South Africa, in providing medication to its infected citizens, and called on the government to declare a national emergency in terms of TRIPS so that ARV delivery could start.

Formal criticism from inside the ANC was slow to emerge, with those who differed from Mbeki scared of reprisals if they spoke out. Most criticism was uttered in hushed tones, but Madisha's and Vavi's relentless public attacks on Mbeki's AIDS stance opened the way for other prominent black figures to join the choir.

Some had kept their own counsel for fear of being lumped with white conservatives who had taken up the AIDS cudgel only because they could use it to bash the 'inept' black government. Thanks to Madisha, Vavi and prominent scientist William Makgoba, the Mbeki-ites could no longer charge that criticism was confined to white reactionaries bent on undermining the black government.

Once the wall of silence had been breached, the AIDS policy came under fire from within. Some of the harshest critics were members of the ANC's health committee, one of the party's constitutional structures, while former health minister Nkosazana Dlamini-Zuma told Mbeki privately that his stance was undermining not only the government's own policy, but his presidency.

The most serious opposition came from individuals serving on the ANC's powerful NEC, but only as late as mid-2000. At an NEC meeting in Johannesburg, Dlamini-Zuma and Shepherd Mdladlana cautiously warned that Mbeki's high-profile international advisory panel on AIDS was adding to confusion over the official AIDS message. They couched their arguments in a way that spared Mbeki from direct criticism, emphasising that the government's message was not being effectively conveyed. They also warned that AIDS had the potential to undermine the ANC's efforts in the 2000 local elections, given that opposition parties and civil movements were threatening to make AIDS, as well as slow social delivery to the poor, central campaign issues.

Mbeki loyalists such as Essop Pahad and Manto Tshabalala-Msimang responded dismissively that government was doing enough, within its capacity, to deal with the AIDS crisis. They listed AIDS education programmes and the amounts spent on them, arguing that it would cost too much to accede to calls by NGOs, trade unions and churches for the government to supply ARVs to all AIDS sufferers. Tshabalala-Msimang reiterated that the toxicity of ARVs had not been unequivocally determined, and cited warnings by the American government that some ARVs were believed to be so toxic that their use could prove fatal.

Mbeki was adamant that he would not backtrack on any of his AIDS statements, and continued to believe that his views were correct.

But he did agree, albeit reluctantly and unhappily, to refrain from further public comment on AIDS, at least until after the municipal elections. His chief policy guru, Joel Netshitenzhe, was assigned the unenviable task of extricating Mbeki from the hole he had dug for himself, without repudiating anything the president had previously said on the subject of HIV and AIDS.

Fully aware of the damage that had been done to the government's reputation, Netshitenzhe fell back on the spin doctor's hardy annual and attacked the media for colluding with critics of the official AIDS policy. Insisting that the government's programmes were fully effective but not 'on message', he got the go-ahead for a R2-million advertising blitz that would somehow make it clear that neither the president nor anyone else in a position of authority had ever said that there was no link between HIV and AIDS.

'We want to put the theorising behind us and programmes to fight the pandemic in front of us,' said one senior NEC member optimistically. Mbeki's international AIDS advisory panel would continue to meet, but behind the scenes, and the president would avoid all public reference to the pandemic until the local government ballots were cast.

The advertising campaign failed to clear up the confusion, not least because no one could admit what lay behind Mbeki's withdrawal from the public AIDS debate. And since the dissidents continued to use his name in support of their own agenda, his silence was widely interpreted as confirmation that he did not agree with the messages imparted by official government policy.

In the wake of the NEC meeting, members of the ANC's parliamentary wing became emboldened enough to make their voices heard on a range of issues, including the economic policy, Mbeki's ineffective 'quiet diplomacy' with Zimbabwe and AIDS.

Nelson Mandela tried to meet with Mbeki to raise his concerns over the AIDS policy, but the president was smarting over what he saw as his predecessor's constant criticism on the subject, and refused to take Mandela's calls.

At a special meeting of the ANC's parliamentary caucus in October 2000,

Mbeki raged against senior leaders who criticised him in public, specifically on AIDS and Zimbabwe, and slammed the media for its coverage of the AIDS debate.

In contrast, he spoke approvingly about a conference in Uganda the previous month, where some sixty dissident scientists argued convincingly that there was no scientific proof that HIV causes AIDS. He quoted from a document stating that the virus had never been isolated, and said reports that Uganda had scored significant successes in the fight against AIDS were untrue.

He told the gathered MPs that if one agreed that HIV causes AIDS, it followed that the treatment lay with drugs manufactured by Western corporations. The pharmaceutical companies therefore needed people to believe that HIV and AIDS were linked, in order to peddle their products. One drug company, which he did not name, had confessed, he said, that it had spent vast amounts of money on the search for an AIDS vaccine, but had abandoned the effort after failing to isolate the virus. This fact remained hidden from the public, Mbeki claimed, because the company's share price would plummet if the truth were told.

He accused the CIA of being involved in a covert plot to spread the belief of an HIV/AIDS link, and cited statistics showing that 10 per cent of Africans died of AIDS. It made no sense, Mbeki argued, to focus the bulk of a state's resources on this 10 per cent, to the detriment of the remaining 90 per cent. Drug companies continually urged governments to pay attention to a growing number of AIDS orphans, but how, asked the president, were the authorities to distinguish between the needs of AIDS orphans and orphans of any other kind?

He claimed he had the support of the editor of South Africa's conservative daily newspaper, the *Citizen*, but said it was less clear that members of his own cabinet stood with him on this issue. They should declare their positions, he said, and the ANC's MPs should join him in fighting off attempts by international forces to undermine him and the government's agenda.

Those within the ANC who criticised him were playing into the hands of the local and foreign media – some of whom had dared to describe his views on AIDS as deranged – and unwittingly supporting the campaigns of the powerful drug companies and their allies, Western governments opposed to Mbeki's vision of success for developing countries.

Before launching his tirade, Mbeki had made it clear to caucus chair Thabang Makwetla that he would take no questions. Deeply shocked by the virulence of his attack, none of the ANC MPs challenged anything he said. According to one, 'there was a stunned silence in the room'.[37]

Throughout his presidency, Mbeki's Achilles heel has been his uncompromising 'you are with us, or against us' attitude. He sees all criticism of government policy as a personal attack, and those who dare express views that contradict his own are categorised as secretly hating him, or, worse, wanting to topple him.

His censure of the AIDS critics choked any further criticism of the government's policy. Not even the bravest ANC leaders would risk being labelled allies of a hostile 'white' media, greedy drug manufacturers or covert Western intelligence conspiracies.

In October 2001, during question time in parliament, it emerged that a number of ANC parliamentarians were taking ARVs, paid for by their state medical aid. The inescapable conclusion among activists was that the government could afford to pay for medicine for its own officials and representatives, but such help was too costly for the masses. Former opposition Pan Africanist Congress firebrand Patricia de Lille openly denounced the government's 'absolute hypocrisy',[38] but Mbeki's response was merely to warn the ANC MPs that the drugs could be toxic.

Having successfully drawn a curtain of silence over AIDS critics within the ANC, the president broadened his attacks to include black intellectuals, activists and individuals of all political persuasions who agitated against the government's policies. A particularly vicious campaign was launched against outspoken physicist and political analyst Sipho Seepe, while Essop Pahad slammed local medical experts as 'pseudo-scientists'.

Mbeki accused William Makgoba of deliberately leaking a long-awaited MRC report on the devastation wrought by AIDS in South Africa to the media before it was handed to him or the cabinet. Tshabalala-Msimang ordered a forensic audit to sniff out the source of the leak.

Achmat and TAC activists, many of them ANC cadres, were next to face Mbeki's ire. He refused to meet any TAC representatives, telling confidants: 'I will not give them the credibility of my presence.'[39] The vilification of Achmat as a pawn in the hands of Western interest groups intensified, and he was publicly accused of defying ANC discipline.

Achmat had infuriated Mbeki by travelling to Thailand in late 2000, buying 5 000 fluconazole pills for 28 cents each, and bringing them back to South Africa in a well-publicised stunt. The government had him arrested for smuggling, and the attacks on the TAC only let up after Mandela visited a very sick Achmat at home in 2002 to plead with him to take ARVs.

Mandela lauded Achmat's commitment to the ANC and praised him as a role model and loyal member, pledging to ensure that his protests were heard in the right government circles. 'We were really under siege,' Achmat later reflected, 'and Nelson has given us protection. It was not for us that he did it. He's not interested in opposing the government. He's interested in doing what is right.'[40]

Mandela had visited a clinic where the international humanitarian agency, Médicins Sans Frontières, was treating 400 patients with ARV and achieving a compliance rate that exceeded that of most AIDS clinics in America. After his emotional meeting with Achmat, the former president broke his own rule of non-interference with his successor's governance and increasingly began criticising both Mbeki and the official AIDS policy in public. Mandela was greatly concerned about a growing perception that 'the ANC does not care about the death of millions'.[41]

He tried again to arrange a meeting with Mbeki, hoping to advise him that he and the First Lady, Zanele, should lead the anti-AIDS campaign. But every time Mandela called, Mbeki's aides would say he was not available.

In November 2001, Mandela, frustrated at his inability to see Mbeki, used a speech at an ANC rally in the Cape Town settlement of Khayelitsha to throw out the challenge to Mbeki and his wife to be the visible faces of government's attempts to combat AIDS. 'We have wasted time,' he said, 'but the more vigorous and focused we are in what we do, the greater the chance we have of moving forward.'[42]

Mbeki was outraged. Yet again, he took the criticism personally, and privately accused Mandela of overstepping the line. He instructed aides to telephone Madiba and demand an explanation. Mandela denied that he had been attacking the president, and Mbeki finally agreed that they should meet, along with the ANC's National Working Committee, to discuss the subject.

At the appointed time and place, however, Mbeki was conspicuously absent. Mandela joked that Mbeki was 'too busy', and told the committee that the government's AIDS policy was creating the impression that it did not care if millions of South Africans died. He urged the immediate introduction of ARVs for pregnant women, as a start.

Jacob Zuma, standing in for the president, assured Mandela that the government was serious about the pandemic, but was not ready to roll out the ARV programme because the effectiveness of the drugs was still being tested in a pilot project. The only problem the government would admit to was one of communication, in keeping with Netshitenzhe's earlier strategy.

Mandela agreed to reserve his doubts and questions for the next NEC meeting, which Mbeki would hopefully attend, but urged Zuma to play a leading role in the fight against AIDS, because Mbeki's busy schedule frequently took him abroad.

Archbishop Tutu, just as exasperated as Mandela over the government's vacillation on AIDS, went public with what was undeniably a rebuke of Mbeki:

It would be tremendous if our president said this is the common enemy. The stance adopted by the president has harmed his image. He has done wonderfully well – the world thinks the world of him, I want to see him succeed. I think it is silly to hold on to positions that are untenable. At the present time, everybody recognises that the president's position is undermining his stature in the world. When the *New York Times* is constantly bashing us over this issue, it is not good for us or for him. He has so much going for him.[43]

Tutu threw his full support behind efforts to prevent mother-to-child transmission of the virus: 'Yes, this means the use of Nevirapine if that is what is available. It is irresponsible of us not to save lives we could save. It makes us appear hard-hearted where we are not. We are seen to be lacking in compassion and uncaring. Women who are raped should be put on a course to ensure that they are not infected.'

He also made the point that whereas AIDS was considered a chronic condition in the United States, it was tantamount to a death sentence in South Africa.[44]

At a January 2001 cabinet meeting, Mbeki finally acknowledged that negative perceptions of South Africa's AIDS policies were based not on bad communication, but on a lack of consensus over what the government's message should be. A year later, he and his cabinet accepted, for the first time, that confusion over the policy was no longer a medical or scientific matter, but a major issue that was undermining the country's interests.

The opposition Inkatha Freedom Party leader, Mangosuthu Buthelezi, decried the lack of leadership on the AIDS front and proposed more stringent monitoring of the activities of Mbeki's international AIDS advisory council. In his State of the Nation address at the opening of parliament, Mbeki hinted at finally putting the issue to rest when he spoke of government's intention to 'intensify its comprehensive programme against AIDS'.[45]

Ahead of the NEC meeting in March 2002, Nelson Mandela was attacked by a number of Mbeki-ites, including one of the president's loudest cheerleaders, Dumisani Makhaye, a KwaZulu-Natal ANC leader. Thami Mazwai, the black entrepreneur in charge of a publishing house, also launched a broadside against Mandela in the mass-circulation Sunday newspaper *City Press*, accusing him of unprecedented interference in government affairs.

The NEC spent a whole day discussing the government's AIDS policy. All the provincial health MECs had been invited to the meeting, but members of the ANC's health committee, who had been critical of the failure to make ARVs freely available, were barred. When Mandela voiced his concerns, he was heckled and jeered by Mbeki supporters.

The loyalists urged Mbeki to bulldoze ahead with the controversial AIDS policies rather than reverse or revise them, lest this be seen as caving in under pressure from Mandela and others. After hearing impassioned arguments from the likes of Peter Mokaba, the NEC resolved that rape victims, health workers and pregnant women should not be provided with ARVs because the effectiveness of the drugs remained unproven. The hardliners also pushed through a bizarre decision that the government would appeal against the recent judgment by Judge Chris Botha in the Pretoria High Court ordering that Nevirapine be given to pregnant women.

This was one of several truly extraordinary reactions by the government to a high court ruling. Immediately after it was handed down, then justice minister Penuell Maduna, a trained lawyer, said the judgment could be enforced only in the province where the case was heard. He later retracted his statement, but Tshabalala-Msimang said on national television that the government would not obey the court order. For Mandela, the NEC's decision to appeal against the ruling was the final proof that people were justified in seeing the ANC as a party that did not care about those who were dying of AIDS.

In the end, economics rather than compassion would force Mbeki's hand on HIV/AIDS. Members of his international investment council warned him at roughly the same time as the NEC meeting that investors found the confusion over the government's approach to the disease unsettling, if not downright frightening. Mbeki's association with the AIDS dissidents was fuelling negative perceptions about South Africa as a potential investment opportunity, and unless a clear and unambiguous change in policy could be discerned, his meeting with the G8 in June to discuss NEPAD could be blown off course.

Trevor Manuel and Reserve Bank governor Tito Mboweni were also starting to feel the pinch as foreign investors probed them on government's AIDS policy, and they, too, began dropping cautious hints to the president of looming economic consequences.

When the cabinet met in April 2002, Mbeki proposed that ARVs be made available to pregnant women and rape survivors without further delay, pointing out that despite the absence of conclusive evidence that they worked, they were already being routinely used by medical staff who suffered puncture wounds sustained from hypodermic syringes.

It was a landmark decision and a radical departure from Mbeki's position to date. He followed through by starting to distance himself from the AIDS dissidents, and gave cabinet an undertaking that no longer would the dissidents or Mokaba be allowed to speak on his behalf regarding the disease.

In an interview with the *Star*, Mbeki denied that there was a lack of government leadership on AIDS. 'Perhaps we are not communicating that message loud enough,' he said. 'But I think there's been very strong leadership on the matter. It is critically important that I communicate correct messages.'[46]

Since then, like many other developing countries, South Africa has increasingly channelled funds into AIDS programmes, albeit at the cost of poverty alleviation or opening up their markets to trade with poorer countries. Development funding is now earmarked almost exclusively to halt the infection rate and treat the victims.

But in fairness, the business community has not been a partner to government in this battle. The South African Business Coalition on HIV/AIDS surveyed 1 006 companies throughout the country on the impact of the disease in commerce and industry, and found that only 25 per cent of them had implemented a formal HIV/AIDS policy. Less than 20 per cent had introduced voluntary counselling and testing programmes, or provided care, treatment and support to infected workers.[47]

Having previously announced with great fanfare that it would make ARVs available to employees free of charge, mining giant Anglo American subsequently withdrew the offer, saying it would be far too costly.[48] Incredulously, trade minister Alec Erwin would claim as late as April 2002 that AIDS had 'no impact on the South African economy or workforce'.[49]

The harsh reality is that South Africa is now faced with creating the largest AIDS treatment programme in the world. The ARV roll-out in the public sector will require a major upgrading of the existing healthcare infrastructure, recruitment and training of a vast corps of health workers, and a well-coordinated national programme for HIV tests and counselling.

It is a daunting prospect, to be sure, but it can be done. In the mid-1980s, the picture looked equally grim in Thailand, but thanks to a dedicated monitoring programme, concentration on high-risk groups, general AIDS education combined with 100 per cent condom use and vigorous efforts to dispel the stigma attached to the disease, the situation has been brought under control and infection rates appear to have stabilised. The secret ingredient to success, however, has been large doses of political will.[50]

Worryingly, Mbeki still firmly believes that those who contract the disease should assume individual responsibility for their care and not simply expect the state to pick up the tab. He remains unconvinced that HIV causes AIDS, and many senior ANC leaders share this view. Said Smuts Ngonyama, the party's official spokesperson and one of Mbeki's closest associates: 'It's based on a scientific assumption, and like all assumptions, it can be disproved.'[51]

Small wonder, then, that Mbeki could tell the world, without blinking an eye, 'I don't know of anybody that died of AIDS' in an interview with the *Washington Post* in September 2003.

Cynics have no doubt that the only reason the government backed down on the ARV roll-out was to deny opposition parties the chance to use the issue as a vote-catcher in the 2004 elections. Many claimed that the ANC still lacked the political will to tackle AIDS head-on, and predicted that the issue would be moved to the back burner again once the election was over.

In August 2004, Tshabalala-Msimang confirmed that the government would not meet its target of supplying ARVs to a paltry 53 000 people by March 2005. After all, she sighed, 'we are just a developing country'. Somewhat tellingly, she added: 'If you say to the nation that you are providing ARVs then you will wipe out all the gains made in the promotion of a healthy lifestyle and prevention.'[52]

Practical considerations aside, there is much work yet to be done, by government, the TAC and other civil society organisations, to destigmatise the disease. Gugu Dlamini was stoned to death by a mob near Durban after she disclosed her HIV-positive status on radio. The veil of secrecy surrounding the deaths of Peter Mokaba and Parks Mankahlana show how pervasive the stigma is.

The Sisulu family proved a rare exception when they went public after a family member died of AIDS. Buthelezi, an arch-traditionalist, also broke the silence by acknowledging that both a son and a daughter had died of AIDS within months of one another in 2004 and publicly speaking of the devastation the disease caused within the family circle. And when Nelson Mandela announced that his son, Makgatho, had died of AIDS in January 2005, it was a move aimed at breaking one of the most stubborn taboos surrounding the pandemic.

It is true that there are cultural taboos against speaking about death, but the continual denials perpetuate the terrible stigma surrounding AIDS in South Africa. The vast majority of the population still see the disease as something that happens to 'other' people – prostitutes, migrant workers and moral lepers. Only those who have done something bad, behaved immorally or been sexually promiscuous get AIDS, and 'decent' folk are right to treat them as outcasts. Sex, too, is something that polite people don't discuss in public. It happens, but one does not talk about it, hence Zuma's mind-boggling statement that those who dare to mention oral sex are 'un-African'.

The fact that Mbeki has never led the way in talking openly about AIDS, as President Yoweri Museveni did in Uganda, has seriously undermined all government efforts to combat the disease. Mbeki's refusal to acknowledge that HIV is sexually transmitted is a major obstacle to facilitating behaviour modification and greatly diminishes the dedicated attempts of sex educators to protect another generation from wholesale infection. A more enlightened leader such as Chandrababu Naidu, chief minister of the Indian state of Andhra Pradesh, for example, insisted that all his ministers should make mention of AIDS in their public addresses, no matter what the topic.[53]

Mbeki's role is crucial. Though South Africa has the most progressive Constitution and Bill of Rights in the world, with women's rights firmly entrenched, gender relations are far from being democratised. Age-old perceptions of women as 'possessions' run deep, and in November 2003, a South African Medical Research Council study offered conclusive evidence of links between gender-based power inequalities and the risk of South African women contracting AIDS.

The study recommended that reducing gender inequalities and making men more respectful of women are crucial weapons in the fight against AIDS and in building a society in which women have the right to live free from violence. As the country's president and leading male role model, Mbeki could be extremely influential in changing attitudes towards women.

Mbeki's handling of the AIDS issue has reinforced his image as a lone, remote intellectual and contrarian battling against the world. It has also illustrated the president's Don Quixote side, which caused his mentor, Oliver Tambo, many headaches. Tambo once told an associate: 'That Thabo is such a clever young man, but I always have to keep a close eye on him, because he tends to wander off [on intellectual pursuits]. He would cause my death, if I am not careful.'[54]

In dealing with AIDS, Mbeki may have wandered off on a deadly diversion that has helped place an entire nation in denial and needlessly taken the lives of millions of its citizens.

# — 8 —

# Comrade Bob

No, the men in suits,
in the Members' Stand
have written the songs,
and the bleeding choirs are conducted
by police batons,
beat the dead horse
the Good Friday effigy
of the honkey again to death,
the straw man you kill
will not cry mercy,
nor the man on the guarded hill
with the new flag
the ridiculous currency,
the not-so-secret police.
              – Derek Walcott, 'The Little Nations', 1974[1]

BARELY A YEAR AFTER HE WAS SWORN IN ON THE MAJESTIC LAWNS OF Pretoria's Union Buildings, an imposing legacy of formidable colonial architect Sir Herbert Baker, Thabo Mbeki's first term as president was on shaky ground.

The ANC's impatient left wing was muttering about blood on the floor, and it was Mbeki's they had in mind unless promises of change to a policy of real redistribution were realised soon. Mbeki's vision of black economic empowerment and a substantial black business class was widely derided within the ruling ANC alliance, as well as outside, for seemingly enriching only a few well-connected oligarchs.

An air of rebellion hung over provinces where Mbeki had hand-picked the premiers, while younger and fresh recruits to the ANC's parliamentary wing were noisily demanding more independence. At municipal level, ANC councillors publicly balked at implementation of cost-recovery measures demanded by the central government's tight macroeconomic policy, GEAR, which would lead to water and electricity supplies to the poor being cut off for non-payment of increased tariffs.

During the elections in 1999, the mainly white opposition DA's 'fightback' campaign had raised the spectre of South Africa being plunged into a black–white confrontation after all. Bitter white expatriates carried the message to foreign lands that the country was coming apart at the seams as criminals ran amok. Meanwhile, Mbeki was desperately trying to persuade notoriously suspicious African leaders to rally behind his Herculean attempt to launch an ambitious programme of economic and political renewal. Many Western powers, businesses and African despots, keen to keep the continent divided in furtherance of their own interests, were working equally hard to spike his ambitions.

A frustrated Mbeki was feeling unappreciated, misunderstood and besieged. Alone at night, smoking his trademark pipe and sipping his beloved cognac, tapping away at his computer keyboard or sharing a private moment with intimate friends such as the Pahad brothers, Joel Netshitenzhe and Nkosazana Dlamini-Zuma, he would ask rhetorically: Why did I take this job?

He must have been aware that some ANC factions were already talking in hushed tones about replacing him, looking with new eyes at the deputy president, political journeyman Jacob Zuma. Perhaps he would not be such a bad choice after all, said some, while others secretly sounded out Mbeki's old rival, Cyril Ramaphosa. Bruised from the bitter leadership battle against Mbeki, however, Ramaphosa made it clear that he was entirely content with his new role in the business community.

As the storm clouds gathered, Mbeki's closest ally and best friend for almost forty years, Essop Pahad, the minister in the presidency, lashed out at the media, which he believed guilty of stoking the political fires that were breaking out over a wide front.

At precisely this juncture, the head of South Africa's northern neighbour threw his full support behind an obscure, ragtag group of 'war veterans' embarking on a controversial and violent campaign to seize white-owned farms.

It was the reckless act of a man determined to cling to power. Zimbabwe's once thriving economy was teetering on the brink of collapse due to monumental mismanagement, kleptocracy and corruption. The country's fiscus was being sucked dry by a doomed military misadventure in the Democratic Republic of Congo, a war that was costing Zimbabwe £1 million a day.[2] Robert Mugabe's post-independence paradise, the erstwhile breadbasket of the region, was becoming so dependent on international aid that by 2004, an estimated 5.5 million people a day would need to be fed by donors.[3]

The first real opposition to Mugabe in two decades spilt onto the streets, with daily protests, strikes and riots reminiscent of the popular uprising that forced Indonesian strongman Suharto's downfall. The trade union wing of Mugabe's ZANU-PF had broken away in February 1999 to form the Movement for Democratic Change (MDC). The ruling party was riddled with factions, many of them openly challenging Mugabe's iron grip. Stalwarts like the respected Edison Zvogbo were brazenly lampooning their leader, and after more than twenty years in power, Mugabe's presidency hung by a thread.

Among the upstarts was an arrogant Polish-trained medical doctor, Chenjerai 'Hitler' Hunzvi, who came from obscurity to dare the ageing Mugabe to condone a bloody campaign to forcefully reclaim land from whites or face a bruising leadership revolt. After his shaky 1996 presidential victory, Mugabe had defiantly proclaimed: 'We are going to take the land and we are not going to pay for the soil. This is our set policy. Our land was never bought [by the colonialists] and there is no way we could buy back the land. However, if Britain wants compensation they should give us money and we will pass it on to their children.'[4]

Mugabe did not follow through on his threat, but Hunzvi, his eyes fixed on the ultimate prize of unseating Mugabe and taking his place, was bent on taking land seizure to its awful logical conclusion. He conveyed his plan to the octogenarian leader towards the end of 1997, claiming massive support among the starving rural peasants, the bedrock of ZANU-PF's constituency.

No one had ever challenged Mugabe so boldly, but, wily as ever, the president calculated that he could manipulate both Hunzvi and the planned campaign to his own advantage. It was true that disproportionate white land ownership was a source of anger among the majority black population, so why not blame Zimbabwe's economic ills on bellicose whites and paint the MDC as the willing or unsuspecting puppets of the former colonialists?

For Mugabe, this would not only present a marvellous way out of the economic and political crisis threatening his reign, but would also be a sure way of revitalising ZANU-PF's failing fortunes and reversing the opposition's fast-rising popularity. Mugabe was outraged at the way he had been ignored by Britain's New Labour prime minister, Tony Blair, and his minister for Africa, former anti-apartheid activist Peter Hain. With their leftist background, he had expected them to be sympathetic to his demand for the long-promised funds for land redistribution, but Blair and Hain would have no truck with the rantings of an old despot.

Perhaps Hunzvi's plan would propel them into action, and if the campaign backfired, Mugabe probably reasoned, Hunzvi could always be blamed and made the scapegoat.

By April 2000, so-called war vets, some no more than teenagers and thus patently not former freedom fighters at all, were swarming onto commercial farms to peg their claims. Mugabe and ZANU-PF openly supported the use of brute force to drive not only the white owners, but also hundreds of their loyal black workers, off the land.

Mbeki and other black leaders in South Africa were horrified, the more so since it seemed the country's intelligence service had slipped up and failed to warn the government of the impending crisis. The ANC leadership had no idea how to react, but Mbeki's instinct was to steer clear of active involvement. 'This is another Abacha all over,'[5] he told his closest allies in exasperation.

The ANC's left wing and its parliamentary caucus insisted that Mugabe and his henchmen should be condemned in the strongest possible terms, while the Africanists expressed sympathy for his position. Mbeki decided the safest course of action would be for foreign affairs minister Nkosazana Dlamini-Zuma and her deputy, Aziz Pahad, to try to sort out the crisis through diplomatic channels. Mbeki warned them to avoid any critical public statements that could inflame the hard-headed men in Harare even more, but there was no need to tell the forceful Dlamini-Zuma not to be too harsh on Mugabe. She was firmly in the Africanist camp and would consistently express sympathy for the Zimbabwean government.

Mbeki opted for 'quiet diplomacy' on Zimbabwe because he was still haunted by South Africa's failure to prevent the execution in 1995 of Nigerian activist and playwright Ken Saro Wiwa.[6] In the ANC government's first foray into African politics, Nelson Mandela had sent his deputy president to persuade the cruel and corrupt Nigerian dictator, Sani Abacha, to spare Saro Wiwa's life. Having served as the ANC's representative in the West African state for much of the 1980s, Mbeki was well acquainted with the Nigerian situation, and had agreed with Mandela that isolating the Abacha regime was likely to prove counterproductive.

But when Mbeki met with Abacha and his cronies, the military strongman made it clear that he was not impressed with newly democratic South Africa cosying up to the West, and accused both Mandela and Mbeki of being puppets.

Saro Wiwa's subsequent brutal execution was a slap in the face and a baptism of fire on foreign policy for the fledgling South African democracy. One of his lawyers later told Mandela pointedly: 'Were quiet diplomacy pursued [in regard to apartheid] I doubt you would be alive today.'[7]

Mbeki replayed the details of his fateful meeting with Abacha over and over in his head in an attempt to figure out how things had gone so wrong. Agonising self-reflection finally led him to conclude that the military junta had acted against Saro Wiwa not because quiet diplomacy as such had failed, but because South Africa had been the sole voice of African criticism against Abacha's regime. Unschooled in the art of continental relations, the ANC government's cardinal error had been a lack of prior consultation with a wide selection of continental leaders.

Never again, Mbeki reasoned, would South Africa go it alone in opposing belligerent African despots. 'This issue [Saro Wiwa's execution] highlighted the potential limits of our influence as an individual country ... and the need to act in concert with others and to forge strategic alliances in pursuit of foreign policy objectives,'[8] he concluded.

As things went from bad to worse in Zimbabwe, Mugabe's government targeted the opposition, the media and civil society. Zimbabwe's ties with its southern neighbour run deep, dating from its colonisation in the nineteenth century, through the troubled years after the last white prime minister, Ian Smith, declared unilateral independence, to cooperation between the guerrilla armies that waged a liberation struggle on both sides of the Limpopo River. In 1922, relations between the two countries were so strong that it took a referendum to reject the prospect of then Rhodesia becoming South Africa's fifth province.

So it was hardly surprising that the embattled MDC turned to South Africa for help when its rapidly increasing membership became the target of unmitigated terror and intimidation by a small army of ZANU-PF thugs. Unassuming trade unionist and party leader Morgan Tsvangirai's first port of call was the ANC. But the ANC was not sure how it should respond, and politely directed the MDC leader to the department of foreign affairs. Dlamini-Zuma, in turn, passed the buck to the presidency, which promptly sent the MDC's envoys back to the ANC's head office.

No one at Luthuli House was prepared to make any commitments without presidential approval, however, and the president preferred to buy time so that he could consult with his counterparts in the rest of Africa.

A frustrated Tsvangirai turned next to the opposition DA and set up meetings with white South African business people who had interests in Zimbabwe. In terms of the unique dynamics of South African politics, it was a monumental blunder. The DA eagerly embraced Tsvangirai as Their Man in Zim and the MDC as a natural ally. The predominantly white party was quick to draw parallels between the ANC and ZANU-PF, playing into the hands of right-wing prophets of doom who warned that Zimbabwe's land grab was a dress rehearsal for South Africa's future. 'In fact,' charged DA leader Tony Leon, 'President Mbeki has become Mugabe's best friend, his foremost ally and his strongest defender. For President Mbeki, human rights are not fundamental.'

Mbeki was infuriated by repeated demands from white groups seeking assurances that South Africa would not face a similar scenario and by what he saw as an unwarranted preoccupation with Zimbabwe. Since far more blood was being shed in the DRC, Rwanda and Sudan, he came to the conclusion that the outcry over the situation in Zimbabwe was directly related to the fact that a handful of white farmers had died and that white livelihoods and lifestyles were under threat. Celebrated South African journalist Allister Sparks argues that many South African whites are indifferent to black suffering. Mbeki agrees, as do millions of black South Africans.

Leon was seen as deliberately arousing passions by playing on white fears that the chaos in Zimbabwe was the forerunner of South Africa's fate under a black government.[9] The ruling elite in Pretoria is extremely sensitive to the seldom stated but broad racist assumption in the West that black governments are inherently incapable of governing democratically, and tarring the ANC and ZANU-PF with the same brush not only angered Mbeki's government, but deeply influenced the way it responded to the crisis in Zimbabwe.

ANC leaders believe that since coming to power, they have done everything possible to reassure white South Africans and Western sceptics that their government represents a break in the pattern of African failure, even though this has been to the detriment, in some respects, of the majority black population. His personal animosity towards Leon aside, Mbeki could not fail to be angered by allusions to failure or mismanagement on racial grounds. Tsvangirai's approach to the DA thus severely undermined his credibility in both ANC and government circles. On the domestic front, it offered Mugabe a new excuse to accuse the MDC of being the political lackey of the West, and specifically the British and American governments. Current events provided a bonus, with Mugabe slyly suggesting that the MDC favoured 'regime change', the term so readily used to describe the US-led coalition's invasion of Iraq.

As deplorable as Mugabe's cynical exploitation of the land question is, it is, however, a very real problem, and one of colonialism's most diabolical legacies. At independence, Britain promised but never paid adequate funding to redress historical land distribution inequalities. For the first twenty years of his rule, Mugabe did nothing to alter the situation, beyond the transfer of relatively small pockets of farmland to ZANU-PF cronies, who generally let the land lie fallow. It was only when his presidency came under fire that the Zimbabwean president saw fit to use the emotionally charged land issue as a lightning rod.

Assumptions that South Africa could face the same fate as Zimbabwe are spurious. Though implementation has proceeded at a snail's pace, South Africa's land restitution policy is both clear and protected by law and the Constitution. Isolated attempts to simulate land grabs as seen in Zimbabwe were crushed swiftly and decisively.

Still, South Africans would have welcomed a statement from either the government or the ANC that unequivocally condemned the human rights abuses suffered by hundreds of thousands of black Zimbabweans and officially denouncing the violent land seizures endorsed by an autocratic Mugabe. Had Mbeki not been so afraid of accusations that he was playing to the opposition gallery, he might have remembered that the very essence of leadership is doing the right thing, even at the risk of being seen as pandering to the enemy.

The ANC government does, after all, have a land problem of its own, notwithstanding the safeguards built into the Constitution. Under apartheid, whites owned 87 per cent of the richest agricultural soil. By the end of 2001, less than 2 per cent of land had been transferred to poor, rural blacks. So, as the situation in Zimbabwe deteriorated, Mbeki's egg-dance had to address both white fears and black expectations.[10] His domestic right wing, rooted in the agricultural sector, was already unsettled by widely publicised attacks on white farmers in what they claimed was an orchestrated campaign to get them off their land, while black communities who had been forcibly removed from their land under apartheid were agitating for compensation to be accelerated. A group of disgruntled ANC supporters formed the militant Landless People's Movement for this very purpose.

The political fallout in South Africa of conditions in Zimbabwe was not lost on Mugabe, whose cunning use of the race card at every opportunity was like a red rag to a bull as far as Mbeki was concerned. When the two heads of state met, Mugabe made a point of embracing Mbeki warmly for the photographers, sending out a potent message of fraternal solidarity.

Both the foreign media and former colonial powers gave Mugabe all the ammunition he needed by focusing on the plight of white farmers. The faceless blacks who were being rendered homeless, tortured, raped and beaten to death rarely made the headlines, even in South Africa, spurring the frustrated mayor of Harare, Elias Mudzuri, to burst out at one point: 'The world must know this is not a black and white issue. It is an issue of the blacks in Zimbabwe suffering.'[11]

On the home front, Mbeki also had to take into account the bonds between ANC alliance partner COSATU and the MDC, born of Zimbabwe's trade union movement. Bad governance and corruption had caused ZANU-PF to lose touch with the grassroots supporters that had made it Zimbabwe's leading liberation movement, and many in COSATU and the SACP fear that the ANC will go the same way.

It was only natural that the workers would forge cross-border links, especially at a time when Mbeki's relations with COSATU were strained. He was well aware that many trade unionists were ready to leave the tent and form a political party that could rival the ANC, and had demanded at several heated internal meetings of the tripartite alliance that COSATU 's leaders should publicly confirm that there were no plans to form a workers' party. Their refusal to issue such statements infuriated Mbeki.[12]

At the height of the Zimbabwean land crisis, COSATU president Willie Madisha and general secretary Zwelinzima Vavi earnestly warned the ANC of the dangers of losing touch with its grassroots supporters. When COSATU launched anti-privatisation strikes in 2000 and 2001, it threw in demands for Mbeki to change his stance on both AIDS and Zimbabwe, but, typically, his reaction was to dig in his heels even further.

Sensitive to regional concerns about South African dominance both politically and economically, Mbeki never intended adopting a 'big brother' approach to Zimbabwe, lest South Africa be accused of throwing its weight around. He needed to secure the support of African leaders for NEPAD and to lay the foundations of good governance as a cornerstone of the African Union.

Mugabe played on these fears, garnering regional support among those who regarded him, rather than Mandela, as southern Africa's leading elder statesman. Troops from several of his allies were fighting side by side with Zimbabwean soldiers in the DRC, and Mugabe had survived several attempts to wrest control of the Southern African Development Community (SADC) security organ from his grip.

One of Mugabe's most powerful weapons was his close association with Libyan leader Muammar Gaddafi, whose 'oil diplomacy' had ranged a number of key African leaders behind his ambition to become the continent's leading head of state. Once loathed as the 'mad dog of Tripoli'[13] Gaddafi had bankrolled ZANU-PF's 2001 election campaign and pledged $900 000 to boost Mugabe's bid to win the 2002 presidential election, notwithstanding a legal ban on foreign funding for political parties in Zimbabwe. Gaddafi had also donated $360 million to alleviate Zimbabwe's chronic fuel crisis.[14] As other foreign countries and companies pulled their investments out of the troubled country, Libya stepped in to fill the vacuum, reportedly taking ownership of vast property holdings, state-financed corporations and the crucial oil pipeline from the Mozambican port of Beira in what amounted to barter trade for foreign currency and oil.

In continental forums, Mugabe and Gaddafi routinely derided Mbeki and his plans for an African Renaissance, placing him in an invidious position as calls mounted for South Africa to support Zimbabwe's eviction from the Commonwealth.

The last thing Mbeki wanted was to be seen as a pawn in the hands of the West, especially the US and Britain, by siding with their leaders in condemning the Mugabe regime's flagrant abuse of the rule of law. He would far rather build a broad African front to put pressure on Mugabe, using moderate regional leaders such as Botswana's Festus Mogae to publicly articulate what the South African government privately felt.

As an unapologetic proponent of African solutions for African problems, and a staunch anti-imperialist, to boot, Mbeki resisted efforts by Britain and Australia to resolve the Mugabe situation through economic sanctions, citing Kenyan author Ngugi wa Thiong'o: 'Africa actually enriches Europe, but Africa is made to believe that it needs Europe to rescue it from poverty.'[15]

On the question of Iraq, Mbeki had favoured action mandated by the UN rather than a unilateral invasion based on Washington and Whitehall's jaundiced view of which world dictators should be toppled and which, like Pakistan, should be spared because of their usefulness as allies. In his weekly newsletter on the Internet shortly before Christmas 2003, he pointedly commented that 'some within Zimbabwe and elsewhere' were treating human rights as a tool to overthrow the Zimbabwean government.[16]

Mbeki was totally opposed to the freezing of Zimbabwean assets or imposing travel restrictions on Mugabe and his officials. Any form of economic sanctions would hurt ordinary Zimbabweans the most, he reasoned, and since it would be all but impossible to muster the support of regional leaders for such drastic measures, South Africa could once again find itself going out on a limb, as with Saro Wiwa.

In contrast to prevailing wisdom, Mbeki actually believed that far more might be achieved if international pressure on Mugabe eased up. According to one of Mbeki's strategists, the thinking was that 'the old man [Mugabe] wouldn't feel so besieged and might open up more'.[17] Mbeki scored a major coup when he persuaded George W Bush, on his first state visit to South Africa, to underwrite his expertise in resolving the situation. It was a fine moment for Mbeki when Bush declared on the lawns of the Union Buildings in Pretoria: 'Mbeki is my point man on Zimbabwe.' But he was less successful at having Zimbabwe rehabilitated when the Commonwealth Heads of Government met in Nigeria shortly before Christmas 2003.

Mbeki was disappointed when the British government publicly censured Zimbabwe after he had obtained private assurances from Blair that Mugabe would be given a period of grace to set his house in order. In January 2001, Hain issued a statement to the effect that constructive engagement by African leaders – by implication Mbeki in particular – had failed to achieve results.[18] Dlamini-Zuma responded: 'We found the comments deeply offensive as the fact that Hain saw it fit to make these public, without discussing it with our government, is confirmation of the contempt in which he holds [our] government.'[19]

Mbeki nevertheless continued building regional opposition to Mugabe, preferring that public criticism come from SADC rather than South Africa. Privately, however, he was losing patience with Mugabe, and on occasion he wistfully sighed: 'Why can't he just leave, resign?'[20]

In November 2001, Mbeki and Nigerian president Olusegun Obasanjo met Mugabe in Harare. Mbeki proposed a package whereby the United Nations Development Programme (UNDP) would fund a lawful land reform strategy, thus allowing both Mugabe and Britain to save face after both had withdrawn promised financial support because of the farm invasions. The US and major Western donors had already agreed to the plan, and Mugabe accepted the offer of an 'honourable' exit. As on numerous other occasions in the cat and mouse game he was playing, Mugabe later reneged on the deal.

Fielding questions after their meeting, Obasanjo said, 'What I think Zimbabwe should do is strictly follow the law. We call on the international community to support materially that compensation, which is also part of the law.'[21]

However, having exploited the land issue to boost his image among die-hard ZANU-PF supporters, Mugabe seemed unable to backtrack as the war veterans under Hunzvi became ever more audacious. In order to break the cycle of violence, Mugabe would have to face down Hunzvi, and he had no stomach for that fight. When Hunzvi died unexpectedly, Mugabe was so far down the path of destruction that he stubbornly believed he could not turn around.

Expectations of free land had been inflamed among his rural constituency, driving Mugabe into a political cul-de-sac from which there was no escape. Any future MDC government would face the same demands for land and would have to find ways of dealing with them.

Not surprisingly, Britain and the West did not make good on the promised funding, arguing that the fickle Mugabe had done nothing to halt the brutalisation of his political opponents. Despite the fact that Mugabe had failed to fulfil his obligations in terms of the UNDP agreement, Mbeki was angered by the non-payment, believing that making at least some of the funds available would have served as an incentive for Mugabe to introduce genuine reform.

For Mbeki, 'quiet diplomacy' means abstaining from public rebuke of Mugabe while telling him privately, over a cup of tea, that some people are a little annoyed with him. He firmly believes that his greatest leverage over the ZANU-PF hardliners is a public pretence that the South African government is Zimbabwe's greatest chum. Those who consider this an unrealistic, naive or simply odd approach to international politics should consider that Blair advances a similar argument in defence of his support for Bush's policies on Iraq and Palestine. The British premier claims he is in a far better position to influence Bush by publicly agreeing with him and sorting out any differences in private. Does this make sense? No, but it is the chosen strategy of certain politicians.

According to Aziz Pahad, ZANU-PF leaders are convinced that Zimbabwe is next in line for a US-led regime change, with Mugabe going the way of deposed Iraqi dictator Saddam Hussein. They believe that the UK and other Western powers are conspiring with America to oust Mugabe because of his shameful human rights record. No doubt many would rejoice if this ever came to pass, and some have thought it so likely that Mugabe's comrade-in-arms, the equally cantankerous President Sam Nujoma of Namibia, made a ludicrous offer to place his armed forces at Zimbabwe's disposal in the event of an attack 'by colonialists bent on removing Mugabe from office'.[22]

Mugabe bought into the paranoia that the MDC, the independent press – especially the embattled *Daily News* – and civil society were in league with the Western devils, forming an embedded fifth column. According to Pahad, fear of regime change caused Mugabe and his cronies to behave irrationally,[23] hence the only way of winning their trust was to behave publicly in a manner that showed South Africa was not party to the perceived threat.

Few things rile Mbeki as much as criticism of his quiet diplomacy on Zimbabwe. 'No diplomacy is loud,' he has been known to respond angrily. Storming Mugabe's fortified posh presidential palace was never a serious consideration, but this didn't stop the president's men from interpreting criticism of South Africa's approach as a call to arms. 'What's wrong with you people? You think we can just go there and take over? Chief, that's another country,'[24] Aziz Pahad pointed out.

The government had painful memories of South Africa's Rambo-like incursion into the tiny kingdom of Lesotho in 1998 with a SADC force consisting primarily of South African and Botswanan troops. Widespread violence, fighting and looting broke out when angry citizens resisted the presence of a foreign force intent on 'restoring order', and Mbeki was haunted by fears of a repetition if South Africa resorted to military intervention in Zimbabwe.

But it was all rather disingenuous. No one ever seriously suggested that Mbeki should despatch a South African National Defence Force (SANDF) contingent across the Limpopo, but everyone involved found it surprising that he was not offering earnest support of some kind to the beleaguered human rights and political activists in Zimbabwe. Foreign assistance had, after all, been a mainstay of the liberation struggle waged by the ANC and a plethora of other organisations during the 1970s and 1980s, as MDC member of parliament, Job Sikhala, pointed out: 'What quietness are they talking about? When we supported the ANC in their fight against apartheid, it wasn't quiet diplomacy.'[25]

Mbeki's position remained unchanged. 'Look, Zimbabwe is a sovereign country, not a province of South Africa. President Mugabe does not take instructions from me. I discuss matters with him as a neighbour.'[26]

It was not that Mbeki did not think the crisis in Zimbabwe serious. On the contrary, he was convinced that if the country descended into economic and social collapse, South Africa would be the first and worst affected. Millions of desperate refugees would flood across the border in search of work, safety and food, thinly stretching already strained resources.

In fact, South Africa had already begun to feel the impact. With food shortages mounting, queues growing longer and the spectre of famine stalking rural areas, more than two million Zimbabweans had entered South Africa, most illegally by jumping the border, and were struggling to make ends meet on the mean streets of towns throughout the country by 2004.

The biggest irony was that Mbeki's reputation for sheltering Mugabe was entirely misplaced. There never was any personal or political affinity between the two men, and, if anything, Mbeki felt contempt for the ailing octogenarian whom he saw as one of the last incarnations of Africa's 'big men' – corrupt leaders who plundered the national coffers to line their own pockets handsomely. In truth, Mbeki believed that everyone concerned would be best served by Mugabe's departure from the political stage, but, to his despair, the old man refused to oblige.

As Mandela's deputy, Mbeki had snubbed Mugabe several times at diplomatic functions, refusing to acknowledge a man well known for craving affirmation and demanding respect. On one occasion, Mbeki enraged Mugabe with his 'bad manners' by using a diplomatic social event to 'lecture' the older man that the application of unwise policies over two decades was responsible for Zimbabwe's economic ills.

Mbeki would later expand on his opinion: 'For two decades, Zimbabwe had very big budget deficits to finance good things such as education, schools, rural and human resource development. For all of these things, Mugabe borrowed money, inside Zimbabwe and from the rest of the world. It couldn't be sustained.'[27]

Mugabe, in turn, holds a dim view of Mbeki, whom he regards as an arrogant young upstart who should defer to him as an elder statesman. Pig-headedly, Mugabe believes he has been passed the baton by great post-colonial leaders like Julius Nyerere, Samora Machel and Kwame Nkrumah, and that a 'youngster' like Mbeki has no right to boss him around. Moreover, Mugabe is convinced that history is on his side, and that by being forced out of office, his legacy will be destroyed. He simply cannot grasp that his legacy has already been irreparably tainted by his own actions.

Mandela's relationship with Mugabe was even more tempestuous, and tensions between the two often spilt over into the public arena. Mugabe disliked Mandela for upstaging him as the elder statesman of Africa, and Madiba's global fame and acclamation were hard for Mugabe to swallow. He especially resented Mandela's reputation as the great reconciler, believing that he had earned this title by inviting whites into his post-independence cabinet and trusting some of his former enemies with key security appointments in the aftermath of the bloody bush war.

The two men had several public spats. Mandela referred to Mugabe as 'Comrade Bob', a diminutive which the Zimbabwean leader saw as an insult, and regularly called on Mugabe to follow his example by retiring from active politics and spending more time with his family.

One of the most serious battles between the two men was over control of SADC's security apparatus.[28] Mugabe used his position to justify the sending of

Zimbabwean troops to the DRC, and it would not be until 2001 that Mandela's successor finally managed to break Mugabe's stranglehold on the regional alliance.

In truth, relations between the ANC and ZANU-PF had always been tense, even when both were fighting for liberation. The Soviet-backed ANC had a more comfortable alliance with Joshua Nkomo's Soviet-sponsored Zimbabwe African People's Union (ZAPU), while the Chinese-sponsored ZANU found common ground with the smaller Pan Africanist Congress. During Zimbabwe's first independent election, the ANC threw its support behind ZAPU.[29] ZANU-PF's victory rankled for a long time, and relations were not improved when Mugabe accused the ANC, during the first few years of his reign, of fomenting opposition to the ZANU-PF government. Hostilities run deep between Mugabe's and Mbeki's parties.

But the Mbeki government believed that if the MDC came to power, an even greater crisis would erupt, possibly even a full-blown civil war on South Africa's doorstep. Zimbabwe's security and intelligence services was packed with ZANU-PF hardliners, Pahad pointed out, and it was not impossible that they would mount a coup against an MDC government. In the interest of avoiding such a scenario, Mbeki had tried to persuade Tsvangirai that talks for a negotiated settlement should include blanket amnesty for Mugabe and his cronies, but the MDC leader was adamant that they would have to return the millions reportedly looted from the state.[30]

Ideally, the ANC would want to see ZANU-PF and the MDC sharing power, at least in the short term. The concept is not unlike the government of national unity that ruled South Africa in the immediate post-apartheid period, but Mbeki would want such a structure to exclude Mugabe and be led by someone new and moderate. The idea found no favour among ZANU-PF hardliners, for whom it amounted to a solution imposed on Zimbabwe by South Africa.

Mbeki viewed both the MDC and its leader with deep suspicion, questioning the solidity of the party's unity and Tsvangirai's leadership acumen.[31] ZANU-PF's propaganda machine had effectively painted the opposition as puppets of the hated 'colonial masters' and, by extension, stooges of South Africa's white conservatives. Other African leaders were also wary of Tsvangirai, whose apparent focus on securing Western support had not struck a chord on his own continent. The image of former colonial powers ruling by proxy was bound to anger those still suffering the consequences of that earlier era.

Based on Tsvangirai's early foreign policy forays, some African leaders were even comparing him with Frederick Chiluba, who came to power in Zambia on the back of the trade union movement, but proved a great disappointment and was eventually accused of mismanagement and cronyism.

To outsiders, the MDC had the look of a one-man show, with prominent figures such as general secretary Welshman Ncube preferring to stay in the background. On occasion, Tsvangirai was his own worst enemy, as when he forged links with the DA and COSATU before trying to build a bridge to the ANC. At other times, the MDC seemed prone to deep internal division.

When Mbeki announced in mid-2002 that the MDC and ZANU-PF were in talks behind the scenes, Tsvangirai strenuously denied that it was so. In fact, talks had indeed been taking place between senior leaders of the two parties, but curiously, Tsvangirai was kept in the dark by his negotiators.

Mbeki's personal distrust of Tsvangirai created a blind spot on Zimbabwe.[32] For him, it came down to better the devil he knew and could control – or so he thought – which meant Mugabe and ZANU-PF. The MDC was untested, and Tsvangirai reminded Mbeki of COSATU leader Willie Madisha, whom he had come to regard as a political foe. Importantly, the president was not convinced that if the MDC came to power it would refrain from taking revenge on ZANU-PF hardliners in the security forces and key business sectors, sparking renewed tension.

On visits to Harare, Mbeki pointedly refused to meet with Tsvangirai, other MDC leaders or civil society groups. This in itself was strange, since no matter how much he might dislike the party or its leaders, there was no escaping the fact that it had commanded almost 45 per cent of the popular vote, even in an election that was almost certainly rigged.

Mbeki's relationship with Tsvangirai improved only in 2004, when it became more evident to Mbeki that the investment he had made in Mugabe would come to nought. Since then, Mbeki has made an extraordinary effort to charm Tsvangirai. It must've worked, for Tsvangirai sang Mbeki's praises in the spring of 2004.

Senior ANC leaders, especially the leftists and parliamentary caucus members, were not comfortable with Mbeki and Mugabe's meetings in Zimbabwe, which the wily ZANU-PF leader shamelessly exploited as evidence that he was taken seriously by his eminent southern neighbour.[33] Conversely, of course, Mbeki's refusal to meet the MDC leader was portrayed to Zimbabweans as a sign that South Africa's leader did not take the opposition in earnest.

Mugabe and his state-controlled media used every visit by Mbeki to drum up support and show images of ZANU-PF loyalists surrounding the two men. Mugabe made a point of warmly embracing Mbeki when they met, to demonstrate their 'close' relationship, and Mbeki never publicly objected.

Every well-publicised trip to Harare by Mbeki or members of his cabinet added legitimacy to Mugabe's land grab and brutalisation of his political opponents, but it was left to Dlamini-Zuma to spell out for the world that South Africa would never condemn him: 'It is not going to happen as long as this government is in power,' she said.[34]

Notwithstanding such lavish support, Mugabe spurned every overture from Mbeki with contempt. At their meetings, Mbeki expressed sympathy with Zimbabwe's land problem, but emphasised that it had to be resolved in accordance with the rule of law; he explained that the land issue was starting to have an adverse effect on investor sentiment throughout the region; he told Mugabe that he was under enormous pressure to apply punitive sanctions against Zimbabwe. Mugabe would mouth predictable agreements and then, like a wilful child, revert to his unacceptable behaviour as soon as his visitors had departed.

Mbeki was conveying the same messages during private meetings with key members of Mugabe's government, such as former finance minister Simba Makoni, parliamentary speaker Emmerson Mnangagwa and ZANU-PF chairman John Nkomo. Mugabe's broken undertakings severely embarrassed Mbeki, since they would inevitably become manifest soon after the president had assured the South African cabinet, ANC and even world leaders that Mugabe had – finally – seen reason. Blair, Bush and Nordic leaders were among those to whom Mbeki offered his personal assurances that Mugabe was a changed man.

When they met at Victoria Falls in 2001, a desperate Mbeki even offered to have the South African government negotiate concessions for Zimbabwe from the World Bank and International Monetary Fund, if only Mugabe would apply the rule of law on land redistribution.[35] He would also try to raise funds from the EU and Scandinavian countries, as well as international organisations, to fund the land reform programme.

Even though the Zimbabwean government owed South Africa's bulk electricity supplier, Eskom, millions in arrears, Mbeki agreed not to suspend the service and to explore the possibility of raising capital for Zimbabwe in the financial markets.

When Mugabe and his financial advisors agreed to implement prudent economic policies similar to South Africa's own, Mbeki once again took him at his word. However, the presidential jet had barely landed at its home airport in Pretoria before Mugabe was up to his old tricks. Mbeki lost his patience and his temper, but Mugabe won the battle of wits, proving yet again that Mbeki was far too naive to deal with African dictators steeped in the Mugabe mould.

Business leaders now began to blame the dramatic weakening of South Africa's currency and the slow pace of investment on Mugabe's reign of terror.[36] They argued that Western investors were unable to differentiate between Zimbabwe and South Africa, since to many of them Africa is just a homogenous land mass of interlinked chaos. Meanwhile, local business was already feeling the impact on their investments in farms and commercial ventures in Zimbabwe as marauding 'war vets' systematically made their way across the length and breadth of the country.

On 24 February 2001, Mbeki's international business advisors warned him that Zimbabwe was at the root of negative perceptions about South Africa, which were blocking foreign investment, prompting him to make his toughest public statement on Mugabe to date: 'Some of the things that have been happening recently are to all of us as South Africans matters of serious concern: things that have been affecting the judges, affecting the press, apart from earlier questions having to do with land redistribution. Apart from anything else it impacts negatively on this country.'

COSATU and the SACP were Mbeki's harshest critics on Zimbabwe, especially after the ANC leadership had been cowed into submission. At COSATU's 2000 May Day rally, Madisha attacked Mugabe's oppression of workers and civil society to thunderous applause, and in Mbeki's presence. He called on the government to take a tougher stand against Mugabe, and endorsed the lament of trade unionists that black farm workers were suffering massive hardship as a result of intimidation by the war vets.

In November 2004, COSATU sent a fact-finding mission to Zimbabwe to establish at first hand just how bad the situation was. Mugabe and his security thugs turned the visit into a headline event by physically throwing them out of the country on trumped-up allegations that they had contravened immigration laws. Mbeki and his loyalists, notably ANCYL president Fikile Mbalula, were livid, and accused the trade unionists of 'adventurism' and 'grandstanding'. Worse, he accused COSATU of undermining his quiet diplomacy, but the unionists stood firm and pledged to return to Zimbabwe and complete their mission.[37]

Africanists such as Nkosazana Dlamini-Zuma, KwaZulu-Natal ANC leader Dumisani Makhaye, former ANCYL president Malusi Gigaba and ANC election coordinator Peter Mokaba were unshaken in their support of ZANU-PF. Mbeki's influential legal advisor, Mojanku Gumbi, a member of AZAPO, had made it clear to Mbeki that the Harare government should be fully supported on the land question. Defence minister Mosiuoa Lekota, on the other hand, called publicly for condemnation in the strongest possible terms of the human rights violations in Zimbabwe and slammed quiet diplomacy as totally ineffective.

Mbeki angrily demanded that Lekota withdraw his comments, but he refused, saying he had expressed a personal opinion. Gigaba quickly responded that as ANC chairman, Lekota had 'no such a thing as a personal view' and should be disciplined.[38]

When Mandela and Archbishop Desmond Tutu entered the fray, senior ANC leaders demanded that Mbeki do more in public to make it clear that South Africa and Zimbabwe were two entirely different matters, and to unequivocally condemn the lawlessness that had taken hold north of the Limpopo.

Just how grave the situation had become was evident when Reserve Bank governor Tito Mboweni abandoned protocol – central bankers generally refrain from pronouncing on political issues – and asserted that the government's stance on both AIDS and Zimbabwe was having a negative impact on South Africa's currency. When Mboweni accused Mugabe and other tyrants of being responsible for a rising tide of Afro-pessimism, Mbeki-ites like Trevor Manuel and Alec Erwin realised that something had to be said and done, if only to protect South Africa's economy. Erwin noted in Harare: 'In a short period in Zimbabwe, industrial capacity has been destroyed. What is happening to ordinary people and workers is absolutely devastating.'[39]

Ahead of Zimbabwe's March 2002 presidential election, divisions in the ANC deepened. The left wing made it clear that going to the polls in the prevailing climate of repression would be a joke, and many mainstream ANC leaders agreed. Mbeki himself believed the election would be a farce, but felt he could not support calls for the process to be suspended. He sent ANC secretary general Kgalema Motlanthe to persuade Mugabe to wait until the explosive situation had been defused, but Mugabe spurned the overture. Mbeki next sent Jacob Zuma, but he, too, failed. All that Mbeki could do was despatch a team of monitors to ensure that the elections were free and fair, though how anyone could imagine they would be, given the relentless bludgeoning of the opposition in the run-up to the ballot, was a mystery.

Controversially, the South African parliamentary observer group stood alone in declaring Mugabe's re-election free and fair. All other observers dismissed the outcome as a fallacy.

Mbeki had carefully selected the members of the South African group, and they knew going in that the president expected a final report that would vindicate the inevitable result. However, as insurance, Mbeki also sent a second, secret observer team, consisting of high court judges Dikgang Moseneke and Sisi Khampepe, to report on conditions in Zimbabwe before the elections. When they turned in an account of widespread violations, Mbeki simply ignored their report.

Following Mugabe's re-election, Mbeki quietly began to sponsor secret talks between select senior leaders of ZANU-PF and the MDC, with Motlanthe acting as mediator. Their task was to set an agenda for formal negotiations, which Mbeki firmly believed would be the quickest way to solve Zimbabwe's problems.

While the ANC tried to strengthen the hand of ZANU-PF moderates, Mbeki held secret talks with the security establishment in the hope of bringing them round to the possibility of an MDC government or co-government. South Africa also spied on key ZANU-PF officials to stay on top of what was happening within Zimbabwe's ruling party. The concept of an interim GNU proved to be the major obstacle during informal negotiations, along with the question of whether the MDC should be brought into government even before the next election. The one point on which the two parties seemed to agree was that presidential and parliamentary elections should take place at the same time in future.

All along, Mbeki's strategy was based on the concept of a ZANU-PF government with a moderate leader who would steer the country through a transition phase leading up to a fresh election. But he never envisaged a quick fix, and took the precaution of drawing comparisons with the protracted negotiations on Palestine and Northern Ireland.

Hardliners from both ZANU-PF and the MDC viewed the process with deep suspicion. One of the chief reasons Mbeki persisted with his quiet diplomacy was the threat of internal military intervention. Several times, South African intelligence reports indicated that a coup was imminent in Zimbabwe, but given the notorious lack of credible intelligence from South Africa's agencies, it would be almost impossible to make an accurate threat assessment. Unfortunately, South African intelligence has proved reliable only when harassing domestic critics of the Mbeki government, such as journalists, trade unionists and civil activists.

Privately, most senior figures in ZANU-PF have long conceded that Mugabe is a liability and that it is a question of when, not if, he goes. The longer he clings to power, the more terrible the suffering of his people and the more devastating the damage to his country's economy. One of Mugabe's litany of broken promises to Mbeki was that he would have resolved the question of succession between July 2004 and ZANU-PF's national conference in December. He gave a similar undertaking to the party's central committee,[40] but, typically, he did not indicate that he would retire immediately, or even announce a date on which he would do so. Nor did he offer any hint as to his future role.

Meanwhile, ZANU-PF was effectively paralysed as competing factions fiercely jockeyed for position in a post-Mugabe era. Mbeki's strategists were hard at work behind the scenes to influence the succession, but no one would hazard a guess about whether or not the battle would turn bloody.

None of the possible contenders could openly announce their candidacy, as to do so would invite immediate retribution by Mugabe. Whatever his decision, it would be designed to safeguard his and his wife Grace's future.

While Mugabe retained the right to anoint his successor, the balance of power was vested in the ZANU-PF hardliners and their control of the security apparatus. Emmerson Mnangagwa, the brash parliamentary speaker, was considered the frontrunner until the middle of 2004, when he was accused of corruption. Just eighteen months earlier, he had scored a major public relations coup when Mbeki gave him the chance to address the ANC's national conference. Afterwards, he never missed an opportunity to remind his rivals that he had Mbeki's ear, a crucial requirement for whoever steps into Mugabe's shoes.

The trump card held by ZANU-PF hardliners is that they have the power to destabilise any transition or future administration. They have amassed vast profits from illicit deals during Zimbabwe's ill-fated military involvement in the DRC, and fiercely oppose Tsvangirai's bid for election because he has made no secret of the MDC's expectation that their ill-gotten gains would be forfeited to the state.

John Nkomo is one of the mainstays of the party's moderate wing. As chairperson of ZANU-PF he is almost neck and neck with Mnangagwa in the popularity stakes, despite residual ethnic prejudice against him, an Ndebele, in a party dominated by Shonas. Many of the hardliners would brandish the race card if pushed into a corner, and talk with ease of Zimbabwe not yet being ready for an Ndebele president.

Vice-president Joseph Msika could have an outside chance, but lacks the party machinery and state apparatus available to either Mnangagwa or Nkomo. As Mugabe's deputy, he should have an almost automatic claim to the presidency, but Mugabe has kept him in suspense, playing him off against the other likely candidates. If Mugabe surprised everyone by quitting politics before his term expires and named Msika as the interim president, Nkomo and Mnangagwa would probably toe the party line. However, should Mugabe decide to serve his full term until 2006, the fight to take his place could turn extremely ugly.

Other possible candidates include the moderate former finance minister Simba Makoni, anti-corruption minister Didymus Mutasa, defence minister Sydney Sekeramayi and information minister Jonathan Moyo. Sekeramayi would most likely capture the support of the military.

Makoni, one of the last remnants of the party's progressive wing, does not have Mugabe's support. Moyo, who left Johannesburg's Wits University under a cloud involving alleged misappropriated research grants, had a meteoric rise up the ZANU-PF power ladder. He invested a great deal in buffing Mugabe's tarnished image and expected to be handsomely rewarded. But many ZANU-PF stalwarts considered him a snooty upstart, and his fortune depended on the whims of a fickle Mugabe. Indeed, Mugabe ousted him late in 2004, following allegations that he was preparing an internal party coup for ZANU-PF's December conference.

In the first week of December 2004, ZANU-PF's old guard, including General Solomon Mujuru, suddenly added new spice to the mix by supporting the old soldier's wife, Joyce, as Mugabe's new vice-president. A heroine of the liberation struggle, she was one of Mugabe's original cabinet appointments and his long-serving minister of water affairs and rural development.

Significantly, thanks to both her own struggle experience and that of her husband, Mujuru commands the support of the country's security establishment, the very group that could make or break the next Zimbabwean president.

Whoever takes Mugabe's place would have to reach some kind of accord with the MDC, and that, indeed, has been Mbeki's hope all along. The problem, however, is that towards the end of 2004, with Zimbabwe's next election looming large, quiet diplomacy had achieved little of any consequence for the country's starving millions or hundreds of thousands of brutalised MDC supporters.

It would be foolish to pretend anything except that the universally reviled Mugabe had outplayed the silky Mbeki at his own game. Quiet diplomacy has failed abysmally to stop the rot in Zimbabwe, but it is not in Mbeki's make-up to admit defeat.

What did surprise observers, however, was Mbeki's apparent myopia on NEPAD. His grand blueprint for an African Renaissance was thoroughly discredited by his handling of the Zimbabwe situation. Blair and Bush continued to pay lip service to the idea of an economic renewal throughout the continent, but funds were not forthcoming,[41] and some of Mbeki's strongest African allies have quietly distanced themselves from Zimbabwe.

Botswana's Festus Mogae did not want his country's spotless democratic record tainted by association, and Mbeki was shocked to discover at the Commonwealth Heads of Government meeting (CHOGM) in late 2003 how many of his other regional allies refused to side with him on Zimbabwe. Mbeki, of course, continues to believe that he will yet be proven right, but in the meanwhile, his NEPAD dream is in danger of falling on the sword of Zimbabwe.

Perhaps the greatest indictment of South Africa's 'softly-softly' approach is its gross betrayal of blacks in Zimbabwe and everything that the liberation movement fought for. As Tutu reminded the former warriors of the struggle: 'What has been happening in Zimbabwe is totally unacceptable and reprehensible, and we ought to say so. The credibility of our democracy demands this. If we are seemingly indifferent to human rights in a neighbouring country, what is to stop us one day being indifferent to them in our own?'[42]

# — 9 —

# NEPAD
# and the
# 'Big Men'

We know it is a matter of fact that we have it in ourselves as Africans to change all this. We must, in action, say that there is no obstacle big enough to stop us from bringing about a new African Renaissance. **– Nelson Mandela**

No renaissance can come out of state legislation and admonitions. States and governments can and should and must provide an enabling democratic environment, and resources. **– Ngugi wa Thiong'o, September 2003**

The programme for Africa's renewal is not a beauty contest on the catwalks of Paris, London or New York; it's about the interest of the ordinary African man, woman and child in Dakar, Abuja, Tshwane, Polokwane, Khartoum and Harare.
**– Joel Netshitenzhe, 2002**

EVERY COW IN EUROPE GETS A SUBSIDY OF $2 A DAY. IT'S EVEN HIGHER IN affluent America, Japan and Canada. In the rest of the world, more than 1.2 billion wretched men, women and children barely survive on half that much.[1] Rich countries give their farmers $320 billion in handouts, more than six times what they give poor countries in aid. The most impoverished countries on earth lose out by around $24 billion a year because of agricultural subsidies.[2]

The irony is that rich countries continually urge poor countries to open their markets, but are not prepared to open their own or reduce the huge subsidies to their farmers. Many rich countries were shocked when developing countries successfully challenged such hypocrisy at the heated World Trade Organisation (WTO) global trade talks in Cancun, Mexico, in September 2003. Outside, an outraged South Korean farmer publicly stabbed himself to death in what a friend called 'an act of sacrifice' to show his disgust at the unfairness of the WTO and international trade rules.[3]

For the first time, developing countries formed a bloc and presented a common bargaining position in the face of unbearable pressure by the rich, and despite differing interests on some issues. The emergence of a new coalition of developing countries, the G20+, which had South Africa, Brazil, China, India and Indonesia at its core, made all the difference. When the exhausted trade negotiators packed their bags and headed for home, they left the traditional powers, the EU and the US, wondering what had hit them. A puzzled deputy US trade representative, Peter Allgeier, incredulously remarked: 'It's really unclear to us what unifying principle there is among these countries.'[4]

It was all the more remarkable in light of the rich countries trying to bully and cajole their poorer cousins into breaking ranks with the G20+. The leadership was told that US trade representative Robert Zoellick had attempted to bribe vulnerable African and Latin American countries with trade incentives to get them to withdraw their G20+ support. Though this was later denied by the US, Costa Rica, El Salvador and Guatemala were offered increased trade quotas if they quit the alliance.[5]

Since 1998, South Africa had been working towards a united bloc of developing countries, so Thabo Mbeki and his trade and industry minister, Alec Erwin, could toast a rare but hard-won victory. Years of shuttle diplomacy from Johannesburg to Mumbai, Beijing, Brasilia and elsewhere had set the seal on the Cancun alliance. 'For the first time in the WTO,' Erwin enthused, 'the developing world united not on ideological grounds, but on key and well-articulated interests, acting in concert to advance its developmental agenda.'[6]

Even so, trade negotiators from some developing countries were deeply suspicious of South Africa's true motives. Some were convinced that the country would instinctively side with the West, and, as a result, despite having spear-headed early efforts to corral the opposition into a single camp, South Africa was excluded from the early horse-trading and caucusing behind closed doors. Only the persistence of Erwin and foreign minister Nkosazana Dlamini-Zuma persuaded the sceptics that without South Africa, any developing world grouping would rapidly come undone.

Obviously, if the wealthy nations of the world are to face a genuine challenge, the bonds between developing countries will have to remain strongly united. The US and EU have worked around the clock since Cancun to weaken the G20+ alliance one country at a time. There have been unprecedented efforts to change minds by suggesting that developing countries will be the biggest losers, and there is a very real danger that, having failed to impose their will on the poor at the WTO, the rich countries will aggressively pursue trade deals on an individual or regional basis. This would certainly be a blow to the cause of the developing world. South Africa knows this, along with the rest of the

G20+ alliance, and their biggest preoccupation is whether they can prevent it from happening.

In foreign policy terms, South Africa's decisive break with its apartheid past came when the ANC government positioned the country as being of the South. Under white rule, South Africa was decidedly Eurocentric and firmly bonded to the culture and character of the northern hemisphere. In May 2001, Dlamini-Zuma told parliament:[7] 'Our foreign policy is not only anchored in our domestic policy, but on the responsibility that South Africa offers hope for all humanity. We have to contribute to the ongoing struggle for a better world. Internationally, we continue to struggle for a world with the following values: democracy, good governance, people-centred development, peace, stability and security, promotion of cooperation, partnership and good neighbourliness.'[8]

Two months later, Mbeki exhorted the party faithful in Port Elizabeth: 'When we decided to address the critical question of the ANC as an agent of change, we sought to examine ourselves as an agent of change to end the apartheid legacy in our own country. We also sought to examine the question of what contribution we could make to the struggle to end apartheid globally.'[9]

Until 1994, South Africa's foreign policy centred on promoting the country's economic interests, widespread sanctions-busting and aggressive defence of apartheid, which translated to destabilising neighbouring states in southern Africa.

In the immediate post-apartheid period, Nelson Mandela was strongly influenced by a 'moralist' outlook. Throughout the liberation struggle, the ANC had received moral, financial and logistical support from countries in the West, Eastern Europe and Africa, many of which were persuaded to impose economic sanctions against South Africa on the grounds that apartheid was a crime against humanity.

A basic tenet of the moralist outlook was the debt owed by the democratic government for that support, hence Mandela's unapologetic defence of the 'new' South Africa's ties with countries such as Cuba and Libya, which had bankrolled the ANC when the British and American governments would not. Famously, Margaret Thatcher, while prime minister of Britain, had called the ANC a terrorist organisation.

Many white South Africans had been brought up to view countries like Cuba as pariahs. A decade into democracy, some could still not understand why the government condemned US interference in the internal affairs of far-flung Haiti, but the new ruling elite in South Africa felt duty bound to stand by poor black countries that lacked the power to stand up to bullies.

In Africa, the moralist position translated into the ANC pursuing mutually beneficial economic partnerships rather than hegemony, even though some of the continent's leaders were sceptical of South Africa's motives and some accused the country of using its economic muscle to bully neighbours into accepting unfavourable trade deals. Zimbabwean president Robert Mugabe was particularly incensed with Mandela on this score.

Under the dour Alfred Nzo, Mandela's foreign affairs department was lethargic, but at its national conference in 1994, the ANC identified the promotion of human rights and democracy, commitment to African development and a just world order as the pillars on which future policy should rest.

The new government lost no time joining the Southern African Development Community (SADC) with a view to shaping a strategy that would link South Africa's economy with that of the region and the global production chain. Early dividends included the transfer of a huge aluminium smelter from a planned site in South Africa to neighbouring Mozambique, at Mbeki's insistence,[10] and the scrapping by Pretoria of Mozambique's and Namibia's debts.

South Africa also negotiated a free trade deal that included other SADC countries with the European Union. It was both controversial and not entirely successful, as the southern African markets were suddenly flooded with cheap, highly subsidised EU products, and many local industries went under.

In 1996, ANC centrists, led by Mbeki, began raising questions about a foreign policy based on human rights. Deputy foreign affairs minister Aziz Pahad, one of Mbeki's closest allies, pointed out the difficulty of translating human rights commitments into diplomatic relations. 'How do we get human rights enforced and implemented in the international environment? There must be interaction between theory and practice,'[11] said Pahad.

Some were surprised that the centrists did not see support for human rights groups as a useful policy tool in undemocratic countries where most human rights violations occur.[12] But 1996 found the Mbeki-ites deflated as a result of the sudden currency crisis and failure to attract foreign investment. Mbeki identified the bogeyman as globalisation, which, he observed, 'is at the heart of international relations today [and] undermines [the] national sovereignty of countries, even more so in the developing world. However, within this international reality there are opportunities that need to be creatively used.'[13]

Amorphous though it was, Mbeki and his supporters began arguing that domestic, economic and foreign policy would have to take globalisation into account. The basic tenet of their thinking was that globalisation was ambiguous. It offered growth opportunities, but these were unevenly divided both within and between nations. Mbeki believed that in order for governments to influence globalisation, they would have to go beyond the 'atomistic nation-state and zero-sum sovereignty' and recognise their interdependence.[14]

Mbeki's foreign affairs team bore little resemblance to Mandela's. In fact, soon after becoming ANC president in December 1997, Mbeki began sweeping out the old to make way for the new thinking on foreign policy. Technocrats were appointed to important posts, with straight-talking Jackie Selebi becoming director-general in the department. The abrasive Dlamini-Zuma, who had alienated various sectors of society as health minister, succeeded Nzo, while the formidable Dumisani Khumalo was appointed ambassador to the United Nations. Trade and industry minister Alec Erwin and deputy president Jacob Zuma became increasingly visible in the international arena, while finance governor Trevor Manuel and Reserve Bank governor Tito Mboweni were frequently in the front line. Mandela was a key, albeit ad hoc, member of the team, using his position to say things that Mbeki, as head of state, was either reluctant or strategically unable to say publicly, such as strongly criticising the US-led invasion of Iraq.

The new foreign policy placed much emphasis on poor governance in Africa, both political and economic, being responsible for negative perceptions in the investor community. As economist Stephen Gelb put it:

> There is some evidence that Africa suffers from being perceived by investors as a bad neighbourhood. Africa as a whole is rated as significantly more risky than is warranted by these [economic fundamentals]. Notwithstanding the evidence that the South African state has some clear dissimilarities from other states in Africa, South Africa's growth and investment performance were affected [by poor governance on the rest of the continent].[15]

After the introduction of GEAR, the new market-friendly macroeconomic frame-work, in June 1996, most exchange controls were abolished, the banking system opened to foreign competition and short-term financial flows rose rapidly as South Africa became a favourite 'emerging market' for institutional investors abroad. In the first six months of 1996, the rand had devalued by 20 per cent,[16] but when Manuel and Erwin[17] pointed out that industrialised countries were not immune to global spillovers either, Mbeki assured the edgy ANC leadership that there was no need to introduce Malaysian-style capital controls. In the global village, it was not only currency and financial crises in one country or group of countries that affected others, but also socio-economic problems such as HIV/AIDS, crime and international terrorism.[18]

By the middle of 1998, the Asian financial contagion reached South Africa. Capital flows suddenly reversed from an inflow of R16 billion during the first four months of the year to an outflow of R7 billion over the next two months. The rand lost an average of 16 per cent against major currencies between May and August, and share prices on the Johannesburg Stock Exchange fell by 33 per cent.

Mbeki again offered assurances that there was no need to panic. 'We must get to the root of the problem,'[19] he suggested. His trusted lieutenant, Joel Netshitenzhe, counselled, 'We need to look at ways to address poor governance in Africa and communicate the difference between the "good governance" African states and the "poor governance" ones.'

'Look,' enjoined Mbeki, 'the world financial architecture is working against developing countries. We must change this.'[20] South Africa had to become actively involved in efforts to transform the world's financial system in order to prevent further economic destabilisation of the country by greedy financiers. On the other side of the globe, Malaysia's Mahathir Mohamed cried out: 'The only thing that can stop this [financial crises] is if we have order in the international financial system. There is total anarchy.'[21]

Erwin agreed wholeheartedly, siding with Manuel and Mbeki's calls for South African resources to be resolutely marshalled to push for reform of the World Bank and IMF, and an equitable new round of trade negotiations in the WTO. The idea was not to abolish these institutions, but to make the rules of global governance more fair and transparent. Only then, South Africa argued, would developing countries have a greater degree of protection and room to manoeuvre in a highly unequal global distribution of power.[22]

New alliances needed to be struck with both rich and poor countries, and South Africa had to reposition itself as a 'bridge' between North and South.[23] To this end, the country needed to secure a more prominent role in multilateral organisations, including a permanent seat in the United Nations Security Council.

Africa was much too divided and chaotic, Mbeki charged. Having lived in various African countries for extended periods while in exile, many ANC members of his generation were disparaging of conditions north of the Limpopo. Africa needed to unite in order to have a more influential voice in international forums and to pool its markets. Those in Mbeki's camp believed that the onus was on South Africa to spearhead this solidarity, since the country would be sub-Saharan Africa's new growth engine.

The consensus of opinion in the North was that better governance was a prerequisite for alleviating poverty and disease on the continent, and South Africa had to accept that it was also a global public good. Moreover, the country's economic strength and democratic credentials made it the obvious, if not only, African state that could offer the leadership required for global initiatives. Gelb argues that one of the strongest motivations for NEPAD was the North's demand for interaction with African leaders, and others from the South, in the context of the annual G7 meetings and other multilateral forums.

Better governance was certainly lacking in much of Africa, with leaders routinely abusing power and plundering the state coffers to line their own pockets, but good governance does not automatically translate into more investment or economic growth. Respected development economist Jeffrey Sachs notes that the US did not withhold development assistance pending good governance in

Afghanistan and Iraq.[24] Furthermore, even a cursory glance at the statistics shows that over a fifteen-year period the African countries that attracted the most FDI, including Angola, Nigeria and Gabon, have some of the worst governance ratings on record. Of course, most of them also happen to have vast oil reserves.[25]

At the SADC summit in Malawi in September 1997, Mandela told the assembled heads of state:

> Our dream of Africa's rebirth as we enter the new millennium depends as much as anything on each country and each regional grouping on the continent committing itself to the principles of democracy, respect for human rights and the basic tenets of good governance. Among SADC's basic principles are respect for the sovereignty of member states and non-interference in one another's internal affairs. This is the basis of good governance on the inter-state level. But these considerations cannot blunt or totally override our common concern for democracy, human rights and good governance in all our constituent states. Can we continue to give comfort to member states whose actions go so diametrically against the values and principles we hold so dear and for which we struggled so long and so hard?[26]

From the moment he became the ANC president, and thus Mandela's heir apparent, Mbeki pondered the question which those in his inner circle claim cost him many a sleepless night. How was he to stamp his own image on the country's highest office when the larger-than-life Mandela vacated it?

The answer, say members of his inner circle, came to him early one morning in the cabin of an aircraft ferrying him to Europe. He would follow his natural calling to lead an economic, spiritual, social, cultural and political renewal of the entire African continent.

By 2001, Mbeki was ready to translate his vision into a policy framework, the New Partnership for Africa's Development (NEPAD), and the African Renaissance could begin. Inspired to change the country, the continent and, indeed, the world, into a caring society and fortified with a new ideology, South Africa rushed to end crippling wars that give Africa a bad name. Vast amounts of time and money were spent on efforts to broker peace in Angola, Burundi, the DRC and the Sudan.[27]

South Africa also offered to export its mediation skills to the Middle East and Northern Ireland, but on the economic front, the priority was to make the SADC region a free trade zone, so that it would have bigger bargaining power when talking to the EU, the North American Free Trade Agreement (NAFTA), Japan and China.

Ultimately, the Mbeki-ites would like to see a free trade zone running the full length of Africa, from Cape Town to Cairo, much as arch-colonialist Cecil John Rhodes dreamt of linking the economies of the northern and southern halves of the continent. The EU has signed free trade agreements individually with SADC, Egypt and the Maghreb, while the US and some countries in sub-Saharan Africa that adhere to its conditions of good governance, including South Africa, have a selective trade pact called the African Growth and Opportunity Act (AGOA). The pact is heavily weighted in favour of America and many African businesses have collapsed against the unfair competition.

Taking a leaf from the Clinton–Gore administration's book, Mbeki has set up bi-national commissions with Nigeria, Egypt and Algeria. South Africa's new strategic allies in the developing world are Brazil, which has the largest economy in Latin America, and India, the world's most populous democracy. Negotiations for a free trade area between the SADC countries and Brazil and between South Africa and India have been launched, which, if successful, would expose the highest number of people on earth to free trade. What excites the Mbeki-ites is that the proposals would facilitate free trade between developing countries, something close to their hearts, but SADC is wary and would have liked extensive consultations on this controversial matter.

South Africa is also behind the ambitious reincarnation of a tri-continental alliance of leading developing countries as the G5. Since inception, the G5 – Brazil, Egypt, India, Nigeria and South Africa – has fought double standards in global trade and financial systems, which place relentless pressure on the poorest countries to open their markets to those of the EU, NAFTA and Japan, while farm subsidies block Third World food exports to the rich North. The group interacts with the G8 as the voice of the Non-Aligned Movement, or G77, and masterminded the G20+ rebellion at Cancun.

The ANC government's focus on the developing world has caused consternation among white opponents accustomed to the North being the standard-bearer for foreign relations. The largely Anglophile DA tends to take its lead on foreign policy from the US and Britain, and is 'disinterested in, and often critical of, the entire non-aligned, developing world focus of the ANC-led government'.[28] But Mbeki is determined that South Africa must be seen as speaking on behalf of the developing world and in empathy with other victims of oppression. The sentiment does not appear to have filtered down to the rank and file, however, and incidents of xenophobia against black émigrés from the rest of Africa have become commonplace on the streets of South Africa's cities.

Driven by economic development, Mbeki's African Renaissance could hold the key to a bright new future for a continent that has known centuries of exploitation, colonialism and fragmentation. But, as respected analysts Peter Vale and Sipho Maseko have argued, the concept is high on sentiment but low on substance.[29]

The truth is, Mbeki wanted it that way. The African Renaissance was never meant to be an ideological objective; it is Mbeki's rallying cry to unite South Africans – black and white – behind a vision of the future. Just as he envisages South Africa surfing the wave of new technology and turning globalisation to its advantage, he sees the rest of the continent following suit.

Both intellectually and emotionally, Mbeki is intent on proving Afro-pessimists wrong.[30] He deems it vital to keep South Africa on the map and at the forefront of international consciousness, firmly believing that a positive image of the country will eventually attract foreign investors.

So the country continues to place itself in the running for major international events like the Olympic Games, and the football and rugby world cups. Some of the Africanists in Mbeki's camp quite literally see the African Renaissance as a romantic embracing of a mythical Africa steeped in culture, literature and folklore.

However, success depends on the support of intellectuals, both at home and further afield. The ANC's Africanist and business wings have heard the call, but black intellectuals have not yet entered the debate. When they do, their concerns are bound to include criticism of Africa's ruling elite, and if that debate is smothered, the African Renaissance will choke.

The ANC's left wing simply dismisses the concept as a diversion from the real problems facing South Africa. At a meeting of the SACP's central executive committee, deputy general secretary Jeremy Cronin slammed the concept as being an escapist ploy to avoid dealing with the hard issues of poverty and unemployment. Essop Pahad, Mbeki's soulmate and minister in the presidency, was incensed. 'How can the [SACP] have a discussion on the African Renaissance without coming to me first?' he demanded. 'I am the minister in charge of the African Renaissance in the Office of the President.'

Cronin sent Pahad a note asking: 'Did the Italian renaissance have someone in charge? Which of the two obvious personalities was charged with that responsibility? Was it Leonardo or Machiavelli? Which one do you think you are?'[31]

However, it would be a mistake to reject the concept out of hand. Certainly, Mbeki's timing has been perfect. Vale and Maseko note:

Most Africans consider themselves to be marginalised from the affairs of their countries, the continent and the world. To succeed, an African Renaissance must end the economic discrimination the continent faces and blunt the anger that people of colour, not only in Africa, but all over the world, feel towards an international system that reinforces what has justifiably been referred to as global apartheid.[32]

Thus, success will lie not in rhetorical flourishes, but in putting bread on the tables of ordinary Africans, giving them a say in how their countries are run, and making their rulers accountable.

Unfortunately, the biggest beneficiaries so far have been those who were already well off, just as was the case with the transition from oppression to democracy. South Africa's white businesses are riding the crest of the African Renaissance wave and the government's outreach to developing countries. NEPAD has been seized on just as eagerly, giving rise to an entire cottage industry of conferences, dinners, workshops and consultancies, and white South African accents can now be heard throughout 'darkest' Africa, as business has conquered the continent.

While new investment has been welcomed, many Africans complain that the white entrepreneurs have carried with them loathsome and uncaring labour practices and racist interpersonal skills. In Mozambique, one of 'white' South Africa's favourite getaways, the pristine shoreline is being systematically destroyed by columns of four-wheel-drive vehicles, now banned on South Africa's own beaches.

Sadly, in many cases, South Africa's black business people are no different and treat local inhabitants of other African states with barely disguised disdain. Parastatals such as Eskom and Transnet have stormed ahead to capture the continent and now have stakes in many African countries. Over the three years from 1998 to 2000, South Africa's trade with the rest of the continent grew by 36 per cent, with an estimated cumulative surplus of R60 billion.[33]

But South Africa's role as a continental powerhouse is viewed with deep suspicion elsewhere on the continent. Concerns that the country instinctively sides with the West were reinforced when South Africa hosted the UN conference on racism in 2001. Most African leaders wanted reparations placed on the agenda, but when countries such as Denmark and Germany threatened to slash aid if this plan went ahead, Mbeki found himself in a quandary. In the end, his ally, Nigerian leader Olusegun Obasanjo, managed a face-saving compromise that saw the issue of reparations watered down.

When South Africa bid to host the 2004 Olympics, not a single first-round African vote was in favour. Likewise, when South Africa won the bid to host the 2010 Football World Cup, none of the African ballots played a role.

With the fuzzy African Renaissance framework in place, the Mbeki-ites turned their attention to the need for fresh leaders and credible economic policies.[34] Finding the new leaders presented the bigger problem, as there was never any doubt that GEAR should serve as the economic model for the rest of the continent.

Mbeki criss-crossed Africa to sound out leaders with the right democratic credentials to champion the plan, courting Senegal's Abdoulaye Wade, Nigeria's Olusegun Obasanjo, Algeria's Abdelaziz Bouteflika, Tanzania's Benjamin Mkapa, Botswana's Festus Mogae and Mozambique's Joachim Chissano.

He put business-friendly accountant Wiseman Nkuhlu in charge of assembling the nuts and bolts of what would ultimately become known as NEPAD, but the entire concept came close to being aborted when Wade, with French backing, came up with a hastily conceived rival plan that would effectively divide French-speaking Africa from the rest. With Obasanjo's help, Mbeki managed to persuade Wade that the two plans should be married, and warned him to beware of falling into the Western trap of divide and rule.

NEPAD was touted as nothing less than the African equivalent of America's Marshall Plan, which rebuilt Europe after the Second World War.[35] Manuel waxed lyrical over the emergence of NEPAD 'when the global economy is pregnant with favourable opportunities'.[36] Its true purpose, however, is to serve as the centrepiece of the Mbeki government's initiatives 'to address what is wrong in the world', as Manuel put it.

Initial response from the ANC's left was derisive. Mbeki would be better served, they argued, by putting his energy into domestic delivery as the best antidote to negative perceptions and Afro-pessimism. In time, the left would come round, if somewhat reluctantly, so that when COSATU's powerful central committee stated that there was 'a need for Africans to undertake an initiative to ensure better governance, end conflicts and embark on sustainable development',[37] the SACP would agree.

Netshitenzhe deflected accusations of NEPAD being a placebo as follows:

This is not merely a matter of African patriotism or some ephemeral love for the continent, but is impelled by profound South African self-interest. How so? South Africa shall never be an island in a sea of poverty. Furthermore, a growing aggregate demand in Africa is critical for South Africa's own industrial development. South Africa has its own medium and long-term needs in respect of such resources as water and energy, and the potential presented by such marvels as the Congo River Basin not only present [sic] opportunities for South Africa, but will help create mutual dependencies that are crucial for true integration.[38]

Few would disagree that only radical action could turn the continent's fortunes. Africa houses 10 per cent of the world's population, more than 30 per cent of the world's poorest people and 70 per cent of the global number of people living with HIV/AIDS. The continent exports 30 per cent more now than it did in 1980, but receives 40 per cent less income than it did then. After more than a decade of structural adjustment programmes, unemployment rates were pegged at an average of 35 per cent continent-wide. Sub-Saharan Africa has a foreign debt of more than $170 million, and pays creditors $40 million a week to service debts accumulated as a result of the Cold War, apartheid and failed projects.[39]

NEPAD was not the first attempt to fashion an Africa-wide development initiative, but several earlier homegrown plans were quickly shot down by international financial institutions like the World Bank. They did not fit into the ubiquitous Washington consensus paradigm.

Critics of NEPAD complain that it too closely mimics the Washington consensus on governance and fiscal management and is likely to further subjugate the continent within the global system, enslaving Africa's economies and leading to further marginalisation of its people.

As George Monbiot, writer and columnist with the London *Guardian*, observes, 'African countries can demand a change of government, but they cannot demand a change in policy. Democracy in Africa is meaningless until its leaders are prepared to challenge the external control of their economies.'[40]

While its supporters claim that NEPAD is the first comprehensive development plan for Africa to come out of Africa alone, critics counter that it is designed to please foreign donors and investors rather than the continent's own governments and citizens.

British prime minister Tony Blair certainly likes it. 'This is the best chance in a generation for us to make the partnership [between the West and Africa] work,' he said effusively while on a tour of four African states.[41]

These were sentiments endorsed by Mbeki when he addressed the UN, but he emphasised that the partnership had to be based on an equal footing: 'We seek to ensure that we move away from the donor–recipient relationship with the developed world to a new partnership based on mutual respect as well as shared responsibility and accountability.'[42]

Partnership in a context of disproportionate power relations amounts to little more than domination. Instructively, a UK Foreign Office briefing proclaimed: 'They have defined a new paradigm for the development relationship. We are dancing to their tune, but at least it is our own dance!'[43]

Some critics argued that NEPAD has given a lifeline to global financial institutions such as the World Bank, IMF and WTO, which face a huge credibility crisis. International financial and currency volatility, such as the Asian crash, no longer affects only rich countries,[44] and civil society groups in developed countries have stepped up pressure on their governments to pursue more equitable policies.

Trade liberalisation is a key aspect of NEPAD, but it is difficult to imagine how this will benefit Africa. Developing countries are subject to tariff barriers that are four times higher than those faced by rich countries.

Global financial structures effectively give the rich world complete economic control over the poor. The richer the nation, the more IMF votes it has. The World Bank is run by 'donor' nations, with all the important decisions being taken in Washington. Inevitably, they come down to the reduction of a state's role to care for its citizens. The consequences for democracy are devastating.

NEPAD's engineers consciously tried to avoid the politically charged language of historical justice and reparations, while nevertheless accepting that colonialism and the Cold War have contributed to Africa's problems. The continent's foreign debt burden, much of it arguably illegitimate, represents one of the single largest obstacles to development. The current international debt relief framework, the Heavily Indebted Poor Countries (HIPC) initiative, has failed to resolve Africa's debt crisis.[45]

NEPAD argues that development is contingent on key local priorities: peace, security, democracy and political governance; economic and corporate governance; a new focus on public finance management; and regional cooperation and integration. African leaders have to commit themselves to good governance, respect for human rights, democracy and sound economic policies, and will monitor one another through a peer review mechanism.

NEPAD sees the state creating an environment conducive to investment by protecting property rights, guaranteeing the rule of law, and providing a social and economic infrastructure. However, the plan fails to recognise that the African state is traditionally weak due to the colonial legacy of fragmentation and the effects of economic globalisation.[46] The 'failing state' is at the heart of Africa's underdevelopment.[47]

With few exceptions, African countries had no proper state to speak of at independence. They had to start from scratch to foster the rule of law and create one regime where none existed, or where there were different systems of religious or ethnic law. 'Building a modern state is much more urgent.'[48]

Many African countries do not have properly elected and constituted national legislatures, but are instead ruled by one-party systems, military regimes and monarchies. This is a crucial issue, since NEPAD's decision-making structures must comprise delegates from national parliaments,[49] and the entire plan is based on the concept of good governance in Africa in exchange for investment from the North. But as the respected scholar Mahmood Mamdani argues,[50] South Africa's paltry post-apartheid FDI should be a warning to the naive.

Nonetheless, NEPAD has a number of admirable goals that essentially reflect those of the UN Millennium Development programme:[51] an annual African growth rate of 7 per cent for 15 years; cutting poverty in half by 2015; reduction of infant mortality rates by 66 per cent; a 25 per cent reduction in maternal mortality rates; and schooling for every eligible child.

To attain these goals, NEPAD has two broad approaches. Firstly, it will focus on specific economic projects, such as building a hydroelectric dam at Inga on the Congo River, and the introduction of new farming techniques. A continental electricity grid is envisaged by 2010, mass production of generic anti-AIDS drugs will be launched in South Africa, and a 'dot force' of specialists teaching computer skills will be created. African leaders will embark on concentrated efforts to identify the continent's comparative advantages and aggressively market them.

Secondly, NEPAD will focus on longer-term political changes designed to entrench the rule of law, good governance and business codes among participating countries.

But the plan is vague on detail and there is much confusion over its policy prescriptions. The architects say vagueness is essential to secure the widest possible backing for the plan, which is still being discussed at the level of heads of state.[52]

Where will the money come from? The hope is that the envisaged 7 per cent growth rate would be achieved on the back of increased exports and by securing an additional $64 billion in investment each year.

The fundamental difference between NEPAD and earlier African development plans is the strong focus on democracy and good governance, and the call for a new international partnership between Africa and the North. NEPAD 'breaks new ground in speaking to Western democracies in Western democratic language'.[53] Proponents of the plan argue that in the prevailing global climate, NEPAD represents the only pragmatic option for getting anything at all from the rich countries, and that a more radical set of proposals would have been a non-starter.

Where does the African Union (AU) fit in?

With the end of the Cold War, African dictators could no longer be propped up by rich Western countries prepared to turn a blind eye as long as their allegiance lay with the West. Even the most brazen African tyrants had to take note that democratisation was the ticket to foreign aid, and with this came a growing realisation that the Organisation of African Unity (OAU) was not up to the challenge of the dawning new era.

The OAU charter placed undue emphasis on the security and sovereignty of states and the principle of non-interference in the internal affairs of member countries. It was ill equipped to deal with the proliferation of coups and authoritarian rule on the continent,[54] hence either a new organisation or radical reform was needed. With the end of apartheid, the OAU had been stripped of its very *raison d'être*, the liberation of Africa.

African leaders opted for reform, and the process began with the review of some elements of the 1991 treaty establishing the African Economic Community, commonly known as the Abuja Treaty. At an extraordinary OAU summit in Sirte, Libya, in 1999, the treaty was revised, placing strong emphasis on popular participation and human security as opposed to the security of states. The AU has no minimum democratic, governance or performance requirements for membership. The changes were adopted at the OAU summit in Togo in 2000.

South Africa entered the debate quite late, having been excluded from OAU membership under apartheid. Democratic South Africa was initially quite sceptical about attempts to reform the organisation, and in the immediate post-1994 period the ANC's foreign policy moralists favoured doing away with the OAU altogether.

However, when it appeared that Libyan leader Muammar Gaddafi's control over the organisation could result in negative spillover for South Africa, Mbeki's foreign policy mandarins began taking more interest. Their chief concern was that Gaddafi's image in the West as a tyrant would damage Mbeki's efforts to market NEPAD.[55]

The ever-pragmatic president persuaded ANC leaders that since the AU had become an established fact, it should be wrested from the clutches of 'bad' leaders with dubious records. Though loosely based on the European Union, the AU model adopted in Durban in July 2002 had South Africa's footprint all over it. Many of Africa's 'big men' were not impressed and resented the manner in which South Africa had usurped control of 'their' baby.

Gaddafi, ailing former Kenyan leader Daniel arap Moi and Zimbabwean strong-man Robert Mugabe were Mbeki's chief opponents. Arab leaders in Africa had fallen out with Gaddafi in 1998, when they refused to endorse an OAU resolution rejecting UN sanctions against Libya for refusing to hand over the two suspects in the 1988 bombing of an aircraft over Lockerbie, Scotland.

Having failed to unite the Arab world behind him, Gaddafi turned to Africa as his new support base. Inaction by the continent's major players, such as Nigeria, South Africa and Egypt, left him with a free hand to dominate AU politics.

Gaddafi has never hesitated to use his country's vast oil and gas riches to promote his foreign policy objectives in Africa and in the Arab world, and his most willing backers have been countries that benefited from Libyan aid. At Sirte, for example, he paid the arrear membership fees of The Gambia, Cape Verde, the Central African Republic, Chad, Equatorial Guinea, Ethiopia, Lesotho, Madagascar, Niger, Malawi and Mali to enable them to meet OAU requirements for participation in the pre-AU proceedings and voting.

Gaddafi's trepidation about Mbeki's rise to international prominence was not misplaced. Although the oil king had been at the forefront of the AU's formation, Mbeki soon eclipsed him. In his reinvention of himself as a man of peace, Gaddafi has increasingly emerged as Mbeki's rival in Africa, and, internationally, in both the economic and political spheres.

Western leaders, previously the Libyan's harshest critics, were charmed by the oil largesse The Leader offered. In April 2004, Tony Blair managed a smile under his stiff upper lip as he sipped tea in the former pariah's desert tent, surrounded by throngs of Gaddafi's trademark women guards. A month later, Gaddafi was enthusiastically received by European Commission president Romani Prodi in Brussels,[56] when he proclaimed that Libya would be the new bridge between Europe and Africa.

Long before, Gaddafi had convinced many African leaders that he genuinely had the continent's best interests at heart. Former Zambian president Kenneth Kaunda warmly acknowledged this, and UN secretary general Kofi Annan told the OAU summit in Lusaka: 'I would like to pay tribute to leader Gaddafi for spearheading this development [formation of the AU].'[57]

Mbeki and the new generation of African leaders saw NEPAD as crucial to a renaissance and fully supported its good governance foundations. Gaddafi and the old guard, on the other hand, viewed talk of good governance with contempt, and dismissed NEPAD as a plot by Western imperialists to yet again hold Africa hostage. 'It's a creation of colonial capitalists and racists,'[58] the Libyan leader raged. The direction in which Mbeki tried to steer the AU galled him.

Libya was one of the backers of a controversial resolution by African foreign ministers on the eve of the AU's Lusaka summit that expressed support for Mugabe's controversial land policies, without a whimper about the ZANU-PF-inspired violence in that country. Mbeki and Obasanjo had to work hard to block the resolution, and finally got it watered down to a fairly innocuous statement supporting continued talks on the issue between Britain and its former colony.

The eventual battle for control of the AU pitted Africa's old guard, personified by Gaddafi, against the Young Turks, associated with Mbeki. The old guard still ranted against colonialism and the need for Africa to carve out a future independent of the West. The Young Turks maintained that the development discourse had undergone a fundamental shift, and that Africa needed to be integrated into the global economic system and engage the West more directly.

Gaddafi wanted the new organisation to be called the United States of Africa, headquartered in Tripoli. He offered a plush palace in the Libyan capital for this purpose, and hinted that Dlamini-Zuma could be the AU's first foreign minister, with himself as the organisation's leader.

The Mbeki camp saw something more like the EU, with member states retaining their own identities, and the AU working closely with the North. The battle extended to which countries would have seats in the proposed Peace and Security Council, modelled on the UN's Security Council. This would be one of the AU's most powerful organs, with the authority to intervene in the affairs of member states and deploy a combined African military force to trouble spots or on peacekeeping missions.

Gaddafi saw the main purpose of the force as protecting the continent from external aggression, while Mbeki's vision was for a peacekeeping force that could intervene in local conflict. The Mbeki camp won the day.

Gaddafi and the old guard were vehemently opposed to inclusion of a prescription for good governance in the AU charter. Last-minute intervention by South Africa ensured that the draft charter made good governance and a culture of human rights prerequisites for accrual of benefit from NEPAD.[59] South Africa also proposed that the AU would have the right to act when human rights were trampled.[60] The proposed charter made provision for the AU to 'intervene in a member state pursuant to a decision of the assembly in respect of grave circumstances, namely war crimes, genocide and crimes against humanity'. Any member state failing to comply with the decisions and policies of the union 'may be subjected to sanctions'.[61]

At the AU's launch, Mbeki and his allies lost the fight over whether or not NEPAD should be placed under the organisation's control, and, by implication, be subject to veto by the likes of Gaddafi. More importantly, the yardstick for good governance, the peer review system, was placed under the AU's direct control. This was a major setback for Mbeki and his allies.

NEPAD will be absorbed into the AU's proposed council on security, stability, development and coordination. Mbeki had hoped to locate a NEPAD secretariat within the UN Economic Commission for Africa, and thus at arm's length from the AU, but it will not be situated within the organisation, and it remains to be seen how independently NEPAD will be able to operate in the circumstances.

Africa's old guard also lobbied successfully for NEPAD's steering committee to be increased from fifteen to twenty heads of state.[62] Mbeki had hoped that only leaders with sound democratic credentials would serve on the committee, but the Young Turks agreed to a compromise that would allow Gaddafi and other members of the old guard into the 'NEPAD Club' in exchange for Durban, rather than Tripoli, being the venue for the AU's launch. Mbeki and his supporters were determined that the AU be launched anywhere but Tripoli in order to protect the credibility of the organisation.

Mugabe, Moi and Gaddafi have made it clear that they will brook no examination by fellow Africans as part of a peer review process, and the AU foreign ministers are treading cautiously on Zimbabwe. This presents a dilemma, for if the AU is to gain the credibility it seeks, it cannot afford to vacillate on the subject of Africa's remaining strongmen.

The new breed of African leaders face the task of succeeding where Ghana's Kwame Nkrumah failed, namely to persuade a majority of African governments to incrementally transfer real power and budgets to the Pan African Parliament and submit to the judicial rulings of a continental court. Only then will they be able to talk about real progress.[63]

The mainstay of NEPAD's plan to hold African states accountable to good governance rests on the peer review mechanism, whereby heads of state and governments will agree to an external assessment of how well they are fulfilling their obligations. The purpose is to encourage the adoption of policies, standards and practices that lead to political stability, high economic growth, sustainable development, and accelerated regional and continental economic integration.[64] Participation 'has to be voluntary – you are not going to be able to get people to live up to specific commitments on the basis of compulsion'.[65]

Whether or not the system has any teeth will be determined by what measures are taken against errant countries. Herein lies the rub. Will Africa have the political will to act against its own when agreement cannot even be reached over how the peer review system should be applied in practice? The old guard favours encouragement rather than public criticism to bring about behaviour change, with Gaddafi, for example, insisting that Africa has its own style of governance, democracy and political culture, which needs to be preserved. 'We don't want imposed conditions.'[66]

Mbeki also advocates use of the carrot rather than the stick, with countries ranked as good performers reaping the rewards of aid, trade and investment.[67]

Would this inspire the bad apples to mend their ways? Think again.

Despite claims that NEPAD is 'African-owned', civil society groups and some governments have questioned where they fit into the new partnership. COSATU general secretary Zwelinzima Vavi summed up popular anger when he slammed the fact that many African statesmen with questionable democratic credentials were spearheading the plan.[68] Leading African intellectuals have commented: 'In spite of recognition of the central role of the African people in the plan, the African people have not played any part in the concept.'[69] To this, Mbeki invited critics to 'join the structures of NEPAD and try to influence it to adopt some of their policy positions'.[70]

The fundamental flaw is that NEPAD was formulated in typical Mbeki policy-making style: small groups of like-minded experts sweat it out in seclusion, shielded from elected representatives and institutions. Bilateral meetings or one-on-one meetings are then held with interest groups to get them on board. Without African grassroots support, NEPAD is doomed to sink beneath the quicksand of a credibility gap. GEAR is a stark lesson in this respect.

What NEPAD's architects omitted is rather instructive. The plan makes little reference to human rights, and, where it does, this is largely rhetorical. Nor does it say much about the crippling HIV/AIDS pandemic sweeping the continent and threatening to lay waste already frail economies and fragile societies.

Nevertheless, NEPAD has been effective in some areas. For the first time, Africa's ills are not all laid at the door of the West, and there is acknowledgment that the continent's own shortcomings have contributed to its precarious position. Moreover, the plan has caught the attention of ordinary citizens, even if only to wonder what the fuss is all about, to an extent that no previous continental proposal has done. NEPAD also placed Africa at the forefront of international debate, albeit fleetingly, until anti-terrorism noise drowned out just about everything else.

But the earliest example of how the good governance concept can be abused by the North confirmed the worst fears of many. While there was fairly widespread support for Zimbabwe's suspension from the Commonwealth, Britain's threat to cut NEPAD's funding if South Africa did not act against Mugabe provoked accusations that colonial attitudes would poison the new partnership. Canadian prime minister Jean Chretien warned that NEPAD would risk losing 9.5 billion Canadian dollars if it did not include a political peer review.[71]

NEPAD's biggest danger is that it could collapse due to a lack of funds. Unless it secures foreign investment, it could become just another pointless product of vanity. While the G8 countries have lauded the plan, they have been in no rush to show Africa the money. Blair, in fact, sought to undermine NEPAD by setting up his own internal commission on Africa.

Ultimately, the solution to Africa's deep-seated but not insurmountable problems lies in the development of the continent's natural resources by its own people. Africa has proved immensely rich in oil, with new reserves being discovered almost every year in certain regions. It also has an abundance of minerals and precious metals, which outsiders are all too eager to exploit. The World Bank would like nothing better than gaining control of the war-torn DRC's vast mining operations.[72]

Until Africans themselves develop and reap the rewards of these munificent riches, and routinely apply good political and economic governance, the future of the continent will never be secure.

# — 10 —

# What's Wrong
# with Being
# Filthy Rich?

What I fear is that the liberators emerge as elitists ... who drive around in Mercedes Benzes and use the resources of this country ... to live in palaces and to gather riches.                              – Chris Hani, *Beeld*, 29 October 1992

THE SELECT CLUB OF SOUTH AFRICANS CLASSIFIED AS 'ULTRA-MILLIONAIRES' jumped from fewer than 150 white, old-money families and individuals in 1994 to 690 of all races in the first decade of democracy.[1]

To join the club, one needs R200 million in cash or assets. Banking watchdog VIP Forum[2] estimates that by 2004 there were 25 000 dollar millionaires living in South Africa, holding at least $300 billion in private wealth. That is more than that the GDP of the Southern African Development Community.

In itself, this might not matter much, but the other side of the coin is that 22 million South Africans eke out an existence in abject poverty.

Business leaders have a special seat at President Thabo Mbeki's fireside. He has overseen this dizzying rise in the number of super-rich, but beyond that, the 'business-friendly president' has little to show for allowing business leaders unprecedented influence in shaping government policy and direction. Very few of the new rich put their money into bricks and mortar; they much prefer to simply acquire more money. Local business has been slow to invest in the economy.

COSATU angrily called it an 'investment strike'.[3] Foreign investors, seeing the reluctance of their South African counterparts, followed suit. Finance minister Trevor Manuel criticised local companies on several occasions: 'Sometimes we in government have to wonder whether our own business people, our own citizens, believe enough in our country,' he has complained.[4]

And this after Mbeki and the ANC government have assiduously pursued business-friendly reforms such as lower taxes, a reduced budget deficit, steady removal of exchange controls, privatisation of state companies and a drop in inflation. The government was even prepared to roll back key labour laws prescribing basic human rights in order to prevent discrimination in the workplace, such as was the norm under apartheid.

Reluctant to extend the social net by, for example, introducing a basic income grant for those left hopelessly destitute as the economy was liberalised, the government also proposed amendments to labour laws that would meet business demands for greater flexibility in hiring and firing, despite massive trade union and civil society opposition and a plethora of studies, including one by the International Labour Organisation (ILO), showing that the South African labour market was already highly flexible.[5]

Mbeki has consistently projected himself as 'pro-business',[6] and has worked hard to transform the ANC from a bloated liberation movement to a modern social democratic party, firmly rooted in the political centre. Manuel says: '[In the past] you couldn't be a social democrat and think like [Ronald] Reagan. Now things are turned on their head.'[7]

Mbeki has drawn heavily on business advice in formulating policy, and has surrounded himself with a selection of consultants divided into five working groups: international investment, business, labour, agriculture and information technology, and international marketing.

His international investment council is undoubtedly the plum. Joel Netshitenzhe, government's chief spin doctor and head of GCIS, says: 'The council provides many insights which help inform the evolution of government's approach to things.'[8]

It was to this group that Mbeki presented his inflation target policy, his growth plan and the government's new marketing campaign intended to lure investment. The star-studded council includes Mitsubishi chairman Minoru Makihara; Unilever CEO Niall Fitzgerald; Commerzbank chairman Martin Kohlhaussen; D-Group chairman Sir Robin Ross; ABB Ltd chairman Percy Barnevik; Alliance Capital chairman Frank Savage; Citibank vice-chairman William F Rhodes; Ashanti Goldfields CEO Sam Jonah; Tata Enterprises chairman Ratan Tata; Petronas CEO Hassan Marican; DaimlerChrysler CE Jürgen Schrempp; Independent Newspapers chairman Tony O'Reilly; and international financier George Soros.[9] Soros is a particular favourite of Mbeki, notwithstanding criticisms by the Hungarian-born financier of his quiet diplomacy approach to human rights violations in Zimbabwe.[10] Senior executives of US-based PC manufacturer Dell Computers and networking equipment manufacturer Cisco have been influential in advising Mbeki on information technology strategy.

Closer to home, the counsel of local captains of industry is very important to Mbeki, who consults both white and black business leaders on policy matters. Not surprisingly, the ANC's left is outraged, since by tilting towards business, Mbeki has distanced himself from the ANC's traditional allies, COSATU and the SACP. Although both COSATU and the Federation of Unions of South Africa (FEDUSA) form part of Mbeki's policy consultation network, COSATU general secretary Zwelinzima Vavi complained to Mbeki that the voice of business seemed to carry more weight than that of organised labour.

Civil society groups, NEDLAC, elected representatives and public institutions also privately complain about marginalisation. NEDLAC's former chief executive Phillip Dexter was alarmed by perceptions that Mbeki's regular policy discussions with business leaders were upstaging the tripartite negotiating forum, established after apartheid to reach consensus between business, labour and government on economic, development and social policies.[11] Mbeki's economic advisor, Wiseman Nkuhlu, says the president has gone to great pains to understand business concerns.[12]

Mbeki has acknowledged that neither the market nor the state alone can tackle the vast poverty and inequality created within the black community over more than 300 years of colonial and apartheid rule. With its extensive skills base, access to capital, resources, infrastructure and mechanisms of delivery, business is seen by Mbeki as a key partner to meet South Africa's development objectives. This has been the driving philosophy behind his efforts to have a hotline to business. The new intimacy between business and government can be seen at NEDLAC negotiations, where the two sides frequently agree on issues at the expense of labour and civil society. Previously, it was business that complained about government's close relationship with labour, but, for some time, it has been the other way round.

The problem, however, is that few South African business leaders share Mbeki's and the ANC's national development objectives. And, importantly, despite the ANC's efficient economic management record, the government is still largely distrusted by business. The belief among many South Africans, especially blacks, was that since white business benefited from apartheid to the detriment of black business and labour, it would make a significant contribution to transformation. However, most corporates have conducted business as usual since 1994, with many business people arguing that since legalised apartheid has been eradicated, no further contribution to social change is needed.[13]

Naively, Mbeki and ANC strategists thought that the implementation of a liberal economy would somehow develop a greater social conscience in the business community, especially since by creating an investor-friendly environment, business has been allowed to prosper as never before. Productivity is up and profits are the highest they have been in many years.

But instead of appreciation, the government has received complaints from business about 'excessive' demands to contribute to development programmes. In addition, legislation such as affirmative action and levies introduced to try to boost the skills level of the black labour force give companies an excuse not to make new investments. The slow pace of privatisation is also frequently cited as a stumbling block.

Mbeki allowed major South African companies to shift their primary listing from the Johannesburg Stock Exchange (JSE) abroad. Since naively allowing the first companies to do so without any preconditions, the government has become more circumspect. Corporate behemoths like Anglo American and De Beers made the shift on the basis that they would be able to raise more capital. The result was the exodus of vast amounts of capital. Companies that retained their JSE listings proved that money could be raised from anywhere.

In 2000, government began closing the loopholes by introducing a new dual listing model, based on that of Australia. Companies wanting to move their primary listing abroad are now obliged to retain head offices in South Africa and invest in the local economy. Niche bank Investec was the first to be subjected to the new rules in 2002.

The government also failed to act on the discriminatory banking practice of 'redlining': refusing to approve home loans for potential buyers in black townships or formerly white suburbs that had seen a post-1994 influx of lower-class residents and criminal elements. Nor did the government impose the all-important recommendation made by the Truth and Reconciliation Commission that a 'wealth tax' – a one-off levy on corporate income or a donation by listed companies of 1 per cent of their market capitalisation – should be imposed on business in order to empower the poor.

For all the concessions, however, the cosy relationship between Mbeki and the predominantly white big business community has taken the occasional dip. Cases in point were Mbeki's controversial handling of the Zimbabwe land-grab crisis and the HIV/AIDS pandemic. However, he managed to patch up his differences with big business through a charm offensive, which included reassuring a SACOB convention in Cape Town that he would not tolerate attempts by the dispossessed to seize land taken from them by colonial powers or the apartheid regime. He reiterated this assurance privately at a meeting of the business-working group on the last day of the conference.[14]

According to some who were present but spoke only on condition of anonymity, there were sharp exchanges, with business leaders demanding that Mbeki get tough on Mugabe and publicly condemn him in the strongest possible terms. Mbeki reportedly responded that he had publicly spelt out his position six times before the meeting, then spent close on an hour explaining again why he believed quiet diplomacy would achieve the best outcome in Zimbabwe.

Mbeki expressed horror at the 'doom and gloom' view of the country's economic perspectives, and business promised to tone down the criticism and initiate a domestic investment drive. Afterwards, SACOB took out half-page advertisements in local and international newspapers pledging support for Mbeki's handling of the Zimbabwe crisis.[15] It was a rare gesture of appreciation in response to Mbeki's overtures that helped restore the equilibrium between business and government. In fact, some were of the opinion that relations between the two had not been so good since the 1960s.

But political analyst Robert Schrire warned that the support of big business should not be taken for granted.[16] Indeed, the biggest shock for Mbeki's government was the lukewarm response drawn by efforts to bring local business into the fold. Month after month, business confidence, as measured by SACOB's index, showed a decline.

Mbeki and his strategists attributed the problem in part to the chasm between white and black business, and argued that unity would go a long way towards propagating a culture of social responsibility in the white business sector.

The high social cost of implementing the government's economic austerity programme was largely borne by a black majority restless for individual economic gain. The trusty struggle tools of mass action, stayaways and service boycotts are back in vogue as ANC supporters take on the government over lack of delivery and increased hardship.

The reason for business pessimism is hard to pinpoint. It has been variously blamed on crime, unemployment and poverty, yet countries such as China, Brazil, Mexico, India and Thailand share many of the same or similar fault lines, but not the negativity.

South African business people have long evinced a strain of pessimism about an ANC government's economic prospects. The dominant mining–finance complex has traditionally espoused the cold, deeply individualistic and unregulated brand of capitalism associated with Margaret Thatcher and Ronald Reagan in preference to continental Europe's capitalism with a social conscience. The dominant view in business circles is of an investor-friendly environment created by weakening the trade unions, rolling back elements of labour legislation reform, reducing government to the bare minimum and letting business do as it pleases, whatever the broader social consequences.

The post-democracy gloom is all the more surprising since South African business suffered no reprisals for having oiled the apartheid machine. 'Businessmen from major corporations acted in advisory roles to the military, especially on manpower issues, and several held high-ranking positions in the armed forces reserves or part-time commando units.'[17] Many banks, computer companies and other businesses have been directly implicated in the still largely unresolved murky activities of the state's death squads, and racial discrimination was rife.

In the mining industry, for example, whites were paid up to ten times more than blacks and received additional benefits, such as housing. Terry Bell, who documented the role of business under apartheid, says: 'These appalling conditions, the meagre rations and even more meagre wages were not required by law; they were a simple outgrowth of racism and the demand for greater profits.'[18] Worryingly for South Africa, racism might be illegal, but such attitudes still flourish.

It is very easy to lose your job in South Africa if you are semi-skilled. Perhaps there is a case for a more rigid labour market at the upper end, but the unemployment problem lies at the lower end.

Whites still hold 80 per cent of the country's corporate positions. A decade ago the figure was 99 per cent. Around 98 per cent of executive directors in JSE-listed companies are white, and they preside over 97 per cent of the exchange's total value, according to *Businessmap*.[19] *Afrobarometer* notes that those who retain good jobs and lifestyles tend to complain loudest about the ANC government. Executives who answer questionnaires about crime, housing, education and the economy usually respond with gloom.

At the Growth and Development Summit in the middle of 2003, the business sector promised to create 72 000 learnerships for unemployed people over a two-year period. Not only would this barely make a dent in unemployment figures, but, as Abedian notes, it isn't even visionary in terms of sheer self-interest, since government would carry almost all the financial costs of the scheme.

South Africa has more than 200 000 registered companies. If only 10 000 took part in a national anti-unemployment scheme and took on 50 apprentices each, up to 500 000 positions could be created in a relatively short time for those who would otherwise have little or no chance of exposure to a formal working environment. Abedian says the wholesale and retail industry and major banks could easily take on between 500 and 1 000 learners. The multiple impact on broad empowerment, economic growth, poverty reduction and development would be phenomenal.

Add to pervasive business pessimism what Kevin Wakeford, former CEO of SACOB, describes as residual white racism against any black government, no matter its merits or successes. Of course, South African society in the past has been fractured along economic, racial and ethnic lines, and building social cohesion cannot happen overnight.

Abedian[20] says mindsets are important in a globalised economy, where movements of people and capital are driven in large measure by prevailing preconceptions and expectations. Interestingly, most of the pessimism is found at the level of small and medium businesses, and among middle management in large corporations. Business leaders at the top end, many well travelled and having been able to observe operations in countries similar to South Africa, are rather more optimistic and positive.

White business organisations have lost some of their traditional cohesion. In the early 1990s, the white business community rallied together, fearing a black ANC government would end capitalism in South Africa. Since 1994, an important section of white business has become more progressive and has worked hand in hand with trade unions to find solutions to the country's economic problems. The results have included new alliances, such as the Millennium Labour Council, which brokered an important compromise on labour legislation.

Sadly, another group has remained steeped in the past, blind to the obscene inequalities fostered by apartheid. They cannot see that creaming profits but refusing to provide employees with rudimentary training, education or housing allowances is a certain recipe for disaster. Some economists sense a rising optimism, though, and an increasing number of business people are asking why they have remained negative in the face of South Africa's improved global status and rising economic resilience.

The government rightly complains that foreign investors have not rewarded South Africa for staying the orthodox economic course despite the major social consequences for its bedrock constituency, the majority black poor. Manuel told Bloomberg news agency in April 2002: 'Developing countries have made many reforms, but the benefits are in fact very slim.' He also complained that rich governments like the US and the EU push poor countries to lower trade barriers, yet maintain subsidies on food and textile products. 'We have undertaken a policy of very substantial macroeconomic reform, but the rewards are few. Are we too stupid, or too poor?'

It was against this background that Mbeki lashed out at Anglo American's Tony Trahar in mid-2004 for commenting that despite all the changes, South Africa was still politically risky. Similarly, Mbeki was angered a year earlier when South African petro-chemical company Sasol reported to the New York Stock Exchange that black economic empowerment posed a business risk.

Mbeki has been unable to persuade business that it is in their own interest to contribute to positive change, that rampant poverty and inequality could be the downfall of South Africa's market-friendly economy. He has failed to achieve a shared understanding of the nature of social and economic problems inherited from the apartheid government. This remains a key challenge, as most nations that have achieved rapid poverty reduction shared a basic understanding between business, labour and government on how to tackle society's problems.

Black business also has a special seat at Mbeki's hearth. He meets regularly with a select group from his black business working group, and things have come a long way since the ANC in exile was strongly influenced by the SACP and deeply suspicious of the capitalistic local black business community.[21] At a historic three-day conference between the ANC and black business people at Mopane Lodge in the

Kruger National Park in late October 1993, a decision was taken to establish a mechanism to forge a more dynamic relationship between the two groups at both national and provincial level. They decided to work together to promote what was still a vague concept, namely black economic empowerment. The consensus was that black business needed to become more organised in order to make a greater impact on the economy.[22] However, the sector has continued to be beset by internecine struggles.

John Friedmann, a professor of urban planning at the University of California in Los Angeles, defined empowerment as an alternative development that aims to redress the historical process of systematic disempowerment. It denies the 'human flourishing' of the disempowered, whose lives are characterised by 'hunger, poor health, poor education, a life of back-breaking labour, a constant fear of dispossession and chaotic social relations'. Empowerment, he argues, has the long-term aim of fundamentally transforming society as a whole, including the power structures.

After independence, many of Africa's new leaders embraced a bold vision of transferring their countries' economic assets from the former colonial powers to local citizens. Many governments introduced economic empowerment programmes, variously labelled 'Africanisation' or 'indigenisation'. However, with the possible exceptions of Botswana and Mauritius, such programmes generally collapsed under corruption and cronyism after initial success. Against the backdrop of relative failure in the rest of Africa, South Africa's new government introduced its own brand of economic empowerment to quickly build sizeable middle, entrepreneurial and business classes among the black majority.

So far, black economic empowerment (BEE) has mainly been measured by how many blacks own shares in blue-chip companies on the JSE – or, as they have become known in South Africa, black-chip shares. Every time a black group acquires shares in previously white-owned companies, the establishment of joint ventures secures an equity stake in government-initiated businesses, such as casinos. This has made BEE companies vulnerable to financial market volatility.

At the end of the financial year in February 2001, black companies accounted for 4.9 per cent of the JSE's total market capitalisation, against 5.2 per cent in November 2000. This represents a 6 per cent decline from the previous quarter. Over the same period, the JSE All Share Index grew by 22 per cent, buoyed largely by non-gold resources.[23] Since 1994, South Africa has seen the emergence of a new black middle class. Almost 10 per cent of the country's top 20 per cent of high earners are black, compared with only 2 per cent in 1990. But there is scant evidence that empowerment has done more than allow a small clique of black South Africans to acquire control, or at least a significant portion, of some of the country's largest companies.

The way that government promoted BEE created a negative perception to start with. Damningly, BEE has since come to be associated with a small and elite group, out to make as much money as they can at the expense of broad black society.

The actions of the new breed of black entrepreneurs reinforce the notion that, instead of benefiting the previously disadvantaged black community, BEE has become a means of self-enrichment for the few. Most BEE deals typically involve the same handful of people, over and over. 'The same people with political connections are always getting the contracts. It is not spread evenly,' complained one struggling black entrepreneur.

The BEE experiment must rank as a huge disappointment. For Mbeki and centrist ANC leaders, establishing a black middle and business class is important as a bulwark against pressure from labour and the poverty-stricken masses for more expansionist policies. Mbeki also sees BEE as crucial for the formation of a black capitalist class, which he believes is the key to a non-racial South African society. Threats by white corporations to move their investments offshore on the eve of the ANC coming to power unless the party applied economic policies that were acceptable to business, left deep scars on ANC leaders. They also made Mbeki more determined than ever to establish a black 'big business' class that would forever lay to rest the ghost of white capital flight and prevent future governments from being held to ransom.

South Africa was one of the few exceptions on the African continent that had a powerful and successful private sector when liberated. Since then, few pan-African companies have thrived, leaving American and European multinationals to corner the continental markets. BEE is thus crucially important as a role model for the rest of Africa. If black-owned and managed companies succeed in South Africa, the entire continent will see what is possible.

But BEE's early track record has been less than exemplary,[24] and the questions dogging Mbeki and his allies have been: What is black economic empowerment really, and how does it fit into the broader economic development strategies?

Since the term was first used in the early 1990s, there have been two interpretations of BEE. The first is a rather narrow view, confined to creation of a new black capitalist or business class in post-apartheid South Africa. The assumption was that once that class had been established, benefits would trickle down to the poor. This approach emphasises increased proportional representation of previously disadvantaged groups, and emphasises the career mobility and advancement of blacks through managerial, professional and business ranks. Essentially, this view focuses on promotion of a new class of wealthy and powerful African movers and shakers through the media and big business, and has become the accepted public interpretation of BEE. Supporters defend this concept of BEE with statements such as 'there is nothing wrong with being filthy rich'. Mbeki's strategic advisor and the public face of the ANC, Smuts Ngonyama, has stated baldly: 'I did not struggle to remain poor.'

They take their cue from Mbeki, who strongly believes that a black capitalist class is one of the pillars of democracy in South Africa, and has publicly declared that there is no reason to be embarrassed about the emergence of a prosperous black bourgeoisie.

'This is the real world,' he told a group of business leaders. 'As part of our continuing struggle to wipe out the legacy of racism, we must work to ensure that there emerges a black bourgeoisie, whose presence within our economy and society will be part of the process of the deracialisation of the economy and the society.'[25]

However, Mbeki has also publicly rebuked those who see BEE as nothing more than a means to acquire 'a grand house, a grand car and a grand salary'.[26] At the same time, he is extremely touchy about internal criticism of BEE. He considers its success to be one of the foundations of the legacy he plans to leave as the post-apartheid leader who brought economic benefits to the previously disadvantaged. When COSATU leaders Zwelinzima Vavi and Willie Madisha, and Archbishop Desmond Tutu, attacked the fact that BEE's benefits were confined to an elite few, Mbeki's response was so virulent and mean-spirited that it demeaned the office of the presidency.

There are many reasons for negative public perceptions about BEE. The proposal in April 1999 by the directors of New Africa Investments Limited (NAIL) to transfer African Merchant Bank share options worth R130 million to its chairman Nthato Motlana and executive directors Dikgang Moseneke, Zwelakhe Sisulu and Jonty Sandler, etched on the public consciousness that black empowerment was being used for self-enrichment of the few.[27]

In many empowerment companies, whites ran the operational and management functions and held the posts of executive directors, with blacks in non-executive positions. Examples abound of black businessmen who lend their faces to white companies so that the latter can satisfy the requirements for government tenders.[28] Red lights should flicker over proposals that the state should use privatisation to kick-start BEE, as unless this is carefully monitored, it could see ownership of state companies being transferred to the same elite and mega-rich black clique, or black businessmen who are nothing more than fronts for white groups.

Expectations that the new black capitalists would become model corporate citizens have been rudely dashed, and, in fact, many BEE companies have been among the worst industrial relations violators.

Many have enthusiastically downsized their workforces, and COSATU president Willie Madisha has slammed black employers for not complying with labour legislation or maintaining progressive labour relations. He charged that black business people were joining the 'chorus of whining white business' who call for more labour flexibility despite the fact that low-skilled workers in South Africa can already be hired and fired with ease. The head of Mafube Publishers, Thami Mazwai, was voted one of the ten worst employers by COSATU members at its 2000 national congress.[29]

Sadly, in a country where the majority of blacks live their entire lives in abject poverty and drudgery, many of the *nouveau noir* rich shamelessly flaunt their wealth. Tokyo Sexwale, the dashing former politician turned businessman, has rebuked many of the 'instant wealth' class for spending most of their time on the golf course.

It isn't even as though newly rich blacks have been stellar philanthropists. Their contribution to social responsibility programmes is negligible, though they enthusiastically swell the ANC party coffers. Sexwale even made a R1-million donation to the New National Party. At the end of 2004, he also paid salaries of staff at the ANC's Luthuli House head office. It is very difficult to see how senior ANC leaders will not feel an obligation to a paymaster.

Having stepped across the threshold into newfound wealth and social cachet, many former black politicians seem to forget the struggling masses with ease. When the TRC demanded that white business should contribute towards reparations, their black counterparts were equally opposed to the idea. Saki Macozoma, a former Robben Island prisoner who went on to become an executive of Standard Bank Investment Corporation, stated publicly that dishing out money to victims of apartheid would be futile.[30]

The path from battlefield to boardroom has been well trodden since Cyril Ramaphosa quit as the ANC's secretary general to join NAIL in 1996. Former Gauteng premier Tokyo Sexwale has carved out a highly lucrative career in the diamond industry, while Mathews Phosa, erstwhile provincial premier of Mpumalanga, is a director of several major undertakings, including Madiba Mills, which is vying for a stake in the state-owned forests. Mbeki's former economics advisor Moss Ngoasheng resigned to join Safika Investment Holdings, a R500-million technology and telecommunications company, of which he has joint control.[31]

The number of ANC politicians and high-ranking public servants passing through the revolving door from government to business so horrified Mbeki that in the winter of 1999, the cabinet debated an ethics code for government employees in a bid to regulate the stampede of leading ANC figures to the private sector. The code aimed at limiting the potential for conflicts of interest by laying down the parameters under which former executive members could do business and barring politicians from using privileged information to the advantage of their business ventures. However, the proposed code stopped short of a 'cooling-off period' between quitting government posts and joining private companies.

The ANC also seems reluctant to enforce the code in practice. In November 2004 the media disclosed that Andile Ngcaba, former director-general in the telecommunications department, and Ngonyama had headed up a consortium that bought a 15.1 per cent stake, worth R7 billion, in public telephone service provider Telkom. Mbeki was mortified, and demanded to know how the pair intended empowering the poor as a result of their deal. Mbeki could not have been satisfied with their response, but he tried to defuse the situation by having the Public Investment Commission (PIC) provide the capital and reduced Ngcaba's stake considerably. The problem, however, is that using PIC funds – which is public money – for this purpose without first consulting public sector employees is in itself questionable.

Given the job reservation policy and widespread discrimination against blacks during the apartheid era, it would be unthinkable for South Africa not to have affirmative action. The question, though, is not whether there should be a system to redress racial inequality in the workplace, but what kind of programme should be adopted.

Mbeki is impressed by the way Malaysia and Singapore have dealt with this problem,[32] namely with government aggressively providing capital and opening up new opportunities.

Waiting for South Africa's large companies to change of their own volition is not an option. Economic policy is an important facet of an accelerated black capitalist class, and this has been done in four ways: legislation to promote BEE in various sectors of the economy; use of government procurement contracts; privatisation; and education and training.

The most obvious example of BEE promotion has been the legislating of targets, such as with the new mineral legislation. It seeks to end the situation in which the historically dominant mining houses stockpile mineral rights but do not exploit them. The new legislation intended transferring all mineral rights to the state, as is the case in most countries, and forcing mining houses to either develop the resources or release them so that other – notably BEE – companies could do so.

Fear of such laws galvanised the industry to develop its own BEE charters, either in conjunction with government or as private initiatives. The charter finally produced after lengthy consultation and a major fall in the share price of many mining companies on the JSE in July 2002 set targets for 26 per cent of the value of the mining industry to pass into black hands by 2012, with 15 per cent being transferred by 2007. Importantly, the charter is based on the willing-buyer, willing-seller principle.

Black entrepreneurs will have to access around R200 billion if they are to meet the 2012 deadline. Even the 15 per cent target would require R100 billion. Government is in a bind over the source of the funding, and the parastatal Industrial Development Corporation is talking with the World Bank and IMF in this regard.

Most major large BEE transactions have taken place in the mining industry. Patrice Motsepe's African Rainbow Minerals (ARM) teamed up with Harmony Gold to buy AngloGold's Free State gold-mining assets for R2.2 billion in a 50:50 venture, while Sexwale's Mvelaphanda entrenched itself in the diamond-mining sector by raising its stake in Trans Hex to 24.5 per cent.

In November 2000, top players – including the South African Petroleum Industry Association, BP, Caltex, Engen, Sasol, Shell, Tepco Petroleum, Excel Petroleum and Total – agreed to transfer 25 per cent of the fuel industry to blacks within ten years. Most oil giants have announced initiatives in their downstream, marketing and retail businesses. However, in the upstream area of the industry, namely exploration and refining, there are as yet few initiatives to promote empowerment. These businesses require substantial financing and few black players have that kind of money. The energy charter was the government's first major BEE success.

The threat of BEE legislation certainly roused the financial services sector. An attempt by then housing minister Sankie Mthembi-Mahanyele to table a Community Reinvestment Bill, which would force banks to provide loans to poor customers, sparked such an outcry that the draft bill was withdrawn for reconsideration.

The industry moved swiftly enough after that to come up with its own BEE charter. Said Bob Tucker, CEO of the Banking Council: 'We've tried to get onto the front foot to make sure we are not unprepared.'

Millions of poor blacks cannot use their homes as collateral for funds to start a business or educate their children. Making matters worse is that almost 5 million black people are blacklisted for having defaulted on credit payments at some time or another and are thus unable to obtain access to bank financing. This means that large numbers of the black poor are effectively excluded from a modern market economy.

The annual R120-billion state procurement budget is an important tool in the quest to establish a black bourgeoisie. Government tenders are the mainstay of several industries, including construction, professional services, advertising, marketing and engineering. BEE contractors will also be favoured for large infrastructure projects until 2009, and state-owned institutions like the IDC and the Development Bank of Southern Africa will increasingly be required to finance such deals.

From a zero base when the ANC came to power in 1994, black business bagged more than 40 per cent of the state's national and provincial contracts between 1997 and 1999. The trend accelerated in the first three quarters of 1999, and between July and September that year, five of South Africa's nine provinces bought more than 75 per cent of their services from black-owned companies, according to the department of state expenditure.[33]

The department says effort to promote participation of black entrepreneurs is paying dividends after a slow start. Additional points are awarded to companies owned or managed by the disabled, blacks or women. Planned new regulations will expand the services of tender advice offices to include matchmaking between big, white-owned businesses and small- or medium-sized concerns.

The state procurement system came under heavy fire at public hearings in the Northern Cape in late 1999. Black small businessmen complained that tender forms are too complex, and accused the government of being a tardy payer. Indignant entrepreneurs reported that numerous small businesses had gone bankrupt while waiting for payment, and professionals argued that official statistics were inaccurate. Black accountants and lawyers, for example, were seeing little government business, and since there was no apparatus to monitor the awarding of contracts by individual government departments, only contracts entered into by the state tender board were being counted.[34]

A common complaint was that shareholding, rather than actual ownership, control and equity, was serving as the hallmark when contracts were awarded.

Renosi Mokate, the suspended chief executive officer of the Central Energy Fund (CEF), alleged that the fund had incurred an actual loss of more than R71 million because it was trying to implement government policy on BEE. One example cited was the sale of two crude oil consignments to a newly formed black oil company, which CEF staff later discovered was not registered. Another was the Strategic Fuel Fund (SFF), which gave BEE company Sky Oil a contract to purchase oil from state reserves. The company defaulted, and the SFF eventually had to sell to Caltex at a much lower price. Mokate claimed the SFF was under pressure to give Sky Oil the contract because it had complained that the SFF was obstructing BEE.

The government has ambitious plans to use privatisation to drive BEE. In the restructuring of electricity utility Eskom, 10 per cent of the generating capacity was set aside for BEE groups. In the telecom sector, 19 per cent of the second network operator was reserved for empowerment groups. Government's intention was to create a new class of black shareholders through Telkom's initial public offering (IPO), and a block of shares was reserved for historically disadvantaged investors. Because the government also wanted to attract foreign capital, its secondary offer on the New York Stock Exchange was marketed on the back of Telkom having US operator SBC Communications as an 18 per cent investor.

But the danger of corruption is ever present. The government had to cancel a deal in which state forests in Komatiland was sold to BEE company Zama Resources for R335 million after allegations of corruption arose. Zama chief executive Mcebisi Mlonzi was accused of paying R55 000 to former public enterprises chief director Andile Nkuhlu before the deal was closed.

The final element of the government's BEE programme is education and training. Several sets of labour market data show that white men continue to hold the cream of top and senior management jobs, most notably but not exclusively in the private sector. According to research published by the University of Cape Town, there are simply not enough black skills to fill the core business roles, including financial management and business strategy. Despite the fact that the public sector had rapidly reshaped itself in racial terms since 1994, the total number of white public service managers had increased by the end of 2001. Based on public sector jobs data and interviews with industry experts, the 2002 Employment Equity Commission report revealed a similar pattern, with white men holding more than 80 per cent of top and senior management jobs. 'Even if every white person were to occupy a management position, we still would not have enough managers in South Africa,' the report noted.

The lack of real change in the structure of the labour force has placed the government under intense pressure to bring black managers into the public service. However, political appointments without the necessary technical skills have frequently been blamed for delivery backlogs. Economic analyst Maja Mokoena warns: 'Economic privilege, manifested in government appointments and government contracts, is extended to those in close proximity to the political elite, regardless of expertise. This is at the expense of quality service. So, South Africa, beware of crony capitalism.'

Indeed, many have warned of the great danger that instead of changing the lives of a broad section of the black majority, BEE has, in fact, led to a few being absorbed into the existing white economic elite and adopting this group's ways of conspicuous consumption, attitudes and norms.

Opposition parties such as the Democratic Alliance and the United Democratic Movement, as well as black left parties like AZAPO, have been quick to capitalise on negative perceptions of BEE. DA leader Tony Leon contends – erroneously – that wealth and income disparities between black and white have nothing to do with colour, but are class-based, as would be the case in countries such as Germany or Sweden.[35]

COSATU leaders have been scathing of this 'narrow' BEE view, with general secretary Zwelinzima Vavi telling an ANC workshop: 'We do not see BEE narrowly as the enrichment of a few black individuals. Rather, we see it as empowerment of the black majority in the context of dealing with the legacy of apartheid. We accept that the process of dealing with [economic] discrimination may ultimately lead to the development of a new black bourgeoisie. Our approach, however, is that for BEE to make sense for the majority of our people, the emphasis must be on blacks as a whole.'[36]

Some in the ANC have argued that despite its flaws, 'narrow' black empowerment has at least provided a psychological boost, in that it showed that blacks like Ramaphosa or Motlana could also become successful super-businessmen. However, this approach consigns the bulk of black society roles as spectators, celebrating the success of a small elite but not sharing in the bounty of increased employment opportunities, skills development, start-up finance or community development.

Mbeki has taken the failure of BEE, which he spearheaded from the start, very hard. To him, failure on the black economic front means failure in the fight against racism. Late in 1999, he told the black management forum in Kempton Park, 'As part of the realisation of the aim to eradicate racism in our country, we must strive to create and strengthen a black capitalist class. A critical part to create a non-racial society is the deracialisation of the ownership of productive property.'

He went so far as to suggest that failure of BEE would amount to failure of the ANC's historic mission of a non-racial society.

The second interpretation of BEE is far broader, and includes the economic and social development of black society as a whole. Following initial outrage over 'narrow' empowerment, Mbeki instructed senior ANC and government economists to find a more appropriate model. The result was the Black Economic Empowerment Commission (BEECom), set up in 1999 and chaired by Ramaphosa. Two years later, BEECom produced a report that accepted the broad definition of black empowerment.[37] The SACP and COSATU lobbied the commission heavily to include the broader definition of BEE in the report. Not surprisingly, government's economic mandarins received it with scepticism, and Trevor Manuel initially dismissed it as short on detail and reading 'like a text out of the Communist Manifesto'.[38]

Since then, government criticism has mellowed and some of the report's recommendations have been accepted. BEECom proposed the setting up of a National Empowerment Commission in Mbeki's office to drive and monitor BEE. Another proposal that found support was an Investment for Growth Accord between business, labour and government to reach consensus on a strategy to raise fixed investment, but this has yet to be implemented. It remains to be seen whether government and business will accept that: government should invest 10 per cent of its productive assets as part of a Targeted Development Investment strategy (TDI). The financial sector, particularly life and retirement funds, would place the same amount of their total assets in productive investments in areas of national priority over a period of five to seven years. The banking sector would set targets for and disclose its investment in underdeveloped areas. Rightly, BEECom urged the trade unions to use joint employer/employee pension contributions to increase worker ownership in industries.

BEECom's broad definition was accepted by the tripartite alliance at a policy workshop in March 2001, providing an official BEE model for the first time. The NEC of the ANC insisted that BEE be placed within the ANC's new growth strategy, and the party's economic transformation committee noted: 'BEE has been hijacked by others who sought to promote a narrow definition for their own purposes and agendas.' The definition of BEE proposed by BEECom is:

> An integrated and coherent socio-economic process, which is located in the context of the country's national economic, social and development transformation programme. It must be aimed at redressing the imbalances of the past by seeking to substantially and equitably transfer ownership, management and control of SA's financial and economic resources to the majority of its citizens. It seeks to ensure broader and meaningful participation in the economy by black people to achieve sustainable development and prosperity.[39]

One of the few victories notched up by the ANC's left was having the broad definition of BEE adopted at the December 2002 national conference. It helped that there was a rising tide of anger among grassroots supporters over reports on an almost daily basis of ANC members becoming wealthy overnight through BEE deals ostensibly designed to improve the lot of the previously disadvantaged. Even Mbeki is gravely concerned about this phenomenon.

The Broad-Based Black Economic Empowerment Act was signed into law in January 2004. The acceptance of BEECom's broad definition opened the way for the government to pursue genuine economic empowerment, which will reduce poverty, unemployment and inequality for the majority of the country's poor. But the process will have to be closely monitored and transparent, with penalties for 'fronting'. Moreover, the government will have to monitor BEE companies very closely to compel them to reach equity, training, investment, job creation and other targets. It can be argued that BEE deals are made because government has made them possible. For example, South Korea's success or 'miracle' is attributed to their government insisting on a return on their investments from companies given state or political support.

Significantly, no one has made a noise about the many existing black-owned and controlled enterprises: small businesses in urban and rural areas and small-scale producers in peri-urban South Africa. Millions eke out a living in the informal sector, and empowering them by providing access to finance and training would arguably go a long way towards mass empowerment. But it would also require the government to come up in a hurry with a plan to find the capital to finance BEE.

For South Africa's black majority to truly become empowered, far greater emphasis on education is needed. In 2003, the Council on Higher Education carried out a survey at universities across the land that showed a disturbing tendency, unchanged in the democratic era, for black students to eschew studies in finance, science and mathematics. An aggressive and focused formal education programme is essential, along with a mass drive to raise literacy levels. Government should be advancing low interest-bearing loans to all those enrolling at tertiary institutions, which can be repaid when graduates enter the labour market. A scheme of that nature would be a sound foundation for genuine black empowerment.

Broad-based BEE is both possible and desirable from both an economic and a political perspective. Two generations ago, the National Party government compelled an almost exclusively English-speaking business and public sector to accommodate Afrikaners, and a prosperous middle class emerged. Under the ANC, however, the focus has been on speeding up job promotion for the black middle and professional class, with attention focused on the needs of the aspirant wealthy rather than on the poor.

Other than proving that blacks are as capable as anyone of being 'big' players, there is no point to pursuing such a course. A broader-based empowerment policy would boost the sprawling informal sector and small business by facilitating access to finance, land and training in the rural areas, launching a massive education campaign, and encouraging employers to give their workers a share in ownership, as well as bursaries for their children.

The hopes of those like ANC intellectual Pallo Jordan that the emerging black bourgeoisie will set a 'new agenda for corporate social and civil responsibility' have been dashed. Yet, it is clear that higher economic growth levels cannot be achieved unless there is meaningful black participation in the economy.

The success of Mbeki's pro-business strategy will rest on whether or not he can convince South Africa's white business community that it is in their own interest to support transformation and acknowledge their responsibility in this regard. The true measure of success will be the extent to which domestic business invests in the economy – not the delusional obsession with foreign investment, which, more often than not, automatically rides on the back of local and state investment.

To some extent, the BEE problem is of the ANC's own making. When it came to power in 1994, nationalisation was high on the economic agenda, and local business leaders were quick to launch programmes aimed at redressing the imbalances of apartheid. The insurance industry, for example, mooted an investment development unit to create employment and infrastructure for the lowest income groups. The obvious route for the ANC was to press the early advantage and encourage more such initiatives.

But when the new government opted for a market- and business-friendly economic policy instead, such initiatives fell by the wayside. A decade and a relatively peaceful transition later, getting business to buy into transformation policies had become a major undertaking. There had been no Malaysian-style riots and the anger of the poor seemed to be well managed, with the exception of an escalation in crime, but even that, while inconvenient and costly, could be controlled by bigger and better security systems.

In Malaysia,[40] the local business community only started taking transformation seriously when angry mobs poured onto the streets to demand their slice of the pie. One of Mbeki's biggest challenges is to get business on board before similar mass action erupts, as it almost certainly will if the stark inequalities persist.

# — II —

# Remaking
# South Africa's
# Politics

The man in the street feels in his bones it cannot be right to vote for a minority
party that stands for the opposite of what he wants the government to do just to
avoid the supposed evil of a majority party getting too strong, or another minority
party being reduced to undue weakness.
— Frederick Ehlers, *Business Day*, 15 April 2004

Our message is that there is life after elections. We invite [opposition parties] to
join the people's contract to make sure all people unite in a national movement
[of consensus].
— Thabo Mbeki, ANC election victory party, Sandton, 16 April 2004

Unity cannot be brought about by enacting a law that all shall be one.
— Rabindranath Tagore, Indian writer and poet, 1902[1]

I T WAS A PARTY HACK WHO SAID OF THE ANC'S LANDSLIDE VICTORY IN SOUTH
Africa's third democratic elections: 'A hurricane has swept this country.'

Thabo Mbeki straddles South Africa's political landscape like the proverbial
colossus depicted in cartoons portraying former Cape prime minister Cecil John
Rhodes at the turn of the nineteenth century.

He was brimming with confidence as he began his second and last presidential
term on 27 April 2004 to the sound of artillery, jets and pop stars. Mbeki had
every reason to be satisfied: the ANC had unquestionably gained control of South
Africa, and he had achieved unparalleled control of the ANC. More people had
voted for the ANC under Mbeki than under Mandela in South Africa's first
democratic elections in 1994. The shadow cast over the Mbeki presidency by
Mandela's popularity had lifted at last.

The ANC bagged almost 70 per cent of the vote and control of all nine provinces. Four ragged opposition parties puffed in the distance with less than 30 per cent of the ballots between them, and more than a dozen tiny parties made up the difference. But the oft-repeated opposition accusation that the ANC was seeking to impose a one-party state by stealth was wildly exaggerated.

Despite the ANC's dominance, South Africa is nowhere near a one-party state. Nor should credence be given to the Afro-doomsayers who insist Mbeki would try, like the cantankerous Sam Nujoma of Namibia, to rig the Constitution to seek a third term, and it is not fair, either, to say that blacks, like sheep, unthinkingly put their crosses behind the ANC for no other reason than support for the party's liberation history. Only the blind cannot see that South Africa is a different place than it was in 1994.

The ANC has not been idle, and many poor blacks have been given housing, water, electricity and telephones. Black people are legally free from racism, though residual bigotry persists in everyday life. The end of apartheid and the establishment of affirmative action and black economic empowerment have given many access to better jobs, but the changes, though immense, fall far short of what was expected, promised and could have been possible.

Yet it is patently unfair to say the ANC has sold out or that Mbeki and party leaders are not committed to providing a better life for the poor. Nor is it true that the ANC has sold its soul to business. The party leaders remain determined to make a difference, but the problem lies with the strategies the ANC has adopted, the way decisions are made to implement them and sensitivity to internal criticism.

The ANC can hardly be blamed for its dominance when the feeble opposition parties have nothing compellingly different to offer voters. This obviously raises questions about the long-term vibrancy and substance of the democracy, but many countries have been ruled by the same party for long periods, yet remain free, democratic and prosperous. Japan under the Liberal Democratic Party is one example.

In response to the racist undertones of those who darkly equate the ANC's dominance to ruling party corruption elsewhere in Africa, it can rightly point to New Labour's staying power in contemporary Britain or the Conservative Party's eighteen-year stranglehold under Margaret Thatcher. It could even throw in social democratic party domination in the Scandinavian countries. In none of these cases does dominance automatically equate to corruption.

The ANC is far from being the patronage machine typical of Africa and Latin America that breeds corruption, like Zimbabwe's ZANU-PF or Mexico's former ruling Institutional Revolutionary Party. For one thing, leaders don't overstay their welcome. Former president Nelson Mandela and the generation of ANC leaders from the 1950s and 1960s retired by choice. By contrast, ZANU-PF and Namibia's SWAPO continue to be led by their founders almost forty years later.

Remarkably, South Africa boasts three ex-presidents still alive, two of whom presided over apartheid governments. They are entirely at liberty to criticise the incumbent, even while receiving handsome pensions and many other perks at taxpayers' expense. This may be the norm in mature democracies, but in Africa and other developing nations, it is a rare occurrence.

Strong, entrenched safeguards protect South Africa's democracy. Power is not wholly concentrated in the state, since an established business sector wields enormous influence, not necessarily in favour of the ANC. The press is free, although at times it dangerously mimics the unstated economic policy consensus around which the ANC and the main opposition parties have seemingly coalesced.[2]

Civil society and pressure groups are energetic, gutsy and bold. The trade union movement is formidable, even if its numbers are in decline, and the judiciary is fiercely independent.

Archbishop Desmond Tutu says South Africa's political system is robust enough to make descent into authoritarianism rather difficult: 'If it were to be the case that the governing party oversteps the mark, we have the Constitutional Court, we have the Human Rights Commission, we have the Public Protector, and I think that more than anything else, we also have a lively civic society.'[3]

For all that, however, when large swathes of power and patronage are concentrated within a single party, those who enter politics for personal gain naturally gravitate towards that party. The swift descent into the abyss of India's Congress Party under the iron-fisted reign of Indira Gandhi is an obvious case in point.[4]

Thus writes Sunil Khilnani: 'The [Indian Congress Party] simply acted as a mechanism for collecting funds, distributing "tickets" or nominations for seats and conducting campaigns. A myopic focus on elections became symptomatic of a deeper malaise. The subtle routines of politics between elections – when support must be nurtured, promises delivered on, things actually done – were neglected. Elections became spasmodic, theatrical events when Indians gathered in hope and anticipation.'[5]

South Africa's Constitution promised both a representative and a participatory democracy, and the system would be reduced to an empty shell if it amounted to nothing more than voters drawing a cross every five years and an opposition that spoke a language foreign to the majority of the electorate.

Turning power into money is relatively easy. Mbeki's determination to quickly create a black business class spawned loud condemnation that the beneficiaries were top ANC figures and those intimately connected to the party, while such advantages continued to elude the ordinary people in whose name BEE is pursued.

And then there is the increasing penchant of ANC leaders to centralise policy-making and appointments; to reward loyalty and sideline critics; to choke off internal opposition; and to pave the way for tough economic reforms the go against the party's own instincts. Such high-handedness inevitably breeds conditions conducive to corruption. Obviously a strong mandate, such as that obtained in 2004, means stable governance and policies between elections, which should please the investors Mbeki hopes to lure and gives the government the muscle to push through prickly policies with less resistance.

But the road ahead is strewn with booby-traps. A powerful mandate carries the risk of complacency, arrogance and touchiness, as Mbeki himself has warned. 'We must now not allow this mandate to encourage an attitude of arrogance among ourselves,' he cautioned amid the lavish and exuberant celebrations that followed the landslide victory.[6]

Some ANC leaders, especially those in Mbeki's inner circle, have displayed a cocky and sneering dismissal of critics, and there have been inexcusable instances of inefficiency and ineptitude: funds left unspent, menial tasks left undone, simple laws and regulations not enforced, and the people treated with disdain.[7] Such arrogance seems to be tempered only when the party leaders go down on bended knee to woo bedazzled voters. Even the incorrigibly aloof Mbeki squatted humbly on the bare floor of a poor family's mud house during the 2004 campaign.[8]

As respected political philosopher Vincent Maphai reminds us, there is ever the temptation that rulers would be 'slow to remedy corruption'.[9]

Mbeki readily admits that he needs to root out corruption. Frustrated and angry with comrades who are not ashamed to dip their fingers into the cookie jar, he slammed 'those who began to act as though our only task as a movement was to win elections and share among the cadres of the movement the benefits of office'.[10] Worse still, he said, 'others have used the opportunity to assume public office as an opening for them to acquire wealth for themselves by corrupt means and not as presenting a challenge to serve the people of South Africa'.[11]

Indeed, an alarming number of ANC politicians, especially in far-flung provinces and local councils, have abused their positions to enrich friends, family members and themselves. Disappointingly, the usual response has been for ANC leaders to close ranks and dismiss whistleblowers as opponents of transformation.[12]

In the summer of 2001, ANC elders were jolted into action by rising public perceptions of corruption and extravagance in the party's ranks, and initiated a drive to inculcate a fresh 'moral sense' among backsliders. 'This is part of a critical effort to build a new society based on a sound value system,' said Mbeki.[13] To be fair, corruption in the new democracy is miniscule compared to the widespread kleptocracy that took place under apartheid, but there is far greater public eagerness to expose corruption than there ever was under the previous regime.

Ironically, soon after Mbeki appointed his deputy, Jacob Zuma, as patron of the ANC's anti-corruption drive, the Moral Regeneration Movement, Zuma himself came under investigation for alleged graft linked to the controversial multimillion-rand arms acquisition programme.

Cedric Mayson, the ANC's religious desk chief and a leading figure in the party's Christian democrat wing, reflects that many great transformations started with a commitment to justice and freedom, but quickly fell into decline:

> It happened to the French, American, Russian, Latin American and Uhuru anti-colonial revolutions. The quest for liberty, equality and fraternity was right and just, but the bloodbath of the guillotine happened. The winds of change that blew the fresh, sweet breath of freedom and justice through Africa did not themselves produce monsters like Idi Amin and Mobutu, but it happened.[14]

Mayson cautions his party against the easy seductions of personal enrichment: 'The focus moves from a social struggle to a personal struggle, from community to individual, from commitment to entitlement, from seeking collective transformation to seeking personal advancement.'[15] The success of any anti-corruption campaign will depend on the example set by senior ANC leaders.

With this in mind, it is crucial for the long-term prospects of a continued healthy democracy that South Africa's opposition parties become relevant, offer serious alternatives and quickly come to terms with the unique challenges of post-apartheid democracy. It is ludicrous to expect that the voters should change and adapt to outdated opposition political parties.

South Africa has an institutionalised party system and a vibrant civil society, unlike countries such as Chile and Venezuela, which also made tumultuous transitions from iron-fisted authoritarian systems to democracy. South Africa's political parties have deep roots in society and party identities are strong. The ANC was formed in 1912 and is well institutionalised. The National Party was formed two years later. The ANC, not unlike the major political parties in Argentina, especially the Peronists, often sees itself as a movement, as the non-institutional embodiment of the whole nation, rather than as a party engaged in winning votes, competing against other legitimate contenders for power.[16]

Indeed, the ANC has always been seen as a broad church, with communists, Christians, conservatives, social democrats, Christian democrats, Christian socialists, liberals, Africanists and traditionalists all claiming it as a political home. Electoral success for the ANC, like the Indian Congress Party, lies in its ability to represent and serve the various social divisions that pervade society.[17] Like the Congress Party immediately after India's independence, the ANC carries the cachet of a former liberation movement and views itself not only as a political party, but also as an 'agent of development and social change'.[18]

It is a dominant catch-all party in a society where race remains an important social cleaver, although most political parties don't explicitly mobilise along racial lines, since South Africa's system of proportional representation does not make it profitable for them to campaign on race-based tickets.

The country's opposition parties are often distinguishable more by the personality and style of their leaders. Changing old habits and modes of operation has been hard for South Africa's beleaguered opposition. Rather than coming up with credible policies, they prefer to noisily, but ineffectively, bark at the ANC like little chihuahuas from behind the safety of the fence. Mbeki often jokes that they are 'Mickey Mouse parties'.

A feature of South African politics over the first decade of democracy was the shifting pattern of sometimes the most unlikely alliances. At one point, the country was being run by a coalition of the ANC, SACP, COSATU, IFP and NNP. But the future of politics in South Africa is not just a matter of forging new alliances. Mbeki has been steering the ANC towards the centre of the political spectrum, and theorists like Joel Netshitenzhe have dubbed as modernisation the dramatic remake of the party from a loose liberation movement to a party with centrist social and economic policies, at ease with the market.[19] The reality is that the ANC has become a liberal social democratic party and a custodian of liberal values.

The grand ambition of Mbeki and the ANC managers is to make the party the natural home of all – black and white – who occupy 'middle' South Africa. The basic contention is that within South African politics there is a cross-racial majority that instinctively espouses moderate politics and values. A centrist ANC would be the fulcrum of a shared programme to remake South Africa's economy and society.

Mbeki often complains about a lack of a national consensus between blacks and whites on the fundamentals of South Africa's transformation, and has been known to quote Disraeli's *Sybil, Or the Two Nations*, in appealing for unity and a sense of common purpose to build a prosperous, modern South Africa.[20]

Mbeki's strategists argue that, once consolidated, a middle ground centred on a 'new' ANC would recast South Africa into 'new left' and 'right' blocs. Thus Mbeki is trying to draw as many opposition parties as possible into his cabinet. Those who spurn the centre – rebels on the ANC's left and white conservatives who dream of rolling back the clock – would find themselves painted as political outcasts. Those prepared to be part of the new national project would have easy access to power, influence and policy-making.

But for all the talk about national consensus, it's still a fuzzy concept. Netshitenzhe says the ANC's driving ambition for the second decade of freedom is to pursue a social compact: 'A partnership of the government, the community sector, business and labour, with clear tasks that each will carry out, variously and collectively, to build an economy from which we all can benefit.'[21]

The institution of economic development is central to Mbeki's new nationalism. In a hostile world with an inequitable trading system and many eager to see a democratic South Africa fail, he dreams that such a compact would fuel nationalism for a shared development project to rebuild the economy. He wants to draw white and black South Africans into a cohesive shared project.

Mbeki-ites point to the economic nationalism that underpinned the rise of the Asian Tigers,[22] such as Japan, Taiwan and South Korea, during a period when their very sovereignty was threatened by hostile big powers. Mbeki's appeal for an African Renaissance rides on the promise of such an economic development project, which would eventually become the motor for continental economic and social renewal.

The paths trodden by Germany, Britain, Spain and the US, following an age of deep division to define a national consensus as the basis for political and regional diversity, excites the Mbeki-ites. The German transformation is particularly alluring, as more than any other example, Germany seems to present a route that South Africa could do worse than follow.

At the end of the Second World War, Germany was highly polarised, but divisions were overcome by a combination of broad agreement on key transformation values, a political system and social equity, all spurred by economic growth. The German example in the 1950s,[23] which saw fringe parties absorbed into two blocks that became the Christian and Social Democrat Parties, is the kind of national consensus that both Mbeki and Mandela had in mind. There, competitors for votes attack each other strongly whenever the opportunity arises, but nevertheless agree broadly on the need for a strong social market economy, on the basics of foreign and trade policy, and on the obligations that arise from the country's recent past.

ANC strategist Firoz Cachalia argues that social democracy succeeded in Sweden through electorally stable parties and a broadly based social consensus.[24]

Ravaged after the Civil War, the US overcame bitter divisions and coagulated around a stable two-party system. All these consensus examples hold deep appeal for the Mbeki-ites.

But does Mbeki have a strategy to turn his dream into reality? He hopes to muster most of the significant black and white groups behind the ANC in its pursuit of the elusive national consensus. He has embarked on a major charm offensive to woo black groups on the right – the bellicose Zulu nationalists in the Inkatha Freedom Party – and the besieged Africanist left – the Pan Africanist Congress and marginal Black Consciousness organisations such as the tiny Azanian People's Organisation (AZAPO) and brittle Socialist Party of Azania (SOPA) – into his bulging political tent.

Thus, he appointed key Black Consciousness leaders to senior government office: Itumeleng Mosala as director-general of arts and culture, Mojanku Gumbi as one of his key advisors, and AZAPO president Mosibudi Mangena as science and technology minister. So far, Mbeki's consistent efforts to sweet-talk the stroppy PAC into government have foundered, but the beleaguered party's crushing defeat in the 2004 elections could tempt it to reconsider as an alternative to spiralling into oblivion.

Similarly, white groups at the political centre and on the right, swearing allegiance to the new democracy, are included in Mbeki's new consensus politics. Arguments that Mbeki is a narrow Africanist are somewhat misplaced. His nationalism is an intricate, pluralist brand of South Africanness that harks back to the days of the ANC under the pioneers of non-racial nationalism: Dube, Xuma and Mahabane. But this does not stop Mbeki, a wily operator, from beating the Africanist drum when it's politically expedient to do so.

Mbeki goes beyond Tutu's 'rainbow nation of God', which Mandela eagerly embraced. Tutu, democratic South Africa's moral conscience, bestows divineness on South Africa's ethnic diversity, while Mbeki's 'I am an African'[25] speech encapsulates what, according to him, a modern South African should be:

> I am formed of the migrants who left Europe to find a new home in our native land … in my veins courses the blood of the Malay slaves who came from the East … I am the grandchild of the warrior men and women that Hintsa and Sekhukhune led, the patriots that Cetshwayo and Mphephu took to battle, the soldiers Moshoeshoe and Ngungunyane taught never to dishonour the cause of freedom … I am the grandchild who lays fresh flowers on the Boer graves in St Helena and the Bahamas … I come of those who were transported from India and China … I am an African.[26]

To Mbeki and his strategists, citizenship is defined by civic and universal rather than ethnic criteria, and is inherently inclusive. Much like India's Nehru, Mbeki is strongly attracted to the political and economic examples of the modern West, but balks at imperialism and is little influenced by Western cultural models.

For Mbeki, reclaiming Saartjie Baartman as part of an African cultural heritage destroyed or impinged on by colonialism, is important. The redemption of early African civilisations is a priority. But Mbeki also makes a point of attending Boer celebrations at the Afrikaner shrine of the Voortrekker Monument.

The promise of an idyllic future is an important element of Mbeki's nationalism. The conflicts of the past should be remembered, but the accent is on looking towards the future of South Africa together. In the process, history might sometimes be glibly glossed over or edited to suit the occasion. The IFP might suddenly become a 'liberation movement',[27] or the SACP could find its contribution to the struggle seriously downplayed.

Mbeki sincerely wants the ANC to provide a political home for Afrikaners and white English-speaking liberals who are unhappy with the divisive conservative politics espoused by the DA under Tony Leon. To this end, Mbeki has held several private meetings with the vast array of Afrikaner groupings to draw them into a new consensus, and, in mid-2001, he appointed ANC chairman Mosiuoa Lekota, a fluent Afrikaans-speaker, as a special emissary to go on a countrywide safari to speak to Afrikaner communities and organisations, especially in rural areas.

Around Christmas that year, Mbeki also embarked on a personal mission to be less hostile to whites: he would refrain from singling them out for attack in speeches and make more symbolic gestures of reconciliation.[28] The result was less convincing than Mandela's efforts in this regard, but genuine enough to indicate Mbeki's acceptance that the contours of South African identity have to be actively plotted.

Sometimes, the bookish president got it wrong, as when he wished the Springbok rugby team well for the 2003 World Cup. He encouraged them to follow the example of JM Coetzee, who had just won the Nobel Prize for literature. As writer Justin Cartwright mused aloud: 'I would doubt that any single one of them had read *Disgrace*.'[29]

Nevertheless, Mbeki has realised that major sporting events are a powerful tool of nationalism, and apart from the economic benefits, securing the right to host the 2010 Football World Cup was a great prize in the nation-building stakes.

The president cast his net ever wider in search of universal symbols of nationalism and made a point of meeting South African actress Charlize Theron after she won an Oscar. On the campaign trail in 2004, he drank tea with Afrikaner *ooms* and *tannies* in their homes with as much alacrity as he showed when visiting makeshift shacks in informal communities, home to thousands of the ANC's more traditional supporters.[30] When IT millionaire Mark Shuttleworth became the first South African to blast off into outer space, Mbeki enthusiastically embraced him as the world's first 'Afronaut' and a role model for the new generation.

These and other well-publicised events have aroused excitement, even within the staunchly partisan Afrikanerbond, about the idea of national consensus.[31] There have been several meetings with the predominantly white trade union, Solidarity, to sell the idea that the ANC would consider an affirmative action pact in an attempt to address the fears of the most vulnerable white workers over a perceived threat to their livelihoods.

Amiable ANC MP Salie Manie, who was given the task of opening secret talks to thrash out an affirmative action accord, pledged that the ANC would 'see that affirmative action was not against whites, while whites would have to accept that affirmative action is necessary to redress the imbalances of the past, and will help reduce the inequality between black and whites'.[32]

Simultaneously, Mbeki has courted white and black trade unions outside COSATU, and has drawn an enthusiastic response from FEDUSA, the country's second largest workers' federation. Should a significant number of disgruntled COSATU members break the tripartite alliance, the ANC would hope to have in place the basis for a realignment of the trade union movement, with a compliant COSATU and FEDUSA as the backbone.

Mbeki envisages a new form of unionism, focused on labour issues rather than the political trade unionism espoused by COSATU, which is seen as inappropriate in the new South Africa.[33] At FEDUSA's 2001 national conference, he called for a new breed of workers.[34]

Sympathetic civic organisations form part of Mbeki's consensus plan. Since the ANC's 2002 national conference in Stellenbosch, he has stepped up efforts to woo groups affiliated to an almost defunct SANCO,[35] not only to halt their constant criticism of government's failures, but also to enlist their active participation in the implementation of policies and delivery of services.[36]

There are certain parallels between the use by Mbeki and India's Nehru of the state as a tool to forge a new nation. Nehru saw the distinctive model of the Indian state as an important framework for identity: a model committed to protecting cultural and religious differences rather than imposing a uniform 'Indianness'.[37]

Mbeki views the state as an important matrix for a new South African identity based on diversity. The peaceful transition from apartheid to democracy is seen as unique, as are the Constitution, Bill of Rights and early government of national unity, all deemed worthy of export to other conflict zones, much as the French Revolution gave rise to the idea of France being a carrier of civilisation to other parts of the world.[38]

However, Mbeki's apparent disregard for parliament could undermine efforts to inculcate respect for representative institutions. Nehru's enduring legacy, for example, was the cultivation of respect for India's parliament as a symbol of the country's new democracy and national identity.[39]

Mbeki's nationalism seeks to endow South Africa with a sense of grand historical necessity – like Nehru impressing upon Indians the importance of their country in the wider world.[40] The subcontinent was the first to achieve independence after the Second World War and had to take up the cudgels on behalf of other oppressed colonies. In the post-Cold War era, the African Renaissance aims to lift Africa out of its economic and social morass. South Africa's new national identity would include being seen as active promoters of a better world, almost as the ANC in exile came to epitomise the heroic fight against the brutalities of racism and oppression everywhere.

Modernity is a key element of the new South African nationalism envisaged by Mbeki. He has a steely determination to modernise both the ANC and the economy, the latter by piggybacking on the IT revolution. Likewise, the institution of traditional leaders must adapt to democracy. Predictably, traditionalists in the IFP and elsewhere cringe.

Mbeki wants the ANC to be the authentic voice of liberation, even while imposing its plural definition of nationalism on South Africa. In a competitive democracy, this is a classic ploy by the mass party that claims to speak for and govern in the name of national interest. The Indian Congress Party tried to be the axis between state and society, organising a multiplicity of social identities within itself. However, when the party ran into difficulties because of its centrist stance, so did the Indian state, and therein lies danger for the ANC. It is politically impossible for a single party to be all things to all people.

A major flaw in Mbeki's quest is the tendency to equate criticism of the state with a campaign to sabotage transformation or, more importantly, questioning the legitimacy and integrity of the state.[41] Netshitenzhe blasted COSATU president Willie Madisha for telling members that if the government undermined workers' rights, the trade union movement would challenge it in the same way as it opposed the apartheid government.

Netshitenzhe responded angrily: 'The very foundation of the legitimacy of this state is put to question. Are we singing our way to self-destruction in the name of free speech? We should debate the question whether there are things to which all of us should collectively pay allegiance, which we should protect and defend. Is the state founded on our democratic constitution one of those things?'[42]

Mbeki's policy guru frets that the real challenge is to build a nation and forge a common statehood in an atmosphere that places these very attributes under threat. Criticism 'adds to the brittleness of a state not only in gestation, but one faced with the challenge of self-expression in a globalising world', says Netshitenzhe.

This is nothing but a recycling of the hoary post-independence argument by African leaders that the state and the ruling party should be insulated from criticism. Progressive white and black critics are accused, at best, of indirectly aiding and abetting international enemies – and local and expatriate white fifth columnists – bent on condemning the infant democracy to failure. Similar arguments were put forward by Julius Nyerere in Tanzania and Kwame Nkrumah in Ghana. The result was the silencing of dissenting voices and an eventual descent into the abyss.

The bitter lessons from Africa should make it clear that heeding Netshitenzhe will place South Africa, too, on the slippery road to disaster. Our guiding light should be allegiance to the Constitution rather than to governments, which are almost never immune to the vagaries of the corrupt. Such a view makes one neither an opponent of nation-building nor unpatriotic.

The fundamental problem is the danger of a false consensus developing. There is already a consensus that includes most of the political opposition, the media and public institutions, and which maintains that calls for more expansionist economic policies as a way to redress the inequities of apartheid engineering are irrational. Those who make such calls are immediately painted as 'ultra', and this form of consensus marginalises an important majority from the mainstream – and therein lies the future fault line of South Africa's democracy.

The cherry on top of Mbeki's efforts to build a new consensus would be to win over the Zulu monarchists in the IFP. He has long dreamt that the IFP would enter a formal alliance with the ANC that would merge the two bitter black enemies of the 1980s and early 1990s. Such a merger would also make up numerically for the irritating rebels in the ANC's current alliance partners, COSATU and the SACP, should they break away to form a left-wing party.

Most importantly, according to the Mbeki-ites, such an alliance would forever end the violence in troubled KwaZulu-Natal. Mbeki argues that the IFP and the ANC share the same roots and are cut from the same political cloth, but although violent confrontations between supporters of the two parties are no longer a daily fact of life, tensions continue to simmer.

Mbeki's offer of the deputy presidency to IFP leader Mangosuthu Buthelezi in 1999 was part of his plan to draw the ageing firebrand into the fold. Musa Zondi, widely seen as the IFP's crown prince, and former IFP heavyweights such as Frank Mdlalose and Sipo Mzimela are key supporters of Mbeki's goal. Mdlalose asks: 'Is there not a way of putting together the IFP, ANC and PAC? Is there no way of setting up a new framework of South African politics based on the principles set out by our founders?'[43]

There are historical precedents. Post-liberation Zimbabwe saw a pact between Robert Mugabe's ZANU and Joshua Nkomo's Patriotic Front to form ZANU-PF. The tearful lesson? Nkomo's PF was swallowed up by Mugabe's ZANU, its voice all but stilled. IFP opponents of a merger with the ANC warn that Buthelezi's party would suffer a similar fate.

Anti-merger groups in both parties have mobilised to spike the idea. An uneasy SACP general secretary Blade Nzimande warned of the folly of striking an alliance with the 'reactionary' IFP, while the ambitious ANC chief in KwaZulu-Natal, S'bu Ndebele, led the bitter opposition in the ANC.

In 1999, Ndebele, a close confidant of Mbeki, led a provincial delegation that strongly urged Mbeki to attach political strings to the deputy presidency. If he was going to offer the post to Buthelezi, they suggested, the IFP should relinquish the KwaZulu-Natal premiership to the ANC, with Ndebele first in line for the job.

Having convinced Mbeki, Ndebele's group deliberately leaked a distorted version of the offer before Buthelezi had been able to brief the IFP leadership. It was a brilliant strategy, and furious IFP hardliners urged Buthelezi to decline.

They warned him that Mbeki intended to curtail the deputy president's authority, and suggested he should take a counter-offer to Mbeki that would see the position upgraded to that of prime minister. In addition, Mbeki would have to look more favourably on IFP demands for greater provincial autonomy and more powers for traditional leaders at local government level.

Mbeki rejected the IFP's demands outright. Buthelezi recalled: 'President Mbeki indicated that I could only take up the deputy presidency if I was willing to give up the IFP premiership of KwaZulu-Natal and allow an ANC member, possibly S'bu Ndebele, to become premier of this province.'[44]

Mbeki appointed Jacob Zuma as his deputy and eventually gave Buthelezi the post of home affairs minister. At its national conference later in the year, the IFP pushed for closer cooperation with the DA. Ahead of the 2000 local government elections, an ebullient Buthelezi told an IFP rally at Osizweni, near Newcastle: 'By now our members should be convinced that we intend remaining as the IFP and not part of any other party.'

The following year, IFP hardliners, led resolutely by Lionel Mtshali, grabbed control of the party at its national conference in Ulundi and set about firing ANC MECs. Several attempts by Mbeki to placate Buthelezi failed. He appointed Buthelezi chairman of two of the six cabinet committees and on occasion made him acting president, but Mbeki's appointment of former ANC intelligence operative Billy Masetlha as director-general of home affairs poisoned the relationship between the two political leaders, perhaps irrevocably.

Buthelezi never forgot what he saw as Mbeki's unwillingness to intervene in the stormy relationship between him and Masetlha, the former spymaster. Threats that he would go to court to prove that Masetlha's appointment was illegal persuaded Mbeki to ask the combative Masetlha to resign in order to keep the peace, and Buthelezi in the fold.

Mbeki, frustrated by Buthelezi's tardy revision of the controversial draft immigration bill, decided in early 2001 to personally oversee the process, which outraged Buthelezi anew. The stage was set for an unprecedented farce that saw the president take one of his own cabinet members to court in 2003 over the immigration impasse. Vindictive as always, Mbeki sacked Buthelezi from his 2004 cabinet, adding insult to injury by appointing junior IFP leaders over his head. It hurt, and the IFP leadership furiously withdrew the party's nominated cabinet ministers.

The IFP's short-lived coalition with the ANC gave it a national footprint, but the more the benefits of democracy reach South Africa's deep rural areas, the more the IFP's bedrock support, the rural peasants, is likely to erode. If the IFP fails to reposition itself, it faces the danger of becoming the party of resistance to rural land tenure reform, ranging from control by chiefs and communal ownership to a more transparent system of allocation, and more secure family or individual ownership, including women.[45] Mbeki and the ANC are determined to bring democracy to South Africa's quasi-feudal rural areas, where chiefs rather than government still rule the roost.

The odd cooperation agreement between the DA and the IFP shocked Mbeki. Indeed, their cooperation is rather strange, given the dramatic differences between their approaches to opposition – the blunderbuss DA under Leon and Buthelezi's vision of cooperation and reconciliation. But the pact was based on the shifting sands of mutual hostility towards the ANC rather than the more durable foundation of principle. Its long-term durability is certainly questionable. Partly in response to the IFP's canoodling with the DA, Mbeki and the ANC leadership put all hands on deck to capture KwaZulu-Natal in the 2004 elections.

Mbeki and the ANC leaders are convinced that Leon's abrasive style threatens plans for a new national consensus. They also believe that a pact between the DA and the IFP will strengthen the hand of dogged Zulu segregationists in the IFP and again polarise politics in troubled KwaZulu-Natal.

During the 2004 election campaign, Mbeki himself canvassed door to door in previous no-go areas. Other party heavyweights were wheeled out too, with Lekota and Zuma campaigning house to house. ANC victories in KwaZulu-Natal and the Western Cape would have huge psychological and symbolic significance, but, more importantly, would forever lay to rest the fallacy peddled by the apartheid regime that the ANC is Xhosa-dominated and enjoys scant support among the Zulu and the Coloureds.

The IFP's disastrous showing in the 2004 elections swung the pendulum back to the ANC, which ended up holding all the cards. Ziba Jiyane's defeat of Mtshali at the IFP's conference in August 2004 put the party hardliners on terms, since Jiyane is instinctively inclined towards closer cooperation between the IFP and the ANC. If the IFP bites, its alliance with the DA is likely to crumble. Mbeki would cheer. In the wake of the 2004 election, he instructed firebrand KwaZulu-Natal premier S'Bu Ndebele to exchange his assegai for a peace pipe and make an all-out effort to lure the IFP back to the ANC. He has been trying hard to do so.

The IFP's cooperation with the DA frustrates Mbeki no end. While he has made overt moves to reconcile with whites in general and Afrikaners in particular, Mbeki goes out of his way to shun Tony Leon. He refuses to speak to the opposition leader or even say his name out loud, referring instead to 'that politician'. Computer-literate South Africans have witnessed the extraordinary spectacle of their president and the chief opposition leader sparring bitterly in cyberspace. Mbeki's open contempt for Leon has even driven Mandela to despair, and on several occasions Madiba has reprimanded Mbeki over his icy attitude towards the DA leader, urging him to meet with Leon because 'that is the only way of settling problems'.[46]

The mere thought is unpalatable to Mbeki.

Although the DA still retains liberal elements, it has undoubtedly become the party of the white right. Its liberalism is not that of traditional continental Europe, but rather the deep conservatism of the American Republicans. Mbeki and the ANC leadership believe that Leon's aggressive criticism of the government has racist undertones, and that he personifies the condescending viewpoint that blacks cannot govern, and that a black South African government must necessarily be as corrupt as any other in Africa.

To the ANC, Leon's attitude is best captured by Justin Cartwright: 'The poverty of their [ANC] education and lack of experience is, of course, the product of apartheid, but the result is predictable: large swathes of government are inefficient and there are many cases of corruption.'[47]

Leon sees the future of South African politics as a strongly adversarial two-party system along the lines of the Democrats and Republicans in the US. He sees the DA being part of one large coalition and the ANC at the centre of another. Ideally, Leon would like to see the DA, the IFP and all other like-minded opposition parties fighting the ANC under one umbrella.[48] Racist or not, Leon is a canny enough politician to know that any realistic ambition to replace the ANC as the governing party would rest on capturing a massive chunk of the black vote.

For a political party to succeed in any democracy, it needs to get the formula right: a charismatic or highly visible leader, coherent policies that distinguish it from other contenders, and high levels of organisation at grassroots, provincial and national levels.

In South Africa, most opposition parties lack one of the vital ingredients.[49] The United Democratic Movement and the Independent Democrats have charismatic leaders, but no effective party structures. The PAC not only lacks a visible leader, but is also mired in internecine squabbles that voters simply have no interest in.

The DA has a forceful leader in Leon, but is perceived as conservative and pro-white, and thus attracts only a specific wedge of the electorate.[50]

In any man's book, on the other hand, Mbeki ran a brilliant campaign in 2004 – clever, humble and positive, admitting that the ANC had failed in crucial areas, and promising to do better. The ANC's undertaking to enter into a 'contract' with the people to deliver, struck the right chord. The genius of the campaign was appointing the unassuming former Northern Cape premier Manne Dipico as election coordinator after the death of Peter Mokaba.

Violence and hard talk were immediately shelved, and campaigners were warned to refrain from attacking the opposition and focus on the future. It worked. The desperately poor crave any sign or message that something will be done to ease their unbearable lot. For the first time, their president came knocking on their humble doors and held conversations with the illiterate, the hopeless and the perpetually poor in which he personally accepted blame for the ANC's non-delivery and mistakes, and promised that a vote for the ANC would bring change just that much closer.

By contrast, Leon told the same voters that his party would stop the ANC from securing the two-thirds majority it would need to change the Constitution. For impoverished black voters wanting to know only how their misery was going to be relieved, the DA's message was meaningless, especially since the ANC already had a two-thirds majority. In any event, the ANC has no wish to be lumped with African politicians north of the Limpopo who do their damnedest to cling to power for life, and is so sensitive to Western perceptions that the DA's message not only shows how far removed the party is from the black pulse of South Africa, but also how crude its electioneering has become.

The DA's rhetoric might appeal to prejudiced white voters inherently afraid of a black government, but to the black balloteer, it comes perilously close to racist implications of inherent duplicity.

Far better to have lured black voters with a message that would hold out some hope of change in their miserable economic fortunes, or boldly explain to white South Africans that in the wake of apartheid job reservation, and the skills and colour bars, justice is not possible without some form of affirmative action. The DA certainly has the intellectual resources to come up with a practical brand of affirmative action that could both please blacks expecting economic redress and reassure whites fearful of reverse apartheid. But that might be difficult to turn into a vote-catcher in the short term.

It's hard to see how the DA is going to lure significant numbers of black voters unless it talks about equity, economic empowerment and redistribution, since all three are necessary, in one form or another, if the crippling legacy of apartheid is to be seriously addressed.

In the 1999 elections, the DA's 'fightback' campaign displaced both the New National Party and the Conservative Party on the right. Many perceived the slogan as being anti-black, and by trudging the low road of driving fear into already insecure whites, the black vote was always going to remain elusive. Equally, the DA faces the dilemma of alienating those same white conservative voters if the party changes course – as it must do if it is to remain viable – to lure the black vote. Dare they risk that?

The DA's strategy suggests that it is a party prepared to remain in permanent opposition. Its aggressive, classic Westminster style might work in the UK, but is anathema to South Africa's blacks, weary of conflict and now drawn to a far more positive brand of politics. Notably, even the Conservative Party in the UK, which perfected the razor-blade form of opposition, has begun searching for a less jarring style. The DA might be well advised to do the same.

Ironically, in 2002 it was the IFP that was talking about finding a new opposition style of politics. The idea was that Buthelezi would act as an elder statesman, praising government when this was due but forcefully criticising it when it went astray. However, that was before the hardliners took control at the 2001 conference and pushed the party firmly towards an alliance with the DA.

In a bid to shed its image as the party of apartheid, the declining New National Party, under its baby-faced leader Marthinus van Schalkwyk, embarked on what it called 'positive' politics. However, the DA's approach had poisoned the political atmosphere so much that any reconciliatory message from the NNP was bound to be seen as weak by whites.

Leon's aggressive message and the freshness of Patricia de Lille's Independent Democrats held far more appeal than the tired and confused whimpers of the once omnipotent Nats. After being led for decades by Afrikaner monoliths like PW Botha, John Vorster and HF Verwoerd, even the party faithful found Van Schalkwyk too weak and boyish. The fatal blow for the party that had ruled South Africa with an iron fist for almost half a century was its humiliating defeat in the Western Cape, where it had thrown everything into the fray.

Van Schalkwyk urged the remnants of the party to disband and join the ANC. A more prudent strategy would have been to overhaul the NNP along the lines of the European Christian democratic parties with a social conscience – the backbone of Western Europe's welfare system – and strike tactical alliances with the ANC, even though this would have cost the party votes in the short term.

The United Democratic Movement (UDM) was born of an unlikely political marriage between former Transkei homeland leader Bantu Holomisa and erstwhile NP crown prince Roelf Meyer. Their mistake was to form the party before South Africa was ready for it. After Meyer quit politics, Holomisa tried to position the UDM to the left, only to encounter internal revolt. The party was badly hit by defections and organisational malaise, and may have a future only if it can form a coalition with other opposition parties or concentrate on becoming a regional force in the ANC heartland of the Eastern Cape.

All in all, it makes little sense for South Africa to have so many splinter groups vying for the opposition vote. Their election platforms differ only marginally from one another, and it would be far more sensible for those with similar goals to unite. After all, if their would-be representatives cannot bury petty differences, grow up and work together, how can voters be expected to take them seriously?

Although about 20 per cent of South Africa's electorate is illiterate, the polls show surprisingly mature voting patterns. From 1994 to 1999, votes for extremist parties on both the left and the right declined from 24 to 9 per cent,[51] while those for centrist parties increased from 64 to 76 per cent.

If the opposition parties wanted to become more credible, they would first have to elect more credible leaders. It would also help if parties seen by blacks as having been complicit in apartheid would publicly apologise for the past before moving into the future.

But one of the biggest problems with South African political parties – including the ANC – is that they go into hibernation between elections and only show signs of life and activity when voters prepare to go to the polls. In their heydays, both the National Party and the ANC had vibrant branches in the most remote hamlets that constantly reminded the community why they were worth voting for.

When the NP was in power, fund-raising fêtes and bazaars were an intrinsic part of social life, with local party representatives in attendance to hear, first hand, what ailed their supporters. ANC party branches offered services ranging from help with family funerals to solving administrative nightmares like missing identity documents or tardy social pension payouts.

Those personal encounters with micro-level politics, with representatives who listen to the bread-and-butter problems of their constituents, are what make the difference to many when they pick up a ballot paper once in five years, and political parties across the board in democratic South Africa either appear to have forgotten this, or no longer see the need to stay in touch with grassroots voters.

The ANC has firmly established itself as the party of black business, the black middle class and professionals. It will instinctively place the needs of these groups before those of the slum dwellers, unemployed, rural constituents and the youth, but if the government continues to deliver at a snail's pace, and the opposition continues to offer no credible alternative, South Africa's politics will plunge into a morass of radical social movements as the disadvantaged seek salvation outside the formal political structures.

Political philosopher Vincent Maphai points out that structural adjustment programmes can usually only be pushed through by military juntas or authoritarian single-party states, as in South America,[52] and inevitably impose incredible hardship on the poorest of the poor. Typically, such programmes involve drastic cuts in social spending, withdrawal of subsidies, such as food or welfare grants, privatisation of services, and the concomitant introduction of higher rates. Such programmes almost always give rise to increased unemployment and a dramatic rise in crime rates.

India, as vibrant a constitutional multiparty country as South Africa, pursued both economic and political reforms. Both came unstuck in the face of popular revolt, and opposition parties successfully campaigned on the back of mass anger to block the campaigns.

The difference in South Africa is that the main opposition parties, such as the DA and IFP, actually campaign for more structural adjustment programmes, which makes no political sense. 'We have already become a one-policy state – many parties, but all offering shades of the same vision,'[53] concludes political journalist Ray Hartley.

The DA strongly supports a basic income grant, and although this reeks of opportunism, it is the right way to go. But the DA needs to go further down the road of redistribution – a scary prospect for a party that has positioned itself to defend white privilege. Be that as it may, until South Africa's opposition parties have something meaningful to offer voters, they will present no real threat to the ANC's supremacy.

Parties are fundamental factors in shaping the political landscape. They not only reflect but also form the social structure, economy and culture of a country.[54] They are the main agents of public representation and are virtually the only players with access to positions of influence in a democracy. But in order to gain control of government, and hence set the policy-making agenda, political parties must win elections.

The way in which they campaign to this end, giving voice to certain interests and conflicts while downplaying others, enhances or diminishes their prospects for effective government, and a stable, vibrant democracy.[55]

Historically, South African politics has been of the fire and brimstone variety. Parties traditionally have a strong racial or ethnic bias, and entered the democratic era after centuries of civil conflict, racial division and violence. Many rightly argue that in societies based on deep group conflict or distrust, aggressive Westminster-style government is likely to exacerbate the situation.[56] The unbridled mutual loathing between the DA and the ANC and their leaders has begun to assume racial undertones, which can only be to the country's detriment.

The ANC's dominance and a mediocre opposition mask a steady but growing alienation of the electorate. Some disillusioned blacks have sought their salvation in religion, as can be witnessed in the phenomenal growth of charismatic churches, or take the law into their own hands, as we saw with the creation of People Against Gangsterism and Drugs (PAGAD). Since 1999, fewer young people even bother to cast their ballots,[57] and overall voter turnout has fallen from 89 to 76 per cent in 2004.

Voter apathy reflects disenchantment among poor Africans and Coloureds who have yet to benefit from liberation, as well as rejection of opposition parties that have nothing better to offer. Ahead of the 2004 election, the Landless People's Movement called on people to boycott the polls. Said one of the organisation's leaders, Mangaliso Kubheka: 'We are sick and tired of being used as pawns by political elites who only care about us at election time, then expect us to suffer our poverty and dispossession in silence for the next five years.'

Disaffected white voters have long since withdrawn from the political process, while the bitter-enders turn to ultra-right splinter groups, such as the obscure Boeremag.[58] Disillusioned white expatriates actively work to discredit the new South Africa abroad,[59] not unlike former Rhodesians after independence. Pieter Mulder, leader of the Freedom Front Plus, cautioned whites 'who predict and hope that South Africa would collapse as soon as possible', and added: 'You also find Afrikaners who enjoy it when everything goes wrong in South Africa. Their personal frustrations with the new South Africa play a role in this. The basis of their thinking is that the old South Africa would be magically reintroduced if everything collapses. This is a negative approach, wishful thinking and brings no solution.'[60]

Race and class present a potential fault line in South Africa's future politics.[61] Group identity can remain dormant for only so long before erupting in response to the behaviour of political parties and their leaders. Maphai and political scientist Keith Gottschalk liken group identity to a virus: 'It can lie deceptively dormant, only to explode under appropriate political conditions.'[62]

The danger is that the DA, bolstered by its performance in the 2004 elections, will continue its aggressive, self-righteous approach, and that a supremely dominant ANC will remain aloof, even arrogant, dismissing opposition from within and without. This would inevitably reinforce the fears of many whites who have voted for the DA because of its perceived 'anti-black' message. At the same time, it could drive black critics into the kraal of conservatism, tribalism and even populism.

The quality of South Africa's leadership is going to be crucial. When the biggest opposition party rails against transformation as a matter of course and aggressively attacks every policy of a black government, whatever the merits, South Africa's politics is in danger of becoming polarised into 'white' versus 'black'. That is the road to certain disaster, since so far the abiding character of the democracy has been its apparent ability to rise above race.

Dormant ethnicity in the former homelands is open to exploitation by unscrupulous politicians, who could blame lack of delivery on tribal discrimination. Increased centralisation, which would require even community leaders in the most remote rural villages to bear Pretoria's stamp of approval, is another potential time bomb. Local leaders passed over in favour of party lackeys by the central leadership could well mobilise popular support against such decisions.

White fears of affirmative action and black economic empowerment are equally dangerous terrain. An absence of economic redress would rouse black anger, and successfully negotiating the political minefield between these two factions will demand a special brand of leadership.

Mbeki's habitual and arrogant dismissal of criticism is not the answer. Certainly he could continue to ignore all opposition – the voters, after all, handed him an iron-clad mandate in the 2004 election – but he should beware not to misinterpret the ANC's landslide victory as a blanket endorsement of anything and everything the government does.

Most of South Africa's opposition parties are situated on the political right, while the majority of the black vote probably lies somewhat left of the centre. Should a new opposition emerge that is prepared to speak out for social justice, redistribution and a better lot for the poor, the centrist ANC could find itself in real trouble. There is neither an ideological nor a cultural guarantee that the nation will stand together, and South Africa's salvation will lie in a broad nationalism that not only accommodates its diversity, but addresses the fears and needs of all its citizens.

Recent African history is strewn with warnings of how badly democracy can go wrong. South Africa has the chance to get it right, but only if the leadership heeds the lessons of the past.

# — 12 —

# Modernising
# the
# Alliance

What need we fear who knows it, when none can call our power to account?
— *Macbeth*, Act V, Scene 1

P ITY THE CONGRESS OF SOUTH AFRICAN TRADE UNIONS AND THE SOUTH
African Communist Party. They are like hopeless men playing the Lotto,
praying that each new draw will see them win the jackpot.

But the tripartite alliance's senior partner, the ANC, shows no sign of
abandoning its relentless pursuit of orthodox economic policies, and Thabo
Mbeki expects nothing less from COSATU and the SACP than to maintain
control over the restless masses and disgruntled workers. He will tolerate token
campaigns for more jobs or rhetoric against greedy capitalists, but nothing more.

Alas, COSATU and the SACP are mere shadows of their former powerful selves.

In 1994, Mbeki and the centrists had to grit their teeth and accept the
Reconstruction and Development Programme, inspired by COSATU, as the
ANC's election platform. To openly oppose it would have been political suicide.
COSATU was the fastest-growing trade union movement in the world; since its
launch in 1984, it had even forced the recalcitrant apartheid regime to back
down. Its deep pockets and able membership oiled the wheels of the ANC's
Uhuru election triumph.

Early in 2001, COSATU won an important victory when the labour laws
were amended to grant employees the right to strike. After tense and protracted
meetings behind closed doors, the organised business community finally agreed
to proposals that were more favourable than those made by the government,
which had opposed COSATU 's demands. The supreme irony was that COSATU
gained more from its traditional adversary than from its long-time ally.

By 2004, COSATU remained the most organised alliance structure in the country, but the mighty had fallen. With an awesome organisational capability, it remained relatively easy for the trade union federation to mobilise members to take to the streets, but membership levels were falling, finances were shaky and influence within the alliance had been seriously eroded.

The decline in the power of the union was reflected across the globe, and perhaps COSATU was fortunate in being able to buck the international trend until well into the 1990s. But its late growth spurt took place in the public sector, off-limits for unions under apartheid[1] and the target of mass retrenchments under the ANC. The manufacturing sector, lifeblood of the unions, also saw jobs tumble as the government abolished trade barriers.

How the trade union federation will deal with another international phenomenon, the shift away from nine-to-five jobs with medical, pension and housing benefits, remains to be seen. Service contracts, off-site workstations and flexible hours have not only changed the pattern of employment, but have reduced the role of trade unions in many traditional sectors.

International trends suggest that governing party links with extra-parliamentary organisations such as trade unions and civil society groups do not necessarily increase their ability to shape party policy or direction. In countries where strong bonds existed between trade unions and political parties, tensions almost always emerged when such parties came to power. Even where the relationship between party and union was strongly institutionalised, such as in Sweden and Norway, labour's influence on government policy was narrowly mapped out.

The British Labour Party's trade union origins fostered a belief that elected officials always carried the flag of the labour movement. By the 1970s this perception was the cause of considerable problems between the Labour government and organised labour.[2] Now the UK Labour Party leadership talks of modernisation, and the unions complain of being ignored as their old left-wing allies embrace privatisation and new corporate friends.

In Africa, experience has shown that civic society and trade unions almost always end up taking back seats after independence. Throughout the continent, unions that were at the forefront of the anti-colonial struggle became subservient to liberation movements and subsequent democratic governments.

COSATU general secretary Zwelinzima Vavi[3] points to the experience of former socialist countries, especially in Eastern Europe, where trade unions were nothing but state conveyer belts:

> They were told, and believed, that in a so-called workers' state it would be counter-revolutionary to be independent; instead, the interests of workers must be subordinated to the interests of the revolution.

Yet in some of these states, nothing was revolutionary. What was prevalent was the accumulation of wealth by the new elite, whilst the living standards of workers and the working class deteriorated, sometimes becoming worse than under a capitalist system.[4]

Mbeki views the trade unions not as privileged allies with exclusive access to government, but as a social partner, like business, who need to compete like any other organisation for the ANC's ear. As he and the centrists steer the party towards becoming a lean, mean machine in favour of both business and the poor, but with a social democratic heart, the SACP and COSATU will just have to accept and adapt to the new dispensation.

COSATU's 1997 September Commission,[5] which studied the future of trade unions in South Africa, identified the need to 'reclaim redistribution as the fundamental goal of economic policy'. This was essential for the eradication of poverty, and COSATU concluded that the ANC, in its 'anxiety to meet the demands of financial capital', had relegated it to less urgent priority. Looking ahead to the first decade of the new millennium, the commission outlined three possible scenarios under an ANC government: dessert, *skorokoro* and *pap 'n vleis* (with gravy).

The first implies no economic development or RDP delivery, while the third suggests massive economic growth and high RDP delivery. *Skorokoro* – township slang for an old and battered car – was, the commission believed, most likely to define South Africa in the new century under the ANC's conservative economic policy. Characterised by a powerful black business elite and an emergent black middle class, but with the vast majority of blacks still drowning in poverty, the country would become 'a *skorokoro* zigzagging from problem to problem' unless the ANC could be prevailed upon to abandon its neo-liberal policies.

The September Commission suggested that the state should greatly extend social services, increase regulation of the financial market, retain exchange controls, reconstruct the Reserve Bank to 'sensitise' it to the country's development needs, and reject high budgetary deficit targets if acceptance meant curbing state spending on social services rather then increased taxation of the wealthy. Such proposals were not welcomed by the ANC.

COSATU's biggest setback has been its inability to stop government's privatisation plans. The federation organised strikes against the plans several times, one protest coinciding with the World Conference on Racism, which Mbeki had hoped to use to showcase to the world how far post-apartheid South Africa had come.

Mbeki was angered, but government went ahead with legislation to convert electricity bulk supplier Eskom into separate entities as a precursor to deregulation and privatisation.

Trade union federation opposition to deregulation of the telecommunications sector, which allowed a second landline operator in competition with Telkom, also failed. Similarly, COSATU tried in vain to halt the privatisation of Safcol, the state-owned forest company.

Ironically, setbacks to privatisation came not from COSATU, but from the markets. Swissair went belly-up, causing 20 per cent of South African Airways to revert to Transnet, and collapse of the TMT sector put an end to the sale of M-Cell shares and delayed Telkom's initial public offering.

Late in 2001, COSATU's central committee took stock and decided that a new strategy was needed to regain influence on government policy-making. Angry union leaders slammed Mbeki and the government's tendency to use COSATU and the SACP as 'shock absorbers to contain dissent and keep the masses in check'.[6] The COSATU leadership debated at length whether to recall unionists deployed by the ANC in government who did not defend the union's policy positions. 'Many COSATU leaders hold senior positions in government, parliament, the public service and in the ANC, but this has little impact on government programmes,'[7] said an exasperated Vavi. In the end, COSATU voted to defer the question until its next congress, but should it proceed, the move will have major ramifications for the already tortuous relationship with the ANC.

Meanwhile, COSATU and the SACP have refocused their energies to tackle the ANC on black economic empowerment and Zimbabwe, described by Jeremy Cronin as 'two very important strategic issues' for the left. Both affect ordinary black South Africans deeply. Many are disgusted that a handful of well-connected elitists are amassing vast fortunes while the majority suffer continued economic deprivation. And many black South Africans feel imminently threatened – rightly or wrongly – by the massive influx of refugees from Zimbabwe. COSATU and the SACP fully intend capitalising on public dissatisfaction over BEE and Zimbabwe, hoping that these issues will allow them to succeed where their campaigns against GEAR and privatisation had failed.

Mbeki believes that COSATU should restrict itself to shop floor issues. 'A trade union is not a political party and therefore must not act as such,' argues one of his closest allies, former Northern Province premier Ngoako Ramatlhodi,[8] in an internal ANC document that outlines the president's thinking on the role of a trade union in a democracy. The document condemns 'the ease with which some union sectors have embraced struggle tactics', referring to COSATU's rolling mass action against the National Party government in the 1980s. However, former deputy general secretary Tony Ehrenreich says COSATU sees itself as having a broader political and social role, almost like a social movement.[9] Vavi believes that

South Africa needs an independent trade union movement to represent the voice of the workers. The trade union movement must contest power within civil society and maintain pressure on the democratic state. If the pressure from the left does not counter the pressure from the right, we will end up on a one-way street to neo-liberalism, sacrificing the workers and the interests, of the working class as a whole.

Within the Alliance, conservative forces argue that if Cosatu criticises their policies, it borders on the counter-revolutionary. These forces seem to yearn for what they saw in Eastern Europe, where Cosatu would be transformed into a harmless and uncritical lap dog – the state's sweetheart, but the worst enemy of workers.[10]

With the ANC repositioned at the political centre, COSATU has been driven into a corner. Should it move even further left, or should it adopt a pragmatic position around the political centre, marked out by Mbeki? The trade union federation is split between the pragmatic centrists and what Mbeki labels the 'ultra-leftist tendency'.[11]

Towards the end of 2004, the pragmatists seemed to be holding sway. They included COSATU president Willie Madisha, Zwelinzima Vavi, Western Cape leader Tony Ehrenreich, parliamentary office chief Neil Coleman, monetary and fiscal policy chief Neva Seidman-Makgetla, NUM general secretary Gwede Mantashe, and South African Clothing and Textile Workers Union general secretary Ebrahim Patel. They had espoused the Dutch and Irish consensus model and formed a joint labour/business Millennium Council to seek solutions to South Africa's economic, development and social problems. COSATU has also energetically used social dialogue institutions, such as NEDLAC, to influence policies in much the same way that trade unions in social democracies like Germany do.

The right to strike agreement was a product of the Millennium Council, while COSATU's biggest affiliate, NUM, negotiated an innovative wage agreement linked to productivity. The hand of the pragmatists was also evident in the joint protest by the trade union federation and the major mining houses in 1999 against the sale of gold by central governments of Western countries, such as the UK, Canada, Belgium and Switzerland, and by the International Monetary Fund. During the dramatic strengthening of the rand in 2003/04, NUM and the Chamber of Mines approached both the government and the Reserve Bank to plead for official intervention to keep the currency at a lower level against the dollar.

COSATU's left was outraged by what they view as compromise with business and opposed the right to strike agreement, accusing the union leadership of trying to ram it through without giving members enough time for debate. The radicals charged that COSATU was selling out the workers by agreeing to proposals that undermined their fundamental rights, and demanded more time to take the proposed agreement back to their constituents to get a mandate. COSATU's central executive committee granted the request, but not before Vavi threatened 'blood on the floor'[12] if the deal was not accepted.

In a document titled *No to Downgrading of Labour Laws*,[13] the South African Municipal Workers' Union (SAMWU), supported by other radical affiliates, slammed the deal 'reached with the bourgeoisie'. They criticised COSATU's leadership for being 'too prone to compromise', and argued that if it signed the deal, COSATU would be agreeing to a two-tier labour market, with different rights for different employees, depending on the size of the employer. Vavi issued a letter, demanding the immediate withdrawal of the document, in which he said: 'The challenge confronting us is to weigh the deal in terms of whether we are advancing or taking a step back. In order to advance we may require trade-offs. It is incorrect to suggest to members that there can be no compromise.'[14]

Mbeki is fully aware of COSATU's internal turmoil over its future political direction, and has pursued multiple strategies to subdue the trade union movement. When he became chairman of the ANC in 1994, he immediately moved to draw key leaders of the trade union movement into his camp. Then COSATU general secretary Mbhazima Shilowa and the trade union's former deputy general secretary, Sydney Mufamadi, were among the early recruits, but when the government introduced GEAR in mid-1996, Shilowa was one of the most outspoken critics.

'Something has gone terribly wrong in South Africa. This is a recipe for certain disaster,'[15] he raged at a seminar marking the SACP's seventy-fifth anniversary. In time, however, Shilowa's criticism grew softer, and eventually he refrained from attacking the government's economic policy altogether.

Vavi, Shilowa's deputy at the time, and former COSATU president John Gomomo were left to do the dirty work. But as Shilowa drew closer to Mbeki, COSATU's leadership became so enraged that he was ordered to leave the room during a 1997 discussion of the trade union federation's response to the economic strategy.

When he was offered the plum job as Gauteng's premier in 1999, Shilowa did not hesitate. He had been bitterly disappointed when COSATU had refused to release him to become an MP in 1994, and Mbeki actually wanted Shilowa to remain with COSATU for another term so that he would have a dependable ally in place during his early presidency, but increasing hostility towards Shilowa by COSATU's rank-and-file membership put paid to that plan.

Another strident voice against the ANC's economic policies was that of Enoch Godongwana, former general secretary of the radical Metalworkers' Union of South Africa (NUMSA). His criticism of GEAR had been so strong that the trade unions had him earmarked as the next secretary general of COSATU. However, after being appointed finance minister in the Eastern Cape, he quickly abandoned such public comments as 'GEAR is a reflection of the conservative consensus in vogue internationally'.[16]

Former South African Democratic Teachers Union (SADTU) president Membathisi Mdladlana was frequently called upon by Mbeki to pacify trade unionists and persuade them to 'keep quiet while the president is looking into your issues'. His reward was the national labour portfolio.

Invitations to take tea or enjoy a barbecue at Mbeki's residence are usually a prelude to rebellious trade unionists being read the riot act, while the president's habit of hand-picking those he wants to serve in his trade union working group causes major rifts, with many union leaders regarding the favoured few with huge suspicion.

Both Vavi and Madisha are old-school unionists, and one of those who stood by them was Gwede Mantashe, general secretary of NUM. Mbeki used the same tactics on Mantashe as he had on Shilowa as part of his strategy to sow dissent among the critics. Mbeki-ites let it be known that Mantashe was the president's 'favourite' COSATU leader, and before long an offer was made for Mantashe to join the presidential labour working group. Mantashe refused to take the bait, and aroused Mbeki's chagrin by continuing to hammer the government's economic policy.

For Mbeki, political differences quickly translate into personal vendettas. He refused to speak to Madisha from December 1999 to August 2001, and could hardly bring himself to mention the COSATU leader's name without becoming angry. Had it not been for the necessity of meeting with COSATU to stop a planned anti-privatisation strike that would coincide with the World Conference on Racism, there is no telling when, if ever, Mbeki would have spoken to Madisha again.

He also refused to meet with COSATU and SACP leaders in bilateral or tripartite meetings for more than a year to show his anger over their public criticism of government policies.

The frosty relationship between Mbeki and COSATU's leadership had a notable impact on the ANC's 2000 local government election campaign, and afterwards the president accused Madisha and Vavi of being 'lukewarm' about the campaign. COSATU's central executive committee hit back in the middle of 2001, saying the unions could not defend the ANC's adoption of conservative economic policies.

As COSATU pointed out, 'Comrades had to answer difficult questions about Igoli 2002 [the privatisation of services in the city of Johannesburg], retrenchments, the labour law amendments and the Growth, Employment and Redistribution strategy'.[17]

Relations between Mbeki and Madisha turned sour in 1997, when Mbeki angrily labelled teachers as drunkards in a keynote address to SADTU. He also tried to spike Madisha's bid to secure the presidency of COSATU in 1999, making it clear that he favoured Vusi Nhlapo, president of the National Education, Health and Allied Workers Union (NEHAWU) for the job. Nhlapo had endeared himself to Mbeki the year before by accepting a compromise wage deal for public servants.

Trade unionists who reject Mbeki's sweetheart deals are quickly marginalised and labelled 'ultra-leftist'. Mbeki is deeply suspicious that Madisha and Vavi harbour ambitions to form a workers' party from the rump of COSATU, and would like nothing more than to neutralise their influence. Smuts Ngonyama was instructed to compile a dossier of all the anti-Mbeki and anti-government statements made over the two-year period by Madisha, Vavi and other senior COSATU leaders, and at a meeting of the ANC's NEC in late 2001, Mbeki spent eight hours lambasting them. Copies of the file were given to all the ANC members who attended a subsequent bilateral meeting with COSATU in January 2002, where Mbeki again singled out Madisha, Vavi and Mantashe as the main culprits in the trade union movement who were trying to discredit his presidency and the government.

Mbeki has also tried to drive a wedge between COSATU and the SACP by meeting separately with their leaders, hoping to secure concessions from the one that he can use against the other. Despite this, a split in the tripartite alliance does not seem imminent. An internal poll by COSATU in 2000 showed that the ANC was still the party of choice for the majority of members, but warned: 'Notwithstanding the high electoral support among workers for the ANC-led alliance in the 1999 election, there has been a trend of declining support for the alliance since 1994.'[18]

'Members see other workers facing job losses as a result of privatisation. Workers ask how can we still be in the same alliance with the very same government who is now privatising?' asks Charles Phahla,[19] shop steward of the Chemical, Energy, Paper, Printing, Wood and Allied Workers' Union (CEPPWAWU).

At the same time, workers see their ANC representatives leading *nouveau riche* lives in the very suburbs where, not too long ago, their mothers earned a pittance in domestic service or their fathers worked as gardeners. Visits to the sprawling urban townships, squatter camps and ghastly hostels that are still home to the poor are rare. Politicians accused of corruption and scandal hog the headlines, while the BEE millionaires and their designer-clad wives grace the social pages of mainstream publications.

COSATU has played a huge role in defence of the poor. It has sharply criticised Mbeki's quiet diplomacy in Zimbabwe and called for a tougher approach against Robert Mugabe, and its leaders have done sterling work in containing mounting grassroots dissatisfaction over job losses and the miserable existence of the poor. Far from attacking Madisha and Vavi, Mbeki ought to thank them.

But COSATU has to define a new role for itself, and find a way to work within a democratic system and a political alliance that see workers' rights as marginal concerns. Information theorist Manuel Castells argues that trade unions are losing their relevance because they continue to doggedly defend narrow interests in fast-changing societies where interests often overlap.[20]

COSATU's venture into business illustrates the dichotomy. Faced with continuing job losses and a government that seems not to have the political will to staunch the flow to the unemployment lines, the trade union federation decided to start creating jobs itself. The September Commission proposed that COSATU should empower ordinary people by investing union retirement funds in employee and community-owned companies, cooperatives and employee share-ownership projects.

Through vast networks and empowerment companies, the unions have invested billions to set up businesses within the pension, insurance, health, gaming, retail, banking, media and information technology fields. Since 1994, COSATU affiliates have started more than twenty companies, and some unionists have gained personal wealth through managing these investments. SACP general secretary Blade Nzimande says the scheme exposed unions to the danger of 'being sucked into the system they fight against', but even the SACP has established an investment arm. One of Mbeki's biggest criticisms of COSATU is the movement's hypocrisy. Despite continuing to call for socialism, he charges, the trade union federation has long since embraced capitalism.

Though elements within COSATU have questioned whether labour should continue to own companies, the scheme has almost certainly passed the point of no return. Late in 2000 the central executive committee accepted that labour-owned companies are here to stay, even though militants such as SAMWU general secretary Roger Ronnie had thought the meeting would sound the death knell of 'this corporatist deviation'.[21] SAMWU was one of the few unions to resist the move into business, despite the fact that COSATU laid down clear guidelines for union-owned enterprises: they must ensure financial sustainability, change patterns of ownership and investment in the economy, and provide benefits to members.

The unresolved question, however, is what role such companies should play in the broader scheme of things. Should their primary goal be to maximise shareholders' investments, or to develop skills and create jobs? And to what extent should unions dictate their companies' investment decisions?

The best-known union companies are the Mineworkers Investment Company (MIC) and the South African Clothing Workers' Investment Group (SIG). MIC has pledged R70 million to its owner, NUM, over a five-year period and is valued at R1 billion, including debt. SIG is worth an estimated R1.2 billion. Both contribute more to union coffers than membership subscriptions.

The remaining companies are smaller, and some are owned as coalitions, such as Union Alliance. For the most part, the companies have declined to use their retirement funds, as this is deemed too risky.

SIG makes R4 million a year available as bursaries for the children of garment workers. Its social investment programme includes pre-and primary school education programmes, computer-literacy training for shop stewards, a workers' college at the University of Natal and an HIV/AIDS prevention programme. MIC paid R15 million into the JB Marks Education Fund and supports the Mineworkers' Development Agency, which trains retrenched miners for new occupations.

Trade and industry minister Alec Erwin,[22] a former unionist, has slammed the union-owned companies, calling them 'unmitigated disasters', and questioning their investment strategies on the grounds that they do little for economic development and do not display a developmental ethos for workers or the nation. According to Erwin, 'They're only investing in financial services and a range of other junk. They are borrowers, not serious investors. Their pension funds have had zero impact on development.' The investment strategies of union companies have been mostly 'equity-based, predominantly paper transactions. Unions have to date not used their pension funds to get involved in any real employment generating businesses,' he adds.[23]

Vavi shares his sentiments: 'In some instances, investment companies have led to a culture of "business unionism" with a confusion of roles and conflict of interest. Unions have to protect members against retrenchments as a result of privatisation or outsourcing, while at the same time their investment companies are bidding for the new contracts.'[24]

Through establishing a federation-wide investment council, COSATU has tried to maintain authority over the executives of union companies. However, this has caused controversy, and some chief executives have quit. 'You can't run a company like you run a shop steward's council,' said one.[25]

So what does the future hold for COSATU? 'Over the last 10 years, and especially since 1994 – the period of democratic rule – the decision to join the alliance has been severely tested,' Vavi admits.[26]

In 2000, despite reasserting its support for the tripartite alliance, COSATU decided to organise a conference of the left. In the early 1990s, some unions, including NUMSA, had called for the establishment of a workers' party, warning that the ANC in government was unlikely to focus on the poor.

Mbeki and the ANC were angered by the proposed conference, claiming it was the product of COSATU's 'ultra-leftist tendency'. At bilateral meetings, he insisted that only the ANC had the authority to call a meeting of civil society groups, and placed immense pressure on COSATU to drop the idea or, at the very least, hand the prerogative over to the ANC.

COSATU renewed calls, first mooted in 1997, to attach conditions to future support of the ANC during elections. It was Shilowa who fought aggressively to have the original proposal watered down to a joint election manifesto, thus costing COSATU a golden opportunity to acquire leverage over the ANC.

If COSATU intends remaining a tripartite partner, it would be naive to let another opportunity pass to pledge conditional support for the ANC. But the trade union federation has no plans to rush headlong into forming a new party. If it decided to go that route, timing would be crucial. If a staunchly leftist party was launched too early, it could backfire. However, COSATU has been testing the waters, exploring the possibility of a united front with disgruntled civil society groups traditionally linked to the ANC. In mid-2000, COSATU entered into an alliance with the South African National Civic Organisation (SANCO), the South African National Non-Governmental Organisations Coalition (SANGOCO), and church, youth and community bodies. The new 'popular front' extended to the trade union federation's rivals, the Africanist National Council of Trade Unions (NACTU), and the conservative Federation of Unions of South Africa (FEDUSA).

If it can be sustained, this alliance could be vitally important in South Africa's near future. Mbeki is fully aware of the significance, and has been working hard to lure SANCO and FEDUSA away from COSATU. The power of the alliance was best illustrated in August 2001 with the watershed strike timed to coincide with the World Conference on Racism and cause maximum embarrassment for Mbeki and the ANC.

Mbeki had planned to use the conference as a showcase for the post-apartheid government's achievements, and was so incensed by the strike that he likened it to the miners' strike in the UK that broke the historic mutual support between the Labour Party and the trade unions. 'The lesson is that COSATU could mount successful strikes against the ANC government policies and get the ANC's own support base to come out in their droves,' says Madisha.[27]

COSATU has been wary of new and more radical social movements, such as the Anti-Privatisation Forum, finding their loud calls for immediate formation of a workers' party jarring. The trade union federation also worries about the blanket condemnation by such groups of the ANC as a sell-out. However, the union leaders are fully aware that they would ignore these civil movements at their peril. They are a long way from having the clout to challenge COSATU, but if the trade union movement fails to offer a credible alternative in the face of widespread unemployment and poverty, they could secure significant support.

Around the middle of 2001, COSATU introduced a new tactic, bypassing Mbeki and the ANC leadership and appealing directly to the party's branches, provincial structures and middle-ranking leaders to support their causes. Mbeki was furious, and in concert with Trevor Manuel, Alec Erwin and Jeff Radebe, then minister of public enterprises, waged a series of stinging attacks on the COSATU leadership. Mbeki had hoped to drive a wedge between the leaders and rank-and-file members by showing that the leadership was out of touch with ordinary members by calling for a strike, but instead COSATU reasserted its independence.

The battle to avert the 2000 anti-privatisation strike broke an almost sacred alliance tradition, namely trying to resolve problems internally while presenting a united front in public. Nevertheless, the leading unionists believe that breaking away from the alliance would be suicidal, due to the deep sentimental attachment of members that transcends their indisputable disappointment over the ANC's U-turn to the right. As Madisha says: 'If I go to heaven, I would not like to be the person explaining to struggle heroes like Chris Hani and Joe Slovo that I was responsible for the alliance being broken up.'

It is exactly that brand of sentimental loyalty that continues to give Mbeki and the centrists control over both COSATU and the SACP.

The bonds of the tripartite alliance run deep. So intertwined are the organisations that a breakaway by any one of the components would split both COSATU and the SACP down the middle, as many of their members are also deeply committed to the ANC. Mbeki and his strategists calculate that a split would hit COSATU the hardest, while COSATU strategists argue that South Africans still largely vote along racial and ethnic lines. 'However,' says Ravi Naidoo, the former head of COSATU's think tank, NALEDI (National Labour and Economic Development Institute), 'as important as a left opposition may be, it is doubtful that a class-based agenda will outweigh race and ethnicity at this stage in the electoral stakes.'[28]

COSATU believes that most members would remain loyal to the ANC rather than join an opposition party. Mbeki believes a split is inevitable in the long term, but that the ANC should manage any division in a way that will be to its advantage. COSATU 's 2003 conference conceded that it must start preparing to go it alone, and adopted a document, *Vision 2015*, compiled by the leading trade union thinkers, that suggests 2015 as a likely date for a separate party, unless the ANC does another about-turn to the left in the interim. However, the conference did not entirely rule out the possibility that a split could occur sooner, depending on who succeeds Mbeki.

Though it is almost certainly in vain, both COSATU and the SACP cling to the hope of one last chance for the ANC to change direction. Both leaderships have embarked on campaigns to turn the party around from within, one branch at a time, while grooming a candidate of their choice to succeed Mbeki and revert to the traditional redistribution policy.

The plan is so far-fetched that it might better qualify as a fantasy. Neither COSATU nor the SACP was consulted when Mbeki chose his 2004 cabinet, and no new representatives of either group made the cut. The tripartite alliance's closest and oldest partners learnt of the appointments in cold, official letters.

Yet Nzimande still dreams that 'the working class will dominate ANC policy'. Mbeki and his allies are keenly aware of this forlorn ideal, and have no intention of lying down and rolling over.

The SACP, the most dominant influence in the alliance for most of the ANC's three decades in exile, is probably even worse off than COSATU. Mbeki has actively pursued a strategy to entice the most critical communists to his side, and by the time GEAR was released, Mbeki-ites were firmly in place on the SACP's central committee. His best friend Essop Pahad has never hidden his credentials, and, from 1996, Mbeki assiduously cultivated a friendship with former SACP general secretary Charles Nqakula. His reward for buttressing communist anger over GEAR was his appointment in 2000 as deputy minister of home affairs, followed by elevation to the prime safety and security portfolio.

When he was elected chairman of the SACP, Nqakula was ideally placed to act as Mbeki's antenna within the party. 'There is nothing wrong with being in Mbeki's inner circle,'[29] he says.

Typically, Mbeki has relied on key 'reformed' communists – persuaded by charm and patronage to his side – to push through difficult and unpopular economic decisions. As public enterprises minister, Radebe, a member of the SACP's central committee, was in charge of privatisation, while Erwin, as trade and industry minister, was responsible for reforming industrial policy, and led the controversial rush to lift trade barriers at a faster rate than even the World Trade Organisation expected.

SACP deputy chair Geraldine Fraser-Moleketi is the public administration minister in charge of restructuring the public service. In her previous post as welfare minister she caused outrage by slashing child grants. Her husband, Jabu Moleketi, the talented SACP leader in Gauteng and tipped to follow Manuel as treasury chief, acted as Mbeki's lightning rod in 2000 when he called the SACP 'irrelevant'. Moleketi's payback was promotion from provincial finance minister in Gauteng to deputy in Manuel's office.

Occasionally, Mbeki handcuffs the SACP by appointing critics to ANC committees presiding over controversial policies. Jeremy Cronin was deployed to the 2004 election manifesto committee, packed with Mbeki-ites who would drown out his voice. Should he subsequently object to policy matters, he would be chastised as having been party to decisions at the time they were made.

The fact that Mbeki uses leading communists in this fashion is a bone of deep contention among rank-and-file SACP members. Cronin told the central committee in July 2001 that the SACP's credibility was being placed on the line.[30] Emotions ran high, and a call by the KwaZulu-Natal region for 'collaborators' to be suspended was narrowly defeated after extraordinary intervention by Nzimande and Cronin, who pleaded for the culprits to be censured instead.[31]

Though Mbeki continues to manipulate alliance partners with impunity, some have proved immune to his patronage, notably Nzimande, Cronin, Madisha and Vavi. He offered Cronin the chairmanship of parliament's transport committee in 1999 in an effort to gag him, but the SACP's deputy general secretary continued to lash out against economic policies. Some of his comments so enraged Mbeki that he demanded an apology, and the SACP leadership put pressure on Cronin to comply. Those who do not kowtow to the president are inevitably labelled unpatriotic and open themselves to malicious rumour or smear campaigns. Cronin readily admits this: 'Blade [Nzimande] and I have been through several tough years in the ANC NEC. We've been marginalised, shouted down, subjected to heavy presidential attacks on us, beginning with Mandela and so forth.'[32]

Since relaunching itself as a legal organisation in 1990, the SACP has come under enormous pressure to remain relevant. 'I have to admit, the party is battling for its soul,'[33] concedes Nzimande.

The makeover has included the shelving of socialist ideals and, perhaps, the most significant shift in the party's history, namely a concerted effort to rid itself of the spectre of being one of the last vestiges of Stalinism. Unlike the more independent Italian Communist Party, the SACP had continued to follow Moscow's edicts without question, but it has now embraced Italian communist Antonio Gramsci as one of its new ideological pathfinders.

Cronin says, 'We do not imagine that South Africa is about to embark upon a major socialist revolution; unfortunately, global and national realities are too stacked against us for the moment. But we in the SACP are not prepared to see ourselves as reserves on the bench, warming up occasionally on the touch-line, waiting for our time to come.'[34]

In a watershed move, the SACP agreed at its strategy conference in 2000 to cooperate with the capital market.[35] Former SACP chairman Joe Slovo was the first to point the way in this regard when he told the directors of Woolworths shortly after the SACP was unbanned: 'Socialism and the market are not, as is commonly supposed, opposed to each other in principle. The market is a mechanism for the realisation of value; there is nothing inherently capitalistic about it.'[36]

The SACP has embraced business partnerships between the private and public sectors, a form of privatisation, as long as this is referred to as 'restructuring' and no jobs are lost.

Central committee member Mantashe says the SACP has adopted certain 'tactical' moves in line with the market reforms introduced by China and Cuba. The party's policies now resemble a form of radical social democracy, and the SACP no longer talks about rejecting capitalism, but rather of transforming it.

At its March 2001 strategy conference, the SACP counselled public sector unions affiliated to COSATU to desist from aggressive quests for higher wages if this would impede the provision of social services for the poor. A conference document noted: 'Public sector unions are unique. The environment in which public sector workers operate is not one in which profits are generated, but rather one in which public resources are consumed in the delivery of services in the form of transfers to those deemed needy.'

Because public sector unions compete for resources with the general public, they need to exercise caution when making claims for such resources, the party argued. While acknowledging that public sector workers are entitled to a living wage and that there is a strong case for closing the apartheid wage gap, the SACP advised that South Africa was confronting unprecedented levels of unemployment, and the emphasis ought to be on ensuring higher levels of employment rather than demanding higher wages, thus echoing Mbeki's sentiments.

Mbeki saw the SACP's relaunch as a mass party on its eightieth anniversary in 2001 as a bid to tread on ANC turf, and accused the organisation of being an 'accomplice to a left rebellion'. The ANC's NEC slammed the SACP decision, and, with Mbeki's approval, the Africanists demanded that NEC members relinquish their dual membership of the ANC and the SACP.

The SACP's decision to become a mass party saw its membership balloon to 200 000 by November 2004. The new recruits are mainly young, with no sentimental or historic ties to the ANC, and feel that the benefits of democracy have passed them by. Already they have indicated, through an internal party survey in November 2004, that the SACP should sever all links with the ANC, but the central committee believes this would be premature. Instead, Nzimande and Cronin urged the party faithful to launch fresh attempts to gain control of the ANC from within by packing branches, executive committees, commissions and all other forums with SACP members.

Wishful though his thinking might be, Cronin insists that the battle for the soul of the ANC is not over, and believes that the SACP can still somehow manage to gain control over such institutions as parliament and the executive.[37] However, previous attempts to do so have been stymied, with local and provincial leaders of both the SACP and COSATU being weeded out by the ANC's selection process. Young Communist League members who tried to infiltrate the ANC Youth League's executive were isolated and read the riot act by the ANC. When SACP branches sought ANC support for their Red October campaign against high commercial bank charges, they were told none would be forthcoming unless they made the issue a pro-ANC platform for local government elections.

Even that failed, with ANC-controlled municipalities refusing to make venues under their control available to the SACP for meetings.

In October 1999, deputy president Jacob Zuma stunned the SACP's central committee by telling leaders: 'The party should consider, on occasion, speaking as communists and not as the ANC in parliament.'[38] The fact that the SACP has since thrown its support behind Zuma as a possible successor to Mbeki has not helped their case in the presidency.

For the moment, Mbeki still needs COSATU and the SACP to manage the dissent, dissatisfaction and anger evoked by the pain and high social cost of pursuing restrictive economic policies. But the SACP might do well to follow Zuma's advice, or even follow the route of the European communist parties and take part in elections as a separate party, forming a post-election alliance with the ANC if it so wishes. Members can then be withdrawn from cabinet if they do not follow party policies.

Of course, that would be contingent on the SACP doing well at the polls, but such strategies have been successfully applied in France and Italy, while the Communist Party of India (Marxist) and the Samajwadi Socialist Party formed a leftist coalition with the ruling Congress Party after elections in May 2004. The CPI (M) had been in power in the Indian state of West Bengal since 1977 and pioneered excellent ideas at state level, such as local democracy, healthcare, human development and literacy.[39]

The missing link in South Africa's politics is that there is no clear voice in government talking for the poor and the marginalised. Voters feel they have limited or no say in what their public representatives do. Most MPs seem to be far removed from the day-to-day problems of their constituents, who have no recourse against individuals who fail to deliver.

The chief defect of South Africa's proportional electoral system is that voters have no say in who goes to parliament, only what parties they represent. Members of the National Assembly are appointed, not elected, and their suitability is adjudged by the party bosses rather than the people in whose interests they are supposed to act.

Consequently, the voices of the poor are heard only on the streets and through the burgeoning civic movements. The masses cry out for opposition political parties with social and economic policies that will deliver them from their misery. A credible party to the left of the political spectrum might be more likely to bring an element of competition – so desperately needed – to South Africa's politics. Only if there is a realistic chance of being voted out do ruling parties become more responsive to voters. Only then, it would seem, will South Africa's politics shift irrevocably towards redistribution.

# — 13 —

# The Poor Strike Back: The 'New' Struggle

The nation of citizens does not derive its identity from some common ethnic and cultural properties, but rather from the praxis of citizens who actively exercise their civil rights. — **Jürgen Habermas**[1]

A real challenge faces the ANC now in trying to recapture something of this [United Democratic Front] culture of democratic participation – not only to hold public officials and political office-bearers to account, but also to ensure that people do not relate to government simply as a delivery mechanism. — **Mkhuseli Jack**[2]

T HE NEW DEMOCRACY HAS BEEN PARTICULARLY HARSH FOR THE ONCE mighty South African National Civic Organisation. Rudderless, embroiled in petty leadership tussles, routinely ensnared in allegations of corruption and shunned from the policy-making process, SANCO is a patient in intensive care. It's a pity. The civic movement played a decisive role in the bitter last decade of the struggle to dislodge the apartheid regime.

When the liberation movements were banned and repression was at its worst, residents of many a township came together to form a 'civic' that could take up their problems with local authorities inured to their plight. At the time, black local authorities were almost always government stooges, nasty types who served as the eyes and ears of the security police in many cases, sniffing out anti-apartheid activists. Many were businessmen moonlighting as councillors or mayors after being issued with licences to run lucrative beer halls or shops.

As part of a wonderful social experiment to create popular democracy in the teeming townships during the 1980s, trade unions, community groups, churches and civics formed a broad alliance under the banner of the United Democratic Front, which helped force the apartheid government to its knees. 'People Power' was the slogan for activities that ranged from agitating against local authorities to refuse removal, soup kitchens and opening peoples' parks.[3] By the early 1990s, most of the civics had gathered under a national umbrella named SANCO.

After ten years of democracy, the traditional civics and their national body had been virtually eclipsed by new, more energetic and dynamic social movements. 'Since the 1994 election, we have been bumbling along,' lamented Mzwanele Mayekiso,[4] the respected former Alexandra civic leader.

The normalisation of South African politics in 1994 saw many once formidable civic groups run out of steam. Former Eastern Cape activist Mkhuseli Jack wrote of the experience in his province: 'It became clear there was a real sense of disillusionment with the "normalisation" of politics: people on the ground felt that the government – whether local, provincial or national – had become increasingly remote, inaccessible, and unresponsive to their needs.'[5]

The integration of the UDF, undoubtedly Africa's most dynamic popular front, into the ANC in 1991 played a huge role, but the civic movement was largely to blame for its own undoing. Unable to find a niche for itself in the new democracy, it became the playground of failed ANC politicians hoping to hitch a ride on the last coach of the gravy train, and a convenient arena in which the ANC alliance's power games were often played out. Winnie Madikizela-Mandela made her return to politics through SANCO when she was elected to the Southern Transvaal leadership in 1993.

How did it go so wrong? In theory, SANCO is a junior member of the ruling ANC alliance, but, in practice, it is generally ignored until an election is due and ANC leaders turn on the charm. Mbeki's repositioning of the ANC as a party of the centre made it increasingly difficult for SANCO to influence local politics, and the organisation was hesitant to take up the battle for better housing, affordable electricity, water and rates on behalf of local communities.

So while townships clamoured for local leadership, SANCO wavered, beset by allegations of corruption. Its controversial investment arm, SANCO Investment Holdings, had made a number of dubious investments, such as putting money into companies poised to take over formerly public functions, such as water supplies. They faced angry community protests over the raising of tariffs, and many township residents were left without basic services.

SANCO suffered even more than COSATU and the SACP when leaders such as former president Moses Mayekiso were given government jobs after 1994. In rural areas, SANCO struggled in the battle over turf with traditional leaders hostile to the new democracy. Stripped of its leadership, its structures in tatters and bickering with the ANC, the civic movement was in no shape to punt for grassroots communities. But the real rot set in when SANCO pledged its support to the ANC in the first democratic election without securing a formal mechanism that would give it a say in decision-making at local government level. SANCO had proposed the inclusion of 'popular assemblies' in the new dispensation, but the ANC was having none of it.

Whether or not the civic movement should be independent from the ANC in government and, if so, how the two should relate to one another, has been a persistent headache for SANCO ever since. Mbeki and other ANC leaders maintain that there is no place in the new democracy for an independent civic movement. 'Now that we have a democracy, why not incorporate SANCO branches into those of the ANC?' asks Smuts Ngonyama.[6]

However, while that would hold enormous benefits for the ANC, it would be a severe blow for democracy if the party swallowed SANCO, even in its ailing condition. Many ANC branches are weak, others paralysed by uncertainty as increasing centralisation has left them in limbo. Mbeki's thinking on the civic movement was set out in the January 2000 edition of the ANC's quarterly journal, *Umrabulo*[7] (a Xhosa term originally used to inspire political discussion and debate on Robben Island). The policy suggested that ANC branches should handle civic matters, traditionally SANCO 's bailiwick, in a bid to inculcate the party's tradition and culture at local government level. In practice, this would sound the death knell of SANCO, as its leaders realise.

Veteran civic leader Godfrey Jack[8] says civics and community organisations must question whether they are 'just an add-on' to the ANC to keep poor constituencies in check. Some SANCO members, who believe that the organisation should operate at arm's length from government, have stood in local elections in opposition to the ANC and many have taken up the call for SANCO to show its teeth.

Mbeki has meddled in the running of SANCO since he became deputy president of the ANC, thanks to significant SANCO support via Madikizela-Mandela at a time when she still counted him a friend. When the time came for Nelson Mandela to endorse his successor, the SANCO leadership again came out in favour of Mbeki.

SANCO has not escaped the battle for the ANC's soul. Indeed, Mbeki-ites have expended much energy on ensuring that the organisation would not block implementation of the tight fiscal policies called for by GEAR at local government level. Opponents were systematically purged or marginalised.

SANCO's top-down, overbearing style of operation not only hampered its success, but made it vulnerable to manipulation from the centre. A somewhat less rigid national structure and more leeway for the local and provincial branches, favoured by some but rejected by the majority, might have been far more effective.

The UDF structure was an ideal model, allowing for overall coordination and organisational coherence, but giving branches ample space in which to exert influence and power and take up parochial issues and campaigns within the national parameters and basic goals.

The pro-independent group gained temporary control of SANCO in 1996 after delegates at the civic's national conference railed bitterly against the newly adopted GEAR, and pushed through a motion ordering senior SANCO leaders to withdraw from government office.

Former president Moses Mayekiso was recalled from parliament, and Mlungisi Hlongwane, mayor in the Vaal Triangle, was also instructed to quit. The Mbeki-ites, aware of the dire consequences if SANCO slipped out of their orbit, swung into immediate action, cajoling, smooth-talking and promising places at the centre of power when Mbeki became president. Hlongwane, Mbongeni Ngubeni, the civic's chief representative Godfrey Jack and veteran housing rights activist Sandi Mgidlana took the bait.

By 1997, Mbeki had the key SANCO leaders in his pocket. Hlongwane was elected SANCO president, Ngubeni became the general secretary. They moved swiftly against dissenters, expelling Mzwanele Mayekiso, leader of the powerful Alexandra civic and one of the main proponents of independence.

Led by Soweto branch chairman Ali Tleane, Mayekiso's supporters broke away in 1998 and formed the National Association of Residents and Civic Organisations (NARCO). They loudly criticised the SANCO leadership's muted response to the government's slow delivery and conservative economic policies. Fumed Tleane, 'SANCO was supposed to be an independent watchdog of civil society. But it can't afford to criticise government. That's a contradiction in terms. SANCO can't speak on behalf of civil society because it take orders from the ANC government.'[9]

However, after the 1999 elections not even SANCO could contain rising grassroots unhappiness, and the Mbeki-ites within the movement appealed to the ANC to take more seriously calls for greater grassroots involvement in policy-making. Like others before them, they had become fed up that SANCO 's only value to the ANC lay in being a vote-catcher at election time.[10]

ANC secretary general Kgalema Motlanthe[11] told the national leadership before the 1999 elections that attempts to regain control over the wayward SANCO had failed, and warned: 'We need to have a serious discussion on the role of SANCO and our relations.'[12]

Early in 2000, Mbeki and the ANC leadership were shocked to learn that a group of SANCO leaders were contemplating the formation of a political party to contest local government elections. A seminal document endorsed by the national executive suggested this as one of five possible future scenarios for SANCO: 'The viability for an option such as this one is because of the lack of a political competitor to the ruling party.'[13]

The document argued that the views of the poor were not sufficiently catered for by the ANC, and that many SANCO leaders believed a civic-based party would attract votes. 'The political space for SANCO to form a political party is readily available. SANCO has to its advantage the appropriate leadership credentials, a large following at community level and a pro-transformation agenda.'[14]

SANCO's other options were to assume the role of political watchdog; 'confusedly' totter on the political fringes; or become a development agency or a 'revolutionary' social movement.[15]

The policy document raised alarm within the ANC, and Hlongwane was summoned to explain it. Under heavy pressure from the ANC, SANCO's leadership was humiliated into distancing itself from the proposals. Branches were not impressed with the easy capitulation of their leaders, and some would take matters into their own hands.

With the ANC campaign for the December local elections in full swing in its traditional Eastern Cape stronghold, a panicky local leader broke the news to Luthuli House that an angry provincial meeting of SANCO had resolved not to support the party at the polls. Already feeling that they were being ignored by the party's central leadership, the final straw for frustrated SANCO leaders was the highly secretive and manipulative compilation of the ANC's list of candidates.

Under the chairmanship of Jacob Zuma, the ANC's national deployment committee had vetted all nominations. Candidates judged likely to cause problems or who had been critical of government policy in the past were relegated to the bottom of the list to ensure that they would not take office, while some of the most popular civic leaders were left off the list entirely.

Madikizela-Mandela was quickly called in from another spell in political Siberia and persuaded to help convince the SANCO rebels that they should return to the fold. Tensions boiled over during meetings to resolve the problem, with local SANCO leaders telling senior ANC figures they were unhappy with government's restrictive economic policies, which they blamed for ongoing hardship in the townships. The ANC was told that 'The water, electricity and telephone cut-offs of those who can't afford the new high rates of many of the privatised agencies are making the pain unbearable in the townships.' SANCO also attacked the slashing of public service jobs, especially at local government level, which saw 'our people being thrown out on the streets'.

Motlanthe promised action. Madikizela-Mandela vowed to personally lobby Mbeki. Some of the loudest complainants were moved higher up on the election list, but about a dozen refused to accept any compromise. The elections went ahead, with dissidents standing as independent candidates on anti-privatisation and pro-poor platforms. But both the Mbeki-ites and the ANC's left had been scared into what would be a fresh skirmish for SANCO 's soul.

Mbeki's earlier efforts to gain control of the civic movement and its subsequent decline had been watched by many with trepidation. Now COSATU general secretary Zwelinzima Vavi and president Willie Madisha set up bilateral meetings with the SANCO leadership to woo them back to the left. COSATU's 2000 conference adopted a resolution to beef up SANCO branches and run joint anti-privatisation campaigns. SACP general secretary Blade Nzimande rushed to offer SANCO counsel, and even Zackie Achmat and the Treatment Action Campaign lobbied the civic leaders.

It all paid off. SANCO joined COSATU and another forty community organisations in an alliance to pressure government on job creation and the rollout of anti-AIDS drugs at public hospitals.

The lobby group would later be at the forefront of efforts to force pharmaceutical companies to halt legal action against the government's proposed import of cheaper ARVs, and would support the TAC's successful court action to make Nevirapine available at public hospitals.

'The debate on economic and social policy needs to be broadened,' explains former SANGOCO executive director Abie Ditlhake,[16] one of the new breed of community activists. 'We need a reconfiguration of the nature of politics in South Africa. A realignment of politics will allow space for fresh input into the economic debate.'

Angered by SANCO president Hlongwane's perceived loyalty to Mbeki, the organisation began casting around for a new leader. The choice fell on former Mpumalanga premier Mathews Phosa, who had gone on to become a successful businessman, at which point the Mbeki-ites drew their line in the sand. There was simply no way one of Mbeki's fiercest rivals could be countenanced in the SANCO driving seat. The ANC offered to secure R2 million in donations to save SANCO from imminent financial collapse.

With debtors lining up and the sheriff just about to knock on SANCO's door, it was an offer the leadership could not refuse. Motlanthe and Ngonyama put the finishing touches to the bail-out, and Hlongwane was duly re-elected.

Nonetheless, SANCO's 2001 national conference was a heated affair, with Mbeki personally addressing delegates. His reconciliatory stance and humble admission of government's shortcomings included the promise of future inclusion in policymaking, and hinted at a more expansionist economic policy. But he also warned that efforts to break the tripartite alliance would hand the formidable enemies of transformation the ammunition they sought to reverse the democratic government's achievements.

Despite having loaded the SANCO executive with allies, Mbeki soon had reason to worry anew. With the 2004 elections on the horizon, there were rumblings within COSATU about forming a workers' party, which could attract the support of both SANCO and the SACP.

At the ANC's 2002 conference, Mbeki pulled out all the stops to charm SANCO, referring in his presidential address to the civic movement as a full alliance partner, holding equal status with COSATU and the SACP. He also hinted at a makeover of civil society that would see SANCO loyalists, sympathetic COSATU affiliates, rival unions such as FEDUSA and NACTU, and various NGOs joining forces in a new centrist civic grouping that would work in tandem with the government to implement transformation.

Dreadlocked, soft-spoken Che Guevara fan and reggae lover Andile Mngxitama is an unlikely fellow to strike terror into the government's heart, except that he is a leading figure in the Landless People's Movement (LPM), one of the new crop of social protest movements that have sprung up from post-apartheid South Africa's grassroots. Formed in 2001 as the result of deep frustration over the slow pace of land and agricultural reform and restitution, the LPM played a major role in the August 2002 march on the World Summit for Sustainable Development in upmarket Sandton, north of Johannesburg. Thousands of delegates and journalists from across the globe witnessed a sea of protestors, wearing T-shirts screaming 'Land!' 'Food!' 'Jobs!', and chanting slogans against imperialists, neo-liberals and anti-poor policies.[17] The march totally eclipsed a simultaneous counter-demonstration, carefully orchestrated by the ANC and addressed by Mbeki, causing him great embarrassment.

That march may yet turn out to have marked the start of a new struggle movement that could redefine South African politics. Although the new movement is still too small and incohesive to 'shut the government down if it doesn't do what the people want', as one of the march leaders thundered to loud cheers, it would be foolhardy to ignore the potential power it could amass.

In an action replay of 1980s confrontations between security forces and anti-apartheid activists, thousands of flag-waving protestors faced the summit venue's heavily fortified perimeter under the watchful eyes of heavily armed police and soldiers with machine guns peering through the portholes of Casspirs. The protestors deliberately chose a route through the neighbouring township of Alexandra, 'the running sore of shacks and open sewers that lies within sight of the gleaming citadel' of Sandton, to show the 'obscene' contrast between shack-land and the plush surroundings where the summit was taking place.[18]

Like the LPM, most of the new social movements are community-based, and vary in size, focus and influence. What unites them is a common determination to help the poor and downtrodden, and therein lies their power.

Growing anger over inequality, poverty and unemployment, combined with disillusionment over the pace of social and economic delivery to the most needy, gives these movements instant appeal. They share a strong aversion to political and corporate bullying and insensitive government bureaucracies and corporate greed, and focus on townships, squatter camps and rural settlements. They raise their voices over issues of direct concern to the poor – HIV/AIDS, evictions, power and water cut-offs, retrenchments, privatisation, and calls for the repudiation of apartheid debt. Their methods are those used successfully by the ANC of old: pamphlets, house visits, marches and defiance campaigns, and they stage their most visible protests in traditional ANC strongholds such as Oswego and Alexandra.

Most are led by ANC dissidents, unionists from COSATU, ex-communists who have given up on the SACP and former civic leaders who have lost faith in SANCO.

The tough and precarious lives endured by most black South Africans due to a combination of colonialism, apartheid, slow change and lack of social welfare for generations make them dependent on family, kinship, religious and mutual-help networks, such as *stokvels* (savings clubs), burial societies and formal community organisations. Recent studies show that there are almost 100 000 non-profit organisations across the country, and in 1998, almost 1.5 million volunteers served them.[19] More than 53 per cent are informal structures rather than non-profit companies, trusts, churches, trade unions or cooperatives.

Some of the new civic movements consider themselves part of the international anti-globalisation community, the so-called Seattle Movement, but are partisan to the poor of countries of the South. They have links with grassroots activists in developing countries such as Brazil, the Philippines and India. Many have structured branches, mandates and leaders, while others consist of no more than extended families or communities with common problems and a shared need to make a better life.

Methods of defiance vary from civil disobedience to violent protest and invasion of land. The LPM caused great consternation in government circles when it warned that unless land reform was speeded up, it would launch a campaign to take back the land. Mbeki acted swiftly to make it clear that the nightmare vision of Zimbabwe-type land grabs would not be tolerated in South Africa, but the LPM has modelled itself on Brazil's Landless Workers' Movement, and might well emulate the South American example of moving thousands of peasants onto farmland without warning.

After being expelled from the ANC in 1999 for his radical anti-privatisation stance, former Pimville councillor Trevor Ngwane founded the Soweto Electricity Crisis Committee (SECC), which was behind Operation Khanyisa (light), the widespread illegal reconnection of electricity supplies cut off by Eskom for non-payment.

'It's criminal to rob people of the necessities of life,' thundered Ngwane.[20] The SECC also campaigns against water cuts, privatisation of services, and the eviction of township residents for defaulting on rent and mortgage payments. Township residents heartily supported the Vula Amanzi campaign to turn on the water, and, the SECC's anti-eviction initiative, Operation Buyel'Endlini (go back to your house), which drew a vitriolic response from ANC leaders. 'Look, these people cannot be allowed to get away with this, the law must deal with them harshly!,'[21] exclaimed Essop Pahad, minister in Mbeki's office.

Ngwane was also the spirit behind the militant Anti-Privatisation Forum (APF), formed early in 2000. The APF favours direct action over appeals for service delivery or poverty alleviation programmes. It aims to mobilise township anger as a powerful force against the slow delivery of basic services, privatisation of essential services, such as water, electricity, sanitation and health, and the slashing of municipal social service budgets.

The APF umbrella shelters some six smaller organisations, including the SECC. Key APF figures include trade unionists John Appolis and Rob Rees, an official in one of COSATU's most militant affiliates, SAMWU. The APF was launched in response to the Johannesburg metropolitan council's Igoli 2002 plan – bitterly but unsuccessfully opposed by SAMWU as a way to slip privatisation in through the back door[22] – and the Witwatersrand University's 2001 retrenchment plan, which was vehemently opposed by the National Education, Health and Allied Workers Union (NEHAWU).

A group of APF supporters dubbed the Kensington 87 were arrested in 2002 after allegedly stoning the home of Johannesburg mayor Amos Masondo during a protest against electricity and water cut-offs.

Ngwane accuses Mbeki of using 'revolutionary-sounding phrases and ANC struggle credentials to implement a capitalist agenda'. Dale McKinley, an APF spokesman, says the new social movements are trying to 'build a new left outside the ANC alliance, speaking to basic issues like water, electricity, jobs and housing'.[23]

In the highly industrialised Vaal Triangle, the Lekoa-Vaal Forum plays much the same role as the SECC, while local resistance groups have sprung up in Katlehong and Katorus. The protests have spread steadily, as far west as Warrenton in the Northern Cape, and to such Western Cape townships as Tafelsig, Khayelitsha, Lavender Hill, Delft, Valhalla Park and Crossroads.

In Durban, the Concerned Citizens Forum (CCF), led by ANC veteran Fatima Meer, has helped form mobile 'defenders of communities', who prevent cut-offs and evictions in areas such as Chatsworth, Mpumalanga and Isipingo. The forum resorts to the courts to halt evictions and has won several cases involving the illegal occupation of empty houses. It scored a ground-breaking victory on council rents and levies, and has launched a major battle against the Durban metropolitan council over plans to relocate rent defaulters.

It is of some concern to the ANC that many of the new social movements have no hesitation about using the law to their advantage, and opposing it when they believe it to be unjust. The CCF has marched on the houses of local councillors who favour disconnection of services for non-payment and openly advocates the illegal reconnection of water and electricity supplies. In fact, the forum has trained what it calls 'struggle plumbers and electricians' to do the job! The CCF was behind a march of more than 5 000 people in 2002 demanding a maximum monthly service fee of R10 for the poor, and has sponsored small independent unions to organise workers in the sweatshops that have mushroomed in the region.

CCF meetings are often lively, with music and dancing by members sporting T-shirts with slogans such as 'Smash GEAR – Celebrate Life'. It has neither a formal structure nor any ideological platform beyond rebuilding 'a sense of community' in townships ravaged by both apartheid and what it calls Mbeki's 'brutal Reaganomics'.[24] The CCF has close links with the LPM and the Anti-Eviction Campaign (AEC) in the Western Cape.

The AEC made its appearance in November 2000, and includes some twenty residents' associations from sprawling townships on the Cape Flats, such as Khayelitsha, Tafelsig, Blue Downs and Mandela Park. Described as a 'grassroots social movement',[25] the AEC caters chiefly for the unemployed. Their chief form of protest is moving into an area where evictions are pending, staging sit-ins to obstruct council officials from carrying out their task and helping evicted residents to reoccupy their homes immediately. In extreme cases, AEC members have rendered properties unliveable for new occupants, arguing that 'if the people cannot have the land, then no one will'. The AEC has recently also taken up the cudgels on behalf of families who cannot pay their children's school fees.

The Khulumani Support Group was launched in 1995 on the back of popular anger at government's failure to provide adequate reparations for the victims of apartheid brutalities, but does double duty as a service NGO.[26] 'There is deep disillusionment with government's failure to keep its promises, especially over reparations,'[27] says Marjorie Jobson, chairman of the group. Khulumani has programmes in all nine provinces to deal with the psychological, educational, medical and long-term socio-economic needs of apartheid victims. Actively involved in various lawsuits against transnational corporations that benefited from apartheid, Khulumani has threatened to go to court if the government declares a blanket amnesty for perpetrators of political crimes who were not granted amnesty by the Truth Commission.

Jubilee 2000 includes influential church leaders, such as Anglican Archbishop of Cape Town Njongonkulu Ndungane, who has borne the brunt of many attacks by ANC leaders for his criticism of government policy that puts economic austerity ahead of development. Jubilee is a branch of the international organisation that has been fighting since 1998 for apartheid reparations.

Of all the new social movements, the TAC is by far the most powerful. Founded in 1998 by Zackie Achmat and Mark Heywood, its aims are access to affordable HIV/AIDS treatment and prevention of new infection. The organisation uses a shrewd mix of civil disobedience, protests and court action to force the hands of government and international drug companies.

Though Achmat is a card-carrying member of the ANC, the TAC is not aligned to any political party, and vigorously decries Mbeki's denial of the link between HIV and AIDS. Good organisation and astute cooperation with other protest groups are the keys to the success of TAC campaigns. In return for the support of COSATU and other civic groups, such as SANGOCO on AIDS issues, the TAC is happy to add its name to trade union and anti-privatisation campaigns or join the clamour for a basic income grant.

Significantly, TAC protests have managed to attract the youth, many of whom have no interest in formal political structures, and have been endorsed by no less a figure than Nelson Mandela in many instances. While this alone angers Mbeki, the TAC does not emulate other dissenting factions by attacking the ANC as a sell-out, but directs its criticism at specific government policies.

Older social movements traditionally associated with the ANC, such as the National Land Committee (NLC), have long since shown signs of rebellion. Launched in 1987 to oppose forced removals, the NLC has branches in all nine provinces and supports all new social movements that share its values. 'Government's land programmes are severely limited and the promises made to the people have not been met,' explains veteran land rights campaigner Zakes Hlatshwayo.[28] 'Our pressure is from below. Unless the government faces the masses, there will be no change.'[29]

In many African countries, radical civil society groups that were influential during liberation struggles lost their power after independence by being drawn into government or pressured into remodelling themselves as narrow interest groups. Mahmood Mamdani warns that this is dangerous for democracy.[30]

South Africa's Reconstruction and Development Programme emphasised 'a commitment to grassroots, bottom-up development which is owned and driven by communities and representative organisations. Beneficiary communities should be involved at all levels of decision-making and in the implementation of their projects. Social movements and CBOs (community-based organisations) are a major asset in the effort to democratise and develop our society.'[31]

The formal political ambit was defined in the 1996 Constitution, which allows for proportional representation based on multiparty competition.[32] An essential feature of liberal democracies is the clear boundary between political and civil society and the designation of the state as a neutral arbiter. Obviously, how democratic the system is depends largely on the internal ethos of the parties and how in touch they are with their constituencies. But it is also determined by the quality of the rules and culture that govern the political chambers, council and committee meetings, as well as their transparency, responsiveness and accountability.[33]

The ANC government enacted a raft of new legislation and policies to provide operating space for civil society groups. Organisations such as the National Lotteries Fund provide financing for groups committed to alleviating poverty, and civil society also benefits from a number of tax advantages.

However, this favourable environment rests on an assumption that civil society groups share government's development agenda and will help government achieve its objectives,[34] hence the demand that existing social movements and NGOs remake themselves or face exclusion.[35]

The exiles, the dominant faction of the ANC from which Mbeki takes his cues, adhere firmly to democratic centralism, with a subservient relationship between civil society groups and trade unions on the one hand, and the government on the other, not unlike the situation in Eastern Europe before the fall of communism. In formal institutions such as NEDLAC, civil society is represented in name only.

As far back as 1990, Mandela rejected calls to retain the UDF's grassroots structures as an independent movement alongside the ANC. The struggle against apartheid had deeply politicised civil society, and the proposal was viewed as an illegitimate challenge to the ANC's position. Following its election victory in 1994, the new government increased pressure on civics to move away from resistance politics to development efforts and service delivery.

Some, especially in SANCO, tried to resist such moves, which had begun when the UDF was disbanded and absorbed by the ANC in 1991, but most civil society groups had been loyal to the ANC all along as part of the Mass Democratic Movement. They supported the party and the RDP, but as large numbers of activists from trade unions, civics and progressive NGOs were given government appointments, the rest had to redefine their future role. Should they work with or in opposition to the ANC government, or focus exclusively on fighting for the interests of the poor?

The one thing the ANC knew was that it did not want radical civil society groups acting as watchdogs over the government, as they had under apartheid. At the party's national conference in 1997, Mandela lambasted organisations and activists, such as SANCO's Mzwanele Mayekiso, younger brother of Moses Mayekiso, the former president of SANCO, for believing that civil society organisations should indeed play such a role and serve as channels for grassroots communities to voice their grievances and expectations.[36]

The adoption of GEAR as South Africa's economic policy in mid-1996 further undermined civil society groups. Not only was one of the mainstays of the policy the outsourcing of state functions to private firms and consultancies, but GEAR ushered in a new style of administration, which sees the government govern and the masses obediently follow.

When Mbeki became president in 1999, he redefined government's relationship with civil society. Stakeholders – women, students, traditional leaders – would be drawn into local development initiatives, and community projects would be tackled by mass-based social movements in partnership with government. ANC strategists advocated the retention of street committees, which had originated in the 1980s to act as community-level 'stakeholder forums'.

The government's Integrated Sustainable Rural Development Strategy (ISRDS) and its urban equivalent, the Urban Renewal Strategy, were among early examples of this new dispensation.[37] The Mbeki-ites were convinced that stakeholder politics would develop a 'new social movement for rural development', firmly under control of central government.

Ironically, the sudden radicalisation of South Africa's civil society after years of quiescence is largely due to growing impatience among the poor and the needy for official attention, empathy and delivery of jobs, services and welfare. For millions of black South Africans, the only difference between their miserable lives under apartheid and their miserable lives under the democracy they fought so long and hard to attain, is that they have the right to vote. Many of the new social movements sprang up in the restless period immediately before the 2000 local elections. Established community bonds, which successfully served as an alternative welfare net to cushion the hardships of apartheid, have been ruptured by a new wave of urbanisation, the dizzyingly swift modernisation of South Africa's economy and the rapid rise of an upwardly mobile population.

Many beneficiaries of the new dispensation have made the trek from the townships to traditionally white suburbs. Few local ANC councillors now even live among their township constituents, and at national level there is an unexpected hardening of attitudes towards the downtrodden by the governing elite. Finance minister Trevor Manuel has frequently made it clear that government will not encourage a culture of 'entitlement', and that people must find their own way out of poverty. As far as the 'haves' are concerned, 'if we could do it [change our material fortunes] they [the poor] can also do so'.[38]

How quickly they forget that political office has been the key to privilege for many. Those trapped in circumstances that have been exacerbated by unemployment, disease and sheer destitution have been forced to form new alliances and networks in a desperate attempt to capture the crumbs from the tables of bounty laid for former comrades who have become deaf, in their new comfort zones, to pleas for solidarity, or answer them with injunctions to be patient.

During the turbulent 1980s, community development forums planted their roots by opening local-level negotiations between residents' associations and civics, many affiliated to the UDF, and white local councils. Their purpose was to resolve disputes centred on evictions, rates and service boycotts – the identical issues that serve as rallying points today.

Some of the older forums proved resilient and continue to operate at local level, while others have adapted and moved into other spheres, notably NEDLAC, in a search for consensus or compromise between government, organised labour, business and civil society on highly contested issues.

It's been a major challenge for civil society groups to remake themselves in order to survive, let alone prosper, while simultaneously taking on added social responsibilities. The government has shifted some of the duties of repairing the fragile fabric of society, already stretched to the limit by the anti-apartheid struggle, to NGOs and churches. By contrast, after the Second World War, many European nations pursued a parallel process of economic reconstruction and rebuilding a social infrastructure ravaged by years of conflict.

With the advent of democracy in South Africa, many community organisations faced financial crisis. Foreign funding dried up rapidly from 1994, and what donor funding continued was diverted to government programmes or the National Development Agency. Most foreign funding was channelled to 'fashionable' causes, such as AIDS, which gets a sympathetic ear in Western countries.

Many NGOs closed down, while others found themselves competing against private firms and consultancies for government contracts. Some successfully reorientated themselves to the point where they could compile government policy documents, conduct research and monitor service delivery projects.

A plethora of new institutions, such as NEDLAC, the Human Rights Commission and the Commission on Gender Equality, assumed the oversight roles previously played by NGOs and community organisations, but as government failed to spend funds earmarked for social upliftment, slashed welfare budgets and limited redistribution, flagging activist entities found a new *raison d'être*.

With the surge in community involvement came new forms of protest. The courts have become a favoured arena in which to fight government policy, claim constitutional rights and agitate for redistribution. Social movements have won stunning legal victories on major issues, such as shelter for children, protection from forced eviction and access to essential medicines.

In what became known as the Grootboom case, residents of an informal settlement outside Cape Town went to the Constitutional Court to force the government to provide their children with alternative housing when they were forcibly removed from their shacks.[39] Community-based organisations and social movements also turned to the law in an effort to block the controversial arms procurement and acquisition deal, arguing that the money should be channelled to social spending.

Protests by the new civil movements are gaining momentum. Some groups seriously considered forming a united party to contest the 2004 election, but although they decided not to do so at the time, it would be dangerous to dismiss their potential support out of hand like Mbeki's closest ally, Essop Pahad, who asks: 'Why all the focus on these little so-called dissident groups?'[40] Intelligence minister Ronnie Kasrils calls them 'the loony left', and Dale McKinley confirms that, initially, the government attitude was 'we don't have to worry about these guys, they're just mosquitoes'.[41]

But as 2004 drew to a close, there were distinct signs that the Mbeki-ites were rather more anxious about the new social movements than they would admit, and that they could well be the president's ultimate ultra-left nightmare.

Not only are the movements in direct competition with the ANC for the support of the poor black masses, they are also led, in many cases, by activists who cut their protest teeth on behalf of the ANC. Some retain their party membership, but have given up on trying to advance their causes through party structures, convinced that the centralisation of policy-making has eroded democracy within the ANC. For Marxists and unionists, this is political anathema, and Mbeki has reason to fear a coalition of the social movements with COSATU, disgruntled ANC left-wingers and the SACP, which could see the rise of a new party along the lines of Brazil's ruling PT, or Workers' Party.

To the chagrin of Mbeki and the ANC leadership, in mid-2004 the SACP resolved to shelter the new social movements under its umbrella and to share anti-poverty platforms. The decision was a pragmatic one, based on the concern that unless the SACP managed to secure some measure of influence on the mush-rooming groups, they could eclipse the party. Prior to this, both the SACP and COSATU had been hesitant about aligning themselves with the new civics, which are often blatantly anti-ANC. The party's alliance partners felt that it was wrong to attack the ANC as a whole on issues such as corruption, being unsympathetic to the poor or selling out to business, as many of the most radical civic leaders do.

Mbeki and ANC strategists are uneasy about the prospect of an alliance between established and new civic movements, the SACP and COSATU, and, at least in part, it is this fear that lies behind the extraordinarily bitter attack on Vavi, Madisha, Nzimande and Archbishop Desmond Tutu in November 2004. The Mbeki-ites are not only deeply concerned that COSATU and the SACP are starting to explore the viability of such an alliance, but also that Tutu's criticism of the ANC's spotty record on poverty alleviation would lend moral legitimacy to such a group and instantly boost their cause.

Mbeki is politically astute enough to foresee a breakaway leftist party at some point in the future, but he would prefer that this not happen during his presidency. So he continues to woo the most militant organisations and pack their leaderships with sympathisers. Should this strategy fail, the next move would be to destabilise the social movements by sowing division within their ranks and demonising the leaders.

Church leaders have been particularly critical of government's economic and social policies, especially GEAR, which they say has increased poverty and unemployment despite attaining macroeconomic stability. Many prominent progressive church groups have rallied behind COSATU's campaigns opposing GEAR and the privatisation of state-owned companies, such as Telkom and Eskom.

In 2001, Mbeki set up a religious working group, ostensibly to advise him on poverty alleviation and social development, as well as to initiate a programme of moral renewal. It is also at least partly intended to draw critical clerics away from rebellious ANC allies and closer to the Mbeki camp. Critical church leaders like Ndungane were invited aboard, and, in a tandem move, Mbeki-ites openly supported candidates known to be sympathetic to the president for election to the South African Council of Churches. General secretary Molefe Tsele, for example, has worked hard to soften criticism of NEPAD.

Senior ANC leaders have repeatedly tried to secure the election of Mbeki sympathisers to SANGOCO's leadership as well. Ngonyama denies that this is part of a campaign to gain control of the organisation, but admits that from time to time the ANC leadership 'engaged with aligned organisations it thought were veering off course'.[42]

Essop Pahad repeatedly called in former SANGOCO CEO Abie Ditlhake for 'discussions' on the organisation's criticism of government policies.

Centralisation of donor funding is a particularly effective mechanism to keep social movements under control. Rebellious activists are simply not likely to receive funding, and, in extreme cases, there have been attempts to cut funding that had already been approved.[43]

The NLC was warned in 2000 that its critical stance against the slow pace of land reform could jeopardise its funding prospects. Shortly afterwards, outspoken NLC chief Zakes Hlatswayo's head was on the block for allegedly not acting against the LPM's Mngxitama for making 'anti-government' statements. The National Rural Network was also read the riot act after linking cholera outbreaks to the privatisation of water services.

Mbeki views the militant social movements with deep suspicion. In his eyes, they could sabotage his vision of a centrist national consensus, so with both the ANC and the government firmly under his control, the next major battle is likely to be against the new civics. Unless official opposition parties find ways of becoming more relevant, social movements could be the greatest threat to the ANC in future. Significantly, young activists disillusioned with party politics and from whom the next generation of leaders will be drawn, are increasingly being attracted to extra-parliamentary groupings.

For the sake of democracy, it is vital for South Africa to have a vibrant, independent, energetic and gutsy civil society that will keep the government on its toes, and any attempts to curtail social activism should be guarded against. Illegal action undoubtedly warrants the taking of appropriate steps, but using them as an excuse to crush dissent should never be allowed to happen.

New civil movements have emerged because they are needed. Opposition parties do not articulate the needs of the marginalised masses, and representative institutions are inaccessible. If delivery remains slow and the ANC continues to choke internal dissent, the first faint stirrings of a new resistance struggle could turn into something of far greater magnitude. If the deep inequalities of the past are not rectified soon, a full-blown and devastating uprising of the poor could be at hand.

# — 14 —

# 'We Are All
# Yes-Men and
# Yes-Women Now!'

Now we, too, ride in official limousines
And humbly get yes-master, yes-sir, yes-minister, yes-everything
The no-people of the struggle have learned
yes-habits swiftly and without explanation
— **Translation of a poem by Mathews Phosa**[1]

O N AN OVERCAST SATURDAY IN MARCH 2002, FORMER PRESIDENT NELSON
Mandela made a passionate plea for the government to distribute the anti-
retroviral drug Nevirapine to all HIV-infected pregnant women at state hospitals.

His presentation at a watershed meeting of the ANC's national executive was
much anticipated, and the party leadership had set aside the best part of a day to
discuss the AIDS pandemic. Prior to the meeting, Mandela had promised that like
'any other loyal member', he would raise his concerns over Thabo Mbeki's
HIV/AIDS policies through party structures.

As the sage elder statesman spoke, candidly stating that the government was
being perceived as uncaring by stubbornly refusing to roll out the desperately
needed drug, he was heckled. A startled Mandela halted, then continued, but the
heckling resumed, louder and bolder and more openly than before.

Ironically, just a few weeks earlier, Mandela had complained at a meeting of
the ANC's National Working Committee that there seemed to be a lack of internal
debate within the party. Not a single cabinet minister, he pointed out, had
opposed Mbeki's views on AIDS.

As soon as he finished his address to the NEC, Mandela left to attend another
engagement. No sooner had he gone than the meeting erupted into a flood of
invective against him. Senior ANC leaders accused the former president of being
ill disciplined for publicly differing from the official line on ARVs. In a charge

led by then deputy speaker of the National Assembly and fervent Mbeki loyalist Baleka Mbete, Mandela was derided as a dissident. Incumbent safety and security minister Steve Tshwete, KwaZulu-Natal leaders Dumisani Makhaye and S'bu Ndebele, as well as election coordinator Peter Mokaba, bayed just as loudly as the pack leader.

Only two NEC members – MP Pallo Jordan and former secretary general Cyril Ramaphosa – defended Mandela's right to criticise and hold his own opinions, and even they were careful not to offend.

When Mokaba stridently challenged anyone among those present to stand up and support Mandela's views, there was an uncomfortable silence. It was common knowledge that Mokaba was Mbeki's lapdog, and no one in that assembly wanted to be seen to be crossing the absentee president.

Apart from the grievous disrespect the outburst showed towards South Africa's iconic first black president, it was a worrying demonstration that the tenets of the ANC's political style in exile have become the mantra of the ANC in government: centralised decision-making, unquestioned loyalty, no public criticism and pre-ordained election of leaders. But the methods required by a clandestine liberation movement facing a ruthless enemy are not the stuff of which a vibrant and dynamic democracy is made. Democracy recognises that in difference and dissent lie strength, that open debate can lead to something other than disarray, that loyalty has to be earned.

When it was unbanned in 1990, the ANC was operating on four levels, each with its own distinct style and culture. Members of all four groups have been accommodated in government, but the exiles, personified by Mbeki, are pre-eminent. Those accustomed to the open and consultative style of the United Democratic Front, trade unions and civics – the inziles – survive in the contemporary ANC only by adapting to the president's style, as Trevor Manuel and Frank Chikane have done, or keeping their heads down, like Murphy Morobe and Cheryl Carolus.

The ANC in exile adopted an almost military command style, as former MK guerrilla Jabu Moleketi explains: 'In exile and in the underground things were run tightly. Information was supplied on a need-to-know basis. If information was leaked into the wrong hands it could cause problems for the movement. People had full confidence in the leadership. They believed that even if they did not have all the information, the leaders who did, had the best intentions.'[2]

Stepping out of line came at a high cost. Chris Hani was temporarily imprisoned for criticising the ANC leadership, though his punishment was later rescinded. Pallo Jordan was incarcerated for some time because he accused the ANC's security apparatus of abusing their power.

He says, 'During its 30 years of illegal operation, security considerations, distance between centres and the dispersal of its membership across the globe, the militarisation of the movement as a result of the armed struggle tilted the balance further away from consultative practices. But within those limitations the movement kept alive a tradition of internal debate and discussion that finds expression in its publications, conference documents and other records.'[3]

But Jordan warns that a monolithic ANC and tripartite alliance, in which no debate is countenanced and internal dissent is suppressed, would deprive it of the 'life-giving oxygen it requires for its very survival'. In his view, 'President Mbeki and his colleagues are as alive to that danger as anyone else.'[4]

While negotiating the future of South Africa, the tactics used in exile came in handy for the ANC. Negotiators often had to make policy decisions on the trot, with no time to consult the rank and file, such as when the armed struggle was suspended and certain sunset clauses were proposed.

However, this brand of policy-making has now become entrenched in the top echelons of the ANC,[5] allowing the government to adopt highly unpopular conservative economic and social policies that clearly go against the welfare of its own mass constituency. Almost everywhere in the developing world, governments embarking on economic reform strategies, known as structural adjustment programmes, like GEAR, have come unstuck amid fierce resistance from the poor masses, who inevitably bear the brunt of such decisions.

So far, except for relatively minor protests, the ANC government has pushed through painful economic reforms unhindered. There have been none of the bloody riots that accompanied economic reform in Zimbabwe, Egypt, India or Nigeria, but this might only be because Mbeki runs a tight ship and none of the opposition parties has the ear of the masses.

The ANC's dominance of the tripartite alliance has also kept the angry poor on a short leash, but Mbeki deserves credit for his shrewd manipulation of avowed leftists into all the strategically important economic posts: the Treasury, trade and industry, public enterprises, public service and administration, labour. If contentious policies must be explained to the masses, who better to do so than those with impeccable leftist credentials, who just happen also to be managing the reforms? To quote Vincent Maphai and Keith Gottschalk: 'Only leftists can confer sufficient credibility on a process of economic reform that is a compromise towards the right, especially within poorer or militant sections of the ANC's constituencies.'[6]

Protests are allowed, provided they can be controlled or managed and have the ANC leadership's approval. Demonstrations against greedy drug manufacturers or the World Bank are even endorsed, as long as the government is left out of the equation. Obviously, protests from the political right – white or black – remain inconsequential, unless they suddenly start agitating for redistribution!

Senior ANC leaders, including Essop Pahad, minister in the president's office, and former Northern Province premier Ngoako Ramatlhodi, launched a bitter personal tirade against Malegapuru William Makgoba, president of the Medical Research Council, when he criticised the government's AIDS policy. Prior to Makgoba attacking Mbeki's denialist views, he was the president's favourite scientist and a frequent guest in the Mbeki home. But in July 2001, Pahad and a group of senior cabinet ministers summoned Makgoba to a meeting, where he faced a relentless intervention by politicians trying to force him to support Mbeki's stance on HIV/AIDS.

A barrage of abusive letters against Makgoba followed, many of them lambasting the highly respected professor for suggesting that Mbeki should leave science to the scientists. One threatening letter contained twenty-two pages of abuse against Makgoba and was signed by Ramatlhodi. He accused Makgoba of 'betraying his race', of not being a 'real' black person and engaging in 'character assassination' of Mbeki. It speaks volumes for Makgoba's strength of character and integrity that he stood firm against such sustained and fierce government-led attacks, and refused to compromise his own convictions, even at great personal and professional cost. But many other black intellectuals were less courageous, and fearing similar treatment, simply fell silent in the face of the onslaught against Makgoba.

Mbeki singled out SACP deputy general secretary Jeremy Cronin for humiliation when he mildly criticised the ANC for losing touch with its grassroots members. Despite being forced by the SACP leadership to offer a public apology, Cronin came in for a severe drubbing from fellow NEC members Smuts Ngonyama and Dumisani Makhaye. Makhaye, an extreme Africanist, made the vicious racist comment: 'We don't need a white messiah.' There was no public rebuttal.

ANC national chairperson Mosiuoa Lekota faced a venomous attack following his public admission that Mbeki's quiet diplomacy was having no effect on Zimbabwean president Robert Mugabe. Mbeki demanded a retraction, but to his credit, Lekota refused, insisting this was his personal opinion. The party bosses moved to stymie his bid for the ANC's deputy presidency at the party's fifty-first national conference in December 2002, and a torrent of abuse rained down on Lekota's head, including leaks to the media that he had not declared certain business interests to parliament.

Juicy and egregious media leaks have become a favourite way of sidelining anyone perceived as a Mbeki critic or opponent. Many watched anxiously as Mbeki trained his sights on Max Sisulu, head of the ANC's transformation unit, who had frequently criticised the fact that many policy decisions are made by a select few. First, Sisulu, son of ANC doyen Walter Sisulu, was redeployed from parliament to arms company Denel as deputy CEO. Then, to rub salt in the wounds, a junior was appointed over Sisulu's head as CEO of the company. Apparently, not even this was enough, as rumours suddenly began circulating that Sisulu was a heavy drinker and not to be trusted to lead a company so closely linked to national security. If it was not so serious, the entire episode would have been laughable, but it brought home to every would-be party critic that not even a revered political name guaranteed immunity.

Nor, as an ugly situation showed in November 2004, did a Nobel Prize or a purple robe and dog collar.

Archbishop Desmond Tutu, who is no man's fool, has never feared to tread where angels will not go, and so it was when he delivered the prestigious Nelson Mandela Lecture in the tenth year of a democracy for which he fought as hard as anyone. South Africa was sitting on 'a powder keg of poverty', he said, as long as black empowerment continued to benefit only a small elite group. Tutu also lamented the fact that the culture of robust debate, which had characterised the anti-apartheid movement, seemed to have given way to servile, self-seeking flattery, with sycophancy coming into its own.

'I would have wished to see far more open debate in the ANC, for instance, on the HIV and AIDS views of the president,' said the feisty cleric.[7]

His words were not yet cold when Mbeki, ANC national spokesman Smuts Ngonyama and secretary general Kgalema Motlanthe launched an astonishingly acrimonious broadside in response.

'Evidently,' fumed Mbeki in his weekly online missive, 'the archbishop thinks there is something wrong with members agreeing with ANC policies that have been decided on within the organisation's various forums, including our national conference. He dismisses the members of our movement as "voting cattle of the party".'[8]

Added the president, 'The archbishop has never been a member of the ANC and would have very little knowledge of what happens in an ANC branch. How he comes to the conclusion that there is "lack of debate" in the ANC is most puzzling.'

Naturally the media had a field day, but behind the sensational headlines lay an incontrovertible truth: no one who dares to criticise Mbeki or the ANC government's policies will escape the wrath of Luthuli House or the West Wing in the Union Buildings.

Many ANC leaders have complained that the NEC has become a rubber stamp.[9] Fear of being seen as opposing or criticising the party line has become pervasive. Some members might privately express reservations about policies, but would not dare raise their doubts at formal meetings. Essop Pahad and others have frequently asked why, if there is as much dissatisfaction with Mbeki or the government as the media suggests, do ANC leaders not express this in party forums?[10] Why, indeed.

Mbeki's victory in having many of his allies elected to the NEC at the Mafikeng conference in 1997 was reprised at Stellenbosch in 2000. The National Working

Committee is also packed with Mbeki supporters. Secretary General Kgalema Motlanthe, former general secretary of the National Union of Mineworkers, was elected by the left to provide a counterbalance to the centrists, but has become totally immersed in rebuilding the ANC and spends long periods on the road.[11]

Independent voices in the NEC, who were critical during the Mandela administration, have been stilled by the retribution against dissenters since Mbeki took office. He and his lieutenants are in total control of the party machinery.

ANC conferences are now held at the same intervals as elections, and are largely stage-managed events. Important decisions are taken well in advance, and though the election of office-bearers is still 'free and fair', only the foolhardy stand against candidates pre-approved by the leadership. Given the public nature of the nomination procedure, delegates who support alternative candidates find themselves marked for ostracisation, marginalisation and exclusion from office. The party leadership frowns on any attempt to mobilise support to remove national or local officials. Unless the ANC leadership sanctions this, it is rejected as factionalism.

At his first NEC meeting after becoming president of the ANC, Mandela memorably told members he did not want lapdogs. 'I want people who are going to criticise me so that, when we go out, we have looked at the matter from all angles and we have the maximum support of our people, including those who had reservations. Once their point of view is expressed without fear or favour, even if it is rejected, a person is satisfied. So we must allow that free debate.'[12] That said, however, Mandela was quick enough to sack Pallo Jordan in April 1996 over the stance he took on curtailment of civil liberties to help police combat crime and against government interference in the national broadcasting service. Mandela also fired Bantu Holomisa when he refused to apologise for telling the Truth Commission that then public enterprises minister Stella Sigcau had accepted a bribe from casino magnate Sol Kerzner while she was the Transkei leader.

But the NEC regularly took Mandela to task. While Mandela was abroad in August 1991, the NEC, offended by signs of 'autocratic leadership' and lack of consultation during the constitutional negotiations, put Ramaphosa in charge of the process, reducing Mandela to a subservient role. The move was reversed, and in time Mandela joked about it, but he got the message and worked more closely with the NEC thereafter. In 1992, he was severely reprimanded at an ANC policy conference for suggesting that nationalisation be scrapped. It took a year of intense lobbying on Mandela's part before he won that particular battle.[13]

Not even Oliver Tambo had as much autonomy as Mbeki. He was often taken to task over lack of consultation with the NEC, and on one occasion, while still in exile, an emotional Tambo even tendered his resignation after being harshly criticised for failing to consult party members. He was persuaded to reconsider his decision, but had to promise that consultation would precede all future decisions.

Tambo also faced fierce opposition at the ANC's first conference in South Africa in 1991, when he suggested that economic sanctions should be called off. Tambo, supported by Mbeki, had hoped to pre-empt plans by the international community to 'reward' former state president FW de Klerk's reforms by lifting sanctions, and had to work hard to persuade the ANC leadership to support his position.[14]

Cabinet ministers almost never challenge Mbeki,[15] lest they lose their privileged positions. Asked for her opinion on a specific matter during a cabinet meeting, Sigcau once responded: 'You decide, Thabo, you know you can count on my support on any issue.'[16] By all accounts, this attitude has become the norm rather than the exception.

Parliamentarians, too, have been cowed into submission. SACP general secretary Blade Nzimande quit the assembly in 1999 amid bitter private complaints that he had been deliberately marginalised for taking Mbeki and the ANC's policies to task.[17]

Several other back-bench rebellions have been quashed. When ANC whip Thabang Makwetla demanded more oversight power for the ANC's parliamentary wing, he was redeployed to the provinces. MPs have long been held in check by a special committee headed by deputy president Jacob Zuma, appointed by the ANC leadership as a 'super whip' who reports directly to Mbeki.

The first to feel the sting of the parliamentary controls was outspoken former MP Pregs Govender. She received a severe dressing down from former speaker Frene Ginwala for criticising the government's AIDS policy. Govender resigned, as did Barbara Hogan, head of parliament's finance portfolio committee, when she was reprimanded over her repeated calls for parliamentary budget oversight. Hogan was persuaded to withdraw her resignation, but has maintained an uncharacteristically low profile ever since.

Ginwala herself quit parliament suddenly in April 2004, frustrated by a lack of open debate. 'We need to reopen the dialogue we had in the eighties and the early nineties instead of going into our laagers and defending our ideas,'[18] she said. It should be remembered, though, that during her ten years in parliament, Ginwala frequently cracked the whip against dissenting MPs.

In April 2001, the entire country was shaken by revelations that the police were investigating ANC stalwarts Cyril Ramaphosa, Tokyo Sexwale and Mathews Phosa for allegedly plotting to overthrow the president. Since the information was supplied to the media by safety and security minister Steve Tshwete, it was given wide publicity and credence, despite the fact that all three of the alleged plotters had quit active politics for the business sector. James Nkambule, an obscure ANC Youth League member who was being investigated for alleged corruption while employed by the Mpumalanga Parks Board, was trundled out as the confidential source. Mbeki seized the chance to accuse white business leaders of conspiring with his rivals in the party to field a candidate to stand against him at the ANC's 2002 national conference.

When the investigation was abandoned without turning up a shred of evidence against the alleged plotters, Mbeki declared that it was wrong to name people accused of such serious offences before a thorough probe had been conducted. To his credit, Tshwete concurred.

It was, no doubt, entirely coincidental that the sensational plot allegations in 2001 drew media attention away from rising criticism of Mbeki's leadership by some in the tripartite alliance, especially on his approach to the crisis in Zimbabwe and AIDS.

Provincial critics have fared no better. In August 2000, Lerumo Kalako, a former Western Cape ANC secretary, had to apologise publicly to the provincial leadership after dubbing it factional and divided. He issued a statement reaffirming that he was 'a committed member of the ANC', and fully acknowledging 'the selfless efforts'[19] of the Western Cape leadership. Mcebisi Skwatsha, minister of transport and public works in the provincial government of the Western Cape, welcomed the retraction, and said: 'We want to reiterate to our comrades not to take issues of leadership to the media because there is enough space for our comrades to lobby inside the ANC.'[20]

Former Soweto local councillor Trevor Ngwane was expelled from the party after criticising the privatisation of township services in a newspaper report headlined 'The People Have Not Spoken'. Lamented Ngwane: 'The mood changed within the ruling ANC caucus. Robust debate became muted; decisions were taken away from councillors and we were discouraged from participating in local community forums.'[21]

Through the use of patronage and punishment, a higher premium has been placed on blind loyalty than principle, and some ANC members are skirting perilously close to cult worship. Already there are party apparatchiks who have turned themselves into 'Mini-Me' clones by studiously adopting Mbeki's dress, speech and mannerisms. Privately, a number of ANC leaders vehemently disagree with the president's stance on AIDS, his quiet diplomacy in Zimbabwe and the government's economic policy, but such admissions are rare and, without exception, prefaced with the stern warning that 'you didn't hear it from me'.

It should be of the gravest concern to all who support democracy that Mbeki has no compunction about mobilising the full resources of the state to crush political opponents. COSATU general secretary Zwelinzima Vavi issued a statement during the furore over the alleged plot to oust Mbeki in which he warned: 'COSATU cautions against any attempt by state organs, including the police, to involve themselves in legitimate internal political contests; such action is both unconstitutional and, in effect, illegal.'[22]

Vavi and COSATU president Willie Madisha have both been on the receiving end of intimidation by the intelligence services, though neither will comment publicly on this. But allegations are rife that their telephones have been tapped, that they have been followed and that their backgrounds have been thoroughly scoured for evidence of any misdemeanours or misconduct that might be used to nail them. At the height of COSATU's anti-privatisation campaign in August 2001, Madisha collapsed during a trade union meeting from the stress of being under constant surveillance.[23]

Intimidation of persons by intelligence agents should set alarm bells ringing throughout the trade union movement, civil society and the media. The terrible abuse perpetrated by the apartheid regime's intelligence agencies left deep emotional and physical scars, and any repetition of such strong-arm tactics, however isolated, can never be tolerated again.

Civil society groups, such as the Landless People's Movement, the National Land Committee and the Anti-Privatisation Forum, also allege widespread monitoring and disruption of their activities by intelligence agents. The message is not subtle, but it is unmistakeable: criticise government policy at your peril.

If such intelligence activities are not ordered or sanctioned via official government channels, they must be the work of rogue operators, but, if that is so, the authorities have a duty to act decisively against them. Should they not do so, the perception will live on that official agents are conducting their shady activities in the name of the government.

Not even the government's own instruments are free of interference. Leaders of the Human Rights Commission (HRC) were called to account by Essop Pahad – Mbeki's chief enforcer – over a 2002 report on government's slack social delivery. The HRC was already in hot water over criticism of the AIDS policy, and at a tense meeting with Pahad and government's chief spin doctor, Joel Netshitenzhe, the top executives were first lambasted over the HRC's research methodology before being reminded that 'the government holds the purse strings'.[24]

Certain policies are simply so sacrosanct that no one dares voice criticism, especially when it comes to the economy. Few, if any, would be brave enough to question the economic power triumvirate of presidency, Treasury, and trade and industry ministry, which is 'a closed partnership'.[25] The finance ministry reduces many ministers to beggars, as it dictates what their expenditure priorities should be. It brooks neither criticism nor unsanctioned policy alternatives.

In 1997, Mandela slammed Cronin for 'continually criticising ANC economic policy'.[26] Manuel has often accused those who call for greater redistribution of espousing 'macro-populism', but reserved his harshest chastisements for proponents of a basic income grant for the poor.

Labelling critics ultra-leftist is bad enough, but accusing them of not adhering to the ANC's 'culture and traditions' is tantamount to being fingered as a 'sell-out' during the struggle. Another favourite discreditation technique is to claim that criticism plays into the hands of 'reactionaries', such as the Democratic Alliance or white right-wingers, who consistently bad-mouth the country.

Understandably, many ANC leaders keep their own counsel rather than be accused of abetting disgruntled white pessimists, but the time has come to set aside fears of playing into the hands of the opposition and accept that silence is a far greater threat to South Africa's fragile democracy in the long term.

Towards the end of 2001, the ANC accused its own left flank of being 'counter-revolutionary',[27] and following the COSATU anti-privatisation strike earlier in the year, Mbeki lashed out at Vavi and Madisha for being in league with 'right-wing forces' bent on destabilising the government.[28] As the SACP later rightly pointed out, attacks by Mbeki and other ANC leaders on party critics have the potential 'to discourage debate'.[29]

An internal ANC survey concurred: 'As policy, the ANC allows for criticism. But its leadership tends to be defensive when responding to criticism, even what appears to be fair criticism.'

Gugile Nkwinti, speaker in the Eastern Cape provincial legislature, put it more bluntly: 'The capacity of the ANC to manage diversity is clearly diminishing.'[30] Rudolph Phala, political education secretary in the Limpopo branch, attributes the formation of factions within the ANC to the stifling of debate by the leadership, and to members' fear of openly voicing criticism through party structures.[31]

NUM office-bearer Walter Mothapo quotes *Revolution and Evolution in the Twentieth Century* by James and Grace Lee Boggs to make the point that 'leaders must never be immune to criticism',[32] and that 'respect for leadership is not given, but must be earned'.

He cites the following passage from the Boggs book: 'The idea of human beings moving simultaneously like a school of fish, with no ideas in their heads and without struggling among themselves over these ideas, provides the basis for a totalitarian dictator who manipulates people as masses, turning elections into plebiscites which deliver mandates to the leader.'[33]

What aggravates the culture of silence is that the major power blocs in South African society – business, the media, think tanks – have coalesced around an anti-redistributionist consensus. They generally support the ANC's economic direction, and often shun calls for more redistribution as being out of step with reality. In truth, however, they have created their own reality, where those who point to the huge inequalities visited on the dirt-poor majority are seen as living in the past or dismissed as unreconstructed communists.

Because of the massive disparity between the 'haves' and the 'have-nots', important opinions are never heard. Those who hold them are too poor to influence party leaders or gain access to the media, and their views have no place in the national consensus. In some cases, the media or public institutions are reluctant to entertain such opinions, lest they be seen as promoting the 'loony left'. The more marginalised people with valid grievances become, the more likely they are to resort to extremism to make their voices heard. The outcome is all too often violent conflict, and should South Africa arrive at that point, many will wonder how we got there, because they will have been deaf and blind to all the warning signs.

By adopting democratic centralism as a guiding principle, the ANC risks destroying a democracy of and by the people, but, says Jabu Moleketi, 'decisions of higher structures bind lower structures, and it is the responsibility of the leadership and cadres to place the interest of the party above self.'[34]

Thus, many NEC members could vote against their consciences on the government's AIDS policy, for example, because they abide by the principle of democratic centralism. Moleketi insists this is what held the ANC together when it was a clandestine organisation in exile. 'Once a decision was taken, whether there was opposition to it or not, everybody needed to support it; it was vital to the ANC's cohesion.'[35]

Former transport minister Mac Maharaj warns that liberation cults develop when people jockey for position by doing the bidding of the leader, who can dispense patronage at will.[36] Things go badly wrong, he says, when leaders come to a decision they are convinced is right, then refuse to accept that it should have been debated by the party membership. He says, 'There needs to be a debate around issues in order to convince people to buy into policies. If there is no such a debate, one will never get people to buy into policies.'[37]

Unavoidably, the curtailing of open debate within the ANC casts a shadow on broader society as well. South Africa's totalitarian past spawned a culture of brutally crushing debate, and the current government should encourage rather than shut down diversity of opinion.

When internal debate is muzzled, a culture of secrecy seeps into society as a whole. South Africa has a model Promotion of Access to Information Act, but trying to gain access to data from government departments is a tortuous undertaking. They obfuscate and drag their feet, cite 'national security' at the drop of a hat, and send applicants from pillar to post. Just try gaining access to documents presented to the Truth Commission, or certain business records that have been declared exempt.

Even the integrity of respected watchdog institutions like the Auditor-General and Public Protector has been questioned, following claims that potentially damaging information had been edited out of public reports on alleged impropriety in South Africa's controversial billion-dollar strategic defence procurement package.

The fallout over the infamous arms deal has done incalculable damage to the much-vaunted goal of transparency. The most dramatic public spat followed accusations by former anti-corruption czar and public prosecutions director Bulelani Ngcuka of bribery involving deputy president Jacob Zuma and his erstwhile financial advisor, Durban businessman Schabir Shaik.

Other senior ANC figures were also drawn into the extensive investigations based on allegations of misconduct, many of which, admittedly, were levelled by unsuccessful contractors. A slew of fiercely contested quasi-judicial probes by parliament, the Auditor-General, Public Protector and South Africa's elite detective squad, the Scorpions, ensued.

Former ANC chief whip Tony Yengeni was charged with fraud related to a heavily discounted luxury vehicle he'd acquired through the good offices of the European Aeronautical Defence & Space Company, one of the major arms suppliers involved in the deal. Yengeni struck a plea bargain with state prosecutors and received a four-year prison sentence, but was granted leave to appeal. He also lost his seat in parliament.

Magistrate Bill Moyses summed up the mounting public anger over the arms deal when he told Yengeni at sentencing: 'Parliamentarians are leaders of the nation and should set an example to their constituents.'[38]

Arms acquisition chief Chippy Shaik, brother of Zuma's financial advisor (who had acted as banker to the ANC in exile), also lost his job when it was found that he had failed to recuse himself from discussions involving a bid by one of his brother's companies to supply combat suites for the navy's new corvettes.

But the probes examined only the awarding of contracts representing some 5 per cent of the total arms deal, and public unease over possible corruption continued. South African contractor Richard Young added fuel to the fire when he won a court battle in 2003 to gain access to documents related to the arms deal, which showed that the results of some investigations had been heavily edited before being made public, apparently in a bid to shield senior ANC members.

In August 2003, Ngcuka dropped a bombshell. With then justice minister Penuell Maduna at his side, he told a media conference that although investigations into Zuma's involvement in the arms deal had produced a prima facie case of corruption, the National Prosecuting Authority had decided not to charge him, as they considered the case 'unwinnable' in court. The crux of the allegations against the deputy president was a R500 000 annual bribe from French arms manufacturer Thales, facilitated by Schabir Shaik.

Shaik went on trial in the Durban high court in October 2004 on charges related to the bribery allegations, but, in the interim, a political storm of biblical proportions washed over ANC luminaries who had become household names.

Zuma's supporters rallied to his defence immediately, while another Shaik brother, former ANC intelligence operative Mo, joined Maharaj in branding Ngcuka a former spy for the apartheid security forces.

The nation was stunned. A relentless smear campaign against Ngcuka threatened at one point to bring down the Scorpions, long considered the country's most effective law enforcement agency. Maharaj was forced to resign as a director of a major investment bank amid allegations that he had taken kickbacks from Shaik while minister of transport, and as 2003 drew to a close, South Africans were treated to the extraordinary spectacle of the country's top prosecutor being investigated as an apartheid spy by retired judge Joos Hefer.

The judicial commission of inquiry was televised live and made for riveting viewing. It turned some of the country's top lawyers into media stars as they systematically broke down the 'evidence' against Ngcuka.

Ngcuka was fully exonerated, but by August 2004, halfway through his term of office, he decided he had had enough, and quit to head up a private forensic investigation team.

Before the Hefer Commission released its findings, Maduna, too, retired from the political arena. The final word on the matter came from Public Protector Lawrence Mushwana, who had investigated complaints that the manner in which Ngcuka had investigated Zuma constituted an abuse of his authority. Mushwana found that this was the case, and recommended that parliament take appropriate steps.

Throughout one of the greatest dramas of his presidency, Mbeki remained silent, apart from lashing out against those who alleged the arms deal was tainted and accusing the media of stoking public perceptions that the government was corrupt.

In a particularly vitriolic outburst, Mbeki warned that he would not abandon the offensive to defeat 'the insulting campaigns that seek to further entrench a stereotype that has, for centuries, sought to portray Africans as a people that is corrupt, given to telling lies, prone to theft and self-enrichment by immoral means, a people that is otherwise contemptible in the eyes of the civilised. What our country needs is substance and not shadows, facts instead of allegations, and the eradication of racism.'

It was left to Motlanthe to punt the party line on whistleblowers: 'The ANC only moves in when your own conscience fails to guide you properly,'[39] he said. Although it was generally accepted that Mbeki was supporting Ngcuka's position behind the scenes, Motlanthe accused the NPA chief of conducting major investigations as if they were 'Hollywood movies'.

At the time of writing, the court had yet to decide if Schabir Shaik was guilty of bribing Zuma in exchange for political favours. If he is convicted, the way would be open for Mbeki to fire his deputy without facing the wrath of his massive Zulu support base.

Appointing the Hefer Commission could turn out to be one of Mbeki's shrewdest political manoeuvres. Long before the first witness was called, the president had access to every intelligence file on Ngcuka and knew that the spy allegations were spurious.[40] However, they gave him an opportunity to pull the political plug on two people he perceived as political opponents: Mac Maharaj, whose alleged private criticism of his leadership style had long irked Mbeki, and Jacob Zuma, whom he suspected of becoming a rival within the ANC.

Both men were too powerful to get rid of in the normal way. It would have been political suicide for Mbeki to fire Zuma without iron-clad cause before the 2004 election, and he could not afford to go head to head with Maharaj either. So strong is Zuma's support within the ANC that Mbeki was forced to reappoint him deputy president even though he would far rather have given the post to Zuma's ex-wife, foreign minister Nkosazana Dlamini-Zuma. Motlanthe was among the prominent ANC leaders who advised Mbeki to bide his time, despite the president's suspicions that his deputy is behind allegations that Mbeki has had clandestine relationships with the wives of various ANC leaders, and conspired with Maharaj and Winnie Madikizela-Mandela to challenge him for the ANC presidency at the 2002 conference.

The 'Travelgate' scandal, in which it is alleged that certain MPs from various parties had benefited from fraudulent travel expenses claims, is another case in which public trust in representative institutions – in this case, parliament – is dashed, because of the perception that these MPs will escape punishment through blanket plea bargains.

Having made the transition from an authoritarian apartheid state to a democracy, South Africa now needs to consolidate its political system. For this to happen, the institutions of state and the political parties have to reflect, practice and embody democratic values, such as accountability, transparency and active engagement with the people. The internal dynamics of the ANC will have a major impact on defining the future and roles of all other political institutions. Undemocratic tendencies in the ANC endanger the consolidation of South Africa's democracy and will leave footprints on the country's infant political system as a whole. The logic that applies to the system of democracy also applies to the internal affairs of political parties. In general, the internal procedures of political parties must be democratic and adhere to the country's Constitution, as the parties are funded and subsidised from the public purse. Germany is one country where the value of internal democracy is taken for granted in the Basic Law of 1949. On the subject of political parties, this mandates that their internal organisation shall conform to democratic principles.[41]

The ANC's soul has always rested in the ability of its ordinary members to shape its policies and direction and determine who should lead them. At the same time, if the central party leadership has no part in selecting candidates, the party could lack unity of purpose, ideological cohesion and organisational discipline. For example, if a political party wants to reflect a certain gender, age or other demographic balance, the central executive must be involved in the overall mix of candidates for election.

Entering its second decade in government, the ANC faces the dilemma of wanting a strong, centralised national leadership to steer the country to a more equitable future, based on the flawed assumption that those at the top know what is best for every region, city, town, village and farm. The approach also assumes that a centralised capacity exists to implement national decisions, policies and leadership choices, but experience has shown that it does not.

All too often, democratic centralism, or 'vanguardism' – which the ANC has adopted as its operational model – serves only to perpetuate the notion of a small group of people operating in the name of democracy, but in fact taking decisions and enforcing them without a mandate from the electorate. A far better route for the ANC to follow would be the decentralisation and deepening of democracy within the framework of strong leadership and agreed values, objectives, codes and goals. This would allow for greater provincial and local diversity within the broad framework, and confirm the party's faith in both the democratic process and the ability of ordinary members and citizens to make decisions for their own good.

If bad leaders who infringe the law or the ANC's code of conduct are chosen, the role of the leadership is to ensure free and fair internal elections so that party members and voters can evict them from office, if they so choose. Centralisation is certainly no insurance against weak or venal administrators.

There are valuable lessons for the ANC in the decline of the Congress Party of India and in what some refer to as 'ZANU-fication',[42] or the danger of a dynamic, popular national liberation movement becoming steadily disconnected from its constituents once in power, as has happened with Robert Mugabe's ZANU-PF in Zimbabwe.

However, what some see as ZANU-fication is seen by the Mbeki-ites as assertive leadership. Jeremy Cronin sums up the approach as follows: 'We are now in power on your behalf. Take a back seat, we will make the decisions and deliver. Mass mobilisation such as strikes, protests and questioning of the leadership's authority get in the way of your government doing the job. In any case, we have a plan; it may be slow, but be patient.'[43]

Of course there are enormous differences between the ANC and ZANU-PF, though the Afro-pessimists love to equate one with the other in order to assuage their own prejudices, but the situation in Zimbabwe serves as a warning of how soon the rot can set in.

Leaders who explain themselves and can be questioned instead of merely issuing dictates and introducing policies that are beyond criticism are far more likely to be followed than those who discourage dissent and crush debate. Pregs Govender condemns disturbing signs that the ANC's proud tradition of debate has been reduced to 'groupthink'.

She says, 'Groupthink is the celebration of the individual above the collective in its naive and unquestioning acceptance of the leader as infallible. It renounces the courage that demands we be honest with those we love, even if they may not like what it is we have to say; loyalty has to be defined not in terms of the party hierarchy in government, but in terms of the poorest.'[44]

In political organisations bonded by affection, friendship and solidarity, such as the ANC, members are often unwilling to be critical for fear that this will prove disruptive and violate the organisation's internal norms. For many in the ANC, however, the rewards for conformity involve salaries, benefits and advancement.

Dissenters might well cause tension, but, importantly, they are also likely to improve the performance of the ANC and its policies. Institutions have a better chance of success if their leaders are subject to scrutiny, and if their actions are continually monitored and reviewed.

If critics in a free society are portrayed as disloyal, unpatriotic or enemies of the state, there is great cause for concern. Freedom of speech is a meaningless right if group pressure demands conformity, but the real victims are those who are deprived of information and views they need.[45]

Self-censorship is a serious social and political malaise, and the cost to society is huge. Already large numbers of black and progressive white intellectuals in South Africa have, to all intents, withdrawn from public debate, and society is the poorer for their silence. The greater danger is a decline in intellectual self-reflection, both within the state and among its critics, about what is actually happening on the ground. This happened in India and ultimately led to the destruction of another once great liberation movement, the Congress Party.[46] As Tutu points out: 'An unthinking, uncritical, kowtowing, party line-toeing is fatal to a vibrant democracy.'[47]

Irving Janis developed the notion of 'groupthink' in the early 1970s and 1980s to describe the kind of decision-making that predictably leads to social blunders and policy failures.[48] So, for example, when US president Lyndon Johnson and his advisors escalated the Vietnam War, it was because the leading group stifled dissent and tried to enforce consensus.

Organisations susceptible to groupthink pressure their members into uniformity and self-censorship, thus creating the illusion of unanimity. This is fostered by direct pressure on any members who argue against the group's stereotypes, illusions and commitments.

In a culture of silence and fear, there is the very real risk that leaders will not receive the information they require to make good decisions. South Africa must have a political culture that encourages disagreement and does not penalise those who depart from the prevailing orthodoxy. When members of the ANC feel free to differ from the president or the party leaders, society is likely to hear a wider range of opinions, and better decisions may result. Cass R Sunstein, a professor of jurisprudence at the University of Chicago Law School,[49] argues that policy errors are most likely to occur when people are rewarded for conformity.

A system of free expression and dissent protects against false confidence and the inevitable mistakes of planners in both the private and public arenas. If there had been more openness and discussion on GEAR, South Africa might not have shed 500 000 jobs in five years. If ARVs had been made available at state hospitals five years earlier, thousands of lives might have been saved and the devastating social consequences of the AIDS pandemic might have been ameliorated. The list of 'ifs' is growing, and time may be running out.

# — 15 —

# The Battle
# for Succession

All power is a trust, we are accountable for its exercise; that, from the people, and
for the people, all springs, and all must exist.                    — Benjamin Disraeli[1]

M BEKI WILL STRIVE TO MAKE HIS SUCCESSION AS RELATIVELY SMOOTH AS
the transition from Mandela was to him. But he would also like the
next president to be a candidate who carries his blessing and will preserve
his legacy.

That legacy includes a competitive economy, creation of a large black business
class, and repositioning South Africa as the champion of poor nations and the
driving force behind continental renewal – his African Renaissance.

At least one of Mbeki's hopes could be dashed. Quite early into his second term
of office the mood within the ANC was shifting towards a contested presidential
election in keeping with the party's established culture and tradition. Many
believe that Mbeki's uncontested rise to the position was a democratic aberration
that should never happen again.

It was not that the ANC believed Mbeki was the wrong man for the job, but
rather that the absence of choice was inherently alien to the democratic process,
regardless of the circumstances. Even Nelson Mandela had conceded that it was
not the ANC's style for an incumbent to choose a successor without putting it
to the vote.[2]

In reality, however, Mbeki was the third ANC president in a row to be elected
unopposed. Oliver Tambo got the job by default, since there was no way for the
ANC in exile to hold elections. Mandela was the consummate struggle icon, fresh
out of prison, and sentiment alone would have made it unthinkable for anyone
else to become president at that specific juncture.

The Mbeki succession is thus fraught with danger. This will be the first time that the ANC has to manage a candidacy battle, and it might well have to do so without the stabilising influence of party elders, such as the ageing Mandela.

As the experience of other liberation movements, such as Zimbabwe's ZANU-PF and Namibia's SWAPO has shown, the choice of second- or third-generation leaders can be a bruising affair. Mbeki will certainly have a say in the selection, but he has yet to show his hand and, for good reason, is not expected to do so until much closer to the election.

To declare his preference too far in advance would place Mbeki's candidate in the invidious position of having to watch his back constantly against those who believe the job should be theirs. Perhaps, more importantly, backing anyone as his successor while the bulk of his term has yet to run would reduce Mbeki to a lame-duck president, something he wants to avoid at all cost, and possibly open him to accusations of manipulating the process. More importantly, Mbeki is not sure whom he should back for the presidency. Taken together, these factors could actually hinder rather than help Mbeki's anointed heir.

However, all indications are that the next presidential election will be a drama-filled event. The ANC had a foretaste of things to come in 2003 during the saga surrounding accusations that Jacob Zuma was bribed and that Bulelani Ngcuka was an apartheid spy. No one, least of all Mbeki himself, had ever considered Zuma a serious contender for succession, but the outpouring of grassroots support when he had his back to the wall told a different story.

Ironically, Mbeki only appointed Zuma as deputy president in 1999 because he was not considered presidential material. Interestingly, Mandela had warned Mbeki against appointing Zuma as his deputy, precisely because Mbeki and Zuma were such close friends. Events during and since 2003 could indicate that his choice of a 'safe' No. 2 has backfired.

In exile, the two men had been close, with Zuma a loyal Mbeki acolyte who dutifully deferred to the chief. After the ANC's unbanning, Zuma did a splendid job of covering Mbeki's back as he fought his way to power. In 1991, Mbeki returned the favour by punting Zuma as ANC secretary general Ramaphosa's deputy, thus placing him in the perfect position to act as an effective foil against Mbeki's biggest rival.

Zuma's current backers unequivocally believe that their man has earned his spurs after a lifetime of doing Mbeki's bidding, rooting out potential challengers and waiting patiently in the wings like the committed cadre he has always been. Now his apprenticeship is over, and it's payback time.

Mbeki has other ideas. Since 2001, relations between the president and his deputy have been positively glacial. By the time Scorpions chief Bulelani Ngcuka announced in August 2003 that Zuma would not be charged with bribery and corruption, South Africa's second most senior politician had been under investigation for more than two years, with Mbeki's full knowledge and support.

Zuma lost favour with Mbeki when ANC leaders, disgruntled over the president's policy lapses on AIDS and Zimbabwe, began murmuring about replacing him with his deputy at the 2002 national conference. The crisis was averted due to intervention by Mandela, and Mbeki, unclear about who was behind the plan to stage a palace revolution, lashed out at his known rivals, Cyril Ramaphosa, Tokyo Sexwale and Mathews Phosa.

He also forced Zuma to declare publicly that he had no interest in becoming president. The two men did not speak to one another for months afterwards, but for Mbeki, it came as a shock to realise that the very man he had thought would never play Brutus to his Caesar was, after all, a threat.

What Mbeki appears to have missed is that Zuma started working on his image as a statesman almost as soon as he took office. Because Mbeki was seen as inaccessible and unapproachable, rank-and-file ANC members took their problems to his deputy, who was almost always available.

When Mbeki fell out with COSATU in 1999 and refused to meet with trade union leaders for more than a year, Zuma acted as a conduit between them and the ANC. At the height of tensions between the partners in the tripartite alliance, Zuma was the point of contact for the SACP leadership to get their message across to Mbeki. He also was the go-between for the civic movement leadership and the ANC. He also played a role in reducing tensions between the government and NGOs. In his traditional stomping ground of KwaZulu-Natal, Zuma intervened to soothe hostilities between the ANC and the Inkatha Freedom Party.

Because Mbeki rarely deigns to grace parliament with his presence, Zuma assumed the role of ANC leader in the National Assembly, engaging directly with opposition parties when Mbeki would not. Zuma lent his patronage to the Moral Regeneration Movement's efforts to break down a culture of political corruption – another delicious irony, since he would later stand accused of taking bribes himself.

What started out as Zuma standing in for the overstretched Mbeki at key international gatherings became an opportunity for Zuma to make his mark in Africa as a conflict mediator and peacemaker. Before long, South Africa's jet-setting president and his deputy were out of the country at the same time so frequently that a raft of cabinet ministers had the chance to act as head of state for brief periods.

Small wonder, then, that when Mbeki came under fire over his controversial stance on AIDS and the Zimbabwe situation, some ANC leaders saw Zuma as a viable alternative. As those who doubt Zuma's sophistication and who like a certain senior ANC leader sniff, 'Imagine Jacob Zuma having to give a comment on the rand.' But he has polished his skills. In plush Stockholm, Sweden, in mid-2003, he smoothly talked up the rand.

And so to the Schabir Shaik scandal, unresolved at the time of writing, but possibly the catalyst that will determine Zuma's fate. The one thing Mbeki wants to avoid at all cost is that Zuma becomes South Africa's next president, and if Judge Hillary Squires finds Shaik guilty of bribing Zuma in return for political favours, Mbeki would have a valid reason to fire him. Indeed, he would be expected to do so.

The problem, however, is that while any other politician's reputation would have been irrevocably tainted by the grave allegations levelled against him, huge numbers of the ANC grassroots supporters and former MK guerrillas have rallied behind Zuma. They remain steadfast in the belief that damaging disclosures about his financial affairs are the result of a deliberate and malicious campaign to discredit him. If Shaik is acquitted, Zuma could well renege on his earlier assurance that he would not seek the highest office.

If he were to stand against a business-backed candidate, he could most likely count on the support of the tripartite alliance's left wing. Zuma is pragmatic and equally at ease among the leftists, Africanists, Christian democrats and the conservative traditionalists within the ANC. In KwaZulu-Natal he has a formidable support base, though young pretenders such as premier S'bu Ndebele are not keen to have him on 'their' turf too often. Ndebele has gone so far as to suggest that in the unlikely event of Zuma becoming the next president, Mbeki should remain president of the ANC, following the example of Namibian head of state Sam Nujoma, so he can manage his successor, Hifikepunye Pohamba, by remote control.

Should Zuma make himself available for election, the intellectuals in the alliance might pull up their noses, but the grassroots party faithful won't. Many view the man who describes his background as 'deprived' with sympathy, if not admiration, for his true-life rags-to-riches journey.

Born on 12 April 1942 at tiny Inkandla, deep in the heart of rural Zululand, Zuma was raised by a single mother who earned a pittance as a domestic worker. His father died when he was a toddler, and by the age of fifteen his formal schooling was suspended by the need to take on odd jobs to supplement the family income. He joined the ANC in 1959 under the influence of a trade unionist kinsman and went underground as an MK operative in 1962, rising through the ranks to become the ANC's intelligence chief.

Should the Mbeki camp be unable to stop Zuma from becoming president, they could possibly try to persuade him to serve only one term and to appoint someone of finance minister Trevor Manuel's calibre as his deputy.

The Zuma factor aside, Mbeki and the party centrists would ideally want the next president to be from the same ideological mould. Mbeki fears the emergence of a strong candidate from the left most, but someone holding overly strong

Africanist views would not be encouraged to stand. Many in the ANC would like once and for all to slay the apartheid-inspired – and incorrect – perception that the ANC is a Xhosa-dominated organisation. Some party leaders contend that pushing a non-Xhosa-speaking leader to the top might do the trick. Moreover, it would also send a strong signal to regimes north of the Limpopo, where ethnicity still sometimes prevents talented leaders from reaching the top of former liberation movements. ZANU-PF in Zimbabwe is a case in point. Indeed, most of the contenders in the race for the presidency are not Xhosa. Mbeki, like most senior ANC leaders, is loath to distinguish on tribal grounds. Another possibility that drives fear into the hearts of the Mbeki-ites is the re-emergence of a populist, such as Winnie Madikizela-Mandela or former Gauteng premier Mathole Motshekga, who would ride the wave of malcontent over government's failure to deliver.

When India's post-independence leader Jawaharlal Nehru died, he was succeeded by his daughter, the populist Indira Gandhi, whose leadership plunged the Congress Party into a downward spiral. The ANC centrists would want to guard against a similar scenario when Mbeki goes.

The ANC's influential new moneyed business wing is also likely to place its imprint on the succession. Numerically in the minority, the combined financial power and patronage this group wields could either make or break a presidential candidate, a situation wholly unfamiliar to the ANC. The group includes all three of Mbeki's 1997 challengers for supremacy: Ramaphosa, Sexwale and Phosa. The combination of wealth and popularity that any one of them can offer could prove an unbeatable formula.

The business wing would certainly want a candidate who would pursue the black empowerment and economic courses set by Mbeki. They would have too much to lose with anyone else, but such a contender might also be drawn from among the powerful mandarins in parastatals and senior government positions. Mbeki's repositioning of the ANC has rested heavily on their influence in policy-making, and they would be unlikely to veer off course on economic issues.

Any candidate who wants to be taken seriously would have to secure the support of ANC strongholds like the Eastern Cape and KwaZulu-Natal, and a home base in either would do no harm. At least some support from the left would also be required, if only because of the numbers and organisational resources that go with trade union backing. ANC Youth League members, once among the major power brokers, are now too focused on making a fast buck to swing the election, but the yuppie politicians could be useful as noisy campaign troops. However, it appears that Zuma has secured influential backing among some provincial branches of the Youth League, who argue that he should automatically become the president. The once mighty Women's League is deep in the doldrums, and the parliamentary wing simply does not have the measure of influence that other social democratic parties, such as New Labour in Britain and the German Social Democratic Party, can offer.

Endorsement by Mbeki would give any candidate a significant fillip, as would support of the ANC's party machinery, and, of course, the nod from Mandela, if he were still around.

The left has not given up hope of capturing the presidency, but strong candidates are thin on the ground. In the rather unlikely event that a last-minute candidate was fielded, the choice could fall on COSATU general secretary Zwelinzima Vavi, or president Willie Madisha. Trade unionist Lula da Silva's conquest of the Brazilian electorate against fierce opposition from pro-business groups caught the imagination of many trade union strategists, but while the names of either Vavi, the former mineworker, or Madisha, the teacher, on the ballot paper could present a serious hazard to Mbeki's health, they would almost certainly be denied the backing of the business wing. The party machinery under erstwhile trade unionist Kgalema Motlanthe might remain neutral and some of the provinces could prove sympathetic, but if the ANC's head office issues a 'hands-off' edict, COSATU would have little hope of success.

The trade union movement has already entered the fray by urging members to ensure that a 'pro-poor' candidate steps onto the podium. At a closed meeting of its central executive committee in November 2004, COSATU declared: 'The battle [for succession] is as much about the leadership as the future trajectory of the ANC.'[3] Almost certainly in vain, the unionists hope that that trajectory will bear left.

The South African Communist Party is highly unlikely to find a suitable candidate within its ranks. Nor would it want to risk the true depth of its support being tested at the polls. So all the frontrunners would probably share Mbeki's ideological pragmatism and outlook, but the ANC alliance is weary of his autocratic style, and his successor is likely to have an established reputation of inclusive, open and consultative leadership.

The feeling among the 'inziles' is that their time has come, and that opens the way for a long list of possible successors. Indeed, few liberation movements have the luxury of depth of leadership that the ANC can draw on.

On all counts, the strongest candidate by far must be Cyril Ramaphosa, if he is hungry enough to re-enter the political fray. He has moved on and become a singularly successful businessman, but among his supporters, the bitterness of what is seen as his unfair earlier loss of the presidency to Mbeki still rankles. They are already pleading with him to put his name forward, and he could muster the support of virtually all the influential factions: the provinces, the business wing, the party apparatchiks, certainly Mandela, and, surprisingly, perhaps even Mbeki himself. Ramaphosa laughs off suggestions that the job is his for the taking: 'Not in a hundred years,' he chuckled. 'I'm having too much fun. Next question please.'

He and Mbeki made their peace after arriving at a tacit agreement that Ramaphosa would defer to Mbeki and recognise him as both the undisputed leader of the ANC and the legitimate president. In return, Mbeki would leave Ramaphosa to pursue his business and other interests. 'The kraal is big enough for both,' explained one ANC leader.

Ramaphosa's camp interprets this as confirmation that Mbeki would not block a bid by their man for the presidency, though some of Mbeki's supporters don't necessarily see it the same way. However, they do point out that Mbeki has always acknowledged that Ramaphosa's politics are not radically different from his own. Their differences lie chiefly in emphasis and leadership style, which, given that Mbeki was an exile and Ramaphosa an inzile, is hardly surprising.

Ramaphosa is unlikely to undo Mbeki's economic reforms, and the president knows that, but before backing Ramaphosa openly, the president would need some assurance that his successor would not allow the critics who are silent now to erode his legacy with retrospective public judgements. Mbeki also worries that old enmities could prevent Ramaphosa from allowing him to play the role of elder statesman in the tradition of Nelson Mandela and Walter Sisulu.

The one person who has Mbeki's unconditional blessing is Joel Netshitenzhe, the highly respected intellectual who has been at the coalface throughout the government's economic and social policy-making. His position as Mbeki's policy czar affords him a unique position both within government and the ANC. Though not a member of the cabinet, ministers defer to Netshitenzhe and it is he who approves their policy proposals.

Most importantly, he is the architect of South Africa's macroeconomic future. Such is Mbeki's confidence in Netshitenzhe that he has been mandated to develop a national vision for the year 2014 along the lines of similar projects that launched the successful Scandinavian consensus social democracies on their way to prosperity.

Netshitenzhe is relatively unknown among rank-and-file ANC members, and support in the provinces could be a problem. The left would view him with suspicion, but the business wing sees him as another Mbeki and would have no problem backing him. The party machine might also be at his disposal. He has long been head of the ANC's political desk, responsible for ensuring that cadres have the right ideological outlook. When given the chance in 1997 to be Mbeki's deputy, he declined, preferring to 'serve the movement in other ways'.

His closeness to the president is both a blessing and a handicap. Mbeki would be guaranteed that his protégé would not only continue his legacy, but ensure that it was protected from criticism. But Netshitenzhe's nomination could trigger a backlash in the party, as those unhappy with Mbeki's style of governance could vote against him as a way of sending a message to the outgoing president. ANC members have a habit of expressing their disapproval in such a manner. In many provinces, for example, they have deliberately voted against those hand-picked by Mbeki as premiers.

Netshitenzhe's other crucial shortfall is that he may be too much like Mbeki. A bright but shy and reclusive intellectual, he also has a master's degree in economics, and has been mentored by Mbeki in much the same way as the president came under Tambo's tutelage. His policy-making style is expected to be just as technocratic as Mbeki's at a time when a return to consultation and open debate are being sought by the ANC.

The lights of ANC national chairman Mosiuoa 'Terror' Lekota have not been dimmed. The former United Democratic Front stalwart remains a darling of the ANC's internal wing, and many believe he personifies the style of leadership that is needed. Despite aggressive attempts by the Mbeki-ites to marginalise him, as national chairman he remains but a heartbeat away from the presidency and could confidently count on having the party machinery at his disposal. Lekota is intimately familiar with the inner workings of the party machine, enjoys huge popularity at provincial level, would be acceptable to both the business wing and the left, and could expect a warm nod of approval from Mandela.

However, he would most likely face fierce opposition from Mbeki and his loyal lieutenants in the Youth League. Mbeki and his allies have not forgiven the gritty Lekota for snatching the national chairmanship away from their chosen candidate, Steve Tshwete, at the 1997 Mafikeng conference. Two years earlier, Mbeki had been behind the unceremonious sacking of Lekota as premier of the troubled Free State after he fired senior ANC members for corruption. Grassroots activists rallied behind Lekota in an unprecedented show of support and sympathy for a leader they thought had been unfairly victimised, but he was sent into the political wilderness anyway, as chairman of the National Council of Provinces.

To the great consternation of Mbeki and the ANC leadership, Lekota, with the backing of the left, made a comeback by standing as national chairman, thus blocking attempts by Mbeki-ites to capture the six top positions in the ANC. This meant Mbeki could not continue to ignore him, and in 1999 he grudgingly gave Lekota the poisoned chalice of the defence ministry in the hope that his impeccable credentials would be tainted by a stint in the hot seat.

Not only did this not happen, but Lekota refused to be cowed, and in 2001 he severely criticised Mbeki's policy on Zimbabwe. When an outraged Mbeki demanded an apology, Lekota refused, saying he had been expressing his personal opinion, thus adding fuel to the fire of the president's anger.

Inevitably, the Mbeki-ites trained their sights on Lekota, with the Youth League launching a blistering attack on him. Lekota dug in, and the next barrage came in the form of revelations that he had not disclosed certain business interests to parliament as required.

Lekota offered a reasonable explanation for the oversight and apologised, but the Mbeki-ites dusted off Northern Province premier Ngoako Ramatlhodi as a possible challenger for the ANC chairmanship at the December 2002 national conference. However, the lawyer failed to strike a chord among the rank-and-file membership, and the challenge petered out even before the conference doors were opened.

Mbeki exacted his revenge by trying hard to push Lekota into the background throughout the conference, usurping the traditional right of the chairman to lead most key sessions. Contrary to expectations, however, the more Mbeki tried to consign Lekota to the political scrap heap, the greater the grassroots support and sympathy he evoked.

He would be a formidable challenger for the top job if he chose to throw his hat into the ring. Many love his consultative style, and he has surprisingly high support among whites. His growing reputation as a reconciliation advocate caused Mbeki to appoint him as a special emissary in 2000 to build bridges with the white community. Lekota was also instrumental in enticing the New National Party to suckle at the ANC's bosom, delivering Mbeki the political coup he craved most: a massive bloc of white voters under the ANC umbrella.

Former Mpumalanga premier Mathews Phosa, perceived by Mbeki and his supporters as an unknown quantity, could be the surprise candidate for the presidency.

Having fallen victim to Mbeki's vindictiveness after accepting a nomination as ANC deputy president in 1997, the independent-minded Phosa could not be counted on to preserve Mbeki's legacy, but he has widespread respect, authority and support within the party.

Like Ramaphosa and Lekota, he has also proved popular with the white electorate, especially Afrikaners. His fluency in their language has seen a volume of his Afrikaans poetry published and he frequently speaks Afrikaans during political speeches. The business wing would find him acceptable, since he would be unlikely to make any major changes to the economic policy, the party machine would not be hostile, and the left, while wary of his business involvement, would probably give him the benefit of the doubt.

Another Mbeki victim, Tokyo Sexwale, is playing his cards close to his chest, but he commands huge cross-racial support both within the ANC and outside. His successor as Gauteng premier, Mbhazima Shilowa, has probably made some inroads into Sexwale's former solid support base in the province, but could not hope to compete for the backing of high finance and money. Sexwale is one of Mandela's favourite sons, not least because when the old man needed a last-minute R1 million bail-out to pay for his birthday bash in 2003, Sexwale paid the bills.

Since being accused of plotting to oust Mbeki, however, Sexwale has become so disillusioned with politics that he might not be interested in returning to the fray. However, Mbeki and Sexwale have made up. Sexwale now frequently supports business projects financially, both at home and on the African continent, that Mbeki feels should be supported by black business. In January 2004, Mbeki's close ally, former spy master Vusi Mavimbela, joined Sexwale's company Mvelaphanda, which indicates the closeness of Sexwale's and Mbeki's new relationship. It can only be good for any future Sexwale campaign. The telegenic former Robben Islander has become extraordinarily wealthy in recent years, but still has the common touch that swept him to prominence in the volatile aftermath of Chris Hani's assassination.

Yet, of all the potential candidates, he would also be the most glamorous. He and his wife Judy are on the guest lists of South Africa's richest and most prominent hostesses, and if South Africa elected its presidents the way Americans do, Sexwale would be a shoo-in.

Saki Macozoma is one of the younger generation of ANC leaders. If he became president, it would be with the unusual distinction of skipping a generation. His greatest advantage is that he enjoys both the support of Mandela and the protection of Mbeki, as the controversy over the appointment of Coleman Andrews as SAA's chief executive showed.

For his two-year tenure, Andrews received more than R220 million at a time when the airline was suffering huge losses. Macozoma was chairman of SAA, but walked away unscathed, while public enterprises minister Jeff Radebe was hung out to dry.

Macozoma's swift rise to the top, his confident nature and his gung-ho business style have made him some powerful enemies in the ANC, however. The role he and Mbeki's former economic advisor Moss Ngoasheng played in the investment arm of the MK veterans' association left many former Robben Islanders and freedom fighters bitter. They were accused of irregularly acquiring shares worth R31 million, which allegedly belonged to former political prisoners, in a hotly disputed deal through Safika Investment Holdings, owned by Ngoasheng, Macozoma and Vuli Cuba. The three have disputed it. At best, Macozoma would be a rank outsider in the presidential race and could expect to find his path blocked by powerful ANC interest groups. He has no provincial support base, neither the left nor the party machinery would be on his side, and his youth would almost certainly count against him.

Tito Mboweni is also a member of the younger generation, but his performance as Reserve Bank governor has earned him plaudits from the financial community. However, his conservative fiscal policies have outraged the left, interest rates remain relatively high and his support of a strong currency, even at the cost of jobs, would deny him grassroots support.

Mboweni is inextricably linked in the public mind to Mbeki's conservative economics, though as recently as 1992 he was a keen promoter of redistribution to drive growth. The sleek and urbane Mboweni has Mbeki's ear, but retains a strong independent streak and has criticised both the government's AIDS policy and attitude towards Zimbabwe for hampering the economy.

Another outsider is Shilowa, former general secretary of COSATU, who has been pilloried by the left and the trade union movement for moving into Mbeki's camp since becoming premier of the country's financial powerhouse. Shilowa has worked hard at reinventing himself, using renowned image-makers such as Thabo Masebe to carve out his niche as a concerned, responsive and caring leader. He regularly holds meetings at community level where he listens to the problems of the people and pledges to resolve them, thus maintaining contact with the grassroots supporters of whom he was one not too long ago.

But Shilowa also holds appeal for the white business community and the ANC's black business wing. Surprisingly, he could more than likely even count on a significant number of votes from the left, which continues to see him as a worker from humble origins who made good.

Manne Dipico, former premier of the Northern Cape, cannot be eliminated as a contender, but perhaps his time has not yet come. He was South Africa's youngest provincial premier and is largely credited with the ANC winning control of a province that was thought to be the natural home of the National and Democratic Parties in 1994.

Dipico would bring a freshness to national politics that none of the other likely candidates can offer. He pioneered the concept of provincial *imbizos,* or small meetings, between his cabinet members and the local community, an innovation that has since been copied successfully by Shilowa, and even Mbeki on occasion.

Dipico has proved to be something of a wizard at running election campaigns, and was brought in by Mbeki after Peter Mokaba died to manage the 2004 national campaign. His efficiency earned him the respect of even the most hostile Johannesburg party bosses, who had not taken kindly to the president plucking a country cousin from the considerable array of available talent for the job.

In the process of securing the ANC's landslide victory at the polls, Dipico managed to build some bridges with COSATU and the SACP, which would stand him in good stead in the future. While it is true that he lacks experience in the ruthless metropolitan political horse-trading ring, this could be to his advantage, as he carries no political baggage. But it would be a pity to lose his talents through a premature bid, and he might be better advised to bide his time.

ANC secretary general Kgalema Motlanthe could come from behind and surprise everyone, especially if the succession battle turns bloody and ugly. Quiet, calm and hard-working, Motlanthe has toiled ceaselessly to rebuild the ANC's shaky party structures. The former general secretary of the National Union of Mineworkers is highly respected within the trade union movement and still retains popular appeal on the left. Whatever he says carries weight.

For much of 2004 he was preoccupied with mediating between the ruling ZANU-PF and the opposition Movement for Democratic Change in Zimbabwe, which required him to spend lengthy periods away from ANC headquarters, leaving some of his normal functions in the hands of Smuts Ngonyama. However, he remains a powerful player, and had a big hand in the selection of Mbeki's cabinet, provincial premiers and the heads of the all-important parliamentary portfolio committees.

Motlanthe's best shot would be as a compromise candidate if the front-runners turn the succession battle into an internecine struggle. His respect, integrity and credentials are accepted by almost all the power blocs in the movement, and he has the obvious advantage of having the party machinery at his beck and call. He would be able to secure the support of the most powerful provincial branches, where he became a familiar figure during the restructuring project, and could probably count on the support of both Mandela and Mbeki. Just how seriously Motlanthe's opinions are taken was illustrated by his suggestion that Mbeki bring the likes of Derek Hanekom and Pallo Jordan in from the cold as members of his 2004 cabinet.

Some ANC kingmakers talk seriously about grooming a queen, instead, to send a message to the macho men of African politics. South Africa has already broken with convention by appointing Nkosazana Dlamini-Zuma as foreign minister, and Mbeki is not averse to a female successor. Much of his 2004 election campaign was devoted to women's issues, though his sincerity was somewhat marred by that awful gaffe when he jokingly said he would slap his sister if she ever dated one of the opposition leaders. He has promoted more women into senior cabinet and top government positions than anyone expected, and it is widely thought that this is partly to test the electorate's readiness for his protégé, Dlamini-Zuma, to become the next president.

Though her domestic reputation is that of being abrasive, she has forced the respect of her counterparts throughout Africa, where foreign policy is the traditional terrain of some of the continent's hardest men. Dlamini-Zuma is nothing if not tough, and her gloves-off dealings with the powerful tobacco and pharmaceutical industries while she was minister of health still inspire awe among the party faithful.

Unless Mugabe's newly appointed vice-president Joyce Mujuru beats her to it, Dlamini-Zuma has an excellent chance of becoming Africa's first woman head of state, and of the continent's most powerful country with the biggest economy to boot. For Mbeki, the idea is more than a little alluring, but while it would be difficult for anyone in the ANC to argue against a woman candidate, she would not have universal support.

Some have watched with anxiety as Dlamini-Zuma has positioned herself firmly in the Africanist camp on Zimbabwe, and her sometimes controversial statements in support of ZANU-PF have not found favour in some important quarters. Some of her harshest critics could muster enough opposition to put her out of the running, not least among them Winnie Madikizela-Mandela, who has not forgotten how Dlamini-Zuma sided with the ANC leadership to oust her.

In addition, there are several other 'Mbeki power women' who are equally competent and generally more popular. They include former housing minister Sankie Mthembi-Mahanyele, land minister Thoko Didiza, and mineral and energy affairs minister Phumzile Mlambo-Ngcuka. All are loyal Mbeki-ites, and Mlambo-Ngcuka's profile was considerably enhanced by the dignified, credible and politically astute way in which she conducted the campaign to help clear her husband Bulelani's name.

Public service and administration minister Geraldine Fraser-Moleketi, a senior SACP leader, is another highly intelligent and politically smart member of Mbeki's cabinet. Her abilities are beyond reproach, but her tough downsizing of the national welfare department as a member of Mandela's administration and the slashing of child grants are still remembered with anger by grassroots members. Her determined efforts to trim the public service have cost her so much support among the trade unions that she was booed off a makeshift stage during the 2004 mass protests over a public service wage dispute. Despite her enduring links to the SACP, the left has become wary of her.

If the consensus is for a woman candidate, both Cheryl Carolus and Naledi Pandor would also have to be considered. Mandela is fond of Carolus, the ANC's former acting secretary general, and his confidence in her is widely shared. She kept a low political profile in the tourism industry on her return from a highly successful stint as South Africa's high commissioner in London, and stepped down as head of SA Tourism in 2004 to take over as chairman of the South African Parks Board after a brief hiatus. But she would unquestionably be capable of promoting Mbeki's dream of developing South Africa as the economic bridge between North and South.

Pandor's chances could depend on how well she handles the perennial political hot potato of education. She performed her duties as leader of the National Council of Provinces with aplomb, and has a sentimental advantage in being the granddaughter of ANC intellectual pioneer, Professor ZK Matthews.

The wild card in the political poker game that is the battle for succession is Winnie. For all her faults, Madikizela-Mandela has an uncanny and enduring appeal among the poor and downtrodden, and as a populist candidate she could throw the best-laid plans into total disarray, as she has done before.

She would have no chance of support from the ANC party machine, firmly under Mbeki's control, but as the voice of the masses, her charisma could be the key if not to her own election, to the success of whatever candidate she might choose to back.

And herein lies the country's future dilemma. The absence of economic and social delivery, or at least the cushioning of hardship and misery while the masses wait for the benefits of the economy to trickle down to them, could feed a grassroots revolt, some observers warn. The less the ANC can offer a convincing and effective strategy for improving the material situation of the black masses, the more many of the most wretched and impoverished members of the population are likely to look to alternative ethnic solutions, which, however retrograde, offer both psychological comfort and, often, immediate economic relief.

Madikizela-Mandela embodies the ANC's worst nightmare of what could go wrong with the battle for succession: if the lives of the poor do not materially change for the better, if political parties remain aloof and inaccessible to the majority, if representative institutions continue not to care, she, or someone in her mould, could find a resonance with the masses that catapults a populist candidate into the presidential suite.

For the moment, however, Mbeki appears confident that he will be able to leave his legacy in the hands of a successor who would maintain his moderate, centrist policies and liberal social democracy. On balance, the most likely candidates espouse these very views. At the opening of parliament in February 2004, Ramaphosa observed: 'Much has already been done, a lot more needs to be done, but in terms of policies, there's not much that needs to change.'

Those are precisely the values that will curry favour within both Mbeki's inner circle and the ANC's powerful business wing. If they go hand in hand with a more open and consultative style of leadership, the succession could be not so much a battle as a benediction.

# Notes

**CHAPTER 1**

1 Brian Willan, *Sol Plaatje: South African Nationalist 1872–1932*. London: Heinemann, 1984.

2 Quoted in Ngugi wa Thiong'o, *Consciousness and African Renaissance: South Africa in the Black Imagination*. Steve Biko lecture, University of Cape Town, September 2003.

3 Quoted in William Malegapuru Makgoba (ed.), *African Renaissance: The New Struggle*. Cape Town and Johannesburg: Tafelberg and Mafube, 1999.

4 Peter Walshe, *The Rise of African Nationalism in South Africa: The African National Congress 1912–1952*. Berkeley: University of California Press, 1971, p. 34.

5 *Ibid.*

6 *Ibid.*

7 Willan, *Sol Plaatje*.

8 Thomas Karis and Gwendolen M Carter, *From Protest to Challenge. A Documentary History of African Politics in South Africa, 1882–1964*. Stanford: Hoover Institution Press, 1977.

9 Willan, *Sol Plaatje*.

10 Walshe, *The Rise of African Nationalism in South Africa*.

11 *Ibid.*

12 Francis Meli, *South Africa Belongs To Us: A History of the ANC*. Harare, Bloomington and London: Zimbabwe Publishing House, Indiana University Press and James Currey, 1988.

13 *Ibid.*

14 Quoted in Meli, *South Africa Belongs To Us*, pp. 41–2.

15 Walshe, *The Rise of African Nationalism in South Africa*, p. 34.

16 *Ibid.*

17 Cherryl Walker, *Women and Resistance in South Africa*. New York: Monthly Review Press, 1991, pp. 32–3.

18 Walshe, *The Rise of African Nationalism in South Africa*.

19 *Ibid.*

20 *Ibid.*

21 Brian Bunting, *Moses Kotane: South African Revolutionary*. London: Inkululeko Publications, 1975.

22 Meli, *South Africa Belongs To Us*.

23 *Ibid.*

24 Walshe, *The Rise of African Nationalism in South Africa*, p. 34.

25 A Lerumo, *Fifty Fighting Years: The Communist Party of South Africa 1921–1971*. London: Inkululeko Publications, 1971.

26 *Ibid.*

27 Walshe, *The Rise of African Nationalism in South Africa*.

28 *Ibid.*

29 *Ibid.*

30 Meli, *South Africa Belongs To Us*.

31 Bunting, *Moses Kotane*.

32  *Ibid.*

33  *Ibid.*; Meli, *South Africa Belongs To Us.*

34  Walshe, *The Rise of African Nationalism in South Africa.*

35  *Ibid.*

36  *Ibid.*

37  *Ibid.*

38  Bunting, *Moses Kotane.*

39  Walshe, *The Rise of African Nationalism in South Africa.*

40  Walker, *Women and Resistance*, p. 87.

41  Walshe, *The Rise of African Nationalism in South Africa.*

42  Bunting, *Moses Kotane.*

43  Walshe, *The Rise of African Nationalism in South Africa.*

44  *Ibid.*

45  *Ibid.*

46  Bunting, *Moses Kotane.*

47  *Ibid.*

48  *Ibid.*

49  Walshe, *The Rise of African Nationalism in South Africa.*

50  Luli Callinicos, *Oliver Tambo: Beyond the Engeli Mountains.* Cape Town: David Philip, 2004, p. 211

51  Adrian Guelke, *South Africa in Transition: The Misunderstood Miracle.* London: IB Tauris, 1999.

52  Martin Legassick, *Armed Struggle and Democracy: The Case of South Africa.* Uppsala: Nordiska Afrikainstitutet, 2002, p. 11.

53  Bunting, *Moses Kotane.*

54  Tom Lodge, *Black Politics in South Africa since 1945.* Johannesburg: Ravan Press, 1987.

55  Baruch Hirson, *Year of Fire, Year of Ash: The Soweto Revolt: Roots of a Revolution.* London: Zed Press, 1979.

56  Walter Sisulu, 'Tribute to the UDF', in *Umrabulo*, special edition, 2003 (www.anc.org/umrabulo).

57  Interview with Murphy Morobe, 10 April 2002.

58  FW de Klerk, *Working on Peace in Multicultural Societies.* FW de Klerk Foundation, 2003 (www.fwd.org.za/db_comm_display.asp?id=55).

59  *Ibid.*

**CHAPTER 2**

1  This chapter is based largely on interviews with sources within the ANC alliance who requested anonymity and reports by the author published in the *Argus* and *Sunday Independent*, or distributed by the Gemini News Agency, London.

2  Thabo Mbeki, toast to President Nelson Mandela on his 80th birthday, 19 July 1998.

3  See also Adrian Hadland and Jovial Rantao, *The Life and Times of Thabo Mbeki.* Johannesburg: Zebra Press, 1999.

4  Quoted in Mark Gevisser, 'The 60s Anti-hero', *Sunday Times*, 30 May 1999.

5  *Ibid.*

6  Anthony Sampson, 'President select', *Observer*, London, 10 June 2001.

7  Anthony Sampson, 'Mbeki: The Anglophile With Roots in a Tangle', *Observer*, 18 April 2004.

8  Also listen to Heidi Holland's account, BBC World, London, 24 April 2004.

9  See *ANC Meeting with South African Business Delegates*, Institute of Commonwealth Studies, London, 1985. Minutes of meeting at Mfuwe Game Lodge, Zambia.

10  Close political associate of Mbeki.

11  See also Sampson, 'President select'.

12  See Stephen Ellis and Tsepo Sechaba, *Comrades against Apartheid: The ANC and the South Africa Communist Party in Exile.* Bloomington and London: Indiana University Press and James Currey, 1991.

13  'The ANC Adopts Gear', *Sunday Independent*, 19 December 1997.

**CHAPTER 3**

1  Machiavelli, *The Prince.* Penguin, 2000, chapter XVII, p. 44.

2  Thabo Mbeki, address to the ANC national conference, 15 December 1997.

3  William M Gumede, *Contrasting the Policy Styles of Nelson Mandela and Thabo Mbeki and the Consolidation of South Africa's Democracy*, seminar presented to Centre for African Studies, Leeds University, 17 March 2004.

4  Interview with Essop Pahad, October 2001.

5  See Larry Collins and Dominique Lapierre, *Freedom at Midnight: The Epic*

*Drama of India's Struggle for Independence.*
London: HarperCollins, 1997, p. 12.

6. Stanley Wolpert, *Nehru: A Tryst With Destiny.* Oxford University Press, 1996.

7 Judith M Brown, *Nehru: A Political Life.*
New Haven: Yale University Press, 2003.

8 Wolpert, *Nehru: A Tryst With Destiny.*

9 Collins and Lapierre, *Freedom at Midnight.*

10 Hadland and Rantoa, *The Life and Times of Thabo Mbeki.*

11 Hein Marais, 'The Logic of Expediency:
Post-apartheid Shifts in Macro-economic
Policy', in Sean Jacobs and Richard
Calland, *Thabo Mbeki's World: The
Politics and Ideology of the South African
President.* Pietermaritzburg: Natal
University Press, 2002, pp. 83–103.

12 Sahra Ryklief, 'Does the Emperor Really
Have No Clothes: Thabo Mbeki and
Ideology', in Jacobs and Calland,
*Thabo Mbeki's World,* pp. 105–20.

13 Gumede, Leeds University seminar.

14 *Ibid.*

15 Howard Barrell, 'A Seriously Kick-arse
New President', *Mail & Guardian,*
28 May–3 June, 1999.

16 Sakhela Buhlungu, 'From "Madiba Magic"
to "Mbeki Logic": Mbeki and the ANC's
Trade Union Allies', in Jacobs and Calland,
*Thabo Mbeki's World,* pp. 179–200.

17 Gumede, Leeds University seminar.

18 See Collins and Lapierre, *Freedom at
Midnight,* p. 12.

19 *The Star,* 10 May 1995.

20 Gumede, Leeds University seminar.

21 Daniel Treisman, *Cardoso, Menem and
Machiavelli: Political Tactics and
Privatisation in Latin America.* Discussion
paper, January 2002.

22 *Ibid.*

23 See Sunil Khilnani, *The Idea of India.*
London: Penguin, 2000; Brown, *Nehru: A
Political Life.*

24 Buhlungu, 'From "Madiba Magic" to
"Mbeki Logic"'.

25 'From Mandela to Mbeki', *Houston
Chronicle,* 8 July 1996.

26 Interviews with senior ANC leaders,
11 November 1996.

27 *Ibid.*

28 *Argus,* 10 to 12 November 1998.

29 'From Mandela to Mbeki'.

30 Anthony Sampson, *Nelson Mandela: The
Authorised Biography.* London: Jonathan
Cape, 1999.

31 Interview with Moss Ngoasheng, 6 March
2000.

32 Adam Przeworski, Luis Pereira and Juan
Maravall, *Economic Reforms in New
Democracies: A Social Democratic Approach.*
Cambridge University Press, 1993.

33 *Ibid.*

**CHAPTER 4**

1 Khoo Boo Teik, *Beyond Mahathir.*
London: Zed Books, 2003, p. 38.

2 Desmond Tutu, speaking on the
American television programme
*NewsHour with Jim Lehrer,* October 1999.

3 Saki Macozoma, 'Black Economic
Empowerment: A New Covenant Forged
in Hope', *Optima* 50 (2), May 2004.

4 Nelson Mandela, statement following
release from prison, cited in the *Sowetan,*
5 March 1990.

5 M Kentridge, *Turning the Tanker:
The Economic Debate in South Africa.*
Johannesburg: Centre for Policy
Studies, 1993.

6 Kaizer Nyatsumba, 'Getting to Grips
with the Mining Industry', *Optima* 50 (2),
May 2004.

7 Dale McKinley, *The ANC and the
Liberation Struggle: A Critical Political
Biography.* London: Pluto, 1997, p. 87.

8 Thabo Mbeki, *Africa: The Time Has
Come.* Cape Town and Johannesburg:
Tafelberg and Mafube, 1998, pp. 23–4.

9 Patti Waldmeir, *Anatomy of a Miracle: The
End of Apartheid and the Birth of a New
South Africa.* London: Penguin, 1997, p. 83.

10 Jonathan Michie and Vishnu Padayachee,
*The Political Economy of South Africa's
Transition.* London: Dryden Press,
1997, p. 176.

11 Stephen Gelb, *The Politics of
Macroeconomic Reform in South Africa.*
Paper delivered at the University of the
Witwatersrand history workshop,
18 September 1999.

12  Sampson, *Nelson Mandela*.
13  Jeremy Cronin, interviewed by Helena Sheehan, 2002.
14  Asghar Adelzadeh, 'From the RDP to GEAR: The Gradual Embracing of Neo-liberalism in Economic Policy', *Transformation*, 31, 1996.
15  Hein Marais, *South Africa: Limits to Change*. Cape Town and London: University of Cape Town Press and Zed Books, 1998, p. 154.
16  Trevor Manuel, quoted in *Business Day*, 27 March, 10 and 15 April 1992.
17  Neil Coleman, *COSATU's Economic Policies*. Internal discussion paper, 1997.
18  Interview with Vella Pillay, 7 November 2001.
19  Saul, 'Cry for the Beloved Country', in Jacobs and Calland, *Thabo Mbeki's World*, p. 37.
20  Peter Limb, *Alliance Strengthened or Diminished? Relationships between Labour & African Nationalist/Liberation Movements in Southern Africa*. Paper presented at conference on Dynamics of Change in Southern Africa, University of Melbourne, 18–20 May 1992.
21  *Ibid*.
22  *SA Labour Bulletin* 16 (2), Oct/Nov 1991, pp. 13–17; *Work in Progress*, No. 79, December 1991, pp. 18–19.
23  'Role of Organised Labour', *New Nation*, 17 January 1992.
24  Interview with Mac Maharaj, 15 August 2001.
25  *Ibid*.
26  Interview with Jeremy Cronin, 17 July 2001.
27  Michie and Padayachee, *The Political Economy*, pp. 6–27; Jonathan Michie and Vishnu Padayachee, 'Three Years After Apartheid: Growth, Employment and Redistribution', *Cambridge Journal of Economics* 22 (5), 1998.
28  Mbeki, *Africa: The Time Has Come*.
29  T Corrigan, *Mbeki: His Time Has Come – An Introduction to South Africa's New President*. Johannesburg: SA Institute of Race Relations, 1999, pp. 77–8.
30  William M Gumede, *South Africa:*

*Is the Economic Miracle Possible?* Lecture delivered at London School of Economics, 27 April 2004; Michie and Padayachee, *The Political Economy*, pp. 6–27; Ben Turok, *Nothing But The Truth*. Johannesburg: Jonathan Cape, 2003.
31  Marais, *Limits to Change*.
32  Gumede, LSE lecture.
33  *Ibid*.
34  Sampson, *Nelson Mandela*.
35  Gumede, LSE lecture.
36  Statistics South Africa; SA Reserve Bank; SA Institute of Race Relations Yearbook, 2000; Michie and Padayachee, *The Political Economy*, pp. 6–27.
37  Julian Ogilvie-Thompson, chairman's statement, Anglo American, 1998.
38  SA Institute of Race Relations Yearbook, 2000.
39  *Ibid*.
40  Interview with Mac Maharaj, 15 August 2001.
41  Interview with Iraj Abedian, 2 December 2004.
42  *Growth, Employment and Redistribution: A Macroeconomic Strategy*. Pretoria: Department of Finance, 1996.
43  Mbeki, *Africa: The Time Has Come*, pp. 82–5.
44  Interview with Iraj Abedian, 2 December 2004.
45  Gelb, *The Politics of Macroeconomic Reform*.
46  Adelzadeh, 'From the RDP to GEAR'.
47  Ryklief, 'Does the Emperor Really Have Clothes', in Jacobs and Calland, *Thabo Mbeki's World*, p. 113.
48  Joel Netshitenzhe, 'A Social Partnership is Required for Growth in the Next 10 Years', *Sunday Times*, 4 April 2004.
49  Department of Finance, *GEAR*.
50  Marais, 'The Logic of Expediency', in Jacobs and Calland, *Thabo Mbeki's World*, p. 91; interview with Alec Erwin, Stellenbosch, 17 December 2002.
51  Thabo Mbeki, *The State and Social Transformation*. ANC discussion paper, 1996.
52  Estelle Randall, interview with Trevor Manuel, *Sunday Independent*, 9 January 2000.

53 Thabo Mbeki, address on the occasion of the annual President's Award for export achievement, 26 November 1996.

54 Marais, 'The Logic of Expediency', in Jacobs and Calland, Thabo Mbeki's World, p. 90.

55 Nelson Mandela, closing address, ANC's 50th national conference, 20 December 1997.

56 Nelson Mandela, State of the Nation address, 6 February 1997.

57 Quoted by Patrick Bond, 'Thabo Mbeki and NEPAD: Breaking or Shining the Chains of Global Apartheid?', in Jacobs and Calland, Thabo Mbeki's World, pp. 53–81.

58 See Ryklief, 'Does the Emperor Really Have Clothes?', in Jacobs and Calland, Thabo Mbeki's World, p. 113.

59 Jacobs and Calland, Thabo Mbeki's World.

60 See also Jeremy Cronin, 'Post-apartheid South Africa: A Reply to John S Saul', in Monthly Review, New York, December 2004.

61 ANC, The State and Social Transformation, 1996, www.anc.org.za.

62 Ibid.

63 Nelson Mandela, address to World Economic Forum, Davos, 29 January 1999.

64 Thabo Mbeki, opening speech at ministerial meeting of Non-Aligned Movement, Durban, 31 August 1998.

65 Thabo Mbeki, statement at African Renaissance conference, Johannesburg, 28 September 1998.

66 Debates with Kenneth Creamer, economics lecturer, University of the Witwatersrand, 1995–2004.

67 Financial Mail, 17 October 1997.

## CHAPTER 5

1 Quoted in Khilnani, The Idea of India.

2 Madeleine Bunting, 'A Very Rare Kind of Hope', Guardian, London, 24 May 2004.

3 SA Government, Towards a Ten Year Review, September 2003.

4 Quoted in Cronin, 'Post-apartheid South Africa'.

5 SA Government, Towards a Ten Year Review.

6 Department of Finance, GEAR.

7 SA Government, Towards a Ten Year Review.

8 COSATU leaders such as general secretary Zwelinzima Vavi regularly accuse the government of following the example of the domestic business community, which has been slow to make significant investments in the economy.

9 SA Government, Towards a Ten Year Review.

10 Interview with Alec Erwin, Stellenbosch, 16 December 2002.

11 Ibid.

12 Trevor Manuel, speech at PSG Online Securities, 6 September 2000.

13 Financial Mail, 5 January 2001.

14 Interview with Francis Wilson, 12 May 2001.

15 Financial Mail, November 2003.

16 SA Government, Towards a Ten Year Review.

17 Department of Public Enterprises, National Framework Agreement, November 1995.

18 William M Gumede, 'To Privatise or Not?', Enterprise, November 2001.

19 Interview with senior public enterprises official.

20 Ibid.

21 Interview with Kevin Wakeford, 5 June 2000.

22 Ibid.

23 Ibid.

24 See Rural Services Network 2002 report, www.rsn.org.za.

25 UNDP, Human Development Report, November 2000, www.undp.org.za.

26 See Ernesto M Pernia and Anil B Deolalikar (eds), Poverty, Growth and Institutions in Developing Asia. Basingstoke: Palgrave Macmillan, 2003, p. 18.

27 Department of Education, Report of the National Working Group on the Restructuring of the Institutional Landscape in Higher Education, 2002.

28 See AIDC, 'Scrapping the Apartheid Debt', 1996, www.aidc.org.za.

29 Ibid.

30 Joseph Stiglitz, Globalisation and its Discontents. London: Penguin, 2002.

31 Interview with Neva Makgetla, 5 March 2000; conversations with Kenneth Creamer, October 1998 and February 2004.

32   'Face Value: South Africa's Cuban Missile',
     *The Economist*, 9 August 2003.
33   UNDP Report, November 2000.

**CHAPTER 6**
1    *Financial Times*, 7 January 1995.
2    Saul, 'Cry for the Beloved Country', in
     Jacobs and Calland, *Thabo Mbeki's World*,
     pp. 27–51.
3    William M Gumede, *The ANC:*
     *From Liberation Movement to Governing*
     *Party – Dither Internal Democracy?*
     Unpublished MA dissertation,
     University of the Witwatersrand, 2001.
4    *ANC – People's Movement and Agent*
     *for Change*. ANC discussion paper.
5    *Financial Mail*, 3 March 2000.
6    Conversation with Phillip Gould, 21 April
     2002.
7    Anthony Giddens, *Beyond Left and Right*.
     Cambridge: Polity Press, 1994.
8    Interview with Patrick Bond, 7 March 2002.
9    Sakhela Buhlungu, 'Ten Years on, Power
     has Distracted SA's Liberators', *Sunday*
     *Times*, 11 April 2004.
10   Trevor Manuel, National Budget Speech,
     20 February 2002.
11   Sampson, 'President select'.
12   Interview with Cheslyn Mostert, 6 April
     2000.
13   *Financial Mail*, 5 April 2000.
14   Phillip Gould, *Unfinished Revolution:*
     *How Modernisation Saved the Labour*
     *Party*. London: Time Warner Books, 1998.
15   Anthony Sampson, *Who Runs This Place?*
     *The Anatomy of Britain in the 21st Century*.
     London: John Murray, 2004, p. 76.
16   William M Gumede, *Thabo Mbeki and*
     *the Remaking of South Africa's Politics*,
     lecture at St Antony's College, Oxford
     University, 20 May 2004.
17   *Ibid*.
18   Gumede, *Dither Internal Democracy?*
19   Ben Maclennan, *Mbeki Campaigns for the*
     *Poor Vote*, SA Press Association, 2 April
     2004.
20   Gumede, *Dither Internal Democracy?*
21   COSATU, *Advancing Social*
     *Transformation in the Era of Globalisation*,
     www.cosatu.org.za.

22   *Integrated Democratic Governance:*
     *A Restructured Presidency at Work*,
     26 March 2001.
23   Sean Jacobs and Farouk Chothia,
     'Remaking the Presidency: The Tension
     Between Co-ordination and
     Centralisation', in Jacobs and Calland,
     *Thabo Mbeki's World*, pp. 145–61.
24   *Ibid*.
25   *Ibid*.
26   *Ibid*.
27   Gumede, *Dither Internal Democracy?*
28   COSATU, central committee statement,
     September 2000.
29   COSATU, *Advancing Social*
     *Transformation*.
30   Jacobs and Chothia, 'Remaking the
     Presidency'.
31   *Ibid*.
32   *Ibid*.
33   Gumede, *Dither Internal Democracy?*
34   CDE, *Policy-making in a New Democracy:*
     *South Africa's Challenge for the 21st*
     *Century*. CDE Publications, August 1999.
35   Helena Sheehan, *Jeremy Cronin*
     *Interviews*, May 2002,
     http://www.comms.dcu.ie/
     sheehanh/za/cronin02.htm.
36   ANC, *50th National Conference Report*,
     December 1997.
37   *Ibid*.
38   Interview with Cheslyn Mostert, 6 April
     2000.
39   Interview with Smuts Ngonyama, 10 June
     2000.
40   *Financial Mail*, 2 June 2000.
41   ANC, *Annual Report*, 1999.
42   Interview with Smuts Ngonyama, 10 June
     2000.
43   ANC, *Annual Report*, 1999.
44   Interview with Jeff Radebe, 7 July 2002.
45   Adelzadeh. 'From the RDP to GEAR'.
46   ANC, *Reconstruction and Development*
     *Programme*, 1994, pp. 4–7.
47   *Ibid*.
48   *Ibid*.
49   Claude Kabemba and Tobie Schmitz,
     'Enhancing Policy Implementation:
     Lessons from the Reconstruction
     and Development Programme'. Social

Policy Series, research report No. 89, September 2001.

50 William M Gumede, Leeds University seminar.

51 Ibid.

52 Adelzadeh, From the RDP to GEAR.

53 Ibid.

54 Interview with Guy Mhone, 14 July 2002.

55 Gumede, Dither Internal Democracy?

56 Gumede, Leeds University seminar.

57 Interview with Zwelinzima Vavi, 25 August 2001.

58 Interview with Willie Madisha, 8 March 2002.

59 William M Gumede, NEPAD and the AU: Good Governance – Whose Good Governance? Paper commissioned by National Economic and Labour Development Institute, September 2001.

60 Interview with Bheki Khumalo, 10 February 2002.

61 ANC, Accelerating Change, 1997, www.anc.org.za.

62 Sheehan, Jeremy Cronin Interviews.

63 CDE, Policy-making in a New Democracy.

64 Sheehan, Jeremy Cronin Interviews.

65 Ashwin Desai and Adam Habib, 'COSATU and the Democratic Transition in South Africa: Drifting Towards Corporatism', South Asia Bulletin XV (1), 1995.

66 Ngoako Ramatlhodi, The Role of the Unions in a Democracy. Internal ANC discussion paper, November 2000.

67 COSATU, Advancing Social Transformation.

68 Ibid.

69 Ibid.

70 Gumede, Leeds University seminar.

71 Interview with Neil Coleman, 10 May 2002.

72 COSATU, Advancing Social Transformation.

73 Quoted in Alex Callinicos, 'South Africa After Apartheid', International Socialism, No. 70, March 1996.

74 Quoted in Pregs Govender, Reasserting Politics as the Power of Love and Courage: Experiments in SA's Decade of Democracy, 21 April 2004.

75 COSATU, central committee statement, September 2000.

76 Ibid.

77 Gumede, Dither Internal Democracy?

78 Ibid.

79 Ibid.

80 Financial Mail, 4 May 2001.

81 Interview with Smuts Ngonyama, 10 October 2001.

82 Firoz Cachalia, Good Governance Needs an Effective Parliament. ANC discussion paper, 2001.

83 Gumede, Dither Internal Democracy?

84 CDE, Policy-making in a New Democracy.

85 Ibid.

86 Gumede, Dither Internal Democracy?

87 Ibid.

88 Ibid.

89 Ibid.

90 Interview with Kgalema Motlanthe, 16 July 2001.

91 Ibid.

92 Gumede, Dither Internal Democracy?

93 COSATU, Draft Resolutions of the National Conference, September 2002.

94 Ibid.

95 Ibid.

96 'All the Provinces' Women and Men', Mail & Guardian, 22 April 2004.

CHAPTER 7

1 William M Gumede, The Politics of AIDS in South Africa. Paper presented at Goodenough College conference, London, 5 May 2004.

2 United Nations, Report on HIV/AIDS, 2000, www.unaids.org.

3 Raymond Whitaker, 'Dying Untreated and Alone: Those I Used to Eat with Shrink From Me Now', Independent, London, 11 April 2004.

4 Cabinet statement on the rollout of ARVs, November 2003, www.gov.za.

5 Pointed out by Kerry Cullinan, respected health journalist and AIDS researcher.

6 SA Institute of Race Relations Yearbook, 2001.

7 Gumede, The Politics of AIDS.

8 Interview with Tony Leon, 16 July 1997.

9 Interview with Essop Pahad, 15 October 2001.

10 Gumede, The Politics of AIDS.

11  Interview with Essop Pahad, 15 October 2001.
12  *Ibid.*
13  Gumede, *The Politics of AIDS.*
14  *Ibid.*
15  Interview with Zackie Achmat, 17 December 1998.
16  See www.actsa.org.uk.
17  Thabo Mbeki, speech to the National Council of Provinces, 20 October 1999.
18  See Kerry Cullinan, 'The AIDS Debate', *Financial Mail,* 14 April 2004.
19  Gumede, *The Politics of AIDS.*
20  Thabo Mbeki, *The AIDS Controversy: Letter to World Leaders,* 3 April 2000.
21  *Ibid.*
22  *Ibid.*
23  Thabo Mbeki, speech at international AIDS conference, Durban, July 2000.
24  Gumede, *The Politics of AIDS.*
25  Whitaker, 'Dying Untreated and Alone'.
26  Rian Malan, *The Spectator,* London, December 2003.
27  UNAids.
28  Interview with Thenjiwe Mthintso, 16 July 2001.
29  *Ibid.*
30  Interviews with members of committee investigating the feasibility of a basic income grant for South Africa, March 2002.
31  Gumede, *The Politics of AIDS.*
32  Cullinan, 'The AIDS Debate'.
33  Zackie Achmat, keynote address at Politics of AIDS conference, Goodenough College, London, 5 May 2004.
34  Cullinan, 'The AIDS Debate'.
35  Willie Madisha, opening address, COSATU national conference, Johannesburg.
36  Interview with Zwelinzima Vavi, 5 August 2001.
37  Interview with ANC member of parliament, 12 August 2001.
38  Interview with Patricia de Lille, 10 October 2001.
39  Interview with senior ANC leader, 17 December 2002.
40  Achmat, keynote address.
41  Gumede, *The Politics of AIDS.*
42  Nelson Mandela, speech at Khayelitsha HIV/AIDS clinic, 17 November 2001.
43  *Ibid.*
44  *Ibid.*
45  Thabo Mbeki, State of the Nation address, February 2002.
46  Mandela interview, *The Star,* April 2002.
47  SA Business Coalition HIV/AIDS survey, 2003.
48  Kerry Cullinan, *Chronicle of HIV/AIDS Treatment in South Africa: 1998–2003.* Unpublished MA dissertation, University of Natal, 2003.
49  Gumede, *The Politics of AIDS.*
50  'Abating or Exploding?', *The Economist,* 17–23 April 2004, p. 57.
51  Sheena Adams, 'We're Behind on ARVs, Admits Health Minister', *The Star,* 17 August 2004.
52  Interview with Smuts Ngonyama, 16 July 2001.
53  *The Economist,* 'Abating or exploding?'
54  Interview with senior ANC leader.

**CHAPTER 8**
1  Bruce King, *Derek Walcott: A Caribbean Life.* Oxford: Oxford University Press, 2000, p. 331
2  Stephen Chan, *Robert Mugabe: A Life of Power and Violence.* London: IB Tauris, 2003, p. 116.
3  Stephane Barbier, *Zimbabwe Leaves Mbeki on the Defensive.* Sapa-AFP, 12 April 2004.
4  Quoted in Chan, *Robert Mugabe,* p. 111.
5  Interviews with senior ANC leaders between 2000 and 2002.
6  ANC, *Developing a Strategic Perspective on South Africa's Foreign Policy.* http://www.anc.org.za/ancdocs/discussion/foreign/html.
7  Quoted in Alex Callinicos, 'South Africa after Apartheid'.
8  Allister Sparks, *Beyond the Miracle: Inside the New South Africa.* London: Jonathan Cape, 2003.
9  Interview with Kgalema Motlanthe, 21 August 2003.
10  See Sean Jacobs, 'The Unfinished Revolution', *FYI,* 5 May 2004.

11  Carolyn Dempster, 'South Africa's "Silent" Diplomacy', BBC News, 5 March 2003.

12  Interview with Zwelinzima Vavi, 7 October 2001.

13  William M Gumede. 'Banking on the AU', *African Business*, November 2001.

14  *Ibid.*

15  *ANC Today*, November 2003.

16  *Ibid.*

17  Interview with senior foreign affairs official, 12 May 2003.

18  'What Dlamini-Zuma Had to Say', *The Star*, 23 January 2001.

19  *Ibid.*

20  Interview with Aziz Pahad, 23 September 2003.

21  Peter Fabricius, 'SA, Nigeria Seek "Honourable Exit" for Mugabe', *The Star*, 30 November 2000.

22  Basildon Peta, 'Mugabe to Launch Newspaper in SA', *Cape Times*, 6 May 2004.

23  Interview with Aziz Pahad, 23 September 2003.

24  *Ibid.*

25  Dempster, 'South Africa's "Silent" Diplomacy'.

26  Interview with senior ANC leader, 17 December 2003.

27  'Mbeki Blames Mugabe for Borrowing too Much', *Daily News*, 28 November 2001.

28  Gumede, 'Banking on the AU'.

29  David Martin and Phyllis Johnson, *The Struggle for Zimbabwe: The Chimurenga War*. London: Faber & Faber, 1981.

30  Interview with Kgalema Motlanthe, 21 August 2003.

31  Interviews with senior foreign affairs officials between 2000 and 2001.

32  *Ibid.*

33  Interviews with ZANU-PF officials in 2000 and 2001.

34  Dempster, 'South Africa's "Silent" Diplomacy'.

35  *Financial Mail*, 5 May 2000.

36  *Ibid.*

37  Rapule Tabane, 'Vavi chastises "Childish Schoolboy" Mbalula', *Mail & Guardian*, 19–25 November 2004; 'COSATU and Zimbabwe: Signalling Left, Turning Right', *ANC Today* 4 (45), 12–18 November 2004.

38  Interview with Malusi Gigaba, 17 December 2002.

39  Quoted in Tim Hughes and Greg Mills, 'Time to Jettison Quiet Diplomacy', *Focus*, first quarter, 2003, p. 9.

40  Interviews with ZANU-PF leaders between 2000 and 2001.

41  Hughes and Mills, 'Time to Jettison Quiet Diplomacy'.

42  Peter Fabricius, 'Tutu Slams SA Stance on Zimbabwe', *Pretoria News*, November 2004.

## CHAPTER 9

1  'Hewitt Targets "Unjust" Farm Subsidies', BBC News, 30 September 2002, http.//news.bbc.co.uk/1/hi/uk_politics/2288452.stm.

2  'Cut Farming Subsidies, says CBI Chief', BBC News, 12 September 2003, http://news.bbc.co.uk/1/hi/business/3102266.stm.

3  *Ibid.*

4  'Rich and Poor Clash over Farm Aid', BBC News, 12 September 2003, http://news.bbc.co.uk/1/hi/business/3102108.stm.

5  *Ibid.*

6  'G20+ Unity Marks new Chapter in Development', *Pretoria News*, 16 September 2003.

7  Nkosazana Dlamini-Zuma, foreign affairs budget debate, May 2001.

8  Hughes and Mills, 'Time to Jettison Quiet Diplomacy'.

9  Thabo Mbeki, keynote address, ANC general council, Port Elizabeth, 12 July 2000.

10  S Gelb, 'Globalisation, the State and Macroeconomic Policy', in J Muller, N Cloete and S Badat (eds), *Challenges of Globalisation: South African Debates with Manuel Castells*. Cape Town: Maskew Miller Longman, 2001.

11  Raymond Suttner, 'South African Foreign Policy and the Promotion of Human Rights', in FGD, *Through a Glass Darkly?*

*Human Rights in South Africa's Foreign Policy. Occasional paper 6*, 1966.

12 Gelb, 'Globalisation'.

13 ANC, *Developing a Strategic Perspective.*

14 Gelb, 'Globalisation'.

15 *Ibid.*

16 Cronin, 'A Reply to John S Saul'.

17 Interview with Jeremy Cronin, 15 July 2001.

18 Gelb, 'Globalisation'.

19 Interviews with ANC NEC members between 2000 and 2001.

20 *Ibid.*

21 Khoo Boo Teik, *Beyond Mahathir*, p. 38.

22 Dot Keet, *South Africa's Official Position and Role in Promoting the WTO and a New Round of Multilateral Trade Negotiations.* AIDC, 2001.

23 Alfred Nzo, statement to parliamentary portfolio committee on international affairs, March 1995.

24 Jeffrey Sachs, 'Doing the Sums on Africa', *The Economist*, 22 May 2004.

25 Thanks to Hein Marais.

26 Nelson Mandela, statement at official opening of SADC Summit, 1997, www.polity.org.za/govdocs/speeches/1997/sp0908.html.

27 Vincent T Maphai and Keith Gottschalk, 'Parties, Politics and the Future of Democracy'. *Development Update*, 2000.

28 *Ibid.*

29 Peter Vale and Sipho Maseko, 'Thabo Mbeki, South Africa and the Idea of an African Renaissance', in Jacobs and Calland, *Thabo Mbeki's World*, pp. 121–42.

30 'African Renaissance', *Southern Africa Report* 13 (1), November 1997.

31 Sheehan, *Jeremy Cronin Interviews.*

32 Vale and Maseko, 'Thabo Mbeki, South Africa and the Idea of an African Renaissance'.

33 SA Institute for International Affairs survey, December 2002.

34 Interview with Adam Habib, 21 October 2002.

35 *Sunday Times*, 12 August 2001.

36 Gumede, *NEPAD and the AU.*

37 COSATU media statement, 25 April 2002, www.cosatu.org.za.

38 Joel Netshitenzhe, *From Liberation to Integration: The Role of NEPAD.* Presentation to Robben Island Leadership School, 21 September 2002.

39 SA Council of Churches, *Unblurring the Vision: An Assessment of NEPAD by South African Churches*, 6 June 2002, http://www.africaaction.org/docs02/nepa0206.htm.

40 Quoted in Gumede, *NEPAD and the AU.*

41 'Africa Sets Economic Plan', BBC, 8 February 2002, www.bbc.com.

42 Thabo Mbeki, *We are the Architects of Africa's Renewal.* Address to the UN, 16 September 2002.

43 Trade & Development Update, 2002.

44 'NEPAD – Who are the Partners in the New Partnership?', *Action for Southern Africa* 2 (3), April 2002.

45 Iraj Abedian, 'Global Financial Regime Needs an Overhaul', *Global Dialogue* 7 (2), July 2002.

46 SA Council of Churches, *Unblurring the Vision.*

47 *Ibid.*

48 Interview with Mahmood Mamdani, 4 October 2002.

49 *Ibid.*

50 Quoted in Gumede, *NEPAD and the AU.*

51 Interview with Mahmood Mamdani, 4 October 2002.

52 *Ibid.*

53 'Africa's Development Plan "Must Succeed"', BBC, 25 March 2002, www.bbc.com.

54 E Maloka, 'Holding Hands, Wielding a Stick', *Sunday Times*, 7 July 2002.

55 *Financial Mail*, 27 April 2001.

56 Tim King, *Gaddafi talks of Olive Branches and Business Deals but the Old Threat of Violence Remains*, 28 April 2002.

57 William M Gumede, 'Oil Diplomacy: Gaddafi and the AU', *African Business*, November 2001.

58 *Ibid.*

59 *Financial Mail*, 27 April 2001.

60 *Ibid.*

61 African Union Charter.

62 'Mbeki Poised to Prove his Worth to Africa', *The Star*, 8 July 2002, www.iol.co.za.

63 Maphai and Gottschalk, 'Parties, Politics and the Future of Democracy'.

64 New Partnership for Africa's Development, 2001, www.nepad.org.

65 'AU Launch May Mark Fresh Start for Africa', *Business Day*, 9 July 2002, www.bd.co.za.

66 Interview with Ron Hope, 18 October 2002.

67 Interview with Bheki Khumalo, 1 July 2002.

68 *Financial Mail*, 27 April 2001.

69 *Ibid.*

70 Interview with Bheki Khumalo, 1 July 2002.

71 Associated Press, 20 November 2002.

72 'World Bank Wants "Control" of DRC Mining', *Mail & Guardian*, 5 May 2004.

## CHAPTER 10

1 Rowan Philp, 'Big Boom in SA's Super-Rich', *Sunday Times*, 9 May 2004.

2 *Ibid.*

3 COSATU president Willie Madisha, speaking at a Workers' Day rally in Johannesburg's FNB Stadium, 1 May 2000.

4 Speaking to PSG Online Securities in Johannesburg on 6 September 2000, finance minister Trevor Manuel unveiled Treasury figures that showed the level of domestic investment, as a proportion of the GDP had declined from 16,5% (1998) to 14,9% (1999).

5 ILO, 'Restructuring the Labour Market: The South African Challenge', *ILO Country Review*, Geneva, 2000.

6 'SA May Not be Ready to Bin the Old Ideologies', *Financial Mail*, 3 March 2000.

7 Manuel's speech to PSG Online Securities.

8 'Lead More, Manage Less', *Financial Mail*, 9 February 2001.

9 'Top-flight Advisors to Raise SA's Investment Rating', *Financial Mail*, 11 February 2000.

10 'Soros Dumps Three Top Mbeki Aides', *Sunday Independent*, 17 December 2000.

11 Interview with author, 21 May 2000.

12 'Scratch Here, Rub There', *Financial Mail*, 17 November 2000.

13 S Mackay and K Shubane, *Down to Business: Government-Business Relations and South Africa's Development Needs*. Research Report No. 69, Johannesburg: Centre for Policy Studies, 1999.

14 Big business representatives at the SACOB convention were: Murray & Roberts chairman Dave Brink; Anglo American deputy chairman Leslie Boyd; Barlows chairman Warren Clewlow; Absa Bank chairman Danie Cronjé; Sanlam chairman Marinus Daling; FirstRand CE Laurie Dippenaar; De Beers chairman Nicky Oppenheimer; Rembrandt chairman Johann Rupert; Stanbic chairman Conrad Strauss; and Johnnic chairman Cyril Ramaphosa. Also present were Eskom chairman Reuel Khoza and Transnet MD Saki Macozoma.

15 *Financial Mail*, 'Scratch Here, Rub There'.

16 *Ibid.*

17 *Ibid.*

18 Terry Bell and Dumisa Ntsebeza, *Unfinished Business: South Africa, Apartheid and Truth*. New York: Verso, 2002.

19 *Ibid.*

20 Rory Carroll, 'Rich Whites Keep Wealth and Poor Beg', *Guardian*, London, 13 April 2004.

21 Iraj Abedian, *Sowetan*, 23 July 2003.

22 Alarmed by the liberation movement's suspicion of its commitment to the struggle, NAFCOC decided at its 21st annual conference to send its president, Sam Motsuenyane, to meet with ANC president Oliver Tambo in Lusaka on 27 May 1986. See *Joint Communique* of the meeting.

23 *Record of Understanding between Black Business and the ANC*, 31 October 1993.

24 'Low Share Prices Continue for Black-controlled Companies on the JSE', *Businessmap*, 22 March 2001.

25 Thabo Mbeki, speech at annual conference of Black Management Forum, Kempton Park, 20 November 1999.

26 *Ibid.*

27 ANC Economic Transformation Committee, *Black Economic*

*Empowerment Policy Workshop Report,*
March 2001.

28 Motlana, a medical practitioner, was
a prominent activist. Dubbed the 'grand-
father' of Soweto politics, he joined ANCYL
in the 1950s and shot to prominence in
the 1970s as founder of the Black Parents'
Association, which assisted families of
those killed during the June 1976 Soweto
uprising. He later led the Committee
of Ten, which became the Soweto Civic
Association. He is now a prominent
businessman. Dikgang Moseneke was
elected deputy president of the Pan
Africanist Congress in 1990, but quit
in 1992. He was the first black member
of the Pretoria Bar. Jonty Sandler was
co-founder with Motlana of NAIL. Cyril
Ramaphosa was secretary general of
the ANC and the movement's chief
negotiator at CODESA. He was formerly
general secretary of the National Union
of Mineworkers. He quit politics for
business in 1995, and chaired the Black
Economic Empowerment Commission.
Zwelakhe Sisulu, former editor of
*New Nation,* is also the former chief
executive of the SABC.

29 Revealed after Mazwai publicly criticised
trade unions for protesting business calls
to trim employee rights in the workplace.
COSATU was infuriated to learn that
Mazwai was not paying his employees
for Sunday work and that he believed
small companies should be exempt
from labour legislation.

30 'The Perils of Ruling-class Amnesia',
*Financial Mail,* 26 January 2001.

31 US businessman Eric Phillips, who
owned a 10% stake in Safika before
being fired, wrote to Mbeki
complaining about Ngoasheng's
involvement. A similar situation arose
when Ketso Gordhan, manager of the
Johannesburg City Council, quit to join
FirstRand Bank, which did business
with the council.

32 Steven Friedman, *The Mbeki Era and
South African Business.* Johannesburg:
Centre for Policy Studies, 1997.

33 'Fast-tracking Black Economic
Empowerment', *Financial Mail,*
28 January 2000.

34 'SA is Still Suffering from Inequalities
from Racial Capitalism', *Parliamentary
Bulletin,* No. 3114, April 1998.

35 BEE policy workshop, 3 March 2001.

36 'Executives Braced for a Little Bonanza',
*Financial Mail,* 16 April 1999.

37 'Whose Fight is it Anyway?', *Financial
Mail,* 6 October 2000.

38 BEE policy workshop, 3 March 2001.

39 BEE interim report, 2000.

40 Harold Crouch, *Government and Society
in Malaysia.* Ithaca and London: Cornell
University Press, 1996.

**CHAPTER 11**

1 Khilnani, *The Idea of India,* p. 150.

2 Ray Hartley, 'How the Hagiographers
Killed South African Politics', *Sunday
Times,* 21 March 2004.

3 Desmond Tutu, Sapa-AFP, 13 April 2004.

4 Khilnani, *The Idea of India,* p. 45.

5 *Ibid.*

6 Duncan Guy, 'Mbeki: There is Life after
Elections', *Mail & Guardian,* 17 April
2004.

7 *Sunday Times* editorial, 6 January 2002.

8 Ben Maclennan, *Mbeki Campaigns for the
Poor Vote.*

9 Maphai and Gottschalk, 'Parties, Politics
and the Future of Democracy'.

10 Thabo Mbeki, statement, 8 January 2000.

11 *Ibid.*

12 *Sunday Times* editorial.

13 *Ibid.*

14 Cedric Mayson, *Towards a Moral
Regeneration.* Internal ANC discussion
document, 2001.

15 *Ibid.*

16 Pradeep K Chhibber, *Democracy without
Associations: Transformation of the Party
System and Social Cleavages in India.*
Ann Arbor: University of Michigan
Press, 2001.

17 *Ibid.*

18 Chhibber, *Democracy without Associations;*
interview with Kgalema Motlanthe,
July 2001.

19  Joel Netshitenzhe, ANC discussion paper, 2000.
20  Patrick Laurence, interview with Sipho Seepe, *Focus*, 23, September 2001.
21  Joel Netshitenzhe, 'A Social Partnership is Required for Growth in the Next 10 Years', *Sunday Times*, 4 April 2004.
22  Meredith Woo-Cumings (ed.), *The Developmental State*. Ithaca and London: Cornell University Press, 1999.
23  Political journalist Stephen Laufer was of great help regarding the German example.
24  Firoz Cachalia, 'Globalisation Limits the ANC's Options for Easing Poverty', *Sunday Times*, 11 April 2004.
25  Thabo Mbeki, statement on adoption of Republic of South Africa Constitutional Bill, 8 May 1996.
26  *Ibid.*
27  Interview with Parks Mankahlana, 12 February 1998; statement by ANC chairman Mosiuoa Lekota, March 2000.
28  Interviews with Bheki Khumalo and Nazeem Mahatey, 2001 and 2002.
29  Justin Cartwright, 'The Rainbow Nation's Miracle Turns a Little Rusty', *Independent*, London, 11 April 2004.
30  Pointed out by political analyst Judith February.
31  Interviews with senior Afrikanerbond leaders, 2001.
32  Interviews with Salie Manie and Bheki Khumalo, April 2002.
33  Ramatlhodi, *Trade Unions in a Democratic South Africa*.
34  *Financial Mail*, 31 May 2002.
35  Thabo Mbeki, presidential speech, ANC's national conference, December 2002.
36  Krista Johnson, 'State and Civil Society in Contemporary South Africa: Redefining the Rules of the Game', in Jacobs and Calland, *Thabo Mbeki's World*, pp. 221–41.
37  Khilnani, *The Idea of India*, p. 184.
38  Frank Fischer, *Reframing Public Policy: Discursive Politics and Deliberative Practices*. Oxford: Oxford University Press, 2003, p. 75.
39  Khilnani, *The Idea of India*, pp. 15–60; Brown, *Nehru*; Shashi Tharoor, *Nehru: The Invention of India*. New York: Arcade, 1998.
40  Khilnani, *The Idea of India*, p. 184.
41  Joel Netshitenzhe, 'National Integrity and National Debate', *Independent Newspapers*, 29 September 2000.
42  *Ibid.*
43  William M Gumede, 'IFP Seeking a New Role', *Focus*, second quarter, 2001.
44  IFP national council, president Mangosutu Buthelezi's report, 2000.
45  Maphai and Gottschalk, 'Parties, Politics and the Future of Democracy'.
46  Interviews with senior ANC leaders between 1 May 2000 and December 2002.
47  Cartwright, 'The Rainbow Nation's Miracle'.
48  Conversation with Tony Leon, Johannesburg, May 2002.
49  Laurie Nathan, Visiting Fellow, Development Studies Institute, London School of Economics, made invaluable suggestions on this argument.
50  *Ibid.*
51  Maphai and Gottschalk, 'Parties, Politics and the Future of Democracy'.
52  *Ibid.*
53  Hartley, 'Hagiographers'.
54  S Mainwaring, G O'Donnell and S Valenzuela (eds), *Issues in Democratic Consolidation: The South American Democracies in Comparative Perspective*. Notre Dame: University of Notre Dame Press, 1992.
55  S Mainwaring and T Scully (eds), *Building Democratic Institutions: Party Systems in Latin America*. Palo Alto: Stanford University Press, 1995.
56  D Horowitz, *A Democratic South Africa? Constitutional Engineering in a Divided Society*. Berkeley: University of California Press, 1991; 'Democracy in Divided Societies', *Journal of Democracy*, 4, 1993, pp. 18–37; A Lijphart, *Democracy in Divided Societies and Power-sharing in South Africa*.
57  Andrew Meldrum, 'Young tell ANC: We're Still Poor, so Why Should we Vote?', *Independent*, London, 11 April 2004.
58  Maphai and Gottschalk, 'Parties, Politics and the Future of Democracy'.
59  *Ibid.*

60  Pieter Mulder, *10 Years of Democracy.* Paper for SRC debate, University of the Witwatersrand, 3 February 2004.
61  Judith February and Donna Andrews engaged with me on this point.
62  Maphai and Gottschalk, 'Parties, Politics and the Future of Democracy'.

CHAPTER 12
1  Ravi Naidoo, *The Union Movement and South Africa's Transition*, 1994–2003. Harold Wolpe Memorial Trust/Centre for Policy Studies seminar, 23 June 2003.
2  Conversation with Phillip Gould, advisor to Tony Blair, 14 April 2002.
3  Interview with Zwelinzima Vavi, 9 August 2001.
4  Zwelinzima Vavi, *Engaging the Democratic Transition*, 30 November 2000.
5  Report of the September Commission into the Future of the Unions, 1997.
6  COSATU central committee discussion paper, July 2001.
7  Interview with Zwelinzima Vavi, 9 August 2001.
8  Ramatlhodi, *The Role of Trade Unions in a Democracy.*
9  Interview with Tony Erhenreich, 6 February 2001.
10  Vavi, *Engaging the Democratic Transition.*
11  Thabo Mbeki, presidential address, special ANC policy conference, September 2002.
12  Interview with Zwelinzima Vavi, 9 August 2001.
13  SAMWU, *No Downward Grading of Labour Laws.* Internal memo, October 2001.
14  Zwelinzima Vavi, response to internal memo on labour laws, October 2001.
15  Sam Shilowa, *SACP: 75 Fighting Years.* Paper presented at UCW seminar, 1996.
16  Interview with Enoch Godongwana, 12 July 1996.
17  COSATU central executive committee internal memo, June 2001.
18  COSATU, *Advancing Social Transformation.*
19  *The Shopsteward*, March 2000.

20  Ebrahim-Khalil Hassen, 'The Role of Unions in a Changing Society', *Naledi*, 3 October 2003.
21  Discussion with Roger Ronnie, 9 July 2000.
22  Interview with Alec Erwin, 16 December 2002.
23  *Ibid.*
24  Vavi, *Engaging the Democratic Transition.*
25  Interview with former CE of a COSATU affiliate's investment companies, 10 May 2002.
26  Vavi, *Engaging the Democratic Transition.*
27  Interview with Willie Madisha, June 2001.
28  Naidoo, *The Union Movement.*
29  Interview with Charles Nqakula, 10 June 1998.
30  Interview with Jeremy Cronin, 14 July 2001.
31  Interview with SACP KwaZulu-Natal provincial leaders, 15 July 2001.
32  Sheehan, *Jeremy Cronin Interviews.*
33  Interview with Blade Nzimande, 15 July 2001.
34  Sheehan, *Jeremy Cronin Interviews.*
35  Draft resolutions for SACP strategy conference, July 2000.
36  *Business Day*, 12 December 1990; Joe Slovo, 'Nudging the Balance from Free to Plan', *Weekly Mail*, 30 March 1990.
37  Cronin, 'A Reply to John S Saul'.
38  COSATU, *Accelerating Transformation: Cosatu's Engagement with Policy and Legislative Processes During SA's First Term of Democratic Governance*, 2000, www.cosatu.org.za.
39  'Who, Me?', *The Economist*, London, 22 May 2004.

CHAPTER 13
1  J Habermas, 'Citizenship and National Identity'. *Praxis International*, 12, 2, 2002.
2  Mkhuseli Jack and Janet Cherry, 'Participatory Democracy: The Legacy of the UDF in the Eastern Cape', *Umrabulo*, 2003, www.anc.org.za.
3  *Ibid.*
4  Interview with Mzwanele Mayekiso, 20 March 1998.
5  Jack and Cherry, 'Participatory Democracy'.

6   Interview with Smuts Ngonyama,
    5 March 2000.
7   www.anc.org.za/ancdocs/pubs/umrabulo/
8   Interview with Godfrey Jack, 5 May 2002.
9   Interview with Ali Tleane, 5 March 2002.
10  *Ibid.*
11  Kgalema Mothlante, *ANC Annual Report*,
    1999. Johannesburg: ANC Publications.
12  *Ibid.*
13  *The Role of SANCO in a Democracy.*
    Discussion paper, 2003.
14  *Ibid.*
15  *Ibid.*
16  Interview with Abie Ditlhake, 5 June
    2000.
17  Rian Malan, 'New Reds Challenge ANC
    and win Skirmish', *Focus* 27, September
    2003.
18  *Ibid.*
19  Edgar Pieterse, *Rhythms, Patterning and
    Articulation of Social Formations in South
    Africa.* Interfund, 2002.
20  'Social Movements: Ultra-left or Global
    Citizens?', *Mail & Guardian*, 4 February
    2003.
21  Interview with Essop Pahad,
    21 September 2002.
22  *Mail & Guardian*, 'Social Movements'.
23  Malan, 'New Reds'.
24  *Mail & Guardian*, 'Social Movements'.
25  *Ibid.*
26  Social scientist Ebrahim Fakir engaged
    me on this point.
27  *Ibid.*
28  *Mail & Guardian*, ' Social Movements'.
29  *Ibid.*
30  Mahmood Mamdani, 'State and Civil
    Society in Contemporary Africa:
    Reconceptualising the Birth of State
    Nationalism and the Defeat of Popular
    Movements', *Africa Development*,
    15 (3/4), 1990, pp. 47–70.
31  ANC. *The Reconstruction and
    Development Programme: A Policy
    Framework.* Johannesburg: Umanyano
    Publications, 1994, pp. 15, 28,
    120–21.
32  *Ibid.*
33  H Blair, 'Participation and Accountability
    at the Periphery: Democratic Local

    Governance in Six Countries', *World
    Development*, 28:1, 1999, pp. 21–39.
34  Thabo Mbeki, *The State and Social
    Transformation*, November 1996.
35  Edgar Pieterse, 'South African NGOs
    and the Trials of Transition', *Development
    in Practice*, 7:2, 1997, pp. 157–66.
36  Nelson Mandela, report by ANC
    president, 50th national ANC conference,
    Mafikeng, 16 December 1997.
37  Pieterse, 'South African NGOs',
    pp. 157–66.
38  William M Gumede, *The ANC Tripartite
    Alliance and Policy Making.* Report
    commissioned by UNDP, April 2002.
39  Pieterse, *Rhythms, Patterning and
    Articulation.*
40  Interview with Essop Pahad, 10
    September 2002.
41  *Ibid.*
42  Interview with Smuts Ngonyama,
    21 August 2002.
43  Interview with Andile Mngxitama and
    Butizi Hlatshwayo, 12 October 2002.

**CHAPTER 14**

1   Free translation of Mathews Phosa's
    poem 'Die Prys van Vryheid' (The Price
    of Freedom), published in a volume titled
    *Deur die Oog van 'n Naald* (Through
    the Eye of a Needle). The original reads
    as follows:
    *Ons ry nou ook in amptelike slap motors
    Ons word ook onderdaning ge-ja-baas,
        ja-meneer, ja-minister, ja-alles
    Die nee-mense van die struggle het vinnig
        en onverklaarbaar
    ja-gewoontes aangeleer.*
2   Interview with Jabu Moleketi, 14 August
    2001.
3   Gumede, *Dither Internal Democracy?*
4   *Ibid.*
5   Tom Lodge, 'Policy Processes Within the
    ANC and Tripartite Alliance', *Politikon*,
    26 (1), 5–32, 1999.
6   Maphai and Gottschalk, 'Parties, Politics
    and the Future of Democracy'.
7   Desmond Tutu, second annual Nelson
    Mandela Lecture, Johannesburg,
    23 November 2004.

8  Thabo Mbeki, 'Letter from the President', *ANC Today*, November 2004, www.anc.org.za.
9  Sheehan, *Jeremy Cronin Interviews.*
10 Interviews with Essop Pahad, August 2001, and Peter Mokaba, July 2001 and May 2002.
11 ANC annual report 1999, www.anc.org.za.
12 Gumede, *Dither Internal Democracy?*
13 Sampson, *Nelson Mandela.*
14 *Ibid.*
15 Interviews with senior cabinet ministers, 2000 and 2003; Sheehan, *Jeremy Cronin Interviews.*
16 Interview with cabinet minister, August 2001.
17 Sheehan, *Jeremy Cronin Interviews.*
18 Jeremy Michaels, 'Storm in a Sari Dithered about Appointment', *Saturday Star*, 9 May 2004.
19 Lerumo Kalako, public apology to the ANC, August 2000.
20 Sapa, 19 August 2000.
21 Quoted in Ebrahim Fakir, 'Institutional restructuring'.
22 *Financial Mail*, 4 May 2001.
23 Interviews with COSATU central executive committee members, 1 August–30 October 2001.
24 Interviews with members of the HRC who attended the meeting with senior officials in the presidency, July 2003.
25 Interview with Blade Nzimande, 15 July 2001.
26 *Ibid.*
27 *NEC Briefing Notes.* Internal ANC discussion paper, 2001.
28 *ANC Today*, August 2001.
29 SACP, central executive committee briefing document, 2001, www.sacp.org.za.
30 Gugile Nkwinti, *A Commentary on Through the Eye of a Needle and the Disbandment of Constitutional Structures.* Internal ANC discussion document.
31 Rudolph Phala, *Tloga Tloga Factionalism, A Third Paper*, 2002.
32 *Factionalism, a Counter-revolutionary Tendency.* Internal ANC discussion document; Walter Mothapo, *On the Question of Collective Leadership.* ANC internal discussion document, 2002.
33 *Ibid.*
34 Interview with Jabu Moleketi, August 2001.
35 *Ibid.*
36 Interview with Mac Maharaj, August 2001.
37 *Ibid.*
38 Justin Arenstein, *The Battle for South Africa's Democratic Soul.* Washington: Center for Public Integrity, 2003.
39 *Ibid.*
40 A letter from Mbeki to his director general, Frank Chikane, and made available to Judge Hefer, showed that the president had already viewed all files and information on Bulelani Ngcuka that existed in the state's intelligence apparatus.
41 Gumede, *Dither Internal Democracy?*
42 Sheehan, *Jeremy Cronin Interviews.*
43 *Ibid.*
44 Govender, *Reasserting Politics.*
45 Cass R Sunstein, *Why Societies Need Dissent.* Cambridge, MA: Harvard University Press, 2003, p. 142.
46 Khilnani, *The Idea of India.*
47 Tutu, Mandela Memorial Lecture.
48 Sunstein, *Why Societies Need Dissent.*
49 *Ibid*, p. 62.

**CHAPTER 15**

1  Quoted in statement from Charles Lewis, executive director, Center for Public Integrity, Washington DC, 29 April 2004.
2  Jacobs and Calland, 'Thabo Mbeki: Myths and Context', in *Thabo Mbeki's World*, pp. 1–24.
3  COSATU central executive committee, assessment of the fourteen months following the 8th national congress in September 2003.

# List of
# Interviews

THE FOLLOWING INTERVIEWS WERE CONDUCTED BY THE AUTHOR FOR THIS BOOK:

Abedian, Iraj (former chief economist, Standard Bank of South Africa)

Andrews, Mercia (former president, South African National NGO Coalition)

Bond, Patrick (associate professor, Graduate School of Public and Development Management, University of the Witwatersrand)

Chikane, Frank (director-general in the office of the president)

Coleman, Neil (head of COSATU's parliamentary office)

Collinge, Jo-Anne (health department media liaison officer)

Creamer, Kenneth (former researcher in COSATU's parliamentary office)

Cronin, Jeremy (deputy general secretary, SACP)

De Lille, Patricia (leader, Independent Democrats)

Dexter, Phillip (director, National Economic Development and Labour Council)

Didiza, Thoko (minister of land affairs and agriculture)

Dipico, Manne (former Northern Cape premier)

Ditlhake, Abie (former chief executive, South African National NGO Coalition)

Dlamini-Zuma, Nkosazana (foreign affairs minister)

Dor, George (Jubilee 2000 South Africa)

Erhenreich, Tony (Western Cape secretary, COSATU)

Erwin, Alec (minister of public enterprises)

Gigaba, Malusi (ANC Youth League president)

Gould, Philip (advisor to British primer minister Tony Blair)

Gumbi, Mojanku (legal advisor to President Thabo Mbeki)

Hlatswayo, Zakes (director, National Land Committee)

Hobongwana, Phaki (ANC Eastern Cape spokesman)

Holomisa, Bantu (United Democratic Movement leader)

Jack, Godfrey (NEC member, South African National Civic Organisation)

Keet, Dot (Alternative Information and Development Centre)

Khumalo, Bheki (President Thabo Mbeki's chief media spokesman)

Leon, Tony (Democratic Alliance and official opposition leader)

Macozoma, Saki (chairman, New Africa Investments Ltd)

Madisha, Willie (COSATU president)

Mahanyele-Mthembi, Sankie (deputy secretary general, ANC)

Maharaj, Mac (former transport minister)

Mahlangu, Dorothy (chairman, NCOP finance committee)

Makgetla, Neva (COSATU economist)

Makhaye, Dumisani (ANC NEC member)

Makwetla, Thabang (former ANC parliamentary caucus leader)

Matlhako, Chris (provincial secretary, Northern Cape)

Mayekiso, Moses (former president, National Union of Metalworkers and SANCO)

Mayekiso, Mzwanele (former SANCO president, Alexandra)

Mboweni, Tito (Reserve Bank governor)

Mdawu, Emmanuel (general secretary, Congress of South African Students)

Meyer, Roelf (National Party's chief negotiator at CODESA)

Mgidlana, Sandi (head of housing, SANCO)

Mhone, Guy (economist, School of Public Management and Development, University of the Witwatersrand)

Mngxitama, Andile (coordinator, Landless People's Movement)

Modise, Joe (democratic South Africa's first defence minister)

Mohlala, Frans (former secretary, ANC interim leadership committee, Limpopo)

Mokaba, Peter (former head of ANC Elections Unit)

Molefe, Popo (North West premier)

Moleketi, Jabu (deputy minister of finance)

Monyobo, Spirit (spokesman for interim Free State leadership

Morobe, Murphy (chairman of Financial and Fiscal Commission)

Mostert, Cheslyn (coordinator, ANC policy unit)

Motlanthe, Kgalema (secretary general, ANC)

Motshekga, Mothole (former Gauteng premier)

Mthimkulu, Mtholephi (executive committee member, ANC Youth League, KwaZulu-Natal)

Naidoo, Ravi (director, National Labour and Development Institute)

Netshitenzhe, Joel (head, Government Communication and Information Service)

Ngomane, Noby (interim coordinator, ANC Free State)

Ngonyama, Smuts (head of the presidency, ANC)

Nhlapo, Vusi (president, National Education, Health and Allied Workers Union)

Ntsaluba, Andile (former director-general of health)

Ntshagase, Khulekane (ANC Youth League and NEC member)

Nyanda, Siphiwe (head, South African National Defence Force)

Nzimande, Blade (general secretary, SACP)

Omar, Dullah (former minister of justice and of transport)

Pahad, Aziz (deputy foreign affairs minister)

Pahad, Essop (minister in the presidency)

Phadine, Mgoato (general secretary South African Students Congress)

Phosa, Mathews (former premier, Mpumalanga)

Pillay, Vella (former MERG director)

Pityana, Sipho (former director-general, foreign affairs)

Potgieter, Febe (former secretary general, ANC Youth League)

Radebe, Jeff (head ANC policy unit, former public enterprises minister)

Ramaphosa, Cyril (former ANC secretary general)

Sathgar, Viswas (provincial secretary, Gauteng SACP)

Schalk, Baba (ANC member, North West)

Seokolo, Tebogo (advisor to North West premier Popo Molefe)

Shilowa, Mbhazima (Gauteng premier)

Sisulu, Max (head, ANC's Economic Transformation Committee)

Stiglitz, Joseph (former chief economist, World Bank)

Stofile, Arnold (former Eastern Cape premier)

Tshabalala-Msimang, Manto (health minister)

Van Heerden, Oscar (former ANC Youth League member)

Vavi, Zwelinzima (general secretary, COSATU)

Wakeford, Kevin (former CEO, South African Chamber of Business)

Zita, Langa (ANC member of parliament and national coordinator, SACP)

Zuma, Jacob (deputy president)

# Index